MW00655779

Wilford Woodruff's Witness

The Development of Temple Doctrine

Jennifer Ann Mackley

Fourth Printing
Copyright © 2014 by Jennifer Ann Mackley
All rights reserved.

ISBN: 0615835325
ISBN 13: 9780615835327

Library of Congress Control Number 2013944033
High Desert Publishing
Seattle, WA

Dedication

To my mother
Alice Clarkson Turley

Table of Contents

Acknowledgments

It would be impossible to thank all those who helped me complete this odyssey. At the risk of leaving some important individuals out, I must begin by expressing my gratitude to husband, Carter, and my children, Tali, Elise, and Eli. They were my inspiration and motivation.

I also want to recognize my muse and writing mentor, the late Ruth H. Maxwell. She was the first to explain why I was the one who had to write this particular book. Quoting the words of Martha Graham she told me, "[B]ecause there is only one of you in all of time, this expression is unique. And if you block it, it will never exist through any other medium and it will be lost. The world will not have it. It is not your business to determine how good it is nor how valuable nor how it compares with other expressions. It is your business to keep it yours clearly and directly, to keep the channel open."[1]

Although the approach is my own and I am solely responsible for any errors in research or presentation, this book would not have been published without the efforts of many other people. At the top of the list are those who gave me feedback on manuscript drafts, including Brian H. Stuy, Gary James Bergera, Jonathan A. Stapley, Richard Latham, editors Kate Coombs, Debi Hales, and Linda Lindstrom, and indexer Rachel Lyon. I depended on the advice of and encouragement from historians Douglas D. Alder, Thomas G. Alexander, Richard E. Bennett, Laurel Thatcher Ulrich, Connell O'Donovan, Amy Tanner Thiriot, Todd M. Compton, Gerald Faerber, Kylie Nielson Turley, David A. Dye, D. Michael Quinn, Steven C. Harper,

Richard E. Turley Jr., Russell Stevenson, Francis M. Gibbons, and Nora Oakes Howard; the assistance of Church History Library specialists Ardis Kay Smith and Anya Bybee and Church History Library archivist William W. Slaughter; access to the library of generous book collector Christine Kelly; the patience of Krystyna Hales; and voluntary research assistance by and inspiration of David L. and Alice Clarkson Turley. Finally, my thanks to members of the Woodruff family, Linda Andrews, Richard W. Price, Laura Woodruff Drew, Carolyn Woodruff Owen, Marge Woodruff Schwantes, Alan J. Hill, Ron Cobia, and particularly Richard N. W. Lambert and W. Bruce Woodruff, for sharing with me their insights, family treasures, and appreciation for the incredible life of Wilford Woodruff.

I gratefully acknowledge the many historians and scholars whose research on the life of Wilford Woodruff, both published and unpublished, gives context to my efforts. Of particular note are: Thomas G. Alexander's *Things in Heaven and Earth: The Life and Times of Wilford Woodruff, A Mormon Prophet* (Salt Lake City: Signature Books, 1991) and Scott G. Kenney's typescript of *Wilford Woodruff's Journal, 1833–1898*, 9 vols. (Midvale, Utah: Signature Books, 1983–1984).

Author's Introduction

I was raised under a microfilm machine, literally at my mother's knee, as she demonstrated the modern turning of the hearts of the children to their ancestral fathers and mothers. When she was a child, her mother read to her the account of Wilford Woodruff's vision of the Signers of the Declaration of Independence in the St. George Temple.[2] The vision made a profound impression on her and led to a lifetime of researching family history.

Interpretation of Wilford Woodruff's Vision of the Signers
"That We May Be Redeemed" by Harold I. Hopkinson

I was similarly intrigued when my mother shared the same remarkable account with me and felt compelled to find out more about Wilford Woodruff's experience. My curiosity led to the reading of his journals, discourses, and available letters as well as contemporaneous sources in Church history. I discovered that the development of temple doctrine in the nineteenth century can be more effectively traced through Wilford Woodruff's life than through any other's. This book is the result of my desire to share what I learned.

The development of temple doctrine began when Joseph Smith was first taught about the mission of Elijah in 1823. Following the restoration of the priesthood in 1829, and the conferral of priesthood keys through other divine messengers in 1836, the temple ordinances were introduced through Joseph Smith. After Joseph's death in 1844, Brigham Young refined the rituals according to Joseph's instructions, administered new ordinances, and suspended others as changing circumstances required.

Wholeheartedly embracing Elijah's mission, Wilford Woodruff was not only a witness to, but a catalyst in implementing temple ordinances and practices. Wilford's experiences in Kirtland and Nauvoo prepared him to receive additional revelation regarding temple worship. He continued the pattern of seeking revelation, clarifying the rites, and effecting changes based on personal experience and new revelations.

The period of time Wilford spent presiding over the St. George Temple from 1877 to 1884 provided an especially focused opportunity. As he and Brigham Young administered all ordinances for the living and dead for the first time in this dispensation, he said their minds were opened and many things were revealed. Under the leadership of John Taylor and Wilford Woodruff, the practices implemented and codified in the St. George Temple were replicated in the temples subsequently completed in Logan, Manti, and Salt Lake City. Finally, as prophet, Wilford received a revelation in 1894 regarding generational family sealings, which made the fulfillment of Elijah's mission possible.

In sharing this chronology of events, my personal commentary is kept to a minimum, so the account is told in Wilford's own words from his own perspective. I use direct quotes and primary sources whenever available. To provide context to his account, I include some discourses of and meeting minutes kept by his contemporaries. Otherwise, the story follows Wilford's view of events as they transpired. This includes Wilford's assessment of the decisions made by Joseph Smith, Brigham Young, and John Taylor in relation to the temple ceremonies and ordinances during their tenures as leaders of the Church.

Although I trace the development of temple doctrine and practices through Wilford Woodruff's life, this is not an exhaustive biography. Thomas G. Alexander's work, *Things in Heaven and Earth: The Life and Times of Wilford Woodruff*, provides a comprehensive account of Wilford's life in the context of American and Church history. Instead, I have chosen to emphasize the more personal side of Wilford's historically significant life to convey the depth of his sacrifices for the things he believed, the importance he placed on the redemption of his extended family—both living and dead—and the impact this focus had on his daily pursuits.

This is a comprehensive look at the development of temple doctrine in the nineteenth century. However, it assumes the reader has a basic understanding of key individuals and events in Church history and it is not a recital of all extant texts relating to the temple. The available journals and accounts that include references to the temple ordinances number in the thousands, and there may be many more yet to be discovered. There are also hundreds of articles and books, dating back to the 1800s, that describe or scrutinize temple practices both positively and negatively. It would be impossible to include all of these valuable perspectives in one volume. Some of these are referenced in endnotes to encourage further study on particular details and to provide current interpretations of events within a broader context.

Wilford firmly believed in revelation and the role of prophets but did not expect or exemplify perfection in either. Writing from his perspective will hopefully give readers a better understanding of the experiment in faith he conducted.[3] To those who look back on Church history and see a straight "line upon line" progression, Wilford's account may come as a surprise. It shows that Wilford and the other early Saints were willing to take one step after another to the limits of their light and knowledge, trusting that if they acted on what they received, they would be given more. The hallmark of Wilford's witness of the development of temple doctrine is his appreciation for the process. Along the way he gained an understanding of the eternal significance of temple ordinances and the essential participation of the living in God's plan for the exaltation of all His children.

For more information see *www.wilfordwoodruff.info*.
Please direct questions and any corrections to *woodruffinfo@gmail.com*.

~ 1 ~

God Moves in a Mysterious Way

The ill-tempered horse bolted down the rocky incline, bucking its rider, seventeen-year-old Wilford Woodruff. Thrown forward, Wilford lodged on the horse's neck and desperately grasped its ears. He braced for the inevitable. The force of the horse hitting the rocks as it stumbled launched Wilford about sixteen feet through the air. He struck the ground squarely on both feet, snapping his left leg in two places and grotesquely dislocating both ankles. Eight hours later, his father arrived with the doctor to set his bones. Knowing he would not have survived if he had been thrown head first, he thanked God for saving his life.[4]

This was not the first time Wilford had survived a life-threatening incident. It was, in fact, the tenth. Wilford later recorded in his journal, "I have been a marked victim as an attack for the power of the destroyer from my infancy up to the present day. I have faced accident, misfortune, and apparently death so many times and in so many shapes and forms from my childhood through life thus far that it has become a proverb with me to say that there has seemed to be two powers constantly watching me and at work with me: one to kill and the other to save me. Thus far the power to save me and preserve my life has prevailed. How long I shall be blessed with this preserving power and care, time must determine."[5]

To illustrate the miraculous preservation of his life, Wilford cataloged the accidents, illnesses and dangerous circumstances he had passed through.[6] The lengthy list of all he suffered and survived from childhood through his adult life is astonishing. Equally as remarkable is what he was able to accomplish and contribute to the Church in the midst of these challenges.[7]

CHILDHOOD CALAMITIES

Born on March 1, 1807, Wilford was the third son of Aphek and Beulah Woodruff. His mother died of spotted fever when he was only fifteen months old and he was raised by his father's second wife, Azubah Hart.[8] His childhood calamities began when he fell into a large kettle of boiling water at the age of three. Although he was pulled out instantly, he was severely burned and it took nine months of painful recovery before his life was considered out of danger. When he was five years old, he fell from the great beam of the family barn, landing face first on the floor.[9] He escaped this fall without broken bones, but three months later he wasn't as lucky.

One Saturday night he and his older brothers, Azmon and Thompson, were roughhousing, in spite of their father's instructions to the contrary. Wilford's misstep sent him to the bottom of the stairs and resulted in a broken arm. Citing Ephesians 6:2 and the commandment to honor one's parents, Wilford commented, "So much for disobedience. I suffered intensely, but soon recovered, feeling that whatever I suffered in the future, it would not be for disobedience to parents."[10] Later that year he broke his other arm, when he fell off his uncle's porch.

Wilford's description of an incident that occurred when he was six years old further illustrates his character as a child. He and his father were feeding pumpkins to their cattle, when one of the bulls pushed Wilford's cow away from the pumpkin she was eating. Infuriated by the bull's selfishness, Wilford picked up the pumpkin to give it to the cow. He wrote, "No sooner had I got it in my arms than the bull came plunging toward me with great fury." His father recognized the danger and told Wilford to drop the pumpkin and run. Instead, "determined that the cow should have her rights," Wilford ran down the hill taking the pumpkin with him. The bull was hot on his heels when Wilford fortuitously stepped into a posthole and fell, catapulting the pumpkin out of his arms. The bull jumped over Wilford to reach the pumpkin, and "tore it to pieces with his horns." Wilford believed the bull would have done the same to him, had he not fallen.[11] He attributed this narrow escape, like the many that followed, to divine protection.

Wilford's boyhood home in Connecticut

Three years later, at the age of nine, Wilford was knocked unconscious after falling fifteen feet from a tree and landing flat on his back. Thinking he was dead, his cousin ran home to tell Wilford's parents of the tragedy. To their astonishment, he revived in time to meet them on their way to retrieve his body. When he was twelve years old, he drowned in the Farmington River. His body sunk thirty feet and another young man, using a rock to weight him down, was able to quickly reach Wilford's body and bring him back to the surface. Wilford said he "suffered much in being restored to life."[12]

At thirteen Wilford nearly froze to death. Crossing Farmington Meadows in the winter snow, he became so chilled he was unable to go on. A passerby saw Wilford crawl into a hollow tree and, by the time he reached him, Wilford had fallen asleep. Understanding the danger, he roused Wilford from his stupor, and helped him find his way home.[13] Before his eighteenth birthday, he also broke his right leg in a sawmill accident, was bitten by a rabid dog, and almost suffocated when trapped under a wagonload of hay that was overturned on top of him.

THE HAND OF GOD

A childhood like his could be written off as the result of parental neglect, bad luck, or simply being accident-prone. The fact that the pattern continued, not only into adulthood but to the end of his life, led Wilford to a different conclusion. At the age of fifty, he wrote that only the hand of God could have rescued him from death in the face of the many dangers and "hairbreadth escapes" he had passed through.[14] His conclusion and God's protection were tested again and again.

While in Zion's Camp in 1834, a rifle was accidentally discharged and the ball passed within a few inches of Wilford's body.[15] A few months later, a heavily-loaded musket that was pointed at his chest misfired. Twice when crossing Lake Michigan he survived shipwrecks.[16] While serving as a missionary, he was caught in a tremendous storm. After wandering for five hours, he described a heavenly light that saved him and his companions from riding off a bluff into a deep gulf, and which continued to shine until they found the right road.[17] Over the next few years he was dragged by runaway horses but broke no bones, escaped being crushed by a sawmill when attempting to de-ice the wheel, and was left unharmed after a tornado removed the building he was standing in.[18]

Wilford Woodruff in 1849

In 1843, Wilford discussed his feelings with Joseph Smith regarding the invisible power constantly looking for some opportunity to take his life. He recorded in his journal that Joseph explained a principle "that few men have thought of."[19] With the understanding that no one can attain salvation unless he or she experiences mortal life and because mortality requires a physical body, Joseph told Wilford that Satan thinks he can thwart God's plans by destroying the physical bodies of God's children on earth. This confirmed Wilford's belief that it was only through God's protection and intervention that his life had been spared.

PRIESTHOOD BLESSINGS

After his conversion to the Church in 1833, Wilford relied on the power of the priesthood to restore his health and prolong his life. In 1842 he was bedridden for forty days with "bilious fever." He struggled between life and death and almost gave up. He wrote, "I felt some of the time like gathering up my feet and sleeping with my fathers."[20] But, after being anointed and blessed by some of the apostles, he felt sure he would recover.

In Winter Quarters on October 15, 1846, Wilford experienced "one of the most painful and serious misfortunes" of his life when he was cutting down trees to roof a shelter for his family. A falling oak tree swung and hit Wilford in the chest, throwing him in the air and pinning him against another tree. His breastbone and three ribs were broken and he suffered extensive internal injuries.[21] Brigham Young and two others administered to him, and by the power of the priesthood "rebuked [his] suffering and distress in the name of the Lord" promising Wilford he would not die.[22] He was unable to move until his breastbone began to "knit together" nine days later and, in less than three weeks, he was able to walk.[23] Within the month he resumed work on the cabin.[24] Tragically their sixteen-month-old son Joseph died from exposure a week later, on November 12.[25] Wilford's wife, Phebe, was six months pregnant at the time of Joseph's death and she prematurely delivered their fifth child, Ezra, on December 8. Ezra only lived for two days.[26]

Wilford Woodruff in 1868

Ten years later, in 1856, Wilford required another blessing. After surviving two difficult journeys across the plains in 1847 and 1850, he had settled in Salt Lake City. While attending to a poisoned animal, his arm became infected. Within eight days the poison had affected his entire body and he began to lose his senses. With the power of the priesthood, Brigham Young administered to Wilford and promised him, "'[Y]ou shall not die but shall live to finish your work which is appointed you to do upon the earth. The Adversary has sought many times to destroy your life from the Earth, but the Lord has preserved you, and will preserve you until your work is done.'"[27]

Even with this assurance, his struggle was not over. In 1859, he was again struck with lung fever. Of this experience he wrote, "My disease, pain and suffering had nearly blown out the lamp of life. . . . Not only the pain and misery of my cough, lungs and side, but all the horrible imaginations that the Devil or disease could invent was heaped upon my feeble spirit which was fluttering between life and death and struggling for the mastery to remain in the tabernacle. These were sufferings . . . which no pen can describe or tongue can tell."[28] His family gathered around him so he could give some final instructions on what to do with his belongings and make arrangements for his burial. After a priesthood blessing in which Daniel H. Wells again promised he would live, Wilford said he would "hold on" to Brother Wells' words and gradually regained his strength.[29]

Wilford continued to serve in his role as an Apostle, as a territorial legislator, and most importantly as a provider for his wives and children. He continued working hard as a rancher, horticulturalist, gardener, and businessman. Then in September 1873, at the age of sixty-four, he vividly describes symptoms of what might have been a mild heart attack. He wrote, "It seemed to be paralysis and death. I felt that I could not live an hour. All my blood, spirit, and life seemed to be leaving my limbs and closing around my heart and vitals." When he felt as if he was "about to give up the ghost," his neighbor gave him a blessing and he was "liberated instantaneously."[30] Thirteen years later, Wilford experienced what may have been another heart attack or stroke. He called it "a very strange turn."[31] This time he wrote that he couldn't see or speak for about thirty minutes, and lost his memory. Yet, he exhibited no lasting effects from either incident. In addition, despite breaking many bones, he never walked with a limp or showed any other long-term physical effects from his injuries.

He was seventy-two when he suffered through a severe bout of bilious colic.[32] He described the attacks through the night that took his breath away and the last attack in the morning that nearly killed him; he did not think his body could have survived another. His whole system was "so badly wracked" that his urine turned to blood. "But," he wrote, "through the mercy of God and the administration of the Elder[s], my life was saved."[33] Fourteen years later, shortly after the dedication of the Salt Lake Temple, he suffered another serious bout of the same ailment. The doctors said he could not live and his family gathered around him as he "lay at the point of death and was breathing [his] last."[34] He felt his work on earth was complete when they finished building the Salt Lake Temple in 1893, but testified that at this time his life was prolonged because of the Saints' petitions to God in his behalf.[35]

A CONSECRATED LIFE

In 1834 Wilford had consecrated and dedicated himself and all his earthly belongings—his precious trunk of books, the clothes on his back, his watch, gun, and even uncollected debts—unto the Lord, that he might be a "lawful heir" to the celestial kingdom of God.[36]

The dedication of his life was unequivocal and unwavering. From 1834 to 1898, Wilford's service in the kingdom included traveling over 180,000 miles, sometimes up to sixty miles a day on foot, through thirty-four of the United States, as well as the countries of Canada, England, Scotland, and Wales. He not only served as a missionary and mission president for more than ten years, but also assisted in setting apart over 5,550 other missionaries. As a missionary and Church leader, he preached over 3,600 discourses. He also administered priesthood blessings to at least 930 individuals, blessed more than 280 children, and participated in the ordination of some 11,000 men to the various offices within the Aaronic and Melchizedek priesthoods, including nine apostles.

Wilford helped build six temples and participated in the dedications of five of them. While presiding over the St. George Temple from 1877 to 1884, he sealed 11,550 couples and was a witness for many of the 33,541 sealings that took place during that time. In addition, he personally acted as a proxy in the sealing of 1,117 couples and officiated in sealing more than 800 children to their parents. He also assisted in 41,398 temple baptisms performed for the living and vicariously for the dead, including 3,188 members of his own family.[37]

In response to the question why Satan sought to take away his life, Wilford responded, "I can find but one answer and that is the devil knew if I got into the Church of Jesus Christ of Latter Day Saints I would write the history of the Church and . . . I would attend to the ordinances of the House of God . . . both for the living and the dead."[38] Wilford did exactly that by faithfully writing over 7,000 pages of personal and Church history in his journal, serving in the Church Historian's Office for thirty-four years, attending to ordinances for thousands of his own family members, and receiving revelations that would expand temple ordinance work and influence millions in the generations to come.

Inventory of property Wilford consecrated to the Church in 1834

Prophetically in 1858 he declared, "[W]henever the Lord has attempted to establish his Church and kingdom upon the earth, He always makes use of instruments whose peculiar circumstances in life will naturally lead them to acknowledge the hand of God in all that is manifested unto them."[39] Wilford was one of those instruments who believed God's hand was evident in every circumstance. After so much personal difficulty—although he may not have understood why God permitted his afflictions—Wilford, like Job, did not blame God or lose faith in Him. On the contrary, he was grateful for his blessings, and prayed that no matter how long he lived he would be able to spend his time in God's service.[40] And he did.

Wilford Woodruff in 1897

Wilford was sustained as President of the Quorum of the Twelve Apostles in 1880, and succeeded John Taylor as president of the Church in 1887, when he was eighty years old. On his ninetieth birthday, after sixty-four years of continual service in the Church, he simply wrote, "It is very remarkable how my life has been preserved . . . God moves in a mysterious way."[41]

Wilford has been recognized as one of the greatest missionaries in the history of the Church. But, for him, the effort to share the gospel with the living on earth was equal to the need to redeem those living in the spirit beyond the veil. Acknowledging God's hand in preserving his life, Wilford dedicated himself to this work and considered his role in the restored Church a miracle.[42]

The following pages tell the story of his particular contributions through his emphasis on temple ordinance work and his understanding of the temple's significance in the lives of Latter-day Saints. This is Wilford's witness of the faith exhibited by the early Saints as they accepted and acted upon each newly revealed doctrine relating to the developing temple ordinances. It is from the record which he kept of "the things which God made known" to him; his testimony of God's mercy, and "the things He has wrought in the lives of men."[43]

~ 2 ~

Entering the Kingdom of God

Wilford Woodruff was introduced to the Church on December 29, 1833, when he heard two missionaries share their testimonies in a schoolhouse near his home. Of this experience he later testified that on that day, although he had listened to many preachers before, he heard a real gospel sermon for the first time. It was what he had been seeking for since he was a boy.[44]

After their sermon, the two missionaries invited those in attendance to share their feelings for or against what they had heard. Wilford immediately stood because, in his words, "[T]he spirit of the Lord urged me to bear testimony to the truth of the message delivered by . . . true servants of God. They had preached to us that night the pure gospel of Jesus Christ."[45] Wilford asked to be baptized the following day. He did not feel this was a hastily made decision, but the culmination of his years of diligent searching and God's promised answer to his prayers.[46] Thus began sixty-five years of complete devotion to the Church as the kingdom of God on the earth.

I AM AFTER SALVATION AND ETERNAL LIFE[47]
In his youth, Wilford's family affiliated with the Ecclesiastical Society of Northington, Connecticut. Reverend Rufus Hawley, who presided over the Northington Church, officiated at the marriage of Wilford's parents and baptized

Wilford and his siblings as infants.[48] Wilford's mother Beulah Thompson died when he was only fifteen months old, and Wilford was raised by his stepmother Azubah Hart. He recognized her good influence and described his father Aphek as an honest man of great charity who "always said yes to anyone who asked a favor at his hand."[49]

His parents strictly adhered to the Sabbath restrictions, which Wilford described as Connecticut's "Blue Laws."[50] He explained that according to these laws, "No man, boy, or child of any age was permitted to play, or do any work from sunset Saturday night, until Sunday night." Not only that, he added, "[A]ll day Sunday we had to sit very still and say over the Presbyterian catechism and some passages in the Bible."[51] Even though he did not appreciate these restrictions as a child, as an adult Wilford was grateful for the time he had spent reading the scriptures.

Wilford wrote that he was taught by Azubah and "the word and Spirit of God" that there had been a falling away from pure and undefiled religion, and that a "great change was at hand."[52] While attending Dr. Noah Porter's Sabbath school, Wilford read the New Testament verse by verse and chapter after chapter. During this time he said he learned of the gospel of life and salvation, a gospel of "power on earth and before the heavens;" that the organization of the church consisted of apostles, prophets, pastors and teachers, "with helps and governments."[53] Wilford also described the people he read about who "had communion with God," who commanded the elements, conversed with angels, and "had the gifts and graces of a religion which had power and salvation in it."[54]

But Wilford could not find a similar church organization or group of people on the earth.[55] It seemed to him that the many different religions of the time were simply different roads to heaven and to hell but none of them resembled the gospel taught by Christ and His apostles.[56] Therefore, he continued looking forward to the "great change."[57] He declared he would "willingly walk a thousand miles to see a prophet, an apostle, or any man called of God," who could teach him the way to be saved; a man who held the power of the priesthood and the blessings of the Spirit, just as the ancient disciples of Christ.[58]

This was a difficult position for Wilford to maintain on his own because, he explained, "The people of Connecticut in those days thought it wicked to believe in any religion, or belong to any church, except the Presbyterian."[59] Robert Mason, a friend of the Woodruff family, was one of the few exceptions to this general view. He, like Wilford, believed it was necessary to have prophets, apostles, revelations, and visions in the church of Christ, with all the gifts, powers and blessings which the church ever had in any age of the world.[60] Mason's example affected Wilford deeply and helped him continue his search for the right church through the years.

Farmington mill of Cowles, Deming & Camp where Wilford worked

OPEN TO THE TRUTH

As a young man Wilford worked in his father's saw and grist mills in Northington until, in 1816, they had to sell their property and move to Farmington, Connecticut. After finishing his common school education at age fourteen, Wilford hired out to other farmers and millers during the summertime and continued his advanced schooling in the winter. While working for Colonel George Cowles in Farmington, he attended revival meetings at the Avon Congregational Church. But he said he was "not happy in the attempt" because they wanted him to "give his heart to God without explaining any principle in a comprehensive manner." Other teenagers joined with the Presbyterians during this local revival, but Wilford "did not wish to make a mockery of sacred things by professing light when [he] had received none."[61]

At one revival meeting Wilford attended, many ministers were preaching. When permission was given for members of the congregation to speak, Wilford stepped forward and queried: "My friends, will you tell me why you don't contend for the faith once delivered to the Saints? Will you tell me why you don't contend for that gospel that Jesus Christ taught, and that His apostles taught? Why do you not contend for that religion that gives unto you power before God, power to heal the sick, to make the blind to see, the lame to walk, and that gives you the Holy Ghost and those gifts and graces that have been manifest from the creation of the world? . . . They had the administrations of angels; they had dreams and visions, and constant revelation to guide and direct them in the path in which they should walk."[62]

One of the ministers responded and told Wilford those were foolish things only given to the children of men in the dark ages of the world so they would believe in Jesus

Christ. The minister then stated his belief that those things were no longer necessary, to which Wilford replied, "'Then give me the dark ages of the world; give me those ages when men received these principles.'" Wilford concluded his account of this experience by stating, "There is where I stood in my youth. I did not believe that these gifts and graces were done away, only through the unbelief of the children of men."[63] He believed every spiritual gift, every priesthood office, and every promised blessing to be just as necessary to constitute the true church of Jesus Christ and kingdom of God in his day as in any age of the world.[64]

Avon Congregational Church where Wilford attended meetings

Though he chose not to affiliate with any specific church, Wilford recognized their positive influence on him and appreciated the good people in his life. He recalled, "Where Presbyterians, Baptists, and other sects have taught the youth and mankind in general good wholesome principles of morality, so far it has had a good effect upon the generation around them."[65] Nevertheless, Wilford did not think they taught the fullness of the gospel and pled with God for light and truth and additional guidance. He explained his belief in this way, "Man possesses a spirit that . . . comes from God; and inasmuch as he is not fed from that same source or power that created him, he is not and cannot be satisfied."[66] Wilford's prayers were answered and he said many things were revealed to him. As a result, he knew he would live to see the true church of Christ established upon the earth and be among a people who would keep God's commandments.

SHARED CONVICTIONS

At the age of twenty Wilford began managing a mill for his aunt, Helen Wheeler. Over the course of the next three years, from 1827 to 1830, he was able to save a considerable sum of money. Then after losing most of his savings to an unprincipled man who would not repay a loan, and helping others who could not repay him, Wilford began reflecting on what was truly worthwhile in life. He became sincerely convinced that real peace of mind and happiness could only be found in serving God and doing His will. He felt that no one could find true happiness without a relationship with God. Wilford therefore resolved to seek Him, know His will, keep His commandments, follow the dictates of His Spirit, and spend the rest of his life "in the maintenance of these convictions."[67]

The earlier answer to his prayers, that he would live to see the true church of Christ established, gave him the hope he needed to continue his search. Robert Mason's influence also reinforced Wilford's efforts. In 1830 Mason shared with Wilford a vision he had seen thirty years earlier. He was in a vast orchard of fruit trees, and in spite of the fact that he was very hungry, he could not find any fruit to eat. Then, in an instant, the orchard was destroyed and immediately thereafter new sprouts grew into large trees. The trees budded and the blossoms became ripe, beautiful fruit. He picked an armful of fruit to eat, but the vision ended before he was able to taste any of it.

When Mason prayed for an interpretation of the vision, the answer he received was that the great trees represented the generation of men in which he lived. God then promised that He would set up His kingdom and church upon the earth, and "the fruits of the kingdom and church of Christ, such as have followed the prophets, apostles, and saints in every dispensation, shall again be found in all their fulness upon the earth."[68] Furthermore, the fruit on the new trees represented the gospel and the reason he had not been able to eat any of the fruit was, although he would live long enough to become acquainted with the fullness of the gospel, he would not partake of its blessings before his death.[69]

Mason then prophesied to Wilford that although he would not be privileged to partake of the gospel in mortality, Wilford would not only live to enjoy its blessings but would become a "conspicuous actor in that kingdom."[70] The fulfillment of this prophecy began three years later and is evidenced by Wilford's remarkable life of service in the Church and the significant impact he had on Church principles and practices over the course of sixty-five years.

A SACRED ORDINANCE

After completing work for his aunt in May 1830, Wilford was hired by Samuel and David Collins to help run their mill in South Canton, Connecticut.[71] During his time in Collinsville, Wilford was able to spend many hours in meditation and prayer and asked God to help him find a people "who contended for the faith once delivered to the Saints."[72] He remembered this period in Collinsville as some of the happiest days of his life and felt that God blessed him because he was "living up to the best light [he] had."[73]

Aware of his own failings and imperfections, he wanted to overcome them in order to merit eternal life. In an attempt to promote gospel principles in the village of Collinsville, he organized prayer meetings where they could pray as a group for light and knowledge. He wrote of his desire to receive the ordinances of the gospel, particularly baptism by immersion, as he could plainly see through his studies of the Bible that baptism was a sacred ordinance.[74] Although Wilford had been baptized when he was three months old, he did not believe infant baptism had any merit. He asserted that baptism of infants was a useless man-made doctrine, which was displeasing to God and entirely wrong. He challenged anyone to find in "any of the records of divine truth any ordinance instituted for the salvation of little innocent children."[75]

Therefore, at the age of twenty-three, Wilford decided he needed to follow Christ's example and be baptized by immersion. In his eagerness to comply with the commandment, "yet being ignorant of the holy priesthood and of the true authority to officiate in the ordinances of eternal life," he asked a local minister to baptize him.[76] In January 1831, Wilford wrote to Reverend George Phippen and asked if Phippen would perform the baptism even though Wilford did not plan to join the Baptist church. In response Phippen expressed his feeling that those baptized should join a church, but said he was ready to baptize all persons who "give evidence of evangelical piety."[77] Wilford waited until his brother Asahel was ready, and both were baptized by Reverend Phippen on May 5, 1831.

Sketch of Collinsville circa 1836 where Wilford lived and worked

SALVATION IS NEAR

After complying with the commandment to be "born of water," Wilford continued to pray, imploring God to lead him by His Spirit and prepare him for His church when it did come. In answer to one of his earnest prayers, the Spirit directed Wilford to go to the scriptures. Upon opening the Bible to Isaiah 56, Wilford read the first verse, "Thus saith the Lord . . . my salvation is near to come, and my right-eousness to be revealed." This scripture gave him such peace of mind that he stopped his searching. He was content to wait until the gospel found him.[78]

Soon thereafter, in early 1832, Wilford read a newspaper editorial about a new church called the Church of Jesus Christ of Latter-day Saints.[79] In one news story from the same time period, the writer described a "Mormonite meeting" he attended in a crowded schoolhouse. The two young missionaries preaching that night were Orson Pratt and Lyman Johnson. The newspaper account stated that these two claimed to be sent out by a prophet named Joseph Smith. Orson Pratt taught of the manner in which revelation comes from God to man, of Moroni's appearance, and the delivery and translation of the plates. Lyman Johnson shared his witness that the new revelation was vital to preparation for the Second Coming of Christ. The article concluded with the writer's opinion, "The speakers were obvious ignorant young men, and the Christians had little to fear, I thought, from their exertions to make the old delusion give place to the new."[80]

Perhaps the editorial Wilford read contained a similar account. Notwithstanding the mocking tone, the story of a religious organization led by a prophet, receiving new revelation from God would have caught Wilford's attention.

GO TO RHODE ISLAND

During this same period of time, in the spring of 1832, Wilford and his brother Azmon were considering relocating to New York to join their brother Thompson. But Wilford felt impressed to go elsewhere. He recorded: "The spirit that was upon me day and night said, 'Go to Rhode Island.' My mind was greatly exercised over the matter for I could not comprehend what it meant."

Wilford decided to settle his personal affairs and move in with his brother and sister-in-law so they could finalize their plans. Upon his arrival at Azmon's house, he shared his feelings with Azmon, and told him, "'I wonder what the Lord wants of me in Rhode Island! The spirit of the Lord has rested upon me for two weeks and said, 'Go to Rhode Island.'"[81]

About an hour later Wilford's half-brother Asahel arrived at Azmon's house. Almost the first words Asahel spoke were: "'I wonder what the Lord wants of me in Rhode Island! The spirit of the Lord has been upon me for two or three weeks and has told me to go to Rhode Island.'" This was astonishing to Wilford and to Asahel particularly because they had not seen each other for several months. Wilford felt sure it was their duty to go there, although at the time the reason why was a mystery to them.[82]

The key to solving the "mystery" was in Kirtland, Ohio, where, in February 1832, missionary calls were extended to Orson Hyde and Samuel H. Smith. As now recorded in Doctrine and Covenants section 75, the Lord instructed Orson and Samuel to go into the eastern states, and proclaim the things which He commanded.[83] They walked a thousand miles from Ohio to Pennsylvania, then on to New York where they began preaching in May. They continued their missionary work in Massachusetts in June and reached Rhode Island in July.

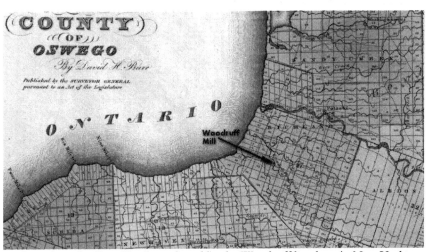

Location of mill and land purchased by the Woodruff brothers in New York

However, these two men did not meet Wilford, Azmon, or Asahel Woodruff during their ten-month mission to the eastern states. Wilford later recognized this was because he did not follow the Spirit and allowed outward circumstances to control him. His brother Azmon thought that because they had already made plans to move to New York and purchase a farm, they should not go to Rhode Island. Wilford consented reluctantly, but later described their decision as "Jonah like."[84]

Instead of going to Rhode Island where Wilford presumably would have heard the restored gospel, he and Azmon moved to Richland Township in Oswego County, New York, and Asahel later settled in Indiana.[85] Consequently, Wilford and Azmon had to wait another year and a half to hear the gospel and to be baptized, and Asahel did not have an opportunity to be baptized before his untimely death in 1838.

THE LORD WILL SHOW ME

In December 1833 God inspired an unlikely candidate, Zerah Pulsipher, to carry the restored gospel to Wilford and Azmon Woodruff. According to the Pulsipher family record, one morning while Zerah was threshing grain in his barn, he felt impressed to leave home immediately and preach the gospel. Zerah did not hesitate to follow the prompting he received. Before lunch he unyoked his oxen, walked into his house, and told his wife he needed a pair of socks and a clean shirt. When she asked him where on earth he was going, he replied, "I don't know, only that I am going to preach the Gospel. The Lord will show me where to go." His wife then asked how long he would be gone, and he responded, "Just long enough to do the work the Lord has for me to do."[86]

Zerah asked his neighbor Elijah Cheney to accompany him on his inspired journey north.[87] They traveled sixty miles on foot through the December snows and the first place they felt impressed to stop was the home of Azmon and Wilford Woodruff. They met Azmon's wife Elizabeth and told her who they were and "what their business was. . . . [S]he said her husband and her brother-in-law both were men who believed those principles, and they had prayed for them for years."[88] They asked if they could hold a meeting that night at the schoolhouse near the Woodruffs' farm.

Zerah and Mary Brown Pulsipher

When Wilford arrived home, Elizabeth told him about the meeting and, without stopping to eat dinner, he headed for the schoolhouse. On his way he prayed for the Spirit so he would know if these men were servants of God and so his heart "might be prepared to receive the divine message they had to deliver."[89] He arrived in time to hear Zerah's opening prayer and said, Zerah "knelt down and asked the Lord in the name of Jesus Christ for what he wanted. His manner of prayer and the influence which went with it impressed me greatly. The spirit of the Lord rested upon me and bore witness that he was a servant of God."[90]

After singing, Zerah preached for an hour and a half of the divine origin of the Book of Mormon and of the mission of the Prophet Joseph Smith. Elijah Cheney then added his witness of the truth of the restored gospel. At the conclusion of their testimonies, when the two missionaries asked if anyone in the congregation wanted to speak, both Wilford and Azmon stood to share with their friends and neighbors their conviction that Elders Pulsipher and Cheney were preaching the pure gospel of Jesus Christ.

Following the meeting, they invited the missionaries to stay at their home, and Wilford sat up all night reading the Book of Mormon. In his journal he wrote that as he did so, he "felt much of the Spirit of God bearing witness to the Book of Mormon." He "believed it was light out of darkness and truth out of the ground."[91] In the morning he told Zerah that he wanted to be baptized because he had a testimony for himself that the principles were true. His prayers had been answered; he had been blessed with the guidance of the Spirit as God had promised; and he had found the Church of Christ with the same principles taught by the ancient patriarchs and prophets of God. The priesthood power was again given to men to act in God's name and the gifts of the Spirit were manifest through it.

Understanding the need to not just be baptized in the proper manner, but to be "born of the water and of the Spirit" by those who had the proper authority, Wilford and his brother Azmon were baptized in Grindstone Creek and confirmed on December 31, 1833.[92] Of his baptism he wrote, "The snow was about three feet deep, the day was cold, and the water was mixed with ice and snow, yet I did not feel the cold."[93]

At the age of twenty-six, Wilford joined a church of 3,100 converts that had existed for only three years, led by a twenty-eight-year-old who declared to the world that he was chosen by God to restore the Gospel of Jesus Christ and establish His church again on the earth.[94] By 1833, the year Wilford was baptized, Joseph Smith had translated and published new scripture—the Book of Mormon—as well as the Book of Commandments containing sixty-five new revelations, reintroduced both the Aaronic and Melchizedek priesthoods with their individual offices, and had begun the literal gathering of Israel. Wilford exclaimed, "The fulness of the everlasting gospel had come at last. It filled my heart with great joy. It laid the foundation of a greater and more glorious work than I ever expected to see in this life."[95]

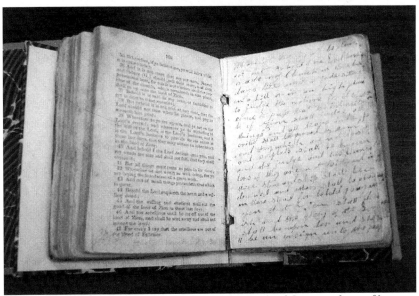

Wilford's copy of the first edition of the Book of Commandments[96]

PROPHECY FULFILLED

Of course Wilford desired to share his newfound knowledge with others and one of the first people he thought of was Robert Mason. A few months after his baptism, Wilford wrote Robert a letter and informed him that he had found the true gospel with all its blessings. He shared his witness that the authority of Christ's Church had been restored to the earth as Robert had prophesied and through the Prophet Joseph, God had again established the Church of Christ upon the earth.[97]

Robert Mason's vision was realized. The Church was restored in his lifetime and yet, because he died shortly after receiving Wilford's letter, he was not able to be baptized and "partake of this fruit in the flesh." His prophecy that Wilford would not only live to enjoy the blessings of the restored gospel, but would become a conspicuous actor in the kingdom of God was also fulfilled. Wilford was ordained an Apostle in 1839, only six years after his baptism, to help lead a persecuted group of 14,000 Saints. After serving faithfully in the Quorum of the Twelve for fifty years, he was sustained as President of the Church in 1889, to preside over more than 183,000 members.[98]

Wilford felt that on the day of his baptism, his mission immediately commenced as a fellow citizen with the Saints in the household of God.[99] Citizenship in the kingdom for Wilford and all other new converts was manifested by the new and everlasting covenant of baptism.[100] But baptism was only the beginning. The revelations Joseph Smith had received to establish the restored gospel and organize the Church prior to Wilford's baptism in 1833, would soon be followed by radical doctrinal announcements regarding the requirements of daily life in the Church and their connection to eternal life. Each new revelation had to be accepted with faith in its divine origin and acted upon, sometimes at great personal sacrifice.

~ 3 ~

Kirtland and the Power of Elijah

Kirtland Temple

The unequivocal commandment that all must be baptized in order to enter the kingdom of God has troubled theologians for hundreds of years. For many, the requirement of baptism presented a dilemma because millions of God's children had died without the opportunity to hear the gospel and comply with this universal mandate.

When Wilford was searching for a church whose teachings were consistent with New Testament scripture he had two theological choices. On one hand were religions that, ignoring the requirement of baptism, taught that the unbaptized would be admitted to the kingdom of God. On the other hand were religions that dismissed God's mercy and declared that without baptism the innocent would be eternally damned.

In 1857 Wilford told the Saints that neither alternative had been acceptable to him. He could not believe that those who lived a life of debauchery and those who had merely not been religious would be consigned to the same hell.[101] Sure that those who died without hearing the gospel would not be punished by a merciful Father, Wilford taught this principle: "Millions of people have been born in the flesh, have lived and have gone to the grave, who never saw . . . a man that was called of God and had power to administer in one of the ordinances of the House of God. Will God condemn them because they did not receive the Gospel? Not at all."[102]

In fact, there was no dilemma. In 1823 God sent Moroni to begin teaching Joseph Smith how all His children could be redeemed. Moroni explained "what the Lord was going to do, and how and in what manner His Kingdom was to be conducted."[103] In his first visit, Moroni instructed Joseph regarding Elijah and the sealing power: "Behold, I will reveal unto you the Priesthood, by the hand of Elijah the prophet. . . . And he shall plant in the hearts of the children the promises made to the fathers, and the hearts of the children shall turn to their fathers. If it were not so, the whole earth would be utterly wasted at his coming."[104]

What this meant and how it would solve the perceived dilemma became clearer in 1840 when God revealed the ordinance of proxy baptism for the dead. This vicarious ordinance would provide those who did not receive the gospel in mortality the opportunity to comply with His commandment.

The significance of Elijah's mission is evident: it was part of the first divine instruction Joseph Smith received after God the Father and Jesus Christ appeared in answer to his prayer in 1820.[105] However, Joseph's understanding of Elijah's mission and its central role in the gospel was not immediate. The doctrine of sealing developed over the course of the twenty-one years following Moroni's 1823 visit. First the priesthood power and then the required priesthood keys had to be restored. These events were followed by revelations regarding each of the preliminary ordinances. Only then could the sealing ordinances be revealed and administered.[106] Understanding their place in the plan of salvation and exaltation did not occur until 1894, fifty years after the death of Joseph Smith, when Wilford Woodruff received a revelation on the sealing of generational families.

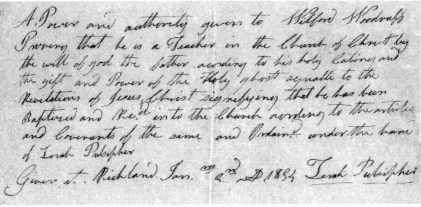

Certificate of Wilford's ordination to the Aaronic priesthood January 2, 1834

REDEMPTION OF ALL MANKIND

Wilford joined the Church the year after God had revealed to Joseph Smith that the destiny of mankind is not irretrievably fixed at death, that the gospel would be preached to the "spirits in prison" and those who died "without law."[107] When Wilford heard of the doctrine, he felt it was the answer to his prayers. It addressed his deep concerns for the salvation of those who, like his mother, had departed this life before hearing the gospel. Subsequent revelations—regarding vicarious baptism for the dead, the endowment, and the sealing of families on earth and in heaven—would provide for the salvation and exaltation of all mankind.

In January 1836, Joseph Smith was shown a vision of the celestial kingdom where he saw Adam, Abraham, his parents, and his brother Alvin, among others.[108] Alvin's presence there surprised Joseph because Alvin had died before being baptized. The Lord explained, "'All who have died without a knowledge of this gospel, who would have received it if they had been permitted to tarry, shall be heirs of the celestial kingdom of God; Also all that shall die henceforth without a knowledge of it, who would have received it with all their hearts, shall be heirs of that kingdom; For I, the Lord, will judge all men according to their works, according to the desire of their hearts.'"[109]

This enlightenment which Joseph shared with the Saints was personally and eternally significant, making it clear that the children of God would have the opportunity to choose their place in the eternities without predestination or limitation.[110] These were, at the time, radical yet scripturally sound doctrines.

Wilford recognized these truths as consistent with his study of the Bible and his long-held beliefs. He remarked that Joseph Smith's vision of the celestial kingdom "opened my understanding and shook off my shackles. There was something in it so different from the old sectarian notion— something that swept away the idea of one heaven, one hell, and that those who do not go to one place must go to the other, and that all in heaven have an equal glory, and all in hell an equal misery." Wilford declared, "[W]hen I got hold of the vision, I saw more light, more consistency, and Godlike mercy and justice than I had ever seen in my life."[111] He said this revelation, in conjunction with the revelation concerning the three degrees of glory, gave him more joy and consolation than any others.[112]

Another four years would pass before God would re- veal the doctrine of vicarious baptism for the dead in 1840, and only then would Joseph Smith understand how his brother Alvin and all those like him could enter the king- dom of God without complying with the commandment to be baptized before they died. Then the scriptures that Wilford had studied throughout his life would finally make sense, the Saints would understand their role in setting free the spirits in prison and how Christ's Atonement would be made available to all.

The role of the living in the salvation of the dead would define and refine the fledgling Church of Jesus Christ of Latter-day Saints. It would set the Church apart from all other churches in existence at the time, as well as those subsequently introduced. Redeeming the dead would also be the catalyst for major changes in Church practices and play a role in the controversial declarations that Wilford would make as President of the Church, including the cessation of polygamy.

PRIESTHOOD ORDINANCES IN KIRTLAND

The first administration of temple ordinances had been in 1836.[113] After several months of instruction in the School of the Prophets, Joseph Smith introduced washing and anointing ordinances. These ordinances were patterned after those described in the Old Testament administered to the priests, such as Aaron, before they performed their duties in the Tabernacle.[114] Joseph Smith instructed the men in Kirtland that participation in the ordinances would prepare them to minister as they preached the gospel.[115]

On January 21, 1836, a group of men assembled first in the printing office and then in the Kirtland Temple to wash their bodies with pure water "in the name of the Lord."[116] This ceremonial washing was followed a week later by the ordinance of anointing. Starting with Joseph Smith Sr., the members of the First Presidency as well as several others, pronounced blessings upon and anointed each other with the oil they had consecrated for the occasion.

On February 6, Joseph called the anointed together to "receive the seal of all their blessings."[117] Soon after, during the dedication of the Kirtland Temple in March and April, the "endowment of power" was manifested through gifts of the Spirit including speaking in tongues, visions, and prophesying. As promised, those assembled received spiritual instruction in order to be "perfected in their understanding . . . in theory, in principle, and in doctrine in all things pertaining to the kingdom of God."[118]

Earlier, in June 1834, God had revealed to those in Zion's Camp that only through this endowment from on high would the Elders of the Church understand their duties and the things that would be required at their hands.[119] For two years Wilford had been looking forward to receiving the "great blessing" God said would be poured upon them once the temple was built.[120] However, on March 27, 1836, when the Kirtland Temple was dedicated, Wilford was not present. At the request of Joseph Smith,

Wilford had remained in Kentucky to preside over the missionary work there so the apostles could return to Kirtland and participate in the endowment. Joseph promised Wilford he would not lose any blessings as a result of missing this Pentecostal occasion.[121]

When Wilford heard the account of the Kirtland endowment, he described it as "glorious in the first degree." Abraham O. Smoot brought the news of the Saints' gathering in the temple. "The heavens [were] opened unto them," Wilford recorded, "Angels and Jesus Christ [were] seen ... great blessings indeed."[122]

PRIESTHOOD KEYS

In fact, on April 3, 1836, one week after the dedication of the Kirtland Temple, two very significant events in the history of the Church occurred.[123] First was the appearance of Jesus Christ to accept His House, the hoped-for ultimate blessing of beholding the face of God in mortality.[124] Second was the bestowal of vital priesthood keys—the knowledge, power and authority to preside over and direct the use of priesthood on God's behalf—by three prophets from prior dispensations.[125] Moses, Elias, and Elijah conferred upon Joseph Smith and Oliver Cowdery the keys to the gathering of Israel, the blessings of the Abrahamic Covenant, and the power to seal on earth and in heaven.[126]

On this occasion, in fulfillment of God's promise to Malachi over two thousand years earlier and to Joseph in 1823, Elijah declared: "Behold the time has fully come, which was spoken of by the mouth of Malachi. . . . Therefore the keys of this dispensation are committed unto your hands."[127] The sealing power Elijah conferred is described by Jesus Christ in Matthew 16:19 as "the keys of the kingdom of heaven." This power was the essential element needed for priesthood ordinances to be efficacious on earth for time and in heaven for eternity.[128] These keys would make it possible to bind the children to their earthly fathers and all mankind to their Father in Heaven, something the Saints had yet to understand.[129]

The three priesthood keys delivered in April 1836—keys to the gathering of Israel, the blessings of the Abrahamic Covenant, and the power to seal on earth and in heaven—provided the basis of temple work. These keys are reflected in the three-fold mission of the Church to preach the gospel, perfect the Saints, and redeem the dead.[130] The literal gathering of Israel would be accomplished through preaching the gospel to every nation.[131] Perfecting the Saints would prepare these converts to make the necessary covenants to qualify for the blessings of Abraham.[132] The sealing of those blessings in the temple—for the living and by proxy for the dead—would then be possible for all those willing to receive the ordinances.

When the Savior appeared to Joseph Smith and Oliver Cowdery in the Kirtland Temple, He referred to the future use of these keys and proclaimed, "the hearts of thousands and tens of thousands shall greatly rejoice in consequence of the blessings which shall be poured out . . . in this house."[133] Indeed, the keys conferred in Kirtland enabled more than just the administration of the ordinances of washing and anointing in the Kirtland Temple. They blessed thousands in Nauvoo—when all the temple ordinances for the living as well as vicarious baptisms were administered—and would bless millions when all ordinances for both the living and the dead could be administered in the temples that followed.[134]

THE HOUSE OF THE LORD

Wilford returned to Kirtland five months after these incredible events, leading a company of twenty-two new converts to join the Saints in Ohio. After traveling 9,805 miles preaching the gospel throughout the South, he had been released from his missionary labors to return to Kirtland and receive the endowment. His little group arrived on foot during a snowstorm on November 25, 1836.[135]

Kirtland Temple

His joy at seeing the temple before they even reached the village was recorded in his journal. That night he wrote, "I spent one of the happiest days of my life at this time in visiting Kirtland and the House of the Lord. . . . I must confess the scenery is indescribable." When he entered the lower assembly room he was overwhelmed with awe; he felt he was walking on holy ground. He also wrote that the priesthood pulpits and the temple's design reflected grandeur, solemnity, order, and the wisdom of God; evidence to him that it was built through inspiration and according to revelation.[136]

The main floor of the Kirtland Temple was used for various religious services, and the second floor was used for the School of the Prophets. The third floor contained a room Joseph Smith used as his office as well as rooms for the "Kirtland High School" during the day and Church quorum meetings in the evening. This pattern of temple design would be followed in subsequent temples. In addition to providing a dedicated space for the performance of ordinances, temples would continue to serve as places for the Saints to assemble throughout the nineteenth century.

Priesthood stands and veil (rolled up) in Assembly Room of Kirtland Temple

Wilford's time in Kirtland was short, but three important events took place in his life while he was there. On January 3, 1837, he was called to be a member of the First Quorum of the Seventy.[137] Wilford met with his Quorum in the Kirtland Temple each week in the School of the Prophets and also took advantage of the opportunity to study Latin and Greek at the Kirtland School.[138] Wilford also met his future wife, Phebe Whittemore Carter, in January 1837. In the spring he was privileged to finally participate in the washing and anointing ordinances in the House of the Lord.

Phebe Whittemore Carter Woodruff in 1849

ENDOWMENT OF POWER

On April 3, Wilford helped gather the perfume and oil that would be used in the temple ceremonies.[139] The following day, during the meeting of the School of the Prophets, he was among those who received an "endowment of power."[140] This endowment was a spiritual experience, not the specific ceremony and narrative practiced in temples today. Those assembled shared gifts of the Spirit, speaking in and interpreting tongues. During these temple meetings angels administered to some and Wilford recorded that the Saints had the image of God in their countenances.

The first week of April 1837, Wilford joined with other men in the temple to be instructed and to prepare for the ordinances of washing and anointing. On April 3 and 4, just as Joseph Smith had directed those who had participated in the ordinances one year earlier, these men followed the Old Testament pattern of cleansing their bodies with water and perfuming themselves, prior to the ceremonial anointings and blessings.[141]

In writing about their experience Wilford recorded the words from the hymn "The Spirit of God" which was sung at the temple's dedication. The composer, W. W. Phelps, included references to a New Testament parable to emphasize the role of those ordained to the priesthood as laborers in the vineyard: "We'll wash and be wash'd, and with oil be anointed, Withal not omitting the washing of feet: For he that receiveth his penny appointed, Must surely be clean at the harvest of wheat."[142]

Wilford both received and administered the washings on the afternoon of April 4 and, in the evening, the group assembled in the temple again to receive their anointings. Zebedee Coltrin anointed Wilford, consecrated Wilford unto God, pronounced additional blessings upon him, and sealed the blessing and anointing.[143]

Two days later, on April 6, Wilford attended the second annual Solemn Assembly in the Kirtland Temple. Wilford recorded their future hope was that, "all official members that can, will meet in the LORD's house annually to attend to the most solemn ordinances of the house of GOD and of receiving the visions and great things of heaven."[144] The purpose of the washing, purifying, and anointing ceremonies was to physically prepare the Saints for the Spirit. Through these intense spiritual experiences, where the gifts of the Spirit were manifest, the ultimate goal was to sanctify themselves and prepare themselves to meet

God. Seeing God was what Joseph wanted all the Saints to experience in mortality.[145]

As they had the previous year, the presidency of the Church, the apostles, and other priesthood quorums, gathered in the upper rooms of the Kirtland Temple to seal their ordinations, washings, anointings and blessings. This time Wilford was included along with other members of the First Quorum of the Seventy. During the "washing of the feet of the anointed" which followed, Heber C. Kimball washed Wilford's feet and pronounced great blessings upon him before they all rejoined the congregation.[146]

Wilford described the instruction from Joseph Smith at that time as vastly important. He wrote that Joseph's language, sentiment, and spirit was powerful enough to "drive into oblivion every particle of unbelief and dubiety."[147] According to Wilford, both day and night were spent gloriously by the Saints. The meeting continued until the following morning and they then returned to their individual homes "with great joy and consolation."[148]

490	MESSENGER AND ADVOCATE.
sea.	DIED—In Ray County Mo. after
I am as ever yours,	a lingering illness, Brother Ezra Har-
J. M. GRANTS.	rington, aged forty seven years.
W. A. COWDERY.	Communicated.
	DIED—In this town on the 28th of
HYMENIAL.	January last Mary Ann Boynton, aged
Married in this town on the 13th	twenty seven years.
inst. by F. G. Williams Esq. Elder	
Jonathan H. Holmes to Miss Marietta	NOTICE.
Carter, Elder Willford Woodruff to	A comference of Elders and members of
Miss Phebe W. Carter, and Elder	the church of Latter Day Saints will be held
George W. Robinson to Miss Athalia	in Rut and Hollow Jefferson Co. N. Y. on
Rigdon all of this town.	the first Saturday in June next at 10 o clock
	A. M.

Wilford and Phebe's wedding announcement in the Kirtland newspaper

Throughout the winter, Wilford continued his courtship of Phebe Carter. In 1836, at the age of twenty-eight, Phebe had left her parents behind in Scarborough, Maine, to gather with the Saints in Kirtland. On April 13, Wilford and Phebe were married by Frederick G. Williams in Joseph Smith's home.

Two days later, on April 15, Wilford received his patriarchal blessing from Joseph Smith Sr. In his blessing Wilford was promised the administration of angels and the Spirit of God to instruct him. He was also told he had a great work to do and by faith he would bring all of his relatives into the kingdom of God.[149]

On May 31, Wilford left his new bride to serve his second mission, because, in his words, "The Lord told me to go, and I went."[150] It was during this mission that he was called to be an Apostle and some of the promises in his patriarchal blessing regarding his family were fulfilled.[151]

SAVING THE LIVING AND THE DEAD

Wilford's greatest desire as a missionary was to share the gospel with his own relatives. He had always shared his religious beliefs with them, but each one had joined with a different church or declined to participate with any organized religion. On his mission he wrote that since he had become a member of the Church of Jesus Christ of Latter-day Saints and entered the new and everlasting covenant, his concern over his father's salvation, in particular, had deepened.

He wanted to declare the message of the restored gospel and thus offer salvation to his father and his father's extended family. In a letter to his brother Asahel he expressed this by saying, "It is one of the greatest desires of my soul that you may see, understand, believe and embrace the work . . . for I feel a deep interest in the salvation of your soul and I beg the privilege of enjoying your society in a celestial kingdom."[152]

In July 1838 he preached the gospel in his hometown, Farmington, Connecticut, and was privileged to baptize members of his own family. He called it a "scene of won-der" and described how through the mercy of God he was permitted to share God's word through the power of the priesthood with his relatives and experience "the living reality of a Father, Mother, an only Sister ... receiving the ordinances of the house of God at [my] hand."[153] He was able to travel to Scarborough, Maine in time to be with Phebe for the birth of their first child, a daughter they named Sarah Emma, on July 14, 1838.

Between 1837 and 1839, while Wilford was teaching the gospel in the eastern states and the Fox Islands off the coast of Maine, the mounting problems in Kirtland forced the Saints from Ohio. Within a year of Wilford's departure from Kirtland, many Church leaders became disaffected or were excommunicated, including three members of the First Presidency and four of the Quorum of the Twelve Apostles. Those who remained faithful followed Joseph Smith to Far West, Missouri, where they laid the corner-stones for another temple and made plans for a new city.

The Saints' plans were not well-received by the locals, and tensions increased to the point of armed conflict in the fall of 1838. Wilford learned through letters and newspaper accounts of the tragedies at Crooked River and Haun's Mill and the Saints' expulsion from Missouri. During the incar-ceration of Joseph Smith and other Church leaders in Liberty Jail, between October 1838 and April 1839, the Saints began to gather in Quincy and then Commerce (renamed Nauvoo), Illinois.

THE FOUNDATION

Twenty years had passed since Joseph Smith's First Vision. As promised, the priesthood authority to act in God's name had been restored. The Church was organized with dea-cons, teachers, priests, elders, seventies, apostles, and patriarchs. The leadership of the Church was organized in presidencies and by quorums. Missionaries were preaching the gospel to the ends of the earth and those who accepted their teachings were being baptized into the Church and kingdom of God on the earth. The first temple had been built and provided a place for sacred experiences. Elijah had returned and delivered the sealing keys as Moroni had prophesied in 1823.

The revelations received in Kirtland, regarding the spirit world, and degrees of glory, set the stage for the doctrinal development in Nauvoo. During the final years of Joseph's life, God would reveal not only the saving ordinance of baptism for the dead, but the endowment and sealing ordinances necessary for exaltation.

~ 4 ~

Baptism for the Dead and Rebaptism

Like other converts, Wilford's desire to share the blessings of the restored gospel with his family members extended to both his living and deceased relatives. Through the revelations in Kirtland, the Saints understood that their deceased loved ones would have the opportunity to be taught the gospel as spirits. Nevertheless, preaching the gospel to those in the spirit world would only be efficacious if the saving ordinances were also made available to them. It was in Nauvoo that God revealed how that could be accomplished, how the living could act on behalf of the dead.

In 1842, Joseph Smith taught the Saints, "if we can baptize a man in the name of the Father, of the Son, and of the Holy Ghost, for the remission of sins, it is just as much our privilege to act as an agent, and be baptized for the remission of sins for and in behalf of our dead kindred, who have not heard the Gospel, or fulness of it."[154] To the incredulous, Joseph responded, "It is no more incredible that God should *save* the dead, than that he should *raise* the dead."[155]

VICARIOUS BAPTISMS
Wilford, along with seven other members of the Quorum of the Twelve Apostles, was serving a mission in England in August 1840 when Joseph Smith gave his first public

discourse regarding baptism for the dead. Phebe was present when Joseph explained the doctrine further in the Church conference on October 5, 1840, and the following day she wrote to share the incredible news with Wilford. Phebe described baptism for the dead as "strong meat;" one of the "strange doctrines" Joseph had brought forth that season. However, she said, he made it very plain and consistent with the gospel. Phebe simply wrote, "How can a spirit be baptized . . . [W]hy not deputise a friend on earth to do it for them?" She added that, according to Joseph's instructions, members of the Church could be baptized for any of their relatives: parents, grandparents, brothers, sisters, children, aunts and uncles who had not had the privilege of receiving the gospel, "but not for acquaintances unless they send a ministering spirit to their friends on earth." She told Wilford that Joseph taught that as soon as the Saints are baptized for their deceased loved ones, they are released from prison and the Saints will then be able to "claim them in the resurrection and bring them into the celestial kingdom."[156]

The Saints accepted the doctrine enthusiastically. They had to be baptized and confirmed separately for every person, and Phebe told Wilford they were "going forward in multitudes" and some were baptized by proxy "as many as 16 times."[157] Indeed, hundreds were baptized in the Mississippi River and local streams around Nauvoo for their deceased relatives and friends.[158]

Joseph Smith matter-of-factly shared this incredible doctrinal development with the apostles in England through a letter of his own written December 15, 1840.[159] Assuming the apostles had heard the news of his announcement from friends and family, as Wilford had from Phebe, and it had inevitably raised some questions in their minds, he wrote to explain it further. Joseph was certain that baptism for the dead had been practiced by the ancient churches, and that he had independent knowledge of the doctrine.

He quoted First Corinthians 15:29 wherein Paul referenced baptism for the dead in his effort to prove the doctrine of the resurrection.[160] Then Joseph closed his letter by stating, "The Saints have the privilege of being baptized for those of their relatives who . . . have received the Gospel in the spirit through the instrumentality of those who may have been commissioned to preach to them while in the prison. Without enlarging on the subject you will undoubtedly see its consistency, and reasonableness, and [it] presents . . . the gospel of Christ in probably a more enlarged scale than some have received it."[161]

Composite of apostles serving missions in the British Isles between 1840 and 1841

Wilford did see the reasonableness and consistency of baptism for the dead, and said that the moment he heard of it his soul leaped with joy. The doctrine of vicarious baptism proved to Wilford that God was reasonable, wise, just, and true, and "possessed both the best of attributes, and good sense, and knowledge . . . consistent with love, mercy, justice, and judgment."[162] As a result, Wilford loved the Lord more than ever. He later testified that the revelation was like a "shaft of light from the throne of God" and "opened a field wide as eternity to our minds."[163]

He had not previously been satisfied with the doctrine taught by others regarding the salvation of those who had not heard the gospel in mortality. Because, Wilford reasoned, there are millions who never had the privilege of being baptized for themselves, and "hence never ought to be punished for not obeying a law which they never heard."[164] The restoration of this part of the gospel was as Wilford imagined it should be: mirroring Christ's Atonement, the Saints could act vicariously to satisfy the law of justice.[165]

THE BEGINNING OF THE WORK

Wilford felt the pieces were now in place. Baptism by immersion for the remission of sins and baptism by the Spirit were essential for admission into Christ's church on earth and entrance into the kingdom of God in heaven.[166] Therefore, gospel truths must be taught to every person so they would have the opportunity to believe and accept these saving ordinances. Wilford knew God is no respecter of persons and would not give the privilege of hearing the gospel to one generation and withhold it from another. Those who died without the law, who did not have the opportunity to hear the gospel in the flesh, would not be held responsible by God for not obeying it, or be under condemnation "for rejecting a law they never saw or understood."[167]

Wilford trusted that these individuals would be taught in the spirit world.[168] Their relatives on earth thus had the privilege and responsibility to act as proxy for them in completing the necessary ordinances, so they "might be judged according to men in the flesh, [while living] according to God in the spirit."[169] Attending to this work for the spirits in prison was vital, for, said Wilford, "[It] takes just as much to save a dead man who never received the Gospel as a living man. And all those who have passed away without the Gospel have the right to expect somebody in the flesh to perform this work for them."[170] The Saints immediately began writing to their extended family members asking for information on their deceased relatives and compiling lists of all those for whom they wanted to act as proxies.

Initially Joseph's counsel was for members of the Church to act as proxy for their own relatives, but he said they could be baptized for those they had "much friendship for" as well.[171] Joseph also set the precedent that would apply to future vicarious ordinances when he told the Saints, "Every man that has been baptized and belongs to the kingdom has a right to be baptized for those who have gone before."[172] Thus only those who first qualified for the ordinance themselves could perform that ordinance on behalf of another.

The baptismal records from this period contain not only the date and name of the proxy and the person for whom the proxy was acting, but also the relationship of the proxy to the deceased person. The majority of proxy baptisms were for relatives, but a few Saints were baptized on behalf of non-relatives with whom they had had a close relationship or for whom they had much respect.[173] For example, Joseph Smith's brother Don Carlos was baptized for George Washington; Sarah M. Cleveland was baptized for Martha Washington; Stephen Jones for Thomas Jefferson; and George Adams for John Adams.[174]

In the case of non-relatives, the relationship of the proxy was listed in the records as "friend." On the other hand, some of those referred to as friends were actually relatives. For example, when Wilford and Phebe were baptized as proxies in 1844 Wilford wrote: "I went to the river in company with Mrs. Woodruff to be baptized for some of our dead friends." They were then baptized by George A. Smith and confirmed by Willard Richards as proxy for five of their relatives in the Hart, Thompson, Carter, and Woodruff families.[175]

REFINING REVELATION
Though the requirement of baptism was absolute, the proper administration of the ordinance of baptism for the dead required years to refine. Reflecting on this fact, Wilford explained, "All was not revealed at once, but the Lord showed the Prophet a principle, and the people acted upon it according to the light which they had. All the perfection and glory of it was not revealed at first; but, as fast as it was revealed, the people endeavored to obey."[176] He added that, because of their enthusiasm for the privilege of acting on behalf on their relatives, they did not wait "to know what the result of this would be, or what the whole of it should be."[177]

This is an early example of what became a familiar cycle—revelation received on a certain doctrine, the Saints' implementation of the related principles and practice, and thoughtful consideration of their experiences—which led Church leaders to seek additional revelation. For instance, even though the vicarious baptisms had been performed by proper priesthood authority, not all baptisms had been witnessed and recorded. This changed after God revealed the importance of witnesses to the ordinances. In letters to the Saints written in September 1842, now part of the Doctrine and Covenants, Joseph Smith explained that all baptisms for the dead must have an eyewitness present who would be able to testify to the validity of the record. "That in all your recordings it may be recorded in heaven . . . [and] held in remembrance from generation to generation."[178]

Later, another refinement occurred after it was determined that men should only serve as proxies for male relatives and women only for female relatives.[179] Wilford recalled that initially, he and others were baptized for both male and female relatives. "[B]ut, afterwards, we obtained more light upon the subject, and President Young taught the people that men should attend to those ordinances for the male portion of their dead friends, and females for females. This showed the order in which those ordinances should be administered, which ordinances had before been revealed, and shows us that we are in a school where we shall be constantly learning."[180]

For example, in August 1844 Wilford and Phebe repeated the proxy baptisms they had performed in 1842.[181] After recording the ordinances in his journal, he explained they had to be baptized for them again, "In consequence of there being no [official] record kept in the above baptisms . . . and women were baptized for men which is not legal."[182]

The reason for the change regarding gender was not evident until additional temple ordinances were revealed. When the Saints began serving as proxies for their relatives in all the vicarious ordinances, they understood that although a woman could be baptized on behalf of a male relative, she could not act as proxy in the other ordinances such as ordination to the priesthood, the endowment, or the sealing ordinance. Brigham Young thought, "It would be very strange . . . if we were called upon to commence a work that we could not finish. . . . [C]onsequently the sisters are to be baptized for their own sex only."[183] Thus a man would commence and complete all the necessary ordinances—baptism, confirmation, ordination, washings, anointings, endowment, and sealing—on behalf of other men, and a woman would do the same for other women.

ANOTHER TEMPLE MUST BE BUILT

In August 1840, the same month that Joseph Smith first taught baptism for the dead, the Saints had begun making plans to build another temple. A letter from the First Presidency addressed "to the Saints abroad" stated, "[I]t is necessary to erect a house of prayer, a house of order, a house of worship of our God, where the ordinances can be attended to agreeably to His divine will."[184] They subsequently located a limestone quarry, and chose William Weeks as the architect.

However, preparations for construction of the temple had barely started when a new revelation was received. On January 19, 1841, only four months after the first vicarious baptisms were performed, the Lord declared that the ordinance of baptism for the dead belonged in His house and must be performed in a font prepared for that purpose.[185] The Lord reassured the Saints that until they could complete the temple, He would continue to accept the vicarious baptisms being performed in the rivers and streams.[186]

After sharing this revelation with the Saints, Joseph stressed the compelling need to build the temple where all the functions of the priesthood could be exercised, and sacred instructions from God could be received. Joseph asked the Saints to concentrate all their powers on these things "which are of such vast importance to this and every succeeding generation."[187] Their enthusiasm and hope in the salvation of all men was evidenced by the monumental task they immediately undertook. The city was divided into four wards and all of the men were asked to tithe their income or labor, working one day in ten on the temple, and the women participated in the effort by providing extra food, clothing and materials for the laborers.

Steel engraving of the city of Nauvoo in the 1840s

In spite of the fact that they were still struggling to build their own homes and care for the thousands who were gathering to Nauvoo, they began to dig the foundation and basement on February 18, 1841. It was completed in ten days. Within seven weeks they were able to build the foundation walls up to ground level using quarried stones four to five feet thick. At a time when the population of the city of Chicago was less than 6,000, an estimated 10,000 people attended the temple cornerstone laying ceremony in Nauvoo on April 6, 1841.[188]

In July, William Weeks began building a temporary wooden font, anticipating a stone font would be built later. His design followed the pattern of the molten sea in Solomon's Temple which was placed on the backs of twelve oxen representing the twelve tribes of Israel.[189] In August he turned the woodwork over to Elijah Fordham who carved the twelve oxen upon which the font would be placed.[190]

SAVIORS ON MOUNT ZION

When Wilford and the other apostles returned from England in October 1841, they asked Joseph to give additional instructions on the doctrine of baptism for the dead. They wanted to understand how they could be instruments in God's hands to bring their relatives into the kingdom of God. Quoting Obadiah's prophecy, Joseph presented baptism for the dead as the only way that men can appear as "saviours on Mount Zion."[191] Joseph made clear that faith, repentance, baptism by immersion and receipt of the gift of the Holy Ghost were the means of salvation to men individually. Serving as proxies to perform baptisms for their relatives meant they were "actively engaging in rites of salvation substitutionally."[192] Nevertheless, Joseph emphasized that although men and women on earth needed to administer this proxy ordinance, only acceptance of the gospel truths would save those for whom the ordinances were performed.[193]

On October 3, 1841, ten months after the Lord revealed that the ordinance of baptism for the dead belonged in His House, Joseph announced that proxy baptisms would no longer be allowed until they could be performed in the temple font.[194] Within a month the pinewood baptismal font, measuring sixteen by twelve by seven feet, was completed and placed upon the twelve carved oxen. The font was dedicated November 8, 1841, and two weeks later was prepared for "the reception of candidates."[195] On November 21 Wilford recorded that forty persons were baptized in this, the first font "erected for this glorious purpose in this last dispensation."[196] Wilford assisted in confirming those who were baptized and described the whole experience as "truly interesting."

Personal worthiness was part of the Saints' preparation to act on behalf of others in this important temple ordinance. For example, paying a full tithing was a requirement for proxies performing baptisms in the Nauvoo Temple.[197] Baptism for the dead was thus an opportunity for the living to revisit their commitment to gospel principles and renew their own baptismal covenants. In fact, baptism for the dead was considered a rebaptism for the person acting as proxy. Some baptismal certificates from this period stated that the individual renewed his or her covenants with God when baptized in behalf of one who was dead. Words to that effect, such as "for the remission of your sins" or "for the renewal of your covenants" were added to the ordinance.[198] When Wilford went to the font on May 7 and baptized about 100 people, he recorded in his journal that he baptized them for the "remission of sins, the healing of the body, and for the dead."[199]

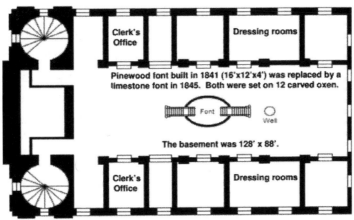

Floor plan of the Nauvoo Temple basement

BAPTISM FOR HEALTH AND HEALING

The commencement of baptisms for the dead in the temple font in 1841 led to the introduction of another type of baptism: baptism for healing or the restoration of health. As with the reinstatement of other ordinances connecting the restored church to the ancient church, Joseph Smith's scriptural precedent for this practice is found in both the Old and New Testaments. The connection between water, or washing, and healing is evident in Elisha's instruction for Naaman to wash in the River Jordan, and the Savior's direction to the blind man to wash in the pool of Siloam.[200]

The first written reference to baptisms for healing in Nauvoo was in an epistle from the Quorum of the Twelve. In October 1841, shortly after their return from missionary service in England, Wilford joined the other apostles in sending a letter to the Saints outside Nauvoo stressing the importance of the temple and asking for the Saints' support in completing it. Their letter included a reference to the healing powers of the pool at Bethesda.[201] It read, in part, "The time has come when the great Jehovah would have a resting place on earth, a habitation for his chosen, where his law shall be revealed, and his servants be [endowed] from on high . . . where the saints may enter the baptismal font for their dead relations . . . a place, over which the heavenly messengers may watch and trouble the waters as in days of old, so that when the sick are put therein they shall be made whole."[202]

The first record of a miraculous healing was at the dedication of the baptismal font in the temple on November 8, 1841. Samuel Rolfe, who attended the dedication, had a very infected finger which the doctors had said would not heal for months. Joseph Smith promised Samuel his finger would be healed if he washed his hands in the font. Samuel did so, and within a week his hand was "perfectly healed."[203] While this "washing" was not a baptism, it began the practice of using the temple baptismal fonts for healing and the restoration of health which continued for over eighty years.[204]

REBAPTISM FOR A REMISSION OF SIN

During the period from 1841 to 1842 there was a general call for reformation of the Church in Nauvoo. Joseph Smith and other Church leaders encouraged the Saints to be rebaptized for the remission of sins and to renew the covenants they had made.[205] This was not the first instance of rebaptism for remission of sins however. The practice of rebaptizing to remit sin evidently began shortly after the Church was organized. The earliest record of rebaptism for a remission of sin was that of David Johnson on May 7, 1832.[206] In most cases, the baptisms were not for specific sins, but for a remission of all sins. These rebaptisms were not considered a requirement for salvation; they were simply a public indication of an individual's personal commitment.[207]

In his journal Wilford recorded hundreds of rebaptisms following discourses on the subject. For example, on March 20, 1842, he wrote that Joseph Smith spoke on the significance of baptism then invited the congregation to pray for the Spirit, humble themselves, and meet him at the river where he would attend to the ordinance. That afternoon Joseph baptized eighty individuals in the river then helped confirm them. That same day, Wilford, with other members of the Quorum of the Twelve, baptized and confirmed eighty more in the temple font.[208]

One week later, on March 27, 1842, Wilford was rebaptized for the remission of sins for the first time.[209] That day Joseph again addressed the subject of baptism for remission of sins. After the meeting, the congregation returned to the Mississippi River and Joseph baptized "all that came unto him," including Wilford. In his journal Wilford recorded that he considered it a privilege to be rebaptized for the remission of his sins at this time, as it had been nine years since his initial baptism into the Church.[210]

At the Church Conference held the following month, April 1842, Joseph Smith set the precedent for generations when he instructed the Saints that baptisms for the dead and for healing must be in the temple font, while baptisms for those coming into the Church and those being rebaptized could be in the river.[211] Wilford refers to being rebaptized and baptizing many for health and healing over the years. Both Wilford and Brigham Young were rebaptized at least six times.[212]

ADOPTION INTO THE FAMILY OF GOD

The individuals who accepted baptism into the restored Church of Jesus Christ understood that baptism by water was for the remission of sins so they could be reborn as children of God.[213] Furthermore, baptism by the Spirit was primarily for the receipt of the Holy Ghost and secondarily for admission into the Church and kingdom of God. Baptism corrected for the lack of birthright in the kingdom of God, "the defect of having no natural and legitimate claim of heirship."[214]

The first written references to adoption into the kingdom of God by baptism were made by Parley P. Pratt in his 1837 publication *A Voice of Warning*.[215] Parley gave the example of Christ's Apostles who were expected to "unlock the door of the kingdom, and to adopt strangers and foreigners into it as legal citizens, by administering certain laws and ordinances."[216] He also indicated that converts will be gathered out and "adopted into the family of Israel . . . and be partakers of the same covenant of promise."[217] Joseph Smith explained—as Paul had written in his epistles to the early Saints—that only through baptism can we "legally call

God our Father, and approach him with the confidence of sons and children of the highest."[218]

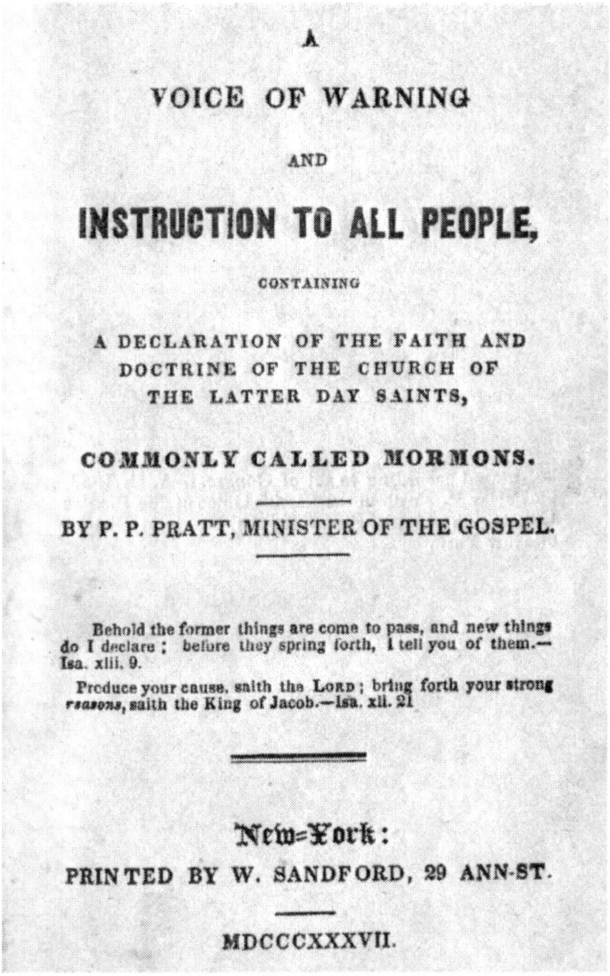

A

VOICE OF WARNING

AND

INSTRUCTION TO ALL PEOPLE,

CONTAINING

A DECLARATION OF THE FAITH AND DOCTRINE OF THE CHURCH OF THE LATTER DAY SAINTS,

COMMONLY CALLED MORMONS.

BY P. P. PRATT, MINISTER OF THE GOSPEL.

Behold the former things are come to pass, and new things do I declare ; before they spring forth, I tell you of them.— Isa. xlii. 9.
Produce your cause, saith the Lord ; bring forth your strong reasons, saith the King of Jacob.—Isa. xli. 21

New-York :

PRINTED BY W. SANDFORD, 29 ANN-ST.

MDCCCXXXVII.

Title page of *A Voice of Warning* written by Parley P. Pratt

In a letter to the Church written September 6, 1842, Joseph Smith taught that the living would be connected or sealed to their ancestral fathers by baptizing them by proxy, thus adopting them into the family and kingdom of God.[219] With reference to Elijah's mission, Joseph reminded the Saints that the earth would be smitten unless there is a welding link of some kind between the fathers and the children. "[F]or it is necessary," he continued, ". . . that a whole and complete and perfect union, and welding together of dispensations, and keys, and powers, and glories should take place . . . from the days of Adam even to the present time."[220] In his letter Joseph stated that the welding link between the fathers and their children was proxy baptism.[221]

Adoption into God's family through baptism would bind the Saints to those in heaven for whom they were being baptized, thus becoming brothers and sisters, a connection created by priesthood authority that would be recognized on earth and in heaven. When Joseph declared God would no longer accept baptisms for the dead performed outside the temple, this nascent doctrine of binding the generations through proxy baptisms became the impetus for accelerating the construction of the Nauvoo Temple.

The relationship of baptism to salvation had been unequivocally established by Jesus Christ.[222] On the other hand, the connection of baptism to the sealing power that Elijah had restored was a novel concept. Accordingly, when Wilford learned of baptism for the dead, he said, "The first thing that entered into my mind was that I had a mother in the spirit world. She died when I was 14 months old. I never knew [my] mother. I thought to myself, 'Have I power to go forth and seal my mother to my father?' The word was, yes."[223] Wilford willingly accepted the responsibility to serve as proxy for his relatives and recorded in his journal the names of others for whom he was baptized. They were, in addition to his mother Beulah, his brothers Philo and Asahel, aunts, uncles, grandparents, and his great-grandparents Josiah and Sarah Woodruff.[224]

Although official records were not kept of hundreds of the initial baptisms for the dead, based on journal entries and other records, an estimated 6,800 proxy baptisms were performed before the revelation requiring witnesses was received in September 1842.[225] The fact that there were only about 4,000 members of the Church living in Nauvoo at the time indicates their devotion to their deceased family members and their acceptance of the doctrine. Before the Saints were forced from Nauvoo in 1846, they recorded proxy baptisms for over 15,700 individuals.

Baptism for the dead was an illuminating and inclusive doctrine. It directed the living to their ancestors and opened the doors of salvation to all people, regardless of their circumstances in mortality. Joseph Smith, Wilford and the other Saints believed they now understood their role in fulfilling Elijah's mission. They were unaware that proxy baptism was only the first piece of the puzzle. The picture would not be complete until baptism was seen in the context of future revelations regarding the endowment and sealing ordinances for both the living and the dead. The Saints' work for the redemption of all mankind had just begun.

~ 5 ~

Temple Ordinances in Nauvoo

On March 30, 1836, after administering the first ordinances of washing and anointing in the Kirtland Temple, Joseph Smith declared to the assembled priesthood quorums that he had given them all the instruction they needed; they had passed through all the necessary ceremonies to go forth and establish the kingdom of God.[226] What Joseph didn't know yet was that the revelations and ordinances in Kirtland were only the foundation upon which God would build. Four years later the ordinance of baptism for the dead was introduced, which began an entirely new focus for the Church. This was the first ordinance revealed and marked the beginning of a period of intense doctrinal development. In January 1841, God promised the Saints that, once the temple was completed, He would reveal all things pertaining to the temple and the priesthood, including additional ordinances.[227]

Over the course of the next three years the promised revelations came one right after another. In 1842 Joseph began teaching a few Church leaders the sacred principles and administering not only the ordinances of washing and anointing, but also the endowment. The endowment ceremony included instructions regarding God's plan for His children from their existence as spirits, through their mortal life on earth, to their future in eternity. It outlined the path for them to follow once they had passed through the "gate" of baptism.[228] The sealing ordinance, required to continue on this path and gain exaltation in the highest degree of the celestial kingdom, was revealed the following year.[229]

During the last ten months of his life, Joseph was able to share the highest ordinances available to God's children on earth with the apostles and their wives, as well as a few other trusted individuals. Of this extraordinary time Wilford wrote, "Truly the Lord has raised up Joseph the Seer . . . and is now clothing him with mighty power and wisdom and knowledge which is more clearly manifest and felt in the midst of his intimate friends than any other class of mankind."[230]

THE BOOK OF ABRAHAM

When the apostles returned from their missions in October 1841 they were asked to take more responsibility for the temporal needs of the Church in order to relieve Joseph Smith of his increasing burden. After so many successful years in the mission field, it was a difficult transition for Wilford to make. At the same time, he was grateful for the opportunity to be with his family in "a city of the Saints in the midst of peace and love."[231] Wilford began hauling blocks from the stone quarry to the temple site in October, then in November he was assigned to work in the provision store. In January 1842 he and John Taylor were asked to run the Nauvoo Printing Office and publish the *Times and Seasons*.[232]

While John Taylor edited the publications, Wilford managed the business side of the office. On February 19, 1842, Wilford recorded how privileged he felt to be setting the type for the first publication of the Book of Abraham in the *Times and Seasons*.[233] At the time only Joseph knew that the truths contained in the Book of Abraham were a significant part of the narrative instruction he would soon teach in the endowment ceremony.[234] Wilford simply included in his journal his solemn testimony that, "The Lord is blessing Joseph with power to reveal the mysteries of the kingdom of God; to translate through the Urim and Thummim ancient records and hieroglyphics as old as Abraham or Adam, which causes our hearts to burn within us while we behold their glorious truths opened unto us."[235]

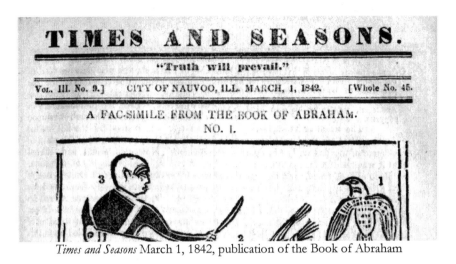

Times and Seasons March 1, 1842, publication of the Book of Abraham

From this book of scripture the Saints learned of their place among the noble and great ones in a pre-mortal existence, their opportunity to prove themselves in mortality, and the impact their earthly decisions would have on their eternal lives.[236] The "gift of knowledge" Wilford and the other Church leaders would soon receive through the endowment would broaden their understanding of these concepts and prepare them to receive further light and knowledge from God.

PRIESTHOOD KEYS

As persecution increased from outside the Church, and dissension within the Church began to reach the highest levels of leadership, Joseph Smith wanted to ensure that the keys of the priesthood he held would be preserved and properly used.[237] On April 28, 1842, when speaking to the newly organized Female Relief Society, he explained that the keys were about to be given to the Church, both to the Elders and to members of the Relief Society.[238]

Accordingly, on May 3, Joseph had the assembly room in the upper floor of his store prepared to resemble the interior of a temple as much as possible.[239] Then, the following day, he gathered nine men whom he felt he could trust—his brother and Church Patriarch Hyrum Smith; Second Counselor in the First Presidency William Law; apostles Brigham Young, Heber C. Kimball, and Willard Richards; Nauvoo Stake President William Marks; bishops Newel K. Whitney and George Miller; and Springfield Branch President James Adams—and instructed them in the "principles and order of the Priesthood."[240]

Joseph Smith's restored Red Brick Store in Nauvoo, Illinois

Joseph recorded that they also attended to "washings, anointings, endowments and the communication of keys pertaining to the Aaronic priesthood, and so on to the highest order of the Melchizedek priesthood, setting forth the order pertaining to the Ancient of Days, and all those plans and principles by which any one is enabled to secure the fulness of those blessings which have been prepared."[241] These men were then able to administer the sacred ordinances to Joseph and Hyrum the following day. Joseph explained at the time that there was nothing taught to these men that the other Saints would not be able to learn as soon as they were ready and a proper place was prepared.[242]

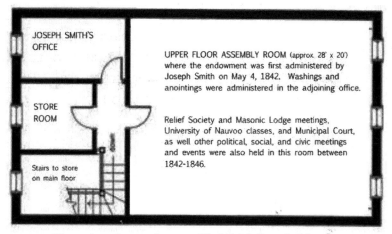

Floor plan of second story of Red Brick Store in Nauvoo

The fact that the Nauvoo Masonic Lodge was established on March 15, 1842, and many members of the Church became Masons—including Joseph Smith, Brigham Young, John Taylor and Wilford Woodruff—is sometimes cited as evidence that Joseph derived the temple ordinances from Masonic rituals. Similarities with Masonry were evident in parts of the ceremonial method Joseph Smith employed. For example, some of the symbols and hand signs used in the presentation of the temple covenants are used in Masonic ceremonies.[243] Yet the symbols used in both ceremonies, such as the compass and square, are universal and represent universal concepts. In addition, some elements Joseph incorporated are found in ancient Christian and Old Testament rituals connected to the priests serving in the Tabernacle—such as washings, anointings, and ceremonial clothing—unrelated to nineteenth-century Masonry.[244]

However, any claim that the temple ordinances were copied wholesale from Masonry—rather than revealed by God to His Prophet—was apparently not something that concerned Wilford or others like him who were introduced to both Masonry and the endowment in Nauvoo. The Saints distinguished between the ordinances and covenants *per se* and their presentation within the ceremonies. Although the Masonic and endowment rituals had common elements, the covenants and ordinances introduced by Joseph had no parallel in Masonry and were unique to Joseph's religious instruction. Freemasonry teaches about the relationship between men as a fraternal brotherhood; the temple instruction concerned the relationship of men and women with God. The two were not incompatible nor were they mutually exclusive.

Wilford's Nauvoo contemporaries within the Church viewed Masonry as a tradition, like other Christian religions in the 1840s, containing fragments of truth preserved from ancient, unadulterated doctrines.[245] Yet, in his 7,000 pages of journals, Wilford mentions Masonry only thirteen times and never in connection with the temple ordinances.[246] He apparently felt comfortable participating in both ceremonies separately but simultaneously.

The purpose of the ceremonies in the Kirtland Temple, which Wilford participated in, were to receive "the visions and great things of heaven."[247] This "endowment of power" in Kirtland—unrelated to any Masonic traditions—involved intense spiritual experiences designed to bring the

Saints into God's presence; to actually see God as Joseph Smith had.[248] The endowment in Nauvoo used ritual to figuratively accomplish the same goal. The instruction associated with the ordinances, helped the Saints understand what they needed to do in mortality to dwell with God for eternity.[249]

Joseph Smith in 1842
Courtesy of Community of Christ Archives

THE MAN IS NOT WITHOUT THE WOMAN

On May 16, 1843, one year after the endowment ceremony was first introduced, Joseph Smith received a vision indicating that within the celestial kingdom there are three degrees of celestial glory. He learned that in order to obtain the highest degree, and eternal increase, a man must enter into the new and everlasting covenant of marriage.[250] Prior to this revelation, only men had participated in the washing and anointing ordinances and endowment ceremonies and been instructed regarding the keys pertaining to the Aaronic and Melchizedek priesthoods. The fact that eternal marriage was required to receive the "fulness of blessings" alluded to in the endowment meant their wives must be full participants in all the ceremonies.[251] As the Apostle Paul taught centuries earlier, the man is not without the woman, nor the woman without the man, in the Lord.[252]

Accordingly, on May 28, Joseph and Emma were sealed for eternity. Hyrum and Brigham were sealed to their wives the following day.[253] Six weeks later, on July 12, 1843, Joseph recorded the details of the doctrines and principles relating to celestial marriage and the need for all marriage covenants to be sealed "for time and for all eternity." These principles had been revealed to him several years earlier, but because of their implications in plural marriage, Joseph delayed sharing them with even his closest relatives and friends.[254]

The revelation, as recorded in 1843, references an eternal covenant made between husband and wife, and the sealing of that marriage covenant, not the sealing of husband and wife to each other. If "a man marry a wife, and make a covenant with her . . . [and] that covenant is not by me or by my word, which is my law, and is not sealed by the Holy Spirit of promise, through him whom I have anointed and appointed unto this power, then it is not valid neither of force when they are out of the world."[255] Their eternal lives end and they do not inherit exaltation. During his lifetime, Joseph sealed marriages, and empowered others such as Brigham Young and Hyrum Smith to perform sealings.[256]

THE LORD HOLDS US RESPONSIBLE[257]

The ability to exercise priesthood power to administer ordinances that would affect their eternal existence was hard for the Saints to fathom. On September 6, 1842, referring to Matthew 16:19, Joseph explained, "It may seem to some to be a very bold doctrine that we talk of—a power which records or binds on earth and binds in heaven. Nevertheless, in all ages of the world, whenever the Lord has given a dispensation of the priesthood to any man by actual revelation, or any set of men, this power has always been given. Hence, whatsoever those men did in authority, in the name of the Lord . . . it became a law on earth and in heaven, and could not be annulled, according to the decrees of the great Jehovah."[258]

Initially the Saints understood the concept of "sealing" through such biblical scriptures as an earthly validation of a priesthood act or ordinance so it would be recognized in heaven.[259] In other words, if an ordinance was sealed or confirmed by one having the proper priesthood authority, God would recognize the ordinance as valid in this life and in the life to come. For example, in 1836 the washing and anointing ordinances administered in the Kirtland Temple were sealed upon those who received them.[260] In addition, priesthood authority could be used to seal individuals to some spiritual status, such as sealing the wicked to damnation and the righteous to eternal life.[261]

However, sealing or ratifying specific ordinances so they would be valid beyond death, and sealing or binding individuals to one another—such as husbands to wives or children to parents—are significantly different. Wilford explained the importance of having ordinances sealed by the priesthood in these words: "The Lord has revealed to us that . . . no ordinance of marriage, no ordinance performed by any man from the days of father Adam, will have any power or force after death, except those ordinances are performed by men holding the Eternal Priesthood. . . . [A]ny man that marries a wife by any other authority than the authority of the Holy Priesthood is simply married for time, or 'until death do you part.' When you go into the spirit world you have no claim on your wife and children. The ordinance of having them sealed to you by one having the authority of the Holy Priesthood must be attended to in this world."[262]

Baptism for the dead had turned the hearts of the children to their fathers and provided a welding link to the family of God, but the sealing of husbands and wives, meant those relationships would survive death and those earthly family bonds would be recognized in heaven.

Wilford and Phebe were sealed on November 11, 1843. Wilford wrote that Hyrum Smith "sealed the marriage covenant between me and my wife Phebe W. Carter for time and eternity."[263] His language reflects their understanding that sealing through the power of the priesthood applied to covenants and ordinances. Sealing of individuals to each other was a new concept that would be reflected months later.[264]

In describing the context of their marriage sealing, Wilford's journal entry includes his conversation with John Taylor regarding this "principle of the celestial world" and Hyrum Smith's presentation about exaltation in the new and everlasting covenant that "reacheth into the eternal world."[265] These were new and incredible notions.

THE PATRIARCHAL ORDER OF MARRIAGE

The introduction of the sealing ordinances relating to marriage necessarily introduced plural marriage, at least in the eternal sense. Many nineteenth century men and women remarried during their lifetimes due to the early death of their first spouses. Brigham Young and Hyrum Smith were among the first taught the doctrine of sealing, and both had remarried after the deaths of their first wives. Thus, after these men were sealed to their living wives, they were also sealed to their deceased wives. Their living wives acted as proxies in the second sealings. Nevertheless, accepting the possibility of plural marriage in the eternities was much further than a step away from accepting the reality of plural marriage as part of their everyday lives.

Although marriage to more than one living wife was a part of scriptural record, it had never been universally practiced in any age and was certainly not an accepted social norm in nineteenth century American society. When Joseph Smith was translating portions of the Bible, he asked God why He permitted the practice of plural marriage by Old Testament patriarchs and prophets, such as Abraham, Moses, David, and Solomon. God's response to Joseph's inquiry—now section 132 of the Doctrine and Covenants—was simple. In this revelation, God explained that the Old Testament prophets were not under condemnation for marrying more than one wife because they were doing what the Lord had commanded, and it was "accounted unto [them] for righteousness."[266] They were only condemned when they took wives not given to them by the Lord.[267]

As explained by Jacob in the Book of Mormon, plural marriage is the exception to the commandment that men should have only one wife, and is sanctioned by the Lord only when He commands His people to raise up righteous posterity.[268]

The sacrifice God was requiring was astonishing to the Saints, but not without precedent. To help them understand, God compared His command to marry more than one wife to His command for Abraham to kill his son Isaac. Abraham's willingness to sacrifice Isaac was in direct defiance of God's universal law not to kill, yet it was "accounted unto him for righteousness."[269] Similarly, God's command to Joseph Smith and the ancient prophets to marry more than one wife conflicted with another of His commandments: "Thou shalt love thy wife with all thy heart, and shall cleave unto her and none else."[270] Nevertheless, God, the lawgiver and ultimate judge, can make exceptions to His own laws and promise blessings rather than condemnation to those who obey Him.

Thus Joseph was instructed to accept and teach the principle of patriarchal marriage as part of the restoration of all things: the New Testament church and the Old Testament practices.[271] This principle meant men would not only be sealed consecutively to multiple wives, resulting in plural marriage in the hereafter, but be sealed concurrently to multiple wives and live it on a daily basis.

In obedience to the Lord's command, Joseph Smith began teaching a few individuals about patriarchal marriage in 1840. When members of the Quorum of the Twelve Apostles returned from their missions to England in 1841, Joseph taught the doctrine to them one by one.[272] As with other doctrines, Joseph asked them to go to God for confirmation. He promised the men and the women that the unions sealed by the priesthood would make future eternal progression possible, not only for them but for their children. Nevertheless, the doctrine was shocking to the Saints and the general public.[273]

WILFORD AND PHEBE'S CONVICTION

Even with the promised blessings, Wilford and Phebe had difficulty accepting the doctrine of plural marriage. Only after receiving confirmation from God that it was His will, did they eventually accept it and live it faithfully for the remainder of their lives. In Phebe's words, "When the principle of polygamy was first taught I thought it the most wicked thing I ever heard of; consequently I opposed it to the best of my ability, until I became sick and wretched. As soon, however, as I became convinced that it originated as a revelation from God through Joseph, and knowing him to be a prophet, I wrestled with my Heavenly Father in fervent prayer, to be guided aright at that all-important moment of my life. The answer came. Peace was given to my mind. I knew it was the will of God; and from that time to the present I have sought to faithfully honor the patriarchal law."[274]

PROCEEDINGS IN MASS MEETING

OF THE

LADIES OF SALT LAKE CITY,

TO

PROTEST AGAINST THE PASSAGE OF CULLOM'S BILL,

JANUARY 14, 1870.

Notwithstanding the inclemency of the weather, the Tabernacle was densely packed with ladies of all ages, old, young, and middle aged.

On the motion of Sister Eliza R. Snow, Mrs. Sarah N. Kimball, President of the Female Relief Society of the fifteenth ward, was elected president of the meeting.

Mrs. Lydia Alder was appointed secretary of the meeting.

The following ladies were proposed and unanimously sustained as a committee to draft

our people by a spirit of intolerant persecution. I watched by the bedside of the first apostle, David W. Patten, who fell a martyr in the church. He was a noble soul. He was shot by a mob while defending the Saints in the State of Missouri, Ray county, on the 25th of October, 1838. As brother Patten's life-blood oozed away, I stood by and heard his dying testimony to the truth of our holy religion, declaring himself to be a friend to all mankind. He sacrificed his life freely to defend the innocent. He had no feelings of hostility to his

Record of rally where Phebe Woodruff spoke in support of plural marriage

Later Phebe would publicly defend plural marriage and her Constitutional right to freely exercise her religion. At an 1870 rally, she posed the question: "Shall we, as wives and mothers, sit still and see our husbands and sons, whom we know are obeying the highest behest of heaven, suffer for their religion, without exerting ourselves to the extent of our power for their deliverance?" Her response was, "No; verily no! God has revealed unto us the law of the patriarchal order of marriage, and commanded us to obey it. We are sealed to our husbands for time and eternity that we may dwell with them and our children in the world to come; which guarantees unto us the greatest blessing for which we are created."[275]

Wilford also gained a testimony of the law of patriarchal marriage and found that it paralleled scriptural precedent. He said, "Father Abraham obeyed the law of the patriarchal order of marriage. His wives were sealed to him for time and all eternity, and so were the wives of all the Patriarchs and Prophets that obeyed that law."[276] In 1867 he described patriarchal marriage as a great blessing, and told the Saints it was not prized by them as it should be. He then testified: "I know that God has revealed this law unto this people. I know that if we had not obeyed that law we should have been damned. ... [T]he kingdom of God would have stopped right where we were when God revealed that law unto us."[277]

Wilford felt those who truly aspired to salvation would want a continuation of family ties after death. Without the principle of patriarchal marriage, the Saints would be like the rest of the world—without any such hope. Because, he explained, until the gospel and fullness of the priesthood was restored through Joseph Smith, not one man could "claim a wife" in the resurrection.[278] All marriages solemnized without priesthood authority would end at death.

However, because the sealing ordinances had been revealed, husbands and wives, parents and children could be eternally united in the family organization back to Adam and Eve. Wilford then added, "We could not obtain a fulness of celestial glory without this sealing ordinance or the institution called the patriarchal order of marriage, which is one of the most glorious principles of our religion."[279]

In a later discourse, while responding to a frequent criticism of plural marriage, Wilford specifically stated his personal reasons for obedience. He said, "Many men suppose that we have obeyed that law to gratify the lusts of the flesh. Bless your soul, if that had been our object, we might have followed the example of the people of the Christian world—committed whoredom and adultery—without bringing upon ourselves the cares, pains, and penalties that we have to bear by obeying this law. . . . I obeyed it because I want my . . . wives and children with me in the morning of the resurrection . . . in the family organization, that I may dwell with them and they with me, throughout all eternity." He then concluded, "We have obeyed the law because God has commanded us, and I bear record of its truth."[280]

WILFORD'S WIVES
The first woman that Wilford considered marrying as his plural wife was Phebe's niece Rhoda Foss. Two years after being taught the doctrine of patriarchal marriage, when Wilford was visiting his family in Connecticut in September 1843, he records the discussion he had with his parents. Wilford talked to his father about taking Rhoda home to Nauvoo with him because she wanted to join the Saints there. His father told him "it would be well if [he] was a mind to do it." Still, Wilford expressed his concern that he didn't yet know what Phebe would think and his mother

cautioned him that he "must not have Rhoda Foss now, for [he] had got one good girl and [he] must not have all the good ones."[281]

Mary Ann Jackson   Sarah Delight Stocking

Wilford waited three more years to marry his second wife, Mary Ann Jackson, on August 2, 1846. They had one son, James Jackson Woodruff, born May 25, 1847. Wilford was most likely sealed to Sarah Elinor Brown and Mary Caroline Barton on August 2, 1846, as well.[282] Then, between 1852 and 1857, Wilford married four more women: Mary Meek Giles Webster, Sarah Brown, Emma Smith, and Sarah Delight Stocking.[283] Sarah Brown bore eight children with Wilford and both Emma and Delight bore seven children. His last plural marriage, to Eudora Lovina Young, was in 1877.[284]

In spite of Wilford and Phebe's determination to honor the patriarchal law, it strained their relationship, and proved very difficult at times for the other wives as well. He and his wives endured separation, deprivation, financial hardship, persecution, and loneliness. His first plural wife, Mary Ann, divorced him after a year of separation while he served a mission. The two younger women sealed to Wilford on the same day as he was sealed to Mary Ann— Mary Caroline Barton and Sarah Elinor Brown—chose to leave his family less than four weeks later. His plural wife, Mary Webster, succumbed to an infection just six months after their sealing when she was only fifty years of age. Eudora Young, a twenty-five-year-old divorcée, left him less than two years after their sealing to marry Albert Hagen. Wilford's first wife Phebe died thirteen years before him, and fourteen of his thirty-four children also preceded him in death.

Wilford and Sarah Brown with three of their eight children in the 1860s

In light of these difficulties, Wilford worked hard to take care of his wives and his families. He built each of them homes and developed relationships with his children and grandchildren in varying degrees. During his frequent absences, he maintained contact with his wives and children through letters. In one letter he shared his philosophy on family life with his daughter Blanche in these words: "We are all expecting to live together forever after death. I think we all as parents and children ought to take all the pains we can to make each other happy as long as we live, that we may have nothing to regret."[285]

Emma Smith   Eudora Lovina Young

At the age of eighty-two, after living the law of patriarchal marriage for forty-three years, Wilford spoke of the eternal nature of families and said, "What a glorious thought that is! I have felt if, when I get through this world, where I have passed through many tribulations and afflictions with my wives and children, I can only have them with me in the next world, in their immortal bodies, to stand with me in the presence of God and of the Savior, and of the patriarchs and prophets, it will pay me for all my labors, if I should live to be as old as Methuselah."[286] He encouraged the Saints to prize their families and the associations they have together, "remembering that if we are faithful we shall inherit glory, immortality and eternal life."[287]

THE FULNESS OF THE PRIESTHOOD

By 1843, the temple rites revealed to Joseph Smith included baptisms, washings and anointings, the endowment ceremony, prayer circles, and sealings.[288] Between 1843 and 1844 Joseph administered or directed the administration of these ceremonies and ordinances to both men and women. On December 2, 1843, the day Wilford received his endowment and instruction from Joseph, he recorded in his journal their discussion of "the light, blessings, and glory that awaiteth Zion."[289] Emma Smith was the first woman to be endowed, and Phebe received her washings, anointings and endowment under the direction of Emma and Mary Fielding Smith, three weeks after Wilford.[290] Throughout Wilford's life he spoke often of receiving his temple blessings and, in 1882, testified that Joseph first made known to him "the very ordinances" which were still being administered to the Latter-day Saints fifty years later.[291]

The final ordinance administered by Joseph Smith was a second anointing, whereby the blessings promised in the first anointing in the endowment were actually bestowed.[292] Through the second anointing men and women are enabled to secure a fullness of all the blessings the Father has, to not only live with Him and become like Him, but to actually become gods.[293] The promise in the initial anointing is that those who prove faithful to their covenants will be kings and queens, in the second anointing they are anointed as kings and queens.[294]

As later explained in the *Juvenile Instructor*, "These additional powers include all the keys that belong to the holy priesthood on the earth, or were ever revealed to man in any dispensation, and which admit men and women within the veil. . . . They make of them kings and priests, queens and priestesses to God."[295] If the Saints qualified for this highest and holiest ordinance they could therefore be sealed up to eternal life, receive the unconditional guarantee of exaltation, and thus make their calling and election sure.[296]

Joseph Smith had talked about this concept as early as June 1839 but had not indicated at the time that making one's calling and election sure would involve a specific ordinance.[297] Peter's New Testament teachings specified the prerequisites of faith, virtue, godliness and charity among others, in order to obtain the fullness of God's blessings.[298] In May 1843, Joseph explained that, in addition to these prerequisites, the temple ordinances specifically "the new and everlasting covenant of marriage" are also required.[299] Then, in August 1843, he further clarified that the temple ordinances would fall under "three grand orders of the priesthood:" the Levitical or Aaronic, the Patriarchal, and the Melchizedek. For the first time he explicitly stated that those "holding the fullness of the Melchizedek priesthood are kings and priests of the Most High God" and through the second and final anointing they would be "called, elected and made sure."[300]

Wilford believed that the second anointing reflected the instruction given in the Book of Abraham.[301] Chapter three contains Abraham's account of his conversation with God regarding the creation and first or pre-mortal estate of man. God showed Abraham the noble and great spirits that existed "before the world was" and told Abraham these individuals would be sent to earth to prove themselves. If they were obedient to God's commands they would be worthy to inherit God's kingdom.[302] Wilford told the Saints, "We are here to fill a probation and receive an education."

He then exclaimed, "Who can comprehend that by obeying the celestial law, all that our Father has shall be given unto us—exaltations, thrones, principalities, power, dominion—who can comprehend it?"[303]

Joseph and Emma were the first to receive their second anointings, on September 28, 1843.[304] Six other couples also received their second anointings later that year, including Brigham Young and his wife Mary Ann on November 22, 1843.[305] After administering the second anointing to Brigham, Joseph asked Brigham to anoint the other members of the Twelve present in Nauvoo. In January 1844, eight of the apostles and their wives received their second anointings, including Wilford and Phebe.[306]

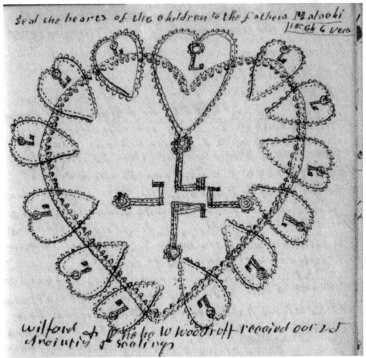

Wilford's January 28, 1844 journal entry regarding second anointing

Wilford described the two parts of the second anointing in his journal. The first was administered January

28, when he and Phebe received additional instruction and priesthood blessings by the laying on of hands.[307] The second part of the ceremony was administered by Phebe in their home on May 5, 1844.[308]

These higher ordinances of sealing and anointing created the "kingdom of priests" Joseph had spoken of, and fulfilled the promise he made to the women of the Relief Society, on March 30, 1842.[309] This followed the Old Testament account in Exodus, when God promised the children of Israel that if they would obey Him and keep His covenant they would be "a kingdom of priests, and an holy nation."[310] The following month, April 1842, Joseph assured the faithful women that they would "come in possession of the privileges, blessings and gifts of the Priesthood"[311] which God had established and the keys of the priesthood would be delivered to them.[312]

Before Joseph Smith's death two years later, sixty-six men and women had been anointed as priests and priestesses to God, received the "fulness of the priesthood," and been promised eternal life.[313]

EXALTATION FOR FAMILIES

These final ordinances were the culmination of all that had been revealed to Joseph Smith: the faithful, as joint-heirs with Jesus Christ, would not only be able to live with God, but be like Him, with the capacity to become gods themselves.[314] These "last and most important ordinances" were significant for several reasons.[315] First of all, sealings and the second anointings could only be administered to couples, with women and men as equal participants.[316] Secondly, they established the principle that exaltation in the highest degree of the celestial kingdom could not be attained alone. Eternal progression was thus established as a joint endeavor requiring both husband and wife.

~ 6 ~

The Lord's House

Nauvoo Temple circa 1847

Wilford's testimony of Joseph Smith's mission on earth was personal and powerful.[317] He declared over and over again that Joseph Smith was what he professed to be—a prophet of God, a seer and a revelator. Wilford said Joseph spent the last winter of his life, day after day, and week after week, teaching the Quorum of the Twelve, their wives, and several others, "the things of the kingdom of God."[318] In total, Joseph imparted the sacred temple instruction to approximately ninety individuals, thus ensuring that the knowledge of these principles and ordinances would be carried on.

Joseph Smith reminded the Saints that, in addition to receiving these saving ordinances for themselves, their ancestors' salvation was essential to their own. He taught that, "we without them cannot be made perfect; neither can they without us be made perfect."[319] In other words, the Saints who did not attend to the temple ordinances on behalf of their deceased relatives jeopardized their own salvation.[320] This responsibility was daunting. Just as the number of individuals for whom the proxy ordinances had to be performed had increased exponentially, the number of ordinances had also increased since Joseph had first introduced baptism for the dead in 1840. By 1844, initiatory and second washings and anointings, the endowment, and sealing ordinances had been revealed in addition to baptism. All these ordinances would need to be administered—in person or by proxy—for each person who had ever lived in order to place every member of the human family "upon an equal footing."[321]

As the immensity of this work became apparent, the apostles asked Joseph if there was a simpler or shorter method of administering the ordinances. Joseph responded that "every man who wishes to save his father, mother, brothers, sisters and friends, must go through all the ordinances for each one of them separately, the same as for himself."[322] Joseph enumerated all the ordinances and made it clear that one could not receive a fullness of salvation without abiding by the whole law.[323]

THE POWER OF ELIJAH

The first divine instruction Joseph received following the 1820 appearance of God and Jesus Christ was in 1823. When Moroni visited Joseph he repeated the prophecy of Malachi regarding the mission of Elijah and its importance. However, it would take twenty-one years for the necessary elements to be revealed before Joseph understood and could teach the Saints about their vital role in God's plan of salvation to connect parents and children.[324] The restoration of the priesthood and conferral of the priesthood keys had to come before the ordinances that would be revealed could be administered with the proper authority. The conversion and gathering of enough Saints prepared to receive the ordinances had to be accomplished. Then temples had to be built before those who had received the ordinances for themselves could officiate by proxy for their loved ones.

By July 1843 there was no doubt that Joseph understood the significance of the sealing power. God clearly stated that the keys and power of the priesthood had been conferred upon Joseph Smith, and through this priesthood power would come the restoration of all things.[325] On March 10, 1844, Wilford recorded what he called "one of the most important and interesting subjects ever presented to the Saints."[326] On this occasion Joseph Smith explained the spirit and power of Elijah to the Saints. He told them that, holding the keys of the fulness of the Melchizedek Priesthood, they could receive and perform all the ordinances belonging to the kingdom of God.[327] In response to the question, "What is this office and work of Elijah?" Joseph stated, "It is one of the greatest and most important subjects that God has revealed."[328] He then told the Saints to "Go and seal on earth your sons and daughters unto yourself and yourself unto your fathers in eternal glory."[329]

In two short years, Joseph had progressed from teaching that baptism was sufficient to bind the fathers and children together, to learning that it was possible to seal individuals to each other on both sides of the veil and thus fulfill Elijah's mission to connect families eternally. His understanding of God's plan made clear that together with their descendants and ancestors, the Saints could be exalted and blessed with eternal increase, and eternal lives. He told the Saints that this restoration of the ancient order of things was what would reconcile the scriptural truths, justify the ways of God, and harmonize every principle of justice and righteousness.[330] In April 1844 Joseph declared, "The greatest responsibility in this world that God has laid upon us is to seek after our dead. . . . [F]or it is necessary . . . that those who are going before and those who come after us should have salvation in common with us."[331]

SEALING FAMILIES

This expansion of ordinances applied not only to the Saints' progenitors, but to their descendants as well. In 1843 Joseph Smith had reassured the Saints that children would not be lost in death, but would be saved by virtue of the covenants of their fathers and mothers. In a sermon given on August 13, 1843, Joseph explained, "When a seal is put upon the father and mother, it secures their posterity."[332] Thus it was not necessary for children to participate in the sealing ordinance if their parents had been sealed; the children would be heirs to the sealing blessings through their parents' sealing.

As comforting as this revelation was, it represented a limited application of the sealing power; the sealing blessings only extended from parents to children. It was not until 1844 that Joseph made it clear that the sealing power was not confined to the living—only binding children through their parents' sealing—but extended from children to deceased parents through the veil between earth and heaven.

Wilford in 1850

Wilford later acknowledged that the principle of sealing and the linking of all dispensations was on Joseph's mind "more than most any other subject that was given to him."[333] He said, Joseph was "wound up with this work," but he did not live long enough to "enter any further upon these things."[334] Although Joseph taught the Saints to have their children sealed to them and to be sealed to their fathers, Joseph did not officiate in any family or multigenerational sealings before his death. It was not until the Nauvoo Temple was dedicated in December 1845 that the first child-to-parent sealings were performed under the direction of Brigham Young.[335] Then children, born before their parents had been sealed to each other and their marriage recognized by God, could be sealed to their parents.[336]

Another sealing ordinance that Joseph Smith alluded to but did not live long enough to explain or administer was what became known as "priesthood adoption."[337]

HEIRS OF THE PRIESTHOOD

In 1832, the Lord had revealed through Joseph Smith that all those who receive the fulness of the priesthood are promised sanctification and all that the Father has.[338] In this same revelation—now contained in Section 84 of the Doctrine and Covenants—the Lord explained that those who obtained the priesthood would become the sons of Moses and part of a patriarchal priesthood chain from Moses through Abraham back to Adam.[339] If they were true to the oath and covenant of the priesthood, they would have the ability to claim the same blessings promised to the children of Israel as the seed of Abraham.[340]

In August 1843, Joseph taught of the relationship of the sealing powers to the "doctrine of election with the seed of Abraham." In one discourse Joseph said the sealing of fathers and children would be "according to the declarations of the prophets."[341] In a second discourse he explained that the priesthood was directly from God, "not by descent from father or mother."[342] The Saints thus needed to seal the patriarchal chain of priesthood back to Adam—who received the priesthood directly from God.[343] Joseph promised the Saints that when they finished the temple they would "receive more knowledge" concerning the patriarchal priesthood.[344]

Most converts to the Church residing in Nauvoo were not only the first generation of their family within the Church, they were the only generation of their family within the Church. Many were adults who had been forced to leave family behind to join the Saints and did not anticipate ever having family members within the Church on earth to whom they could be sealed. Without parents who were able to participate in the sealing ordinance to link the generations, they were afraid they would be left without a priesthood connection to the family of God.

Similarly, married converts who joined the Church, but had spouses who did not join, could not be sealed to each other and, consequently, could not have their children sealed to them. There were also few men who had been ordained to the priesthood, and even fewer who had received all the temple ordinances. Only those men who had been ordained, washed, anointed, endowed, and sealed had the "fulness of the priesthood" required to be a part of the patriarchal priesthood chain.

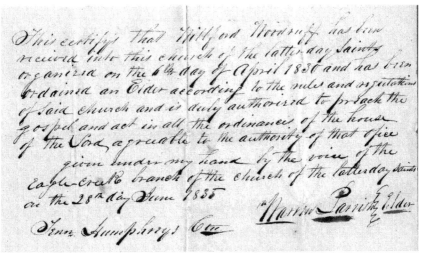

Certificate of Wilford's ordination to the Melchizedek Priesthood

The conundrum was solved in part through the law of adoption, which linked non-relatives together if traditional family ties had been severed. Adoption ceremonially created father-child priesthood relationships for those who had no biological father within the Church to connect to. The practice of adoption also alleviated the concern that, if the Saints' ancestors did not accept the gospel in the spirit world, the Saints would not have a connection to the family of God. In addition, adoption to priesthood leaders, rather than relatives, allowed individuals to be sealed into a priesthood line when fathers or husbands appeared unworthy to lead their families to salvation and exaltation.

Being sealed, through marriage or by adoption, to a worthy man ordained to the Melchizedek Priesthood was vital to the Saints' eternal membership in the kingdom of God. During Joseph Smith's lifetime the only sealings into priesthood lineage were of women. (Men were not adopted into the priesthood lineage of other men until the Nauvoo Temple was completed.) Understandably, women desired to be sealed to one holding a high priesthood office hoping that it would be an indication of the man's faithfulness.

At least ten women in Nauvoo chose to be sealed to Joseph Smith spiritually (for eternity, not mortality) in order to be connected to his priesthood lineage, yet remained physically with their husbands.[345] Some of these women were married to men who supported the Church but were not baptized members. Others were married to men who were members of the Church but were not Church leaders. One was the wife of an apostle. Joseph's assurance to these women was that being sealed to him and adopted into his priesthood line would assure their own exaltation and benefit their husbands and children as well. After Joseph Smith's death four more women chose to be sealed to their husbands for mortality only and to Joseph for eternity.

The application of these sealing principles, and the ability to receive the ordinances required for exaltation hinged on the Saints' ability to administer the ordinances. On March 4, 1844, with an unending list of concerns ranging from poverty to mob violence, Joseph set the priorities when he told the Twelve "we need the Temple more than anything else."[346] Three months later, the exterior walls of the temple were only partially completed when he and his brother Hyrum were murdered.[347] Joseph did not live to administer any sealing ordinances within the temple.

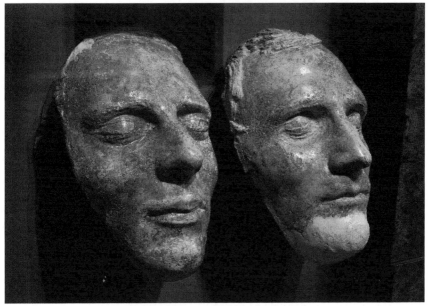

Joseph and Hyrum Smith's death masks

In spite of the heartbreaking tragedy of their Prophet's death, the Saints were able to maintain their faith and hope amid the ensuing confusion and intense persecution. Construction on the temple only stopped for a few days, astonishing those who did not understand the purpose and significance of the temple ordinances. On July 7, 1844, the Saints voted to support the decision to finish building the temple as quickly as possible, thus making it evident that killing Joseph and Hyrum Smith did not rescind the Restoration or alter the mission of Elijah any more than crucifying Christ could destroy Christianity.[348]

THE SUCCESSION

Wilford was among those whom Joseph had sent to various eastern cities in the spring of 1844 to raise money for construction of the temple and to spread word of Joseph Smith's candidacy for President. Wilford learned of the martyrdom through a newspaper account when he was in Portland, Maine, on his way back to preach the gospel in the Fox Islands.[349] He immediately planned his return to Nauvoo. He arrived in Nauvoo on August 6, with Brigham Young, Heber C. Kimball, and other apostles, to find the Saints in a state of confusion and several individuals claiming authority to lead the Church.[350]

The leadership crisis that followed Joseph's death threatened to splinter the Church.[351] The three principal claimants were Sidney Rigdon, based on his former position in the First Presidency; Brigham Young, as the senior member of the Quorum of the Twelve Apostles; and James Strang, a recent convert who produced a Letter of Appointment from Joseph Smith.[352] A meeting had been set for August 8 at which Sidney Rigdon planned to speak and explain why he should be chosen as Joseph's successor. Brigham and the other apostles countered his claim with their conviction that Joseph had conferred all the priesthood keys and ordinances on the Twelve and they were the only quorum authorized to lead the Church.

Wilford supported Brigham and later testified that Joseph had "called the Twelve together the last time he spoke to us . . . and upon our shoulders he rolled the burden of the Kingdom, and he gave us all the keys and powers and gifts to carry on this great and mighty work. He told us that he had received every key, every power and every gift for the salvation of the living and the dead, and he said: 'Upon the Twelve I seal these gifts and powers and keys from henceforth and forever.'"[353]

DEATH OF JOE SMITH, THE MORMON PROPHET.

[From the Quincy Herald.]

DEATH OF THE PROPHET—*Joe and Hyrum Smith are Dead.*—The Steamboat Boreas, just in from Warsaw, brings shocking intelligence from the scene of the Mormon war. The following slip from the office of the Warsaw Signal explains the dreadful tragedy:

Joe Smith and Hyrum are dead—shot this afternoon. An attack from the Mormons is expected every hour. Will not the surrounding counties rush instantly to our rescue?

Warsaw, June 27th, 1844.

It seems that the circumstances attending the killing the Mormon Prophet and his brother Hyrum are as follows: On yesterday Gov. Ford

Article published July 12, 1844 in the *Portland [Maine] Tribune*

Furthermore, Brigham told the Saints that they could not make the decision to "fill the office of a prophet, seer and revelator: God must do this."[354] Wilford indicated his belief that God had done this by revealing to Joseph Smith those who should be called to serve as apostles, and which of those would be given a "fulness of the priesthood." In this context of receiving temple ordinances, Wilford noted it was significant that Sidney Rigdon had lost Joseph's confidence the year before Joseph's death. As a result, Sidney was not allowed to receive the fulness of the priesthood through the higher ordinances of sealing and the second anointing.

Following Brigham's remarks, Wilford pointed out that Sidney Rigdon was also not with Joseph and members of the Quorum of the Twelve when they "actually received the keys of the kingdom of God, and oracles of God, keys of revelation, and the pattern of heavenly things."[355] James Strang had been converted to the Church in February 1844, only four months before Joseph's martyrdom, and had also not received all the ordinances, or "fulness of the priesthood."

HANG ON TO THE TRUTH
Although his own sister, brother-in-law, and later his stepmother chose not to follow the Twelve, Wilford unequivocally stated, "I can say with every sentiment of my heart, and feeling of my soul, as has president Young, 'that if there are but ten men left, who hang on to the truth, to Joseph and the temple, and are willing to do right in all things, let me be one of that number.' If it cost me my life to defend the truth of the everlasting gospel of the Son of God . . . let it go; I want to be among the number."[356] Wilford was true to his word. He did hang on to the truth and the temple.

As difficult as it was to imagine the progress of the Church without the leadership of Joseph and Hyrum Smith, Wilford knew the work did not depend on them. He said, "All the world thought if they could only slay Joseph Smith there would be an end to Mormonism, and so there would have been had it not been the work of God Almighty; if it had been the work of man it would long since have ceased to exist on the earth. The power that has sustained this work from the beginning sustains it now. . . . The Lord Almighty has set his hand to accomplish his purposes, and he is feeling after the honest and meek throughout the world, in order to find those who are willing to take hold and help to build up his kingdom in the latter days. He has found a few, and he will find many more."[357] It was God's church and God's work, and it would go on.

In the end, although some Saints followed Sidney Rigdon to establish a new church in Pennsylvania, and many prominent members of the Church—including most of Joseph Smith's family—denounced polygamy and supported James Strang and others, the majority of the Saints chose to sustain the Quorum of the Twelve.

The Apostles' counsel was to gather in Nauvoo and complete the temple because it was the work of God and "we have to rush it forth against the combined powers of earth and hell."[358] Brigham reminded the Saints that they needed to carry out Joseph's plan. Unless they followed the pattern Joseph had given them to work by, they would not be able to get any further endowment.[359] He then added, "We want to build the Temple in this place, if we have to build it as the Jews built the walls of the Temple in Jerusalem, with a sword in one hand and the trowel in the other. . . . I would rather pay out every cent I have to build up this place and get an endowment, if I were driven the next minute without anything to take with me."[360]

THE RESUMPTION OF ORDINANCES

On August 9, 1844, Wilford recorded in his journal, "It is gloomy times in Nauvoo as the Prophet and Patriarch are gone and there appears to be but little ambition to do anything only they are at work very busy on the temple."[361] Three days later, on August 12, Wilford was asked to move his family to England to preside over the missionary work throughout Europe and to gather the Saints to Zion. He later explained the wisdom of leaving in the midst of the turmoil in Nauvoo by saying that in order for the kingdom to stand, it must "spread itself abroad, and gather unto itself strength."[362] Aware of the fragile situation of the Church, he met with the Saints and reassured them that Joseph Smith's death could not destroy the gospel nor could it take away the power of God. Truth had not been annihilated.[363] He counseled them to be faithful, to remain united, and to focus on building the temple so they could get their endowments.

Wilford also felt that redemption of the dead should remain a priority in spite of the turmoil.[364] He believed that Joseph only had time to lay the foundation before he was taken away so he could go to the spirit world and organize the efforts on the other side of the veil. By gathering together the Elders of Israel in the spirit world to accomplish the missionary work there, Joseph would enable the Saints to continue the proxy work on earth. Therefore, the Saints needed to be prepared to do their part, because those in the spirit world who heard and accepted the gospel would need someone on earth to attend to the ordinances of the House of God for them.[365]

Wilford recognized the uplifting and motivating influence Elijah's mission had on the Saints during their most difficult times. Reflecting on this in his journal, he recorded that the Saints had "been called to pass through scenes of sufferings and privations that would have discouraged an Alexander. They have had to combat earth and Hell, wicked men and devils, sickness and death, burnings, drivings, and persecutions. . . . What has sustained us and inspired us to action in the midst of these difficulties? We have been upheld by the power of God that we might fulfill his purposes [and] . . . been moved upon by the spirits of our fathers and progenitors . . . now waiting for the redemption of their bodies."[366]

On August 24, 1844, several of the Twelve Apostles were baptized for their dead in the temple font, and the work continued.[367] Two days later Wilford and Phebe went to the Mississippi River to be baptized for some of their relatives.[368] Then, three short weeks after he returned to Nauvoo, he, Phebe and their children, left to fulfill his calling as President of the European Mission until January 1846. Before they left, Phebe received a blessing from Brigham Young. He promised Phebe that she would be preserved to "return and meet with the Saints in the temple of the Lord and shall rejoice therein."[369]

TEMPLE ENDOWMENT

While the Woodruffs were in England, Wilford learned of the progress on the temple through letters from Brigham Young and others. In the summer of 1845, Brigham wrote that the Saints' prayers had been answered and they had been granted the peace to continue work on the temple. The capstone of the temple was laid by the Twelve on May 24, 1846, and Brigham told Wilford, it would have pleased Wilford to have witnessed the occasion and heard the Saints' hosannas. Brigham concluded his letter by saying, "There is the most perfect union prevailing among the Saints, and every man seems determined to do all he can to roll on the work of the Temple as fast as possible."[370]

July 30, 1848 sketch of the stone baptismal font in Nauvoo Temple

Brigham thought they would be able to finish the stone baptismal font and top floor of the temple that summer, but the persecution and conflict in and around Nauvoo interfered. By October 1845 the tension had increased to the point that a truce had to be brokered. One condition of the truce was the Saints' agreement to leave the state of Illinois in the spring.

Recognizing the urgency and the desire of many Saints to receive their endowment, Brigham dedicated the upper floor of the temple on November 30.[371] Their focus then shifted from proxy baptisms to ordinances for the living. On December 10, thirty men and women participated in the washings, anointings, and endowment ceremony. All had previously received the temple ordinances under the direction of Joseph Smith, but wanted to go through the ceremonies again in the Temple.[372] The group included Heber C. Kimball, George A. Smith, Orson Hyde, John Smith, Newel K. Whitney, Brigham Young, Parley P. Pratt, Amasa Lyman, John Taylor, John E. Page, and their wives, as well as Willard Richards, Joseph C. Kingsbury, Hyrum Smith's widow Mary, and Don Carlos Smith's widow Agnes Smith. Significantly, Emma Smith was not among them.[373]

These individuals began administering the washings and anointings, and officiating in the endowment ceremony for others on December 11, 1845. On some days more than 100 people received their endowment and by the end of the month over 1,000 individuals had been endowed.[374] This was an incredible achievement given the fact that, depending on the size of the group, completing the endowment ceremony could take four to six hours. Sometimes the ceremonies lasted into the night.

To help make it possible for more people to participate, temple clothing was washed and ironed during the night in preparation for ceremonies the next day. Ordinance work continued daily from December 10 through December 25, when it was stopped for three days, in part because the supply of anointing oil had been depleted.[375]

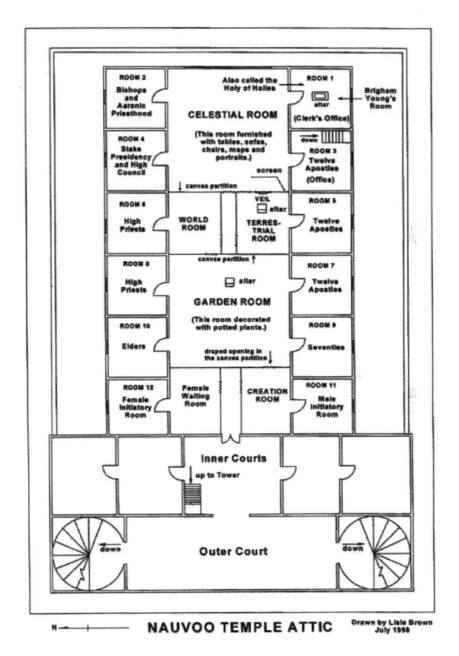

Over the course of the few weeks that the Saints were able to use the Temple, more than 2,000 couples were united for eternity.[376] Sometimes two types of sealings were performed in the same ceremony. For example, a widow would be sealed for eternity to her worthy yet deceased husband and be sealed to a living man for mortality only. Although the spiritual purpose of sealing was the main motivation in most cases, some of these relationships were formed for practical purposes. These unconventional relationships made it possible to provide for women and children emotionally, financially, and physically in difficult circumstances. As a result, some polygamous and polyandrous-type sealings were simply spiritual, ceremonial connections, and the couple did not have any further interaction, while other couples were sealed in conjugal relationships and had additional children.[377]

MAKING PERFECT THE PRIESTHOOD

In January 1846 the Church leaders in Nauvoo made the decision not to wait for spring, but to begin the exodus from Nauvoo in February due to reports that their anticipated departure would be sabotaged.[378] This decision to leave Nauvoo only increased the Saints' desire to receive temple ordinances before they had to abandon the temple. On January 12, 1846, Brigham Young recorded, "Such has been the anxiety manifested by the saints to receive the ordinances, and such the anxiety on our part to administer to them, that I have given myself up entirely to the work of the Lord in the Temple night and day . . . going home but once a week."[379]

In addition to the washings, anointings, endowments, and sealings, priesthood adoptions were also being performed.[380] Brigham explained that if the priesthood had been retained through every generation, the law of adoption would not have been necessary, all would have been included in the covenant without it.[381] Wilford's journal entry recording Brigham's instructions sheds additional light on the practice: "President Young said the priesthood had been on the earth at different times. When the Priesthood had not been on earth, men will have to be sealed to each other until we go on to Father Adam. Men will have to be sealed to men so as to link the chain from beginning to end and all children [born before their parents received their endowments] will have to be sealed to their parents. . . . But this must be in a temple and nowhere else."[382]

Later Wilford explained to the Saints that Joseph Smith came through the loins of ancient Joseph and, as his literal descendant, was heir to the priesthood keys by birthright.[383] When Joseph Smith was adopted into the priesthood line, by virtue of his ordination to the Melchizedek Priesthood by Peter, James and John, he bridged the gap created between the dispensations when apostasy occurred and the priesthood was taken from the earth.[384]

Logically it followed then that, just as one must be adopted into the House of Israel through baptism in order to become an heir to Abraham's blessings, one must be adopted to Joseph as head of this dispensation to inherit the blessings of the fulness of the priesthood.[385] The thinking at the time was that after being sealed to their fathers within the Church the Saints would then seal their forefather to Joseph Smith by adoption. Doing so would reconnect their families on earth to the eternal priesthood chain, through Joseph's "priesthood fathers," back to Adam.[386]

In practice, the integration of priesthood lineage into the sealing rituals meant that, in addition to the sealing of husbands to wives and children to parents, a priesthood link had to be established through a separate sealing ordinance.[387] On January 7, 1846, Brigham Young dedicated the altar around which those being sealed could kneel. Four days later he solemnized the first child to parent sealings and the first priesthood adoptions of men.[388] A total of 211 persons were adopted and more than seventy children were sealed to their parents in the Nauvoo Temple in 1846.[389]

The relative age of the individuals was not a factor in priesthood adoption; it was based on perceived righteousness and therefore the ability of a man to lead the members of his biological and adopted family to exaltation in the eternities. Most of those who were adopted to a priesthood leader chose to be linked to members of the Quorum of the Twelve and their wives, such as John and Leonora Taylor, Willard and Jennetta Richards, Brigham and Miriam Young and Heber C. and Vilate Kimball.[390]

Five women were sealed to Joseph Smith posthumously for eternity when they were sealed to their husbands for mortality in the Nauvoo Temple.[391] However, there is only one recorded posthumous priesthood adoption of a man to Joseph Smith in Nauvoo. John M. Bernhisel wrote that on February 3, 1846, he was sealed to Joseph Smith "to become his son by the law of adoption and to become a legal heir to all the blessings bestowed upon Joseph Smith pertaining to exaltations."[392] The fact that John was sealed by adoption only to Joseph, not to Joseph and Emma as a couple, may explain the reason this was a singular occurrence. Emma Smith did not participate in the temple ordinances after her husband's death.[393]

Priesthood adoptions and the sealing of children to parents were not performed again for thirty-one years. The Saints would have to wait until another temple was finally completed in 1877 to take part in these ordinances.[394]

Brigham Young circa 1851

FINAL TEMPLE ORDINANCES IN NAUVOO

On February 2, 1846, Brigham Young announced that the Saints must prepare to leave and temple ordinances must cease. In spite of this, there was a large group waiting when he arrived at the temple the next day. He tried to reassure them that there would be more temples built in which to perform the ordinances when they were resettled, then informed them that he was going to get his wagons and "be off." Brigham walked some distance away from the temple, assuming the group would disperse, but when he returned, the temple was "filled to overflowing." Understanding the Saints' intense desire to receive the temple blessings, Brigham resumed work and administered another 295 ordinances that day.[395]

Although the exodus of Saints began on February 4, temple ordinance work continued around the clock for two more days, and the Nauvoo Temple records show that more than 600 people received ordinances on the final day, February 7. Thus the temple they had labored five years to build was only used for forty-six days. During that short period between December 10, 1845, and February 7, 1846, more than 5,600 Saints received their endowments.[396]

Recalling this time, Brigham Young explained the charge he had been given by Joseph Smith when Joseph first administered the endowment in May 1842. He said, "[A]fter we had got through Brother Joseph turned to me and said, 'Brother Brigham this is not arranged right but we have done the best we could under the circumstances in which we are placed, and I wish you to take this matter in hand and organize and systematize all these ceremonies with the signs, tokens, penalties, and key words.'" Brigham felt he had done that as he administered the ordinances to others in Nauvoo between 1842 and 1846. Each time he did so he said he "got something more," so when they officiated in the Nauvoo Temple, they "understood and knew how to place them there." Although the circumstances in the temple had also been less than ideal, Brigham believed, "We had our ceremonies pretty correct."[397]

A WEIGHTY RESPONSIBILITY

Thirty-one years would pass before the next temple would be completed in St. George, Utah. There, for the first time, all the temple ordinances would be administered, not only to the living, but also by the living on behalf of the dead. Although Joseph lived long enough to establish the foundational framework for the redemption of all mankind, he was murdered within months after the sacred ordinances and principles were revealed, before their implications could be realized, and before their administration to both the living and dead could begin.[398]

If revelation had ceased with the death of Joseph Smith and the ordinances had remained as he introduced them, the mission of Elijah would have failed. God's work "to bring to pass the immortality and eternal life of man" would have been frustrated. In spite of Joseph's efforts to communicate the knowledge that had been revealed to him, he acknowledged that the Saints were not ready. God would continue to reveal additional instruction, and the Saints had to be prepared to receive it.[399]

What may have appeared to some as loose ends or unanswered questions, were markers of progress in the continuous unfolding of the restored gospel that had been taking place since 1820.[400] Brigham Young was in the first group of Church leaders who received the ordinances from Joseph Smith in May 1842. On that occasion Joseph asked Brigham to organize and perfect the ceremonies according to the pattern revealed from heaven.[401] Dutifully, Brigham then directed the intense period of ordinance work in the Nauvoo Temple, and presided over the limited ordinances administered in the Endowment House and other temporary locations between 1847 and 1877. Brigham's role in conveying the temple ordinances as well as the sealing power was a sacred obligation that weighed on him. Nevertheless, although Brigham's presidency spanned thirty years and was critical to the survival of the Church, he only lived four months after administration of all the ordinances began in the St. George Temple in 1877.[402]

As with Joseph Smith, if God had closed the heavens when Brigham Young died in August 1877, the work would have been impeded by the Saints' limited understanding of the breadth and scope of God's plan of salvation. As the Saints' comprehension of the restored gospel matured, as membership in the Church increased, and as the Church expanded geographically, changes in the Church organization were necessary. At the same time, some of the temple ordinances would be adapted, others refined, several suspended, and a few discontinued altogether.

~ 7 ~

Exodus to a New Beginning

The Saints' ability to dismantle their lives and prepare themselves for an unknown future, both physically and spiritually, was tested again in 1846. This transition would be exponentially more difficult than the flight from Ohio to Missouri and their escape from Missouri to Illinois. They planned to establish a refuge outside the borders of the United States where they could be protected in their isolation. But they only planned to be there long enough to accomplish what God required so they could return to Zion and usher in the Second Coming of Christ. In order to complete those eternally significant tasks, they first had to survive the journey, provide for their necessities, and establish a new society. Building temples in order to receive the blessings of exaltation and redeem the dead would have to wait.

LET THE SAINTS ARISE AND GO OUT
As the Saints were preparing to evacuate their beloved city, Wilford and Phebe were planning their departure from England to join the main body of the Church on its journey west. At a special conference in Manchester, England on December 15, 1845, Wilford told the British Saints he had to bid them farewell because he could not think of the Church leaving the United States with his family "un-

gathered." He and Phebe had left their daughter with Phebe's family in Maine, his elderly father and stepmother were still in Connecticut; and Wilford Jr. had remained with their friends in Nauvoo. Wilford felt called back to America by a sense of duty to ensure that his extended family was not left behind "in the midst of Babylon."[403]

Wilford sent Phebe and two of their children ahead with a group of emigrating Saints, and he followed them on January 23, 1846. Before he left, Wilford published his feelings regarding the exodus in the *Millennial Star*. "I am perfectly willing that these things should be," he wrote, "and that America should have the credit of banishing so many of her citizens from her midst for conscience' sake. There is no safety under the government of the United States. It is time to go where we can enjoy our rights, and no longer be hemmed in. . . . Let America go ahead with her present measures, but let the Saints arise and go out of her midst. If we are called to make sacrifices, the Saints are the people that can make them."[404]

When Wilford's great aunt learned that her brother Aphek and other members of the extended family were leaving with Wilford to head west, she asked if they would find any other Christians to associate with. Wilford told her he hoped not, because the Christians they had known in the United States had persecuted the Saints, burned their homes, murdered their family members, martyred their prophet and patriarch, and "driven the remainder from their midst."[405] Wilford declared that he would rather be in the midst of the grizzly bears of the Rocky Mountains than remain in the United States.

NAUVOO TEMPLE DEDICATION
Upon his arrival in Nauvoo on April 13, 1846, Wilford recorded that the temple "truly looked splendid," but he

found a half-empty city where thousands were "struggling for life, as it were, to gather with the Saints in the wilderness."[406] Some Church members, including Wilford's sister Eunice and her husband Dwight, were still trying to decide whether to follow Brigham and the apostles or one of the other men who had claimed authority to lead the Church. Wilford was "much grieved in spirit" when Eunice, Dwight, and his stepmother Azubah, chose to stay behind and, in his words, "turn away from the Church and walk no more with us."[407]

Nauvoo, Illinois in 1846

A few days later, Wilford was able to take Phebe and others through all the rooms in the temple from the font in the basement to the top of the tower.[408] Knowing they would not be able to stay in Nauvoo, the Saints nevertheless completed the temple because the Lord had said if they did not build the temple they would be "rejected as a church."[409]

In fulfillment of the promise Brigham had made two years earlier, Phebe joined with the other Saints on April 30, when Wilford and Orson Hyde dedicated the completed temple in a private ceremony. They followed the dedicatory prayer with the Hosanna Shout, "which entered the heavens to the joy and consolation of our hearts."[410] Speaking at the temple dedication Wilford said, "The Saints had labored faithfully and finished the Temple and we're now received as a Church with our dead. This is glory enough for building the Temple and thousands of the Saints have received their endowment in it. And the light will not go out."[411]

That same day Wilford loaded his wagons to leave Nauvoo and follow the Saints across the Mississippi River into Iowa.[412]

House Wilford built in Nauvoo (which he lived in for only six weeks)

PRIESTHOOD ADOPTION DURING THE EXODUS

Having left the intimate society of Nauvoo, the need arose for all Saints, but especially those who were gathering from other states and countries, to have the financial, physical, and emotional support and strength usually provided by family. Since many of these converts had left behind their extended families when they emigrated, Church leaders struggled to meet the needs of those without necessary personal resources. During the exodus, the law of adoption was used as means of organizing the Saints into "families," which could then provide the needed support and stability. These priesthood families were led spiritually and temporally by their adoptive fathers.[413]

The first such families were formed by the leaders of the Church according to revelation received by Brigham Young.[414] The formation of these families was based in part on the limited number of sealings and adoptions that had taken place before they left Nauvoo. In addition, because adoption ceremonies could not be performed outside a temple, the majority of people in these priesthood families simply covenanted with each other to keep certain rules and maintain particular standards as they traveled together. The Saints' plan and expectation was to formally solemnize these relationships in temple ceremonies, as soon as another temple was built, so their priesthood families would be eternally connected.[415]

On January 18, 1847, Brigham Young met with his company comprised, in part, of those who had been adopted to him in the Nauvoo Temple or planned to be officially adopted to him when a new temple was completed. Brigham told them that "no man should come into his company to work iniquity. They should break off from all their sins. And they did enter into a covenant with uplifted hands to Heaven with President Young and each other to walk in all the ordinances and Commandments of the Lord our God."[416]

The following day Wilford recorded the organization by Heber C. Kimball of his company of about 200 persons through this same process of covenanting absent the temple adoption ordinance. Later that night Wilford organized the members of his company, forty men who covenanted with him to keep the commandments and sustain him as their leader.[417] Wilford's "adopted" family included his father Aphek, Abraham O. Smoot (one of his mission companions), John Benbow (one of the English converts Wilford baptized), and Zerah Pulsipher (the man who baptized Wilford). Following their family meeting, Wilford recorded that they parted in good spirits. The experience must have had quite an effect on him, because after falling asleep he had a "singular dream" wherein he was "with child and ready to be delivered."[418]

In February Brigham Young reiterated the reason adoption was necessary. "I have gathered a number of families around me by the law of adoption and seal of the covenant according to the order of the priesthood," he said, "and others have done likewise, it being the means of salvation left to bring us back to God." He then explained that adoption would not be necessary if the keys of the priesthood had been handed down from father to son through all generations because "all would have been included in the covenant without it and would have been legal heirs instead of being heirs according to promise."[419] Adoption was the means of reconnecting the chain of the priesthood.

In theory, the inter-family sealings and priesthood adoptions were initially intended to parallel each other. However, the Saints' circumstances in the 1840s made that approach practically impossible. Their limited understanding of the principles and covenants involved in the ordinances also contributed to the complicated sealing protocols that developed. As the Church leaders struggled to comprehend the implications of these ordinances on earth and through eternity, they recognized their incapacity to implement them perfectly.

Although Brigham Young was absolute in his pro-
nouncements and unequivocal in his demands, he told the
Saints that knowledge and understanding come slowly and
that none of the revelations revealed everything about a
subject. He conceded that the "revelations of God contain
correct doctrine and principles, so far as they go; but it is
impossible for the poor, weak, low, groveling, sinful inhabitants of the earth to receive a revelation from the Almighty
in all its perfections. He has to speak to us in a manner to
meet the extent of our capacities."[420] In fact, Brigham said
he did not believe there was "a single revelation, among the
many God has given to the Church, that is perfect in its
fulness."[421]

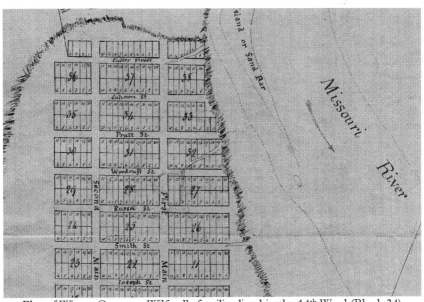

Plat of Winter Quarters: Wilford's families lived in the 14th Ward (Block 34)

Accordingly, during 1846 and 1847, when the Saints
were scattered between Nauvoo and the Salt Lake Valley,
Brigham sought additional instruction on the law of adoption. On February 23, 1847, in a meeting with Wilford and
other apostles, Brigham shared a dream he had had the

previous week. In his dream, he went to see Joseph Smith to tell him about their great anxiety to understand the law of adoption and the sealing principles.[422]

Brigham simply said, "[If] you have a word of counsel for me I should be glad to receive it."[423] In response, Joseph's instruction was, "Tell the people to be humble and faithful, and be sure to keep the Spirit of the Lord and it will lead them right."[424] Joseph explained that, even though the Saints were disorganized and in great confusion, if they would follow the Spirit they would "find themselves just as they were organized by our Father in Heaven before they came into the world."[425] Although Joseph then showed Brigham the pattern of organization in the beginning, Brigham could not describe it. Brigham did see when the priesthood had been taken from the earth and how all "must be joined together, so that there would be a perfect chain from Father Adam to his latest posterity."[426]

Perhaps this dream served to remind Brigham Young, the apostles, and the Saints that God would continue to reveal the needed direction regarding these vital ordinances if they were willing to listen to the Spirit.

A few months later, on August 15, 1847, Wilford recorded another discourse on the law of adoption by Brigham. Among many other "interesting and important items," Brigham told them that as all the gospel ordinances administered by the world since the apostasy were illegal, all the marriage ceremonies were illegitimate and children born to those marriages would have to "enter into the law of adoption and be adopted into the Priesthood in order to become sons and legal heirs of salvation."[427] This new information extended the work of the Saints to not only connect their own family members to the priesthood, but to connect every member of every family to the priesthood.

COMPLICATIONS AND IMPERFECTIONS

The application of adoption to facilitate the exodus from Nauvoo was not a sustainable practice. Although its purpose was to unite the family of God, its application sometimes led to jealousy, competition, and division. Furthermore, it raised significant questions about the organization of eternal families. Instead of a direct line from one generation to the next, it created convoluted links within biological families and connections to individuals outside one's family. These connections were complicated further when those chosen for their worthiness subsequently left the Church or did not live up to their responsibilities. New adoptions, to reconnect through the priesthood lines of others, led to more confusion.

Some of those adopted as "sons" expected special treatment from their "fathers," such as advancement within Church leadership or financial assistance.[428] In a few cases, the status given to those sought after as family leaders led to the idea that the larger one's adoptive family became, the greater one's heavenly glory would be. Initially any individual could propose an adoption as the father or the child. However, due to the desires of some to "build kingdoms," the instruction was changed so that only the adult seeking the adoption could request it; a man could not ask others to be adopted to him.[429]

Even though the use of adoption as a means of organizing the Saints decreased significantly by 1848, the effects, both positive and negative, remained. As a result, the priesthood connections formed in Nauvoo and on the plains during the migration both facilitated and complicated the settling of the Salt Lake Valley and surrounding areas.[430]

Brigham's 1853 discourse on the right of heirship in the priesthood chastised men who sought a second wife when they were not honoring their first wife. "If you cannot keep the jewel you already possess," he told them, "be cautious how you take more, lest you lose them both." He further explained that, although it is natural for men to "be miserly with regard to their religious blessings," they must not make the sacred ordinances a matter of speculation "to administer to their avaricious dispositions." Specifically, they should no longer ask to marry young girls, and never tell women, "You must be sealed to me or you cannot get an exaltation." In addition, those marrying widows were instructed not to interfere with the eternal birthright of her children. His advice to the sisters was never to be sealed to any man "unless they wished to be."[431]

A NEW BEGINNING IN THE SALT LAKE VALLEY

Wilford entered the Salt Lake Valley with the vanguard company on July 24, 1847. True to form, he spent the afternoon planting a half bushel of potatoes.[432] On July 28, four days after their arrival, as they laid out the plan for the city, Wilford helped drive a stake into the ground to mark the spot where Brigham indicated the next temple should be built.[433] The next few weeks were spent exploring the area and constructing a fort to protect and house the Saints who were already on their way.[434]

On August 6, after spending the day cutting timber to build cabins, Wilford could hardly stand up, so he went to his wagon and "flung himself" upon his bed to rest. But shortly thereafter, Heber C. Kimball came to inform him that the Twelve were going to be rebaptized for the remission of their sins to set an example to the Church. On this, the occasion of Wilford's third rebaptism, he wrote that after coming into the glorious valley to build up Zion, they felt like renewing their covenants before God and each other. They considered this opportunity to be rebaptized a duty and a privilege.[435] Brigham Young rebaptized the

Twelve, reconfirmed them in the Church, and sealed upon them their apostleship with "all the keys, powers, and Blessings belonging to that office."[436] Heber C. Kimball then rebaptized and reconfirmed Brigham Young. The following day, fifty-five members of the camp were rebaptized. On August 8, Wilford helped to rebaptize and reconfirm the remaining 224 camp members.[437]

These rebaptisms were not intended to call into question the validity of their original baptisms or to function as an empty gesture. Brigham made it clear that before the Saints entered the waters of baptism, they needed to confess their sins and repent.[438] He also hoped that at rebaptism they would feel the same Spirit they had at baptism when they "first embraced the religion of Jesus."[439] Wilford said their entrance into the Valley symbolized a new beginning for them, and a new birth. Church leaders had allowed the "non-observance of certain regulations" while the Saints were crossing the plains, but as the Saints arrived in the Valley they wanted each member to show by rebaptism that they were willing to strictly adhere to instructions and the principles of the gospel.[440] This pattern of rebaptism and reconfirmation upon arrival in Utah continued for decades.

Saints' route from Nauvoo, Illinois to the Salt Lake Valley

WHATEVER THE LORD INSPIRES

One month after their arrival in the Salt Lake Valley, Wilford and the other apostles began retracing their steps back to Iowa and the families they had left behind. In early September, they met the Abraham O. Smoot Company at the Sweetwater River in Wyoming. Wilford was able to see his second wife, Mary Ann Jackson, and their three-month-old son James, who were traveling west under the care of Wilford's father, Aphek.[441]

As they traveled, Brigham felt "led by the Spirit" to seek Wilford's counsel on appointing one of the apostles as President of the Church and naming two counselors.[442] The apostles had discussed reorganizing the First Presidency of the Church in the months following the death of Joseph Smith, but deferred the decision. On October 12, 1847, Wilford recorded his response to Brigham in his journal. He believed that, because the Quorum of the Twelve had been appointed and confirmed by revelation, it would require a revelation to change the Quorum and told Brigham, "Whatever the Lord inspires you to do in this matter, I am with you."[443]

Wilford arrived back in Kanesville, Iowa on October 31. After traveling 2,500 miles and being absent for six months, he "truly rejoiced to once more behold the face[s]" of his wife Phebe and their children: Wilford, Jr., age seven, Phebe Amelia, age five, and Susan, age four.[444] Phebe had also given birth to a daughter, Shuah, three days before Wilford's arrival so he was able to welcome her to the family. (The Woodruffs had buried their two other sons, Joseph and Ezra, in Winter Quarters, Nebraska in 1846.)

On December 5, 1847, six weeks after their return to Kanesville, nine apostles gathered in Orson Hyde's cabin and organized the First Presidency. Brigham Young was sustained as President, with Heber C. Kimball and Willard Richards as his counselors.[445] A few weeks later, at the Church Conference held on December 27, the First Presidency was accepted by the Saints and Wilford recorded,

"We learned from President Young's teaching that it was necessary to keep up a full organization of the Church through all time, as far as could be. At least the three First Presidency, Quorum of the Twelve, Seventies, and Patriarch over the whole Church so the devil could not take advantage of us."[446]

First Presidency of the Church as organized in 1847

Organizing the First Presidency, the highest decision-making quorum in the Church, meant the Twelve could return to the mission field and continue the work of the Gathering. The following spring Wilford was called to serve his seventh and final mission. This time it was to gather the Saints from the eastern states. So on June 21, 1848, Wilford headed east with his family and several other individuals.[447]

This mission lasted almost two years and was significant for the Woodruffs in several ways. Wilford and Phebe's sacrifices included the death of their nine-month-old daughter, Shuah, on July 22, 1848, as they traveled through Illinois.[448] On the other hand, they were able to share the gospel with members of their own families. Wilford baptized more than twenty individuals, including his father-in-law Ezra Carter on March 22, 1849.[449] When the Woodruffs left Maine in the spring of 1850, they had gathered about 100 Saints, among them Phebe's sister Sarah Foss and her children. Their company was later joined by another 125 Saints and they arrived in the Salt Lake Valley on October 14, 1850.[450]

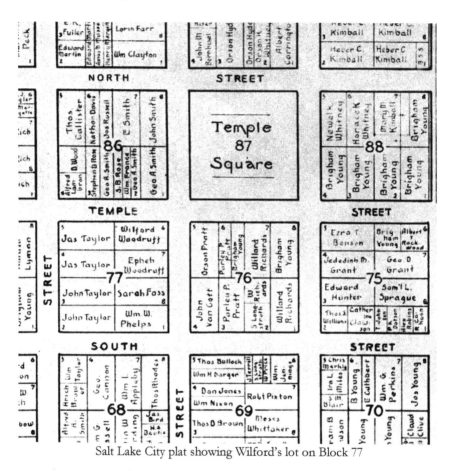

Salt Lake City plat showing Wilford's lot on Block 77

THIS IS THE PLACE FOR US

Although Wilford's family moved into the two-room cabin he had built three years earlier, the rest of the city looked very different.[451] Over 11,000 people occupied the Salt Lake Valley in 1850. When Wilford left with the vanguard company in 1847, there had only been a few hundred Saints in the area. Another major difference was the fact that the Salt Lake Valley was now within the boundaries of the United

States. One month before Wilford arrived back in Salt Lake City, the Territory of Utah was created under the Compromise of 1850.

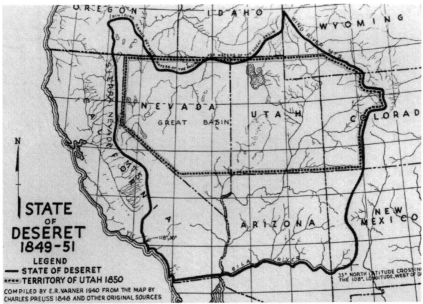

Proposed State of Deseret from which Utah Territory was created

In spite of this turn of events, after enduring twenty years of persecution, Wilford wanted the Saints to appreciate their current situation and the relative calm they were enjoying in Utah. Speaking to those who were too young to remember what the Saints had been subjected to in Ohio, Missouri, and Illinois, Wilford told them, "I am glad we are here, and our enemies where they are. [You] . . . cannot realize the great contrast between Utah and the rest of the world."[452] On another occasion he said, "If this people could comprehend the position they stand in and their true relationship to God, they would . . . not only enjoy, but . . . prize the privileges that are afforded us—prize the day that we live in, and the City of Great Salt Lake where we dwell."[453]

ORDINANCES WITHOUT A TEMPLE

When the Saints left Nauvoo, they hoped when they reached their new home in the West that they would have time to gather the faithful, build a new temple and have the peace needed to engage in the sacred ordinances required for exaltation. In the interim, until a temple could be completed, some exceptions were made to continue administering ordinances. Sealings were performed for a limited number of couples as the Saints journeyed west. For example, some men called to join the Mormon Battalion were sealed to their wives before they left the main body of the Saints.[454] Brigham Young also sealed others in Winter Quarters, including Wilford to three plural wives.

Baptisms for health and healing were occasionally performed between 1846 and 1847. However, the only baptism for the dead recorded during the exodus was performed by Wilford on April 4, 1848, in the Missouri River.[455] The first post-Nauvoo endowment was not administered until October 21, 1849. On that day Brigham Young dedicated the top of Ensign Peak, a hill just north of the settlement in the Salt Lake Valley, in order to administer the endowment to Addison Pratt who had been called to serve a mission but had not yet received his endowment.[456]

In the early 1850s, Brigham authorized several temporary locations for the administration of temple ordinances to the living, including his office and the Territorial Council House, located across the street from the Temple Block.[457] The Council House, completed in December 1850, was the first public building of consequence constructed in the Territory and served many roles over the ensuing thirty-three years.[458] As a governmental building it housed federal offices, the district court, and the city police headquarters. It also functioned as the meeting place for the Territorial Legislature, of which Wilford was appointed a member.

Reflecting their homogenous society at the time, the top floor of the Council House was used for religious meetings and dedicated especially for ceremonial functions.

Territorial Council House on Main Street in Salt Lake City circa 1850s

The temple ordinances of washing, anointing, and endowments for the living, as well as marriage sealings were performed in the Council House. Other priesthood functions, such as the special blessing and anointing Wilford received on February 20, 1851, also took place in the Council House.[459] The first endowment ceremonies began there in February 1851.[460] Between 1851 and 1855, 2,222 members of the Church, including members of Wilford's family, were endowed in the Council House.[461] Wilford also recorded going there to be resealed to his first wife Phebe, and sealed to Emma Smith and Sarah Brown as plural wives on March 13, 1853.[462]

The Council House served an important role as a place for those who had received the ordinances in Nauvoo to administer some of them to the living. However, the use of the Council House for sacred ordinances was problematic. It was not conducive to privacy because, in addition to its government functions, the Council House held the public library and even housed the University of Deseret for a short time.

In addition, as Brigham explained, "There are many of the ordinances of the house of God . . . that will not be received, and ordinances that will not be performed according to the law that the Lord has revealed, without their being done in a temple prepared for that purpose." These other ordinances included proxy endowments, the sealing of children to parents, and adoptions "to connect the chain of the Priesthood."[463]

Brigham's direction was consistent with Joseph Smith's instructions given in Nauvoo. On June 11, 1843, Joseph taught, "[T]here are certain ordinances and principles that, when they are taught and practiced, must be done in a place or house built for that purpose."[464] Proxy endowments were not administered in Nauvoo and, because the temple had not been completed, Joseph did not perform any priesthood adoptions or any child to parent sealings before his death.

The ordinances had been revealed to Joseph Smith. Priesthood authority to officiate in those ordinances had been restored. But, as the gathering of the Saints continued and they struggled to regain the ground they had lost, the administration of the temple ordinances was interrupted. In Nauvoo, the Saints had administered baptisms, confirmations, ordination, washings, anointings, the endowment ceremony, sealings, and second anointings. Baptisms for the dead would not begin again, in earnest, until 1867; and second anointings, for both the living and the dead, were suspended for twenty years. Proxy ordinations and the initiatory ordinances of washing and anointing accompanying the first proxy endowments were delayed until 1877.

~ 8 ~

The Endowment House

I n a discourse delivered in 1855 Wilford asked the congregation if they realized and appreciated the privileges they had been granted. These privileges included the priesthood, the "keys of the kingdom" and the fact that "the world of mankind [is] dependent upon you for salvation?"[465] This theme of recognizing the responsibilities that accompanied these privileges was one he would emphasize for the next forty-three years, as an Apostle, a temple president, and as president of the Church.

Temple Block in Salt Lake City in 1855: old tabernacle (left) on site of present day Assembly Hall and bowery (right) on site of current Tabernacle completed in 1867

A TEMPORARY TEMPLE
Although the site for the temple in Salt Lake City had been dedicated on April 6, 1853, and the cornerstones laid in 1854, the Saints knew the envisioned structure would take

many years to complete. In the interim Brigham Young asked Truman Angell to design a "temple pro tempore" to provide a sufficiently private place for some of the ordinances and ceremonies to be performed. Brigham had talked about it as early as 1847 and, in the spring of 1854 shortly after the cornerstones for the temple were laid, the Saints began building what would become known as the Endowment House.[466]

Endowment House and 1856 additions with granite blocks for temple in front

By September 1854, the foundation was laid in the northwest corner of the Temple Block. The Endowment House was the first structure built with separate rooms for each ordinance and the various phases of the endowment ceremony. By comparison, canvas partitions had been used to divide the areas used for ordinances in Nauvoo—both in Joseph Smith's Red Brick Store and in the temple—as well as in the upper floor of the Council House. Rooms in the Endowment House, such as the Garden Room, were also painted to reflect the scenes depicted in the ceremony, setting the precedent for future temples.

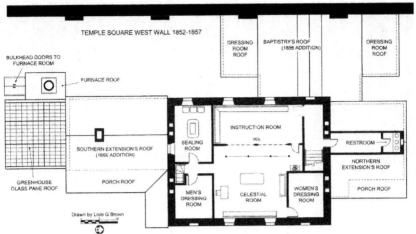

Layout of the second floor of the Endowment House

The first floor of the Endowment House had a room for washing and anointing, and also rooms representing the Garden of Eden, the world, and the terrestrial kingdom. Steps and stairs led from one room to the next, symbolizing the upward progression throughout the ceremony. The sealing room and the room representing the celestial kingdom were on the second floor. The northern addition, added in 1856, served as a reception area, and the southern extension was used as an "official's room" and as a place where those attending and officiating in the ordinances could eat.

On May 5, 1855, when the Endowment House was dedicated, eight people received their endowments and three couples were sealed.[467] Wilford records the events in his journal, stating that Brigham Young wanted to refer to the Endowment House as "the House of God" and when the temple was completed he would call it "the Temple of our God."[468] Wilford was one of the many workers called to officiate in the Endowment House, along with apostles Joseph F. Smith and Daniel H. Wells. Women who had been endowed in Nauvoo, such as George A. Smith's wife

Bathsheba and Orson Hyde's wife Marinda, administered ordinances to other women in the Endowment House.

On March 18, 1856, Wilford and Phebe were able to take their two oldest children to the Endowment House to receive their endowments. Wilford officiated in washing, anointing and ordaining his son Wilford Jr. to the office of an Elder and "sealed upon him all the blessings of his ordination, anointing, and my birthright."[469] Recalling the patriarchal blessing Wilford received from Joseph Smith, Sr., wherein he was promised he would live to have posterity who would receive the priesthood, he wrote of his gratitude that this blessing had been fulfilled. On February 26, 1857, he records the first time he took his family to "the altar in the House of the Lord." On this occasion he had his three living wives—Phebe, Emma, and Sarah Brown—resealed to him, and Phebe's deceased sister, Mary Carter, sealed to him by proxy.[470]

The primary ordinances performed in the Endowment House between 1855 and 1889 included sealings of living couples and proxy sealings; baptisms for the living and by proxy; washings, anointings, endowments, and second anointings for the living.[471] Proxy baptisms were sporadically performed after a baptismal font was built next to the Endowment House in 1856, but these baptisms did not take place on a regular basis until 1867. Second anointings were not recommenced until 1866, after a twenty-year hiatus. It would not be until 1877, when the St. George Temple was completed, that all the ordinances performed in the Nauvoo Temple were again administered, and proxy endowments were administered for the first time.

The completion of the Endowment House in 1855 was important not only for temple work, but also the beginning of a general reformation of the Church in Utah. The California Gold Rush and Salt Lake City's position on the trail west, among other things, brought the outside world closer and Church leaders felt the need to reinvigorate Church members' dedication. Similar to the reformation in Nauvoo fifteen years earlier, the Utah reformation simultaneously increased and tested the Saints' faithfulness and commitment. Rebaptism was an important symbol of the Saints' recommitment to the Church and gospel principles.

In an October 1855 address, the Saints were instructed that, "[A]ll the children that are 8 years old and all young persons and all old people and strangers that have not been baptized ... and also those who have commit[ed] sins for which they should be baptized for . . ." ought to be baptized in order to be considered candidates for the "fullness of Celestial Glory."[472] A few months later, on March 17, 1856, Wilford rebaptized all his family members over the age of eight: "three wives, three children and a Lamanite boy called Moroni." He then returned to his house where he confirmed them all.[473]

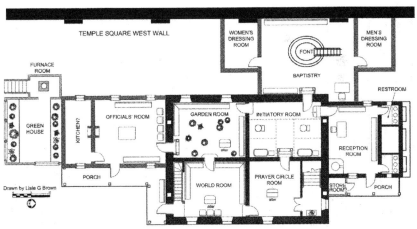

Layout of main floor of Endowment House with baptismal font

THE 1850s REFORMATION

During the summer of 1856 a stone baptismal font was carved and installed on the west side of the Endowment

House.[474] On September 21, 1856, referring to the need for a reformation among the people, Brigham Young promised, "When we get the baptismal font prepared that is now being built, I will take you into the waters of baptism if you repent of your sins. If you will covenant to live your religion and be Saints of the Most High, you shall have that privilege ... [but] a separation must take place, you must part with your sins."[475]

Heber C. Kimball dedicated the font on October 2, using language reminiscent of the description of the font in the Nauvoo Temple and alluding to the blessed waters of the pool of Bethesda.[476] Wilford recorded the words of Heber's prayer in his journal as follows: "Let thine Angel, O Lord, touch this water and this font with his finger that it may be holy unto Thee Lord." Heber C. Kimball also asked that the people would feel the power of God so they could bring about a great reformation among the Saints. He then dedicated the font to baptize the living and the living for the dead and "that the generations which are dead and passed away may be saved and that the sins of the living may be washed away and that the sick may be healed of every infirmity, that we may be renewed in body and spirit in all things."[477]

Exemplifying the reformation, the dedication of the baptismal font was celebrated with the rebaptism of Brigham Young and members of the Quorum of the Twelve, including Wilford. This was the second time the Quorum of the Twelve had been rebaptized as examples to the general membership of the Church; the first took place upon entering the Salt Lake Valley in 1847. Once again Wilford did not hesitate to demonstrate his commitment and devotion to the Church and to God.

Brigham Young went down into the water first and baptized his two counselors, Heber C. Kimball and Jedediah M. Grant, then laid hands upon them and confirmed them. Brigham then baptized Wilford and all three members of the First Presidency laid their hands upon Wilford. Jedediah M. Grant reconfirmed Wilford a member of the Church and sealed upon him "all the gifts and blessings of the Apostleship and priesthood and every blessing" which had ever been sealed upon him.[478] Jedediah then blessed Wilford that he might be healed from his infirmities and be able to fulfill his responsibilities in the Church. Following the dedication of the font, they had a "soul stirring meeting."[479]

Speaking in conference the following Sunday, Wilford added his support to the reformation and said, "[T]he Presidency had called upon us to reform our ways, to renew our covenants, and commence to live the lives of Saints."[480] Wilford then records that after the meeting ended, many went to the font and Brigham Young baptized about seventy-five members of his own family. Heber C. Kimball then baptized another seventy-five, including some members of Wilford's family. Others followed, and all those who had been rebaptized were then confirmed.[481] Although official records were not kept of every baptism, journal entries indicate children of at least eight years of age were baptized in the Endowment House font, and baptisms for health and renewing covenants were performed for individuals of all ages.[482]

Thousands of Church members were rebaptized and recommitted themselves to more fully live the principles of the gospel during the 1850s. For example, in October 1856, Wilford rebaptized sixty-five missionaries and their families, and the bishops in Salt Lake. In addition to the font next to the Endowment House, baptisms were performed in many other locations. When the baptismal font was dedicated at Wilford's own ward building, the Fourteenth Ward, he wrote that the day was spent rebaptizing members of the Ward.[483] "The spirit of Reformation lives in their hearts," he wrote, "and brings forth fruit in their lives."[484]

When the original font next to the Endowment House began leaking, it was replaced and a new font was dedicated by Brigham Young. On June 4, 1864, Wilford's record shows that, after working in the Endowment House all day, they dedicated the baptismal font unto God for baptisms "for the remission of sins, for the healing of the sick, and for baptism for the dead."[485] On August 19, 1865, he baptized Mary Woodard Sprague for Eliza Caroline Everett Sprague, stating that this was the first proxy baptism in the new font.[486] By 1876 over 134,000 proxy baptisms were completed in the Endowment House font.[487] On a few occasions more than 1,000 baptisms and confirmations were administered in a single day.

At the height of the reformation, on December 30, 1856, Wilford, a member of the Territorial Legislature of Utah, records a unique occurrence in the history of governmental affairs in the United States. During a Joint Session of both houses of the Legislature, after speeches by several leaders including Brigham and Wilford, a motion was made for all members of the Legislature to repent of their sins and go to the Endowment House font and be baptized for the remission of their sins. The motion was carried unanimously and all fifty-five members of the Legislature met at the font that evening at 6:00 p.m. to be rebaptized and reconfirmed.[488] In his journal Wilford stated the obvious: "This was a new feature in Legislation." He then explained, "We believed that if we could get the spirit of God we could do business faster and better than with the spirit of the Devil or the spirit of the world."[489]

LIVE YOUR RELIGION

During this time of reformation, Wilford's discourses, like those of Jedediah M. Grant and other Church leaders, were constant reminders of what the Saints' priorities needed to be in order to withstand the world's influence. However, instead of the harsh approach employed by others, Wilford emphasized the need for righteous examples and a willingness to help one another.

For example, on December 7, 1856, he said the Spirit of God was in his "tabernacle" like fire in his bones. He told the priesthood leaders it was not necessary to "jump and shout and stomp off 50 cents worth of sole leather" or "knock the people in the head" in order to get them to wake up or reform. Instead, he encouraged the bishops and home missionaries to rely on the Spirit of God, and treat the people in a "fatherly" way in order to save them.[490]

The following day Wilford reiterated that the priesthood leaders were using the sledgehammer too much, and told them, "The people will live their religion when you live it yourselves."[491] The short amount of time the Saints spent in mortality would determine their eternal destinies and, he suggested, that thought alone should guide their decisions.[492] Determined to do his duty with God's help, Wilford asked the Saints to do the same. In response to his own question, "What is man's life good for, or his words or work good for when he stands in the way of men's salvation, exaltation, and glory?" he replied, "They are of no use at all."[493]

During the reformation a list of twenty-seven questions was developed for the home missionaries to use as a guideline to determine the level of faithfulness of each member in their wards.[494] The questions addressed topics ranging from murder and adultery to bathing habits and the use of irrigation water. Questions regarding the payment of tithes and the frequency of family prayer were included along with inquiries into the payment of debts and the cutting of hay. Wilford described the catechism as "containing a part of the law of God."[495] Yet, indicative of the focus at the time, the temple covenants and ordinances were not mentioned at all. The rise of temple consciousness was still twenty years in the future.[496]

QUESTIONS TO BE ASKED THE LATTER-DAY-SAINTS

1. Have you committed murder by shedding innocent blood or assenting thereto?
2. Have you betrayed your brethren or sister in anything?
3. Have you committed adultery by having any connection with any woman that was not your wife or any man that was not your husband?
4. Have you taken and made use of property not your own, without the consent of the owner?
5. Have you cut hay where you had no right to, or turned your animals into another person's grain or field, without his knowledge and consent?
6. Have you lied about or maliciously represented any person or thing?
7. Have you borrowed anything you have not returned, or paid for?
8. Have you borne false witness against your neighbour?
9. Have you taken the name of the Diety in vain?
10. Have you coveted anything not your own?
11. Have you been intoxicated with strong drink?
12. Have you found lost property and not returned it to the owner or used all dilligence to do so?
13. Have you branded an animal that you did not know to be your own?
14. Have you taken another's horse or mule from the range and rode it without the owner's consent?
15. Have you fulfilled your promise in paying your debts, or run into debt without prospect of paying?
16. Have you taken water to irrigate with, when it belonged to another person at the time you used it?
17. Do you pay your tithing promptly?
18. Do you teach your family the gospel of Salvation?
19. Do you speak against your brethren, or against any principle taught us in the Bible, Book of Mormon, Book of Doctrine & Covenants, revelations given through Joseph Smith the Prophet and the Presidency of the Church as now organized?
20. Do you pray in your family night and morning and attend to secret prayer?
21. Do you wash your body and have your family do so as often as health and cleanliness require and circumstances permit?
22. Do you labor six days and rest, or go to the house of the worship on the seventh?
23. Do you and your family attend Ward meetings?
24. Do you preside over your household as a servant of God and is your family subject to you?
25. Have you laboured diligently and earned faithfully the wages paid you by you employers?
26. Do you oppress the Hireling in his wages?
27. Have you taken up and converted any stray animal to your own use, or in any manner appropriated one to your benefit, without accounting therefor to the proper authorities?

In answer to the above questions, let all men and women confess to the persons they have injured and make restitution, or satisfaction. And when catechizing the people, the Bishops, Teachers, Missionaries and other officers in the Church are not at liberty to pry into sins that are between a person and his or her God, but let such persons confess to the proper authority, that the adversary may not have an opportunity to take advantage of human weaknesses, and thereby destroy souls.

Questions to be asked by home missionaries and Church leaders of all members during the 1850s reformation in Utah. Transcribed from holograph of broadsheet made by Andrew S. Gibbons.

Wilford later noted that, although the world "marveled" that the Saints' religious discussions included temporal matters, "two-thirds of all the revelations given in this world rest upon the accomplishment of this temporal work." The example he gave to illustrate this was their duty "to cultivate the earth, to take the rocks and elements out of the mountains and rear Temples to the Most High God."[497] The Saints believed their spiritual unity embraced both the temporal and spiritual, because temporal things were done for the purpose of building the literal kingdom of God on the earth.[498]

Members of Utah Territorial Militia

THE UTAH "WAR"

The efforts to strengthen the Church and support the Saints by blending their daily religious, political, personal, and family lives were viewed as a threat by some outside the Church. This perceived threat, coupled with false reports submitted by government appointees, influenced President Buchanan's decision to remove Brigham Young as Governor of the Territory and send a newly appointed governor to replace him. On July 24, 1857, as the Saints gathered to celebrate the ten-year anniversary of their entrance into the

Salt Lake Valley, they received word of President Buchanan's intention to have 2,500 soldiers escort the new gover-governor to his new post and suppress the "rebellion" in Utah.[499]

The Saints believed that the Constitution guaranteed the free exercise of their religion. But they had also experienced the failure of the federal government and state governments in Ohio, Missouri, and Illinois to protect them or their rights. Upon hearing the news of President Buchanan's decision to send the Army, Brigham Young told Church leaders he was "determined no more to submit to oppression either to individuals, towns, counties, states or nation." However, he also said, "If the Governor and officers wished to come and would behave themselves well, they would be well treated."[500]

Wilford's journal entries over the years reflect the growing gulf he observed between the inspired men who drafted the Constitution, and the men in the federal government who failed to govern by its precepts.[501] As a result, he and the Saints in general felt they needed to not only defend themselves, but the Constitution itself.[502] As the army approached, Wilford told the Saints he believed they were ready to shoulder their guns in defense of the Constitution of the United States and the rights "which both the laws of God and man guarantee to us."[503]

After an extended standoff, when the Saints abandoned Salt Lake City and buried the temple foundation, a brokered peace was reached in 1858. The army was allowed to peacefully enter the city with the new governor. Nonetheless, the truce between the federal government and Church leaders did not stop attempts by Congress to change the judicial, political, and personal practices of the Saints including forcing an end to polygamy. The 1862 Morrill Anti-Bigamy Act gave the federal government the power to disincorporate the Church and take any property owned by the Church in excess of $50,000.[504] Although the Morrill Act was signed into law by President Abraham Lincoln on July 8, 1862, he did not provide funds or the manpower to enforce it. Another twelve years would pass before the Poland Act provided a basis for the prosecution of polygamists.[505]

Wilford in 1862

THE CIVIL WAR

The 1860s brought many changes in Wilford's family life with the death of his father, the return of his son James Jackson to his household, the marriages of his daughters Susan and Phebe, the births of ten more children, and the birth of his first grandchild. This was also a time of tragedy as the Civil War raged in the East. The Saints received the news of the secession of the Southern States, the Emancipation Proclamation, the end of the Civil War, and then, shortly after Abraham Lincoln's second inauguration, word of his assassination. Wilford was asked to deliver one of the eulogies when the Saints gathered to mourn Lincoln's death in April 1865.

In the midst of these difficult times Church leaders made extra efforts to help refocus the Saints on their eternal goals and the ordinances necessary to achieve them. Efforts to invigorate the Saints included the 1867 reorganization of the Female Relief Society for women, and the School of the Prophets for instruction of priesthood leaders.[506]

Brigham Young also reintroduced the second anointing after a twenty-year hiatus. Wilford's journal contains Brigham's instructions to the Quorum of the Twelve on December 26, 1866, regarding the proper procedures to use in administering the ordinance.[507] Over the course of the ensuing twelve months, Wilford then records the names of those individuals and couples asked to come to Salt Lake City to receive their further anointings.[508] In his synopsis of the year 1867 he states that he personally administered second anointings to 259 individuals.[509]

Speaking to the Saints on May 19, 1867, Wilford stressed the importance of obeying all the principles of the gospel. He said, "No part of the Gospel is superfluous . . . and all the inhabitants of this world and all others have got to be saved by it, if saved at all."[510] Wilford recalled his joy as the principles and ordinances had been revealed to Joseph Smith one by one, and his hope that the Saints would recognize that every principle the Lord reveals is good for them and applicable in time and eternity.

First picture taken of Church Presidency and Quorum of Twelve Apostles (1868)
Front row from left to right: George A. Smith, Brigham Young, and Daniel H. Wells.
Back row seated by seniority from left to right: Orson Hyde, Orson Pratt, John Taylor,
Wilford Woodruff, Ezra T. Benson, Charles C. Rich, Lorenzo Snow, Erastus Snow,
Franklin D. Richards, George Q. Cannon, Brigham Young Jr., and Joseph F. Smith.

UNITED ORDER

As the Transcontinental Railroad neared completion in 1869, Church leaders took additional steps to prepare for the societal changes that would naturally follow the influx of "outsiders." Brigham Young re-implemented the Law of Consecration and Stewardship through the United Order movement and introduced other measures to assist the poor and maintain economic unity within individual communities and the Church as a whole.[511] In the Church Conference held on May 8, 1874, Wilford endorsed Brigham Young's decision to re-establish the United Order of Zion, saying, "I feel that it is our duty, as a people, to unite our interests together, also our time, talents, labor, and all that we are stewards over, that as men who have faith in God, we may be prepared for those things which await us, and for the coming of the Son of Man."[512]

The rules of each Order differed slightly but the underlying purpose was for the Saints to consecrate themselves unselfishly to the good of the entire community in order to build up of the kingdom of God on the earth and establish Zion.[513] In 1874 and 1875, during the establishment of more than 200 United Order movements throughout Utah and in communities in Arizona, Idaho, and Nevada, rebaptisms again occurred en masse. The words used in the rebaptism ceremony for entrance into a United Order were, in part: I baptize you "for the remission of your sins, for the renewal of your covenants with God and thy brethren, and for the observance of the rules that have been read in your hearing."[514]

New tabernacle (left) and Endowment House (right) circa 1872 with granite blocks cut for Salt Lake Temple in the foreground

On July 13, 1874, after meeting with the First Presidency, Quorum of the Twelve, and general priesthood membership, Wilford wrote that nearly all agreed to renew their covenants and be rebaptized.[515] A year later, on July 17, 1875, Wilford recorded being rebaptized for his seventh and final time. Brigham Young and five members of the Quorum of the Twelve, including Wilford, were baptized for the renewal of their covenants and their commitment to the United Order.[516] The other members of the Quorum of the Twelve had been rebaptized several weeks earlier.

The following day, the Church leaders traveled to Farmington, Utah, and met with the Saints there. After several speeches, George Q. Cannon read the rules of the United Order, and the majority of the congregation voted to abide by them. At the close of the meeting, twenty-seven of the leading men of Davis County, including the bishops and their counselors, were rebaptized by George Q. Cannon, and Wilford assisted in their confirmations.[517] Wilford records similar meetings in August where, after the rules of the United Order were read, the congregation would gather at a body of water for rebaptisms and reconfirmations.[518]

Sign above ZCMI store in Salt Lake City

Wilford assisted in the dedication of Zion's Cooperative Mercantile Institution (ZCMI) in Salt Lake City on March 31, 1876, and similar cooperatives were set up in smaller communities as part of the United Order system. The establishment of the first United Order in St. George was a critical factor in the building of the St. George Temple.

Salt Lake Temple foundation in front of old and new tabernacles in 1873

Thirty years had passed since the first Saints arrived in the Salt Lake Valley to establish a refuge "in the tops of the mountains."[519] Their work building the temple in Salt Lake had been interrupted by the necessities of daily life, and slowed by the federal government's interference. But by 1870 despite the obstacles and opposition they faced, Church membership had grown to more than 90,000. The population of the Territory of Utah had reached 86,000 and Brigham Young had directed the establishment of towns and cities throughout the region. And, with the coming of the railroad, the number of Saints able to immigrate would certainly grow. The need for temples and the resources to build them would increase simultaneously.

~ 9 ~

Utah's First Temple

The Saints had made extreme sacrifices to build temples in Kirtland and Nauvoo. By 1870, they had been struggling for almost twenty years to build the Salt Lake Temple and were just beginning to see progress beyond the foundation. Church leaders were keenly aware that the generation who had received the "fulness of the priesthood" in Nauvoo was passing away. And although they had been officiating in ordinances in the Endowment House for fifteen years, the "organization and instruction of the Priesthood," as Brigham described it, could only be completed in a temple.[520]

In 1871 Brigham's health was deteriorating and, because he worried the Salt Lake Temple would not be finished in his lifetime, he proposed building a temple in St. George. He spent winters in St. George beginning in 1869, and was impressed with the Saints' workmanship as they constructed the St. George Tabernacle. He hoped they could apply those same skills to building a temple, which would have the added benefit of providing a continued means of support for the struggling community.

Brigham Young's proposal to begin constructing a temple was approved in the Church Conference held October 6, 1871, two months before the final stone of the tower on the St. George Tabernacle was set in place.[521] The first United Order, organized in St. George, facilitated this new project. Ground for the St. George Temple was broken five weeks after approval, and construction on the temple moved forward. The cornerstone was laid April 1, 1874, and in less than a year the red sandstone walls were erected.[522]

St. George Temple construction in 1875

As had been done in Nauvoo, as soon as the basement was constructed, the baptismal font was installed. The font and oxen were cast in Salt Lake City. Then in July 1875, the font was transported in sections to St. George, first by train and then on carts drawn by oxen. It was assembled in the basement of the partially completed temple in August 1875. Erastus Snow dedicated the font, and on August 11, it was used to rebaptize those entering the United Order in St. George. Charles L. Walker records the event in his journal stating that those who accepted the rules of the United Order, read before the congregation on August 8, were invited to be baptized. Erastus Snow performed the baptisms for the remission of sin, the renewal of covenants, and "for the Observance of the Rules of the Holy United Order."[523] Two days later Charles then assisted in rebaptizing and confirming a "goodly number of persons" including his own family members.

WORTH EVERY SACRIFICE

As construction progressed on the temple in St. George, Church leaders encouraged the Saints to prepare themselves to go to the temple and officiate by proxy for their deceased relatives. Joseph Smith had stressed the vital importance of the Nauvoo Temple as the only place designated for receipt of the "fulness of the priesthood": all the sacred ordinances for the Saints and their deceased relatives by proxy.[524]

The same emphasis was echoed by Wilford when the St. George Temple was being constructed thirty years later. In 1875 he told the Saints, "We are held responsible for all this, and for building Temples to the Most High, wherein we can enter and attend to ordinances for the salvation of our dead. . . . [F]or this is what the Priesthood is for. The God of heaven has ordained this from eternity to eternity. These persons in the spirit world died in the flesh without the law, without the Gospel, and they are shut up in prison. . . . [T]here is no baptism there; there is no marrying or giving in marriage there; all these ordinances have to be performed on the earth. . . . The Lord holds us responsible . . . for the salvation of the dead."[525]

Wilford constantly reminded the Saints of this privilege and duty and the blessings promised if they would wield the sealing power appropriately. On one occasion he asked them if they realized their "responsibilities before the Lord." He then explained those responsibilities saying, "The Lord has raised up a kingdom of priests here in the last days to establish his Church and kingdom, and to prepare the way for the Second Coming of the Son of Man, and the God of heaven has put into the hands of his servants the keys of the kingdom . . . power to bind and to seal both on the earth and in heaven."[526]

Later, with this overwhelming task in mind, Wilford encouraged the Saints by emphasizing that it was a great work, a glorious work, and one in which they should rejoice. He reminded them that it gave them the privilege of being instruments in the hands of God, of helping to build up His kingdom on the earth. In addition, he told the Saints that the promised blessings they would receive as a result of their efforts would sustain them and bring them consolation, hope and joy.[527]

TURNING THEIR HEARTS

Wilford's own motivation to do this work was clear. From the day he was introduced to the restored gospel, he continuously tried to share its principles with his extended family in person.[528] Reflecting on this he said, "All men who have obeyed this Gospel for the love of the truth, and whose minds have been inspired by the Spirit and power of God, have felt . . . a great desire to spread the knowledge of its principles among their fellow men. When first embraced by them it has seemed to them as though they could convince the world; and they have been anxious to lay these principles before their father's household, their uncles, aunts, cousins, neighbors and friends, believing that they would receive it. I felt so myself."[529]

His desire to offer salvation by proxy to his family members in the spirit world was no less focused. When speaking of the celestial law, he said, "I desire to keep that law, so that when I have finished my probation here, I may get into the presence of my Heavenly Father, where our Savior is . . . [and] I desire the same for my family."[530]

St. George Temple construction in January 1876

In order to have this privilege of serving as instruments in God's hands to offer salvation to their family members, the Saints first needed to gather information and family records. In 1872 Brigham stated that once the temple was completed they would be able to obtain endowments for "relatives, friends and old associates, the history of whom we are now getting from our friends in the East. The Lord is stirring up the hearts of many there, and there is a perfect mania with some to trace their genealogies and to get up printed records of their ancestors. They do not know what they are doing it for, but the Lord is prompting them; and it will continue and run on from father to father, until they get the genealogy of their forefathers as far as they possibly can."[531]

Wilford, like others, had been researching and gathering his family records for years in anticipation of the opportunity to perform ordinances for his relatives. Speaking in the April 1876 Church Conference, Wilford said if there was anything he desired to live for, it was to get the genealogical records of his family so he could receive ordinances for them.[532] His journal entries reflect his ongoing efforts between 1874 and 1876, which had intensified as the construction of the St, George Temple progressed.[533] He felt he "held the keys of the dead of my father's house," and therefore dedicated many hours to genealogical work.[534]

In 1874 he obtained a book containing the history of New Britain, Connecticut, and his birthplace, Farmington, from 1600 to 1850.[535] In it he found information on his Woodruff ancestors, his mother Beulah Thompson's family, and the Harts, his stepmother's family. This book even contained the names of his father Aphek, his uncle Ozem and his brother Azmon. He later records his efforts to write the genealogy of this ancestry from Matthew Woodruff, the progenitor of the Woodruffs in Farmington, Connecticut, to his own father. From this one book he filled eleven pages with notes, and extracted 303 names of the Woodruff family.[536] He was then able to go to the Endowment House on September 4, 1875, where, for the first time, he had an opportunity to perform baptisms for the Woodruff family.[537] His daughters served as proxies for 141 relatives.

The following year, Wilford describes a history he purchased containing all the descendants of his stepmother's ancestor, Stephen Hart, who was born in England in 1605. In February and March he spent many days studying this book, extracting Hart family names for baptism.[538] Finally, on June 20, 1875, he records, "Glory

Hallelujah for this day! For in spite of the Devil, through the blessing of God, I have had the privilege this day of going into the Endowment House and with my family have been baptized for 949 . . . of my dead relatives and friends." He "felt to rejoice" that he was able to go into the baptismal font with his eldest brother Azmon and his own children to redeem their family members.[539] Two days later he was personally able to act as proxy for 110 ancestors, and with the help of family and friends, completed baptisms and confirmations for 924 more family members.

Wilford in 1874

Azmon Woodruff circa age 60

The opportunity to redeem their own deceased family members was a blessing he hoped all the Saints would embrace. Wilford shared with them his desire that no one who could find family records would go to his grave without attending to the ordinance work for each individual. He testified that, "[I]t will take all the ordinances of the gospel of Christ to save [one] soul as much as another. Jesus himself obeyed all the ordinances of the Gospel that He might fulfill all righteousness."[540] Wilford then wondered aloud, "How would I feel, after living as long as I have, with the privileges I have had of going into these temples, to go into the spirit world without having done this work? I meet my father's house, I meet my mother's house, I meet my progenitors, and they are shut up in prison; I held the keys of their salvation, and yet did nothing for them; what would be my feelings, or what would be their feelings toward me?"[541]

In conclusion, he shared his conviction that because the Lord had blessed the Saints with the priesthood and opportunity to perform these proxy ordinances, every man and woman in the Church that had any faith in God and in the Gospel should attend to this duty. He testified, "These are glorious principles—principles which the Latter-day

Saints should not neglect while they have the privilege and power." In fact, he asserted there is no calling greater than to save souls by preaching the gospel to them, by administering the ordinances of the house of God to them, so all God's children may be prepared to "go into the kingdom of heaven and into a celestial glory."[542]

St. George Temple on February 28, 1876
showing lower half of the sandstone prepared for plaster and whitewash

THE END OF AN ERA
In October 1876 Brigham directed the closure of the Endowment House in Salt Lake City. He instructed the Saints to travel to St. George, once the temple was dedicated, to participate in further endowments or sealings for the living and dead. Consequently, in the final week of work in the Endowment House, a record number of sealings, endowments, and baptisms were performed. On October 10,

ninety-one were endowed. The following day 1,207 proxy baptisms were completed. On October 12, Wilford performed 125 proxy sealings for couples and wrote, "Total sealed at the altar 300 couples. . . . [T]he most sealings ever performed in one day by two men in this dispensation, if not during the age of the world."[543] Wilford officiated in the Endowment House on October 19 when they sealed 250 couples and baptized 1,300. He worked until his lungs "entirely gave out and [he] had to leave the House."[544]

He then made preparations to move to St. George and assist in the final preparations for the commencement of work in the temple there. Wilford left Salt Lake City with Brigham and other members of the First Presidency on November 1, 1876, to commence an unprecedented year of temple ordinance work. Finally, as Joseph Smith had said in 1842, with a temple in their midst the Church could be put in "proper order."[545]

On November 9, 1876, the apostles arrived in St. George to help make the final arrangements so ordinance work could begin. As they approached the city, the temple—a "glorious sight"—came into view.[546] Wilford's recorded reaction to seeing the St. George Temple was reminiscent of his experience forty years earlier when, returning to Kirtland from his mission in the Southern States, he rejoiced upon seeing the House of the Lord there for the first time.[547]

The day after he arrived in St. George, Wilford was able to visit the temple and go through "every department of it from the baptismal font in the basement to the top of the roof." The painstaking efforts of the Saints in its construction and decoration were evident to him, and he described the temple "as white as snow both inside and out and . . . a beautiful contrast with the red appearance of the surrounding country."[548]

Town of St. George, Utah

The exterior of the St. George Temple was built to look like a castle, symbolic of the royal priesthood and the divine birthright of God's children. The defensive architecture, with buttresses and crenulations, symbolizes the spiritual protection provided by the ordinances administered in the temple. In designing the interior of the St. George Temple, Truman Angell followed the layout of the Nauvoo Temple. The lowest floor held the baptismal font and related rooms for changing before and after the baptisms. The main floor and the fourth floor were designed as open assembly rooms. Just as in the Kirtland Temple, pulpits were constructed at both ends of the assembly rooms; the Melchizedek priesthood on the east end and Aaronic priesthood pulpits on the west. The third and fifth floors were divided into smaller rooms that could be used as sealing rooms or offices and even sleeping quarters.[549]

Wilford spent his first few weeks in St. George helping set up the main hall of the temple for the endowment ceremonies. He made arrangements for the curtains and partitions to be used to divide the hall into areas representing the Garden of Eden, and the telestial and terrestrial kingdoms.[550] He also assisted John D. T. McAllister in writing some of the ceremony "for work in the temple."[551]

He then spent Christmas day in the temple, along with forty women who were still sewing the carpets and other men who were there to make sure specific rooms were ready for the dedication on January 1.[552] The following week he also spent his time "mostly at the Temple."[553]

BLESSED WITH A PRIVILEGE

On January 1, 1877, almost 2,000 Saints assembled within the walls of the temple for the dedication of the baptismal font, the endowment area on the main floor, and one sealing room.[554] Wilford called the meeting to order and explained how rare a privilege temple worship had been through the ages: "[W]e are this day blessed with a privilege that but few since the days of Adam have ever enjoyed, but few of the sons of Adam have ever had the privilege of entering into a Temple built by the commandment of God in which to administer ordinances both for the living and the dead."[555] Wilford's journal entry recording the day's events reflects his understanding that this was "a very important day to the Church and Kingdom of God on the earth."[556]

In his dedicatory prayer Wilford asked God to accept the gratitude of the Saints for preserving their lives so they could enter another temple "to organize the Holy Priesthood, and to administer the ordinances of the gospel of the Son of God both for the living and the dead."[557] He then asked God to bless with His spirit and power all who would administer "ordinances of life and salvation" within the walls of the temple. His prayer continued with a plea that the Saints might accomplish the work that only they could do and "unto which they are ordained:" to build up Zion and prepare the earth for the Second Coming of Christ.[558]

Erastus Snow, in his dedication of the main hall, asked for God's blessings upon those who helped build the temple: "[M]ay they and their generations after them, and through them the Fathers before them, enjoy the blessings and Exaltation which flow through the ordinances of thy House and the administration of thy Holy Priesthood."[559]

Finally, the congregation was asked to remain in the main hall while members of the Twelve and "a few others of the priesthood" went upstairs to the sealing room. After singing a hymn, Brigham Young Jr. dedicated the sealing room for "performing the ordinances of sealing women to men, children to their parents, and man to his fellow man, that the bond may reach unto heaven . . . that we may legally claim the relationship of husbands and wives, parents and children, and be crowned sons and daughters of God and joint-heirs with Jesus our Elder Brother."[560]

Speaking to those attending the dedication, Brigham Young wondered if they understood the privilege of participating in temple ordinance work that had not been done "since the days of Adam that we have any knowledge of."[561] Announcing that the Saints could finally receive the endowment for their deceased relatives, he told them, "All the angels of heaven are looking at this little handful of people."[562]

It was decided that baptismal work would be attended to on Tuesdays and Wednesdays and endowments and sealings would be administered on Thursdays and Fridays.[563] Accordingly, a week later, on Tuesday, January 9, 1877, the first proxy ordinances were performed in the temple.[564] Wilford baptized Brigham's daughter, Susa, in behalf of 141 women. Brigham served as a witness to the work and others in attendance shed tears of joy.[565]

RETURNING TO THE TEMPLE

Although many Saints made incredible sacrifices to finish the Nauvoo Temple so they could receive the temple blessings before heading west, only those administering the ordinances were able to hear the ceremonies and eternally significant instructions more than once. Likewise, those who were fortunate to participate in the ceremonies in the Endowment House between 1855 and 1876 did not have the opportunity to repeat the endowment unless they were called to officiate as administrators of the ordinances. The concern expressed by Church leaders was that even the Saints who were privileged to receive all of the ordinances in Nauvoo did not have sufficient time to understand the information, and whatever they might have internalized earlier had probably been forgotten.[566]

In 1847, Brigham had said that because everything in Nauvoo "went with a rush," when the next temple was built he wanted the Saints to be able to "take time enough about it to understand it" at each step.[567] Later he even proposed administering only the Aaronic priesthood portion of the endowment to ensure the Saints' understanding of its importance. Then, after they proved themselves worthy of those initial covenants, allowing them to receive the endowment relating to the Melchizedek Priesthood.[568] Although this approach was not implemented, Brigham's concern was evident in the training of those officiating in the temple and his oversight of the record made detailing the procedures to be implemented in all subsequent temples.[569]

WORK FOR THE LIVING AND THE DEAD

On January 11, 1877, the first endowments for the dead in this dispensation were performed, ushering in a completely new era of temple work. The first proxy ordinations occurred the same day: Wilford ordained eight to the office of Elder vicariously.[570] The Saints could now return to hear the ordinances over and over again by serving as proxies for their relatives. In this capacity they could review the purpose of pre-mortal and mortal life and the significance of those probationary experiences during the dramatization of the endowment, and thus understand their "true condition and relation" to God, as described by Joseph Smith.[571]

Serving as proxy for the endowment was also an opportunity for them to recommit to the covenants they had made when they received their own endowments. Proxy endowments significantly broadened the circle of temple experience by increasing the number of individuals participating in the ceremonies and thus their ability to share the temple experiences with others. The temple also became a place where the Saints could gather in peace, a sanctuary as the world closed in.[572]

The focus of sealings in the Endowment House had been for the living, and had been a temporary, although long-lasting, substitute for a temple. Because of the limited space, couples were permitted to be sealed without first being endowed. But with the completion of the St. George Temple, the order of administering ordinances to the living returned to that practiced in Nauvoo—first, washings and anointings, then endowment prior to sealings. (The exception to this was children under the age of twelve who were only being sealed.) The Saints who had only been sealed in the thirty-one intervening years between the two temples could now be endowed. Furthermore, all these preliminary ordinances could be performed vicariously by those who had been waiting to be sealed to their deceased parents. In addition to the first proxy endowments on January 11, Brigham and Wilford sealed thirty-two living couples. Proxy sealings began on January 12.[573]

Wilford began the administration of second anointings for the living on January 16.[574] Although over fifty individuals were privileged to receive this ordinance between

December 1866 and November 1867, second anointings had not otherwise been administered since February 1846. During the month of January 1877, seventy-three individuals received their second anointings.[575] The first proxy second anointings in the St. George Temple were given on February 7.[576]

CHURCH REORGANIZATION

By 1877 there were over 100,000 Saints living in the area comprising the Utah Territory that only 12,000 had occupied twenty-five years earlier. Some of these Church members were no longer officially affiliated with any particular ward.[577] Following the dedication of the St. George Temple in 1877, In accordance with Joseph Smith's teaching that the Church cannot be "organized in its proper order" without a temple, Brigham Young instituted a complete reorganization of the priesthood leadership, creating new ward and stake boundaries.[578] He wanted to not only "unite the Saints" but to allow more efficient priesthood administration.

Under Brigham's direction, the Saints had established communities throughout the region and he wanted their priesthood leaders to be in a position to understand the needs of "everyone calling himself a Latter-day Saint."[579] The existing 101 wards were reorganized into 241 wards, and Brigham directed that, whenever required, members should be rebaptized into a specific ward.[580] This process of enrolling all members in a ward or branch made it possible for them to be "numbered among the people of the church of Christ . . . that they might be remembered and nourished by the good word of God, to keep them in the right way."[581]

Although many Saints had been rebaptized during the implementation of United Orders in the early 1870s, those who had not taken advantage of that opportunity were asked to renew their covenants in 1877 during this Church-wide reorganization.[582] Twenty stakes were created from thirteen and the new ward and stake leaders were rebaptized along with the members of their congregations.

David H. Cannon's summary of St. George Temple baptisms from 1877 to 1894

As part of the reorganization of boundaries, a uniform system of record-keeping was introduced. Although records had always been kept, 1877 was the first time a standard membership record form was printed for use in all wards. Rebaptism was so prevalent that a separate column was included on the membership record to differentiate between first baptisms and rebaptisms. The baptisms, rebaptisms, and baptisms for the dead performed in the temple were also recorded according to type. The diary of David H. Cannon, second counselor to Wilford in the St. George Temple presidency, shows the total number of baptisms performed between 1877 and 1894. In his record of temple baptisms during this period, he lists 617 first baptisms, 966 baptisms for the renewal of covenants, 2,951 baptisms for health, and 265,770 baptisms for the dead.[583]

WORTHINESS TO ENTER THE TEMPLE

Permission to enter the temple was proven by a certificate of good standing which included a recommendation from one's bishop or stake president and was countersigned by the President of the Church. In Nauvoo, worthiness included, at a minimum, the payment of tithes. From the 1850s through the 1870s, during the Endowment House era, rebaptism was a prerequisite to entering the House of the Lord. Upon the completion of the St. George Temple, Brigham Young instructed bishops that only those who "kept their covenants, said their prayers, paid their Tithing donations and lived their religion" should be recommended to enter the temple and receive their blessings there.[584]

In the 1880s, the standards for temple admission were augmented. In addition to paying tithes and being rebaptized, individuals were expected to donate to the poor, keep the Sabbath Day holy, attend all public Church meetings—including the Thursday fast meetings—contribute to construction of the temple, and be "firm believers" in plural marriage.[585] Bishops were instructed to ask those who wanted to receive temple ordinances if they observed the Word of Wisdom, "according to the meaning and the spirit thereof," if they had preserved their chastity, and if they had committed any grievous offenses by breaking God's laws.[586] This emphasis on a higher level of commitment to the principles and ordinances of the gospel in order to participate in temple service underscored its importance.

THE TRANSFORMATION OF TEMPLE WORK

The administration of all the temple ordinances for the living and by proxy for the dead required a new approach. The Saints' intense but brief experience administering ordinances in the Nauvoo Temple was not comparable to the temple practices required in St. George. Although the

St. George Temple was designed with the same open assembly areas as the Nauvoo Temple, it would immediately become apparent to Church leaders that the temple would be for ceremonial purposes, not gatherings. The vast majority of Saints would also have to travel long distances to work in the temple, which meant additional adjustments. The revealed answers to the practical questions that arose became a constant part of the experiences that would follow.

~ 10 ~

A New Era Begins in St. George

St. George Temple

Although Wilford officially presided over the St. George Temple for seven years, the most intense period of temple ordinance work for him was from January to August 1877.[587] Wilford worked in the temple every day it was open with the exception of two weeks in May when he was sick.[588] Some weeks he spent seven days in the temple. As a result, he was able to complete thousands of ordinances for his family members and officiate in or witness tens of thousands of other ordinances. Wilford was the only prophet to have such a unique privilege.[589] His journal entries and discourses reveal that this opportunity to focus almost exclusively on the temple allowed him time to more deeply understand and appreciate its importance.

During this time, Wilford had three significant experiences that led to changes in temple practices that remain part of temple worship today. The first experience was a series of revelations that guided the preparation of a written record of the temple ceremonies and procedures. The second was a revelation regarding who could serve as proxy for a deceased individual. The third, his now iconic vision of the Signers of the Declaration of Independence, reiterated for whom vicarious work must be performed. This singular experience has been a catalyst for countless individuals to serve in temples for their own deceased progenitors as well as many others.

A SACRED TRUST

The 1877 transformation of temple work began with record keeping: the ceremonies and ordinances were written down for the first time. On Sunday, January 14, Brigham asked Wilford, his son Brigham Young Jr., and his secretary, L. John Nuttall, to "write out the ceremony of endowment from beginning to end."[590] Previously, the ceremonies had been passed orally from those who received them under the hand of Joseph Smith to those who officiated in the Nauvoo Temple and then the Endowment House. The Saints who had participated in these ordinances in Nauvoo were aging, along with Brigham and the other Apostles. A written record was needed ensure that the ordinances and ceremonies were correct and would be uniformly administered by all future temple workers.

Brigham was among the nine men who first received the temple ordinances from Joseph Smith on May 4, 1842. He recalled that it was on this occasion that Joseph turned to him and said, "Brother Brigham this is not arranged right, but we have done the best we could under the circumstances in which we are placed, and I wish you to take this matter in hand and organize and systematize all these ceremonies.'"[591] Understanding that teaching the revealed principles was more important than the manner in which the knowledge was imparted, Joseph Smith continued sharing the eternal truths with other Saints in this makeshift setting. And those individuals were thus prepared to officiate in the ordinances and teach them to others after his death.[592]

Brigham Young in the 1870s

When the Nauvoo Temple was sufficiently complete in 1845, Brigham directed the administration of the ordinances and began the process of perfecting the manner of instruction and the presentation of the ceremonies. In recounting this experience to the Saints, Brigham said that each time he went through the process, he "got something more." After working in the Nauvoo Temple from December to February, he believed the presentation of the temple ceremonies was "pretty correct."[593]

Yet, thirty years later, Brigham recognized that changes were required for the administration of the ordinances in the St. George Temple because the Saints were operating in different circumstances and administering some ordinances for the first time. In the Nauvoo Temple and in the Endowment House in Salt Lake City, the only proxy work the Saints were able to perform was baptisms and sealings. Some ordinances, including priesthood adoptions for the living and the dead as well as all sealings of children to parents, had been suspended since 1846 when the Saints had been forced to leave Nauvoo. Most significantly, the endowment had never been administered by proxy for the dead.

Thus, in St. George, Brigham felt the same burden Joseph Smith had felt in Nauvoo: to instruct and properly train those who would carry on the work after his death.[594] In order to accomplish this, whenever his health permitted, Brigham instructed the workers and then met almost daily with those officiating in the temple to discuss the day's work and make any necessary adjustments. As the work continued during the winter, Wilford spent at least five and as many as seven days a week officiating in the temple and also presided over the work whenever Brigham was absent. He also spent many evenings discussing and recording the ceremony.[595] L. John Nuttall also wrote down Brigham's lecture at the veil, first delivered on February 1, 1877, "for safekeeping and reference hereafter."[596]

WE ARE AFTER LIGHT AND TRUTH[597]

As these men worked together, questions would arise and they would consult with each other and God to determine how to proceed.[598] Some questions were simple enough. For instance, what clothing children should wear when they came to the temple to be sealed to their parents, or if temple workers should be dressed in temple clothing when they administered certain ordinances. Other questions were more complex.

One question had to do with ordinances for children who had died at a young age. Many of the Saints, including Wilford, suffered the loss of babies and young children as they endured the hardships of pioneer life and the trials and constant moving that followed their conversion to the gospel. God had revealed to Joseph Smith that children are not accountable until the age of eight, and were therefore not to be baptized until then. Likewise, proxy baptisms were not required for children who died before attaining the age of eight.[599]

Brigham Young taught that the only temple ordinance necessary for young children was to seal them to their parents if they had been born before their parents' marriage was sealed in the temple.[600] More specifically, after the dedication of the St. George Temple, some individuals wondered if they needed to complete temple ordinances in behalf of stillborn children, "who the mothers state have quickened." Brigham's answer was, "[T]hey are all right without having anything done for them."[601]

One practical question that arose was whether ordinances previously administered outside a temple should be repeated. But although those endowed and sealed by Joseph

Smith before his death had repeated those same ordinances in the Nauvoo Temple after its completion, Brigham instructed the Saints that ordinance work for the dead administered in the Endowment House in Salt Lake City, specifically sealings and proxy baptisms, should not be repeated in the St. George Temple.

Other questions posed were more hypothetical and Brigham answered these queries with, "Wait until we see one that is." Or, as Wilford later put it, "We cannot anticipate all cases of this kind, and prefer to give no decision on a question of this character until there is a necessity for it and all the circumstances connected with it are known."[602]

IMPROVEMENTS AND REFINEMENTS

Previously Wilford had stated he was confident that they would be "more fully instructed" by those in the spirit world, including Joseph Smith, and that the answers to their questions would come as the need arose.[603] He was not only comfortable with the idea of continuing revelation; he counted on it. As the Saints faced new situations and changing circumstances, the detailed instructions they were given by revelation followed accordingly.

In Wilford's mind, the fact that over the years the presentation of the eternal principles had changed—whether that is defined as refined, modified, or updated—did not change the principles themselves. As a comparison, he pointed out that Christ's Atonement ended the practice of animal sacrifice, but did not change the law of sacrifice or the laws of justice and mercy.[604] The eternal principle in that case was simply taught in a different manner: the sacrifice required by God's children changed from the "firstlings of the flock" to a "broken heart and a contrite spirit."[605] Similarly, Wilford did not believe it inappropriate, for example, for the presentation of the covenants made in the endowment to be altered. In fact, just the opposite. As they worked together in a new setting administering new ordinances, it was assumed that they would learn and adjust as they implemented new procedures.

L. John Nuttall	John D. T. McAllister
Recorder in St. George Temple	Counselor in Temple Presidency

After a day of working in the temple as recorder, L. John Nuttall wrote in his journal that he "found everything very agreeable," yet Brigham Young suggested a few changes "for the better working."[606] Those who had received their endowments under Joseph Smith not only recognized the modifications to the ceremonies, but accepted them as inspired improvements to the manner of instruction. Wilford testified of the continuity of the endowment from the principles revealed to Joseph in Nauvoo, to the inspired administration of the ordinances under Brigham's direction in St. George: "I bear record to this congregation . . . that Joseph Smith first made known to me the very ordinances which we give to the Latter-day Saints in our endowments.

I received my endowments under the direction of Joseph Smith. . . . [He] himself organized every endowment in our Church and revealed the same to the Church, and he lived to receive every key of the Aaronic and Melchizedek priesthoods from the hands of the men who held them while in the flesh, and who hold them in eternity."[607]

Those same priesthood keys had been conferred on the members of the Quorum of the Twelve, and President Brigham Young exercised them in the temple in St. George. Wilford told the Saints, "The spirit of inspiration was with Brigham Young. . . . I bear testimony to these things. There never has been a time, either in these temples or anywhere else, but the Lord has made manifest His will on any point on which light was desired. To my certain knowledge, the Lord gave revelations in the St. George Temple to His servants there upon points of doctrine we did not understand. President Young was there. I was there. Brother McAllister and others labored there, and we knew these things."[608]

When they finished writing the endowment ceremony on March 21, Brigham said, "Now you have before you an ensample, to carry on the endowments in all the temples until the coming of the Son of Man."[609]

THE ONLY TEMPLE THERE IS ON EARTH[610]

Among those Brigham Young called to officiate in the St. George Temple beginning in January 1877 were Wilford; John D. T. McAllister, who would serve as Wilford's counselor in the temple presidency; L. John Nuttall, John Taylor's nephew and Wilford's personal secretary; Sarah Ann Pulsipher Alger, the daughter of Zerah Pulsipher, the missionary who first taught Wilford the gospel; Brigham's son Brigham Jr.; and one of Brigham's plural wives, Lucy Bigelow Young, who presided over all the female temple workers.[611] However, it was not until the final dedication in April that Wilford was officially called to preside over the temple in anticipation of Brigham's return to Salt Lake City.[612]

Those trained in the St. George Temple were later called to officiate and train other workers in the Logan and Manti Temples when they were completed in 1884 and 1888 respectively. The practices implemented and codified in the St. George Temple were replicated in subsequent temples. In 1893, as President of the Church, Wilford called the temple presidents to Salt Lake City when it became necessary to harmonize the various procedures and administrative styles being employed in the four temples. At that time, the written record kept in the St. George Temple was still the standard by which all temples operated.

Another practice that had been introduced in Nauvoo and became customary in St. George was the wearing of white clothing while officiating and serving in the temple. On January 13, 1877, twelve days after the dedication of the St. George Temple, a letter was sent to bishops with instructions regarding proper temple clothing. Women were directed to bring two or three white skirts with them to the temple. The men were asked to have appropriate long shirts made for them to wear while in the temple.[613] Then, on February 1, 1877, Wilford, as Temple President, and Lucy Bigelow Young, as President of the Sister Workers, dressed in white to officiate in the St. George Temple. Wilford recorded that it was "the first example in any temple of the Lord in this last dispensation."[614]

Changing from regular clothing to all white clothing upon entering the temple, to administer ordinances or participate in temple ceremonies, was not yet a requirement. This became part of temple practice in the 1890s. One hundred years later, in the 1990s, this policy was reversed in part so those observing, but not participating in a sealing ceremony, could attend wearing regular clothing. Changing into all white clothing then became optional in that one instance.

A NEW EPOCH[615]

Wilford's understanding of the Saints' unique position in God's plan for the redemption of His children was evident in his discourses. In preparation for the completion of the temple in St. George, Wilford wanted the Saints to understand that Christ's work on both sides of the veil depended on their willingness to first receive the ordinances for themselves and then as proxy for others.

On one occasion he spoke of how glorious it was that they, "like the ancient Saints," could be baptized for the dead, and "thus open the prison doors and set the prisoners free!" He testified that the dead are not going "to remain in the eternal world without the privilege of hearing the Gospel . . . [and] somebody must administer for them in the flesh, that they may be judged according to men in the spirit, and have part in the first resurrection . . . . The Lord has revealed this to us, and commanded us to attend to this duty."[616]

In another discourse, referring to the millions who lived "when God had no Church on the earth," he promised they would not perish spiritually because they would be preached to in the spirit world. He then encouraged the Saints to "go forth and use" the power placed in their hands to attend to ordinances for the salvation of the living and the dead. In conclusion he said that the unbelief of the world "will not make the truth of God without effect. These ordinances have been revealed to us; we understand them, and unless we attend to them we shall fall under condemnation."[617]

Wilford in 1878

THIS IS A REVELATION TO US

After he arrived in St. George, Wilford spent several more weeks preparing genealogy records in order to perform 360 sealings for the Hart family and "a good many for the Woodruffs."[618] To the Saints he expressed his motivation to do this work in these words: "I would not like to go into the spirit world and meet my friends who have died without the Gospel and have them reproach me for not doing my duty towards them. . . . [L]et us labor diligently to fulfill our mission and do our duty and not sell our birthright or make [a] shipwreck of faith."[619] Because they held "the keys of salvation to their Father's house to the endless ages of eternity," he told the Saints they "ought to prize the blessings which God has put in our hands."[620]

Wilford had instructed the Saints many times regarding the anxiousness of those waiting for redemption in the spirit world saying, "We have a great work before us in the redemption of our dead. The course that we are pursuing is being watched with interest by all heaven." He reminded them that the waiting spirits could not be baptized, endowed, or sealed in the spirit world. Therefore, unless someone on the earth performed the ordinances in the flesh, those spirits could not take part in the first resurrection and be worthy of eternal life. "It takes as much to save a dead man as a living one," he told them. And those waiting spirits "are watching over these Latter-day Saints."[621]

The Saints responded. Between January and March 1877, while the remainder of the temple was being completed, 581 living individuals were endowed and 3,208 proxy endowments were administered. More than 200 of the proxy endowments were for members of Wilford and Phebe's families. In addition, 195 couples came to be sealed and 961 couples were sealed by proxy. In the twenty-four days designated for baptismal work during the first three months of 1877, the Saints performed 8,733 baptisms, an average of 363 a day.[622]

INQUIRE OF THE LORD FOR ALL WE EXPECT[623]

After the recording of the ordinances and ceremonies, the second significant change in the administration of temple ordinances came about as a result of Wilford's desire to offer salvation to his own ancestors. Through his devoted research, Wilford had gathered information on over 3,100 family members. He felt the urgency to attend to all the ordinances required for his ancestors' salvation and exaltation. However, because of the sheer number of individuals and ordinances required for each person, Wilford did not know how he could complete such an enormous task. Furthermore, the fact that at the time the Saints were only allowed to perform temple ordinance work for their own deceased relatives meant they were not available to help him. Because his wives and children were not living in St. George, it seemed impossible.

On February 23, while Wilford was praying in the temple to know what to do, he received a significant revelation.[624] He later testified, "When I inquired of the Lord how I could redeem my dead . . . not having any of my family there, the Lord told me to call upon the Saints in St. George and let them officiate for me in that temple, and it should be acceptable unto him. Brother McAllister and the brethren and sisters there have assisted me in this work, and I felt to bless them with every feeling of my heart. This is a revelation to us. We can help one another in these matters, if we have not relatives sufficient to carry this on, and it will be acceptable unto the Lord."[625]

WE CAN HELP ONE ANOTHER

Upon receiving this important revelation, Wilford exclaimed, "Light burst upon my understanding. I saw an effectual door open to me for the redemption of my dead. And when I saw this I felt like shouting glory hallelujah to God and the Lamb. . . . This principle has given me great joy unspeakable at the thought that I can live on the earth to behold my numerous friends redeemed who are in the spirit world."[626] With Brigham Young's permission, a week later on the occasion of Wilford's seventieth birthday, 154 women assembled in the St. George Temple to complete the washings, anointings, and endowments for his relatives.[627] One of those women was Eudora Young Dunford, Brigham and Lucy Bigelow Young's daughter. She served as proxy for Wilford's sister Eunice.[628] (Eudora and Wilford were sealed on March 10, 1877.[629])

Martha Cragun Cox was also among the group of women who assisted as proxies in the ordinances performed for Wilford's family on March 1. The instruction that only the eldest family member or "heir" could act as proxy led Martha to fear that she would never be able to experience the temple ordinances again. Yet, in her patriarchal blessing, she was promised she would "do a mighty work" for the dead. She made it a matter of prayer, hoping that she might be allowed to go to the temple as a "spectator or visitor" so she could learn more. After hearing of President Woodruff's revelation, she was thrilled to be called to assist him and serve as a proxy for his family members. She said she spent every spare day in the temple working "on the Woodruff lists."[630]

Wilford's admonition to the Saints a few years later was to enter the temples and redeem not only the dead of their own families, but "the dead of the whole spirit world." He also wanted to emphasize the Saints' unique position and privilege. Acknowledging that their numbers were few compared with the total number of people whose work needed to be done, he concluded, "Still, with the help of God, we have power to redeem the world. This is our work."[631]

Although this practice of acting as proxy for the relatives of others is commonplace among members of the Church today, it was a revolutionary idea at the time. The revelation Wilford received on this subject, making it possible for the Saints to assist each other in the sacred work, would change the future administration of temple ordinances, and the scope of temple work. Subsequently, not only could the Saints help each other redeem their deceased relatives, they could perform the work for everyone they could identify by name. Those who were unable to trace their biological family members could still return to the temple again and again to offer saving blessings to their "brothers" and "sisters" in the eternal family of God.[632]

Some of the women who led the administration of temple ordinances:
Middle row from left: Bathsheba Wilson Bigler Smith (presided over sisters in Endowment House); Mercy Rachel Fielding Thompson Smith (Nauvoo Temple clerk); Zina Diantha Huntington Jacobs Smith Young (Matron of the Salt Lake Temple); Lucy Bigelow Young (Matron of the St. George Temple); Minerva White Snow (Matron of the Manti Temple).[633]

Because women were not yet able to serve as missionaries and preach the gospel to the living, many were enthusiastic about their ability to serve in the temple and offer the gospel to those "on the other side of the veil." Lucy Bigelow Young moved to St. George in 1870 and, among other things, helped in the construction of temple. It made the temple "all the more precious to her."[634] Lucy was the first to officiate in administering the endowment ordinance for the dead because, as she explained, "the brethren were not ready to begin as soon as the sisters."[635]

After her appointment to preside over the work of the women in the St. George Temple, "she worked side by side with her husband [Brigham Young] . . . administering the saving ordinances to the living and for the dead, as they passed under the hands of blessing." Their daughters Susa and Eudora also served with them in the temple. Lucy said this began the "great spiritual climax" of her life.[636] After the Manti and Logan temples were dedicated, Lucy was asked to go and help train new ordinance workers.

THE WOODRUFF FAMILY

On March 27, Wilford was joined by Phebe and three of their children.[637] They came to St. George to witness the dedication of the temple on April 1 and to attend the Church Conference that was held in St. George to celebrate the temple's completion.[638] Wilford's family stayed in St. George for three weeks and assisted him in the ordinance work for many of their relatives. On March 30, Wilford served as a proxy for the first time when he was endowed for Robert Mason, the family friend in Connecticut who foretold of Wilford's prominent place in the restored Church before Wilford had even been taught the gospel.[639] That same day, his son Wilford Jr. served as proxy in the endowment for Wilford's brother Asahel who died in 1838, and received the second anointing in behalf of Phebe's father Ezra Carter.

Wilford performed the first post-Nauvoo priesthood adoptions on March 22 when he adopted two couples to Brigham Young. Of the experience he wrote, "This day was the first time in my life that I ever heard or performed the ceremony of Adoption."[640] On April 11, Phebe served as proxy for Wilford's grandmother Dinah Woodruff. This also marked the first time anyone outside his family was adopted to him: two couples, Josiah G. Hardy and Samuel

B. Hardy and their wives.[641] Robert Mason and many of their relatives were vicariously adopted to Wilford and Phebe on April 13 and Wilford and Phebe were then adopted to Wilford's deceased father Aphek Woodruff.[642] The following day his family members left to return to Salt Lake City.

Wilford and Sarah Brown's sons
David Patten and Brigham Young Woodruff

After the Church conference and dedication of the temple, Brigham Young left St. George on April 16. As he headed north to Salt Lake City, he dedicated the site for the Manti Temple on April 25 and the site for the Logan Temple on May 18.[643] In Brigham Young's absence, Wilford felt the weight of responsibility for "the only Temple on the

earth where the Saints of God can administer in the ordinances of the House of the Lord for the salvation of the
living and the dead."[644] However, in this capacity he was
afforded an opportunity no other prophet had before him
or would have in the future: to spend almost every day and
many evenings in the temple for a period of eight months.

Wilford was consumed by the work. His temple focus
is evident in his journal entry regarding the tragic death of
his twenty-year-old son, Brigham. Upon learning that
Brigham had accidentally drowned on June 16, 1877, Wilford first acknowledged, "We cannot always comprehend
the ways of Providence." He then continued, "I have felt
calm, composed, and reconciled in this bereavement. I have
thought that as I was doing so much for the dead here in
the Temple in St. George, that it might be necessary to have
one of the family in the spirit world."[645]

By 1885 Wilford recorded that 3,188 of his family
members had been baptized by proxy, and 2,518 proxy
endowments had been completed for them. Wilford continued to correspond with relatives and organizations,
including the New England Historical and Genealogical
Society, seeking additional family information throughout
his life.[646]

Wilford's focus on his own family was entirely appropriate. In fact, Joseph Smith's initial instruction in 1840 on
proxy work for the dead was for the Saints to be baptized
for their immediate relatives. They were not to be baptized
for other deceased individuals unless those individuals sent
a "ministering spirit for their friends on earth."[647] Wilford's
third revelatory experience in St. George was regarding
temple work for deceased individuals he was not related to.
Why these spirits chose Wilford to be their "friend on
earth," and how they changed his temple focus, helps explain the next peak in temple ordinance work.

~ 11 ~

The Eminent Men and Women

August 1877 marked Wilford's third experience in the St. George Temple that would impact temple ordinance work for generations.[648] This experience—the appearance of the Signers of the Declaration of Independence to Wilford—changed not only his view of temple work, but has become an important symbol of the universal nature of temple work. His experience underscored the role of the living in providing the opportunity to accept Christ's salvation to all who have ever lived. It also reminded the Saints that those in the spirit world expected them to fulfill their responsibility.

St. George Temple circa 1877

Eight months earlier, at the January dedication of the St. George Temple, Brigham Young had asked the Saints, "What do you suppose the fathers would say if they could speak from the dead? Would they not say, 'We have lain here thousands of years, here in this prison house, waiting for this dispensation to come?' . . . What would they whisper in our ears?"[649] The answer to Brigham's queries came to Wilford when he spoke to "the fathers." In describing his experience to the Saints in September 1877, Wilford told them, "The dead will . . . seek after you as they have after us in St. George. They called upon us, knowing that we held the keys and power to redeem them."[650] Those fathers Wilford spoke of were the Founding Fathers. Wilford said every one of the men that signed the Declaration of Independence with George Washington "waited on him" for two days and two nights.[651]

In a second Conference address to the Saints, Wilford testified that they called upon him in the temple as an Apostle of the Lord Jesus Christ and demanded that he "go forth and attend to the ordinances of the House of God for them." He then stated, "Would those spirits have called upon me, as an Elder in Israel, to perform that work if they had not been noble spirits before God? They would not." Wilford shared his belief that those men who laid the foundation of the American government and who signed the Declaration of Independence were "the best spirits the God of heaven could find on the face of the earth. They were choice spirits . . . inspired of the Lord."[652]

VISIONS AND DREAMS

Wilford testified often of God's ability to communicate with His children on earth and of the importance of dreams and visions. His first prophetic dream occurred when he was only eleven years old.[653] This experience with the Signers of the Declaration of Independence was only one of the many visions and dreams Wilford wrote about in his journal, but has become the most well-known of those he shared with the Saints.

In clarifying the many ways in which divine communication can occur, Wilford differentiated between those dreams that the Lord has nothing to do with and those "of a very different character" which are inspired by God and teach a principle or prepare one for the future. He also spoke of experiences he felt were different than visions because they involved speaking face to face with a resurrected being or a personage of spirit, as when Peter, James, and John appeared to Joseph Smith.[654]

Wilford's description of his experience in St. George was specific.[655] He said the Signers not only conversed with him, but were with him for two days and two nights. In his testimony of this experience, shared on numerous occasions between 1877 and 1898, he stated his belief that the Founding Fathers were inspired in their combined efforts to establish the United States while they were alive.[656] Yet, none of these men had the opportunity to hear the restored gospel or accept it in mortality.[657] The fact that they came to Wilford and asked him to attend to the temple ordinances for them suggested to Wilford that they had accepted the gospel in the spirit world.

Inspired by his experience, Wilford spent Sunday evening, August 19, 1877, preparing a list of some of the "noted men" of the seventeenth and eighteenth centuries using Evert A. Duyckinck's volumes entitled *Eminent Men and Women of Europe and America*. He added the names of the signers of the Declaration of Independence and presidents of the United States to those he had gathered from Duyckinck's books.[658]

Aug 21, 1877

I Wilford Woodruff went to the Temple of the Lord this morning and was Baptized for 100 persons who were dead including the signers of the Declaration of Independence all except John Hancock and I was Baptized for the following names

William Hooper	Benjamin Franklin
Joseph Hewes	John Morton
John Penn	George Clymer
Button Gwinnett	James Smith
Lyman Hall	Francis Lightfoot Lee
Edward Rutledge	George Taylor
George Walton	James Wilson
Thomas Heyward Jr	George Ross
Thomas Lynch Jr	Caesar Rodney
Arthur Myddleton	George Read
Samuel Chase	Thomas M Kean
William Chase Paca	Philip Livingston
Thomas Stone	Francis Lewis
Charles Carroll of Carrollton	Lewis Morris
George Wythe	Richard Stockton
Richard Henry Lee	John Witherspoon
Thomas Jefferson	Francis Hopkinson
Benjamin Harrison	John Hart
Thomas Nelson Jr	Abraham Clark
Francis Lightfoot Lee	Josiah Bartlett
Carter Braxton	William Whipple
Robert Morris	Samuel Adams
Benjamin Rush	John Adams

Wilford's journal entry with list of Signers of Declaration of Independence

Aug 21 1877

Robart Treat Paine	Samuel Huntington
Elbridge Gerry	William Williams
Stephen Hopkins	Oliver Wolcott
William Ellery	Mathew Thornton
Roger Sharman x Baptized for the following Eminent Men	
Daniel Webster	Edward Gibbon
Washington Irving	David Garrick
Michael Faraday	Sir Joshua Reynolds
William Makepeace Thackeray	Robert Burns
John Calwell Cahoon	Johann Wolfgang Goethe
Baron Justus Von Liebig	John Philip Kemble
Henry Clay	Frederick Von Schiller
Edward George Earl Lytton Bulwer	Henry Grattan
George Peabody	Robert Fulton
Charles Louis Napoleon Bonaparte	Lord Horatio Nelson
Thomas Chalmers	John Filpot Curran
William Henry Seward	George Stephenson
Thomas Johnathan Jackson	Frederick Henry Alexander Von Humboldt
David Glascoe Farragut	Sir Walter Scott
Hiram Powers	Lord Henry Brougham
Lewis John Rodolphe Agassiz	Lord George Gordon Byron
David Livingstone	William Wordsworth
Christopher Columbus	Daniel O'Connell
Americus Verpucius	Count Camillo Benso di Cavour
John Wesley	Richard Cobden
Samuel Johnson	Thomas Babington Macaulay
Oliver Goldsmith	Benito Juarez
Frederick 2d King of Prussia	Count Demetrius Porup d

Wilford's list of other Eminent Men for proxy ordinance work

On Tuesday, the day designated for baptismal work, Wilford took his list to the temple and asked John D. T. McAllister to baptize him for the Signers and forty-five other eminent men. Included in this group were John Wesley, Christopher Columbus, Daniel Webster, Charles Louis Napoleon Bonaparte, and three generations of George Washington's extended family. Wilford then baptized John for all the deceased presidents of the United States, except Martin Van Buren and James Buchanan because of their actions against the Saints.[659] That night Wilford recorded the day's labors in his journal.[660]

EMINENT WOMEN

Along with the list of eminent men, Wilford also compiled, or directed the compilation of, a list of sixty-eight eminent women.[661] He asked Lucy Bigelow Young, the supervisor over the female temple workers, to act as proxy and he baptized her on behalf of all the women on his list. The eminent men he listed in his journal are well-known and, for the most part, their lives are well documented. The eminent women, on the other hand, range from infamous to unknown. Some were admired figures, including the poet Elizabeth Barrett Browning and novelists Jane Austen and Charlotte Brontë. Others, such as Charlotte de Corday and Marie Antoinette, were more controversial historical figures.[662] Eleven of the women were members of George Washington's extended family.

Thirty-seven of the women on his list were wives of the eminent men Wilford had chosen. Another twenty-four of the women were married; however, he did not include their husbands on the corresponding list of eminent men, and proxy ordinances were not performed for them. The husbands of the eminent women on his list included men such as Lord Palmerston, Thomas Moore, Patrick Calhoun, and Arthur Wellesley, the Duke of Wellington.[663]

St. George Temple record book of proxy baptisms on August 21, 1877

Although proxy baptisms and a few sealings for some of the eminent men and women had been completed by non-relatives in the Endowment House, these were exceptions to the general practice of performing proxy ordinances only for relatives and close friends.[664] On August 21, Wilford was baptized in the temple for fifty-four of the fifty-six Signers, excluding William Floyd and John Hancock who had been baptized by proxy in the temple on March 13 and May 29 respectively. Most importantly, before August 21, 1877, only one of the eminent men, John Hancock, had been endowed by proxy. John Hancock's third cousin Levi Ward Hancock had received the endowment on his behalf in May.⁶⁶⁵

During the first eight months of ordinance work in the St. George Temple, Wilford participated in or presided over 24,384 baptisms, 11,597 endowments, the sealing of 3,706 couples and 268 children to their parents, 309 second anointings, and 53 priesthood adoptions.⁶⁶⁶ After the appearance of the Signers, Wilford commented, "I thought it very singular, that notwithstanding so much work had been done, and yet nothing had been done for them. The thought never entered my heart, from the fact, I suppose, that heretofore our minds were reaching after our more immediate friends and relatives."⁶⁶⁷ Wilford was apparently referring to all the higher ordinances—washings, anointings, ordinations, endowments, priesthood adoptions, and second anointings— that the Saints had not been able to perform by proxy until the St. George Temple was completed, and could now perform for all the "worthy dead."⁶⁶⁸

It was through such experiences that Wilford gained his understanding of the vital role of the living in the redemption of the dead. The lesson he took from this experience, and the message he repeatedly shared with the Saints was of universal salvation. All of God's children will be taught the principles of the gospel and all will need to complete the saving ordinances. The Signers' request reminded Wilford of this and expanded his circle of awareness. In addition to those who appeared to him, he chose others he felt were worthy of the blessings of the temple ordinances. The list is perplexing because he included some men but not their wives, and some women without their husbands. Wilford also excluded two of the former presidents of the United States based on their

actions that he felt made them unworthy. Controversy
surrounds some individuals for whom ordinances were and
are performed.

St. George Temple record of proxy baptisms for eminent women

Proxy endowments for the eminent men and women,
as well as proxy ordinations for the men, were performed
for the majority of the 168 individuals over the next few
days.[669] The endowments for the remaining eminent men
and women were finally completed after Wilford returned
to preside over the St. George Temple in February 1878.

All of the eminent men were ordained to the office of Elder, except George Washington, Benjamin Franklin, Horatio Nelson, John Wesley, and Christopher Columbus, who were ordained to the office of High Priest.[670] Even though no children were sealed to their parents at this time, there were several marriage sealings performed, including Martha Dandridge to her first husband Daniel Parke Custis, and to George Washington, her second husband.[671] In addition, George Washington's parents Lawrence and Mary Ball Washington were sealed on August 22.[672]

The work in the temple ceased on August 27 when Wilford received word that Brigham Young was extremely ill. Wilford gathered the Saints in the temple to pray. They prayed for two days until the telegram came with the news that their prophet of thirty years was dead. Wilford left immediately for Salt Lake City, accompanying Brigham's wife Lucy Bigelow Young and daughter Susa on their journey north. Following the funeral on September 2, Wilford was asked to dedicate Brigham's grave.

ONLY A BEGINNING

Two weeks later, when Wilford spoke to the Saints about his experiences in St. George, he concluded by saying, "I have felt to rejoice exceedingly in this work of redeeming the dead. . . . I look upon this portion of our ministry as a mission of as much importance as preaching to the living."[673] Wilford shared his increased understanding of the temple's significance and promised the Saints that when they completed the temples in Manti, Logan, and Salt Lake City they would "begin to see the necessity of building others, for in proportion to the diligence of our labors in this direction, will we comprehend the extent of the work to be done, and the present is only a beginning."[674]

The importance of the work in the St. George Temple during 1877 and its impact on the rise of temple consciousness among the Saints would not be recognized for dec-decades. Over the course of the previous thirty-seven years, more than 120,000 proxy baptisms and confirmations had been performed, offering the possibility of salvation and membership in the Church and kingdom of God to these deceased individuals. However, the higher ordinances of sealing and proxy endowments—administered for the first time in the temple in St. George—were necessary for exaltation. Baptism was only the gate that allowed the Saints to start on the path to exaltation.

The eternally significant instruction repeated in these higher ordinances not only offered exaltation to those in the spirit world, but maintained the Saints' focus on exaltation when they served as proxies. Furthermore, the need to qualify for a recommend to return to the temple included remaining faithful to gospel principles, paying tithing, and devoting their time and resources to building the kingdom.[675] Wilford believed that the inspired system of proxy service in temples gave real meaning to Joseph Smith's statement that the salvation of the dead is necessary and essential to the salvation of the living.[676]

GLORIOUS PRINCIPLES

On one occasion, in his effort to help the Saints understand the privilege and duty of temple ordinance work, Wilford asked them, "Can you point me to any emperor, king, priest, denomination or power on the face of the whole earth, outside of the Church of Jesus Christ of Latter-day Saints, who has power to go forth and redeem one of their dead? There never was a soul anywhere that could do this until God organized His Church upon the earth."[677]

He then reminded them of his experience in the St. George Temple and said, "The signers of the Declaration of Independence and the men that laid the foundation of this great American government know full well that there has not been a power on the earth where they could apply to have this principle carried out in their behalf, only the Apostles that held the keys of the kingdom of God in this generation."[678] These men came to him and pled with him to redeem them because "there was no other power on earth that could do it." "There is no more glorious principle given to man," he concluded, "than the power which you have while holding the Priesthood, to go forth and redeem your fathers, your mothers, your progenitors. . . . Such principles are worthy of contemplation."[679]

Wilford's commitment to temple ordinance work was solidified during his time in St. George and his messages to the Saints reflected his focus. He wanted them to grasp the eternal significance of the temple and told them that their mission was more extensive than they realized. As His sons and daughters, God expected them to accomplish His work. Wilford reminded them that building the temples and redeeming the dead were blessings. The work was a privilege as well as a duty, particularly on behalf of their family members. He said, "Our forefathers are looking to us to attend to this work. They are watching over us with great anxiety, and are desirous that we should finish these temples and attend to certain ordinances for them, so that in the morning of the resurrection they can come forth and enjoy the same blessings that we enjoy. . . . We occupy a position in this capacity . . . of Saviors upon Mount Zion."[680]

In October 1877 Wilford again expressed his firm belief that each member of the Church would be held responsible for their individual efforts. He told the Saints,

"This labor is not to be performed by other hands. . . . [W]hen our time comes to take our departure for that life behind the veil, none of us will regret having devoted our time, talents, and labor for the accomplishment of this great object. . . . We hold the Priesthood for that purpose, and we have no business to use it for anything else but to offici- ate in the ordinances of the house of God."[681]

Salt Lake Temple construction in 1877

OUR AIM IS HIGH[682]

John Taylor, as the new presiding officer of the Church, acknowledged Wilford's influence on the rising awareness of temple work.[683] In November 1877 he said, "Brother

Woodruff has been operating a long time in the Temple at St. George and you have perhaps heard him testify of visits that he has had from the spirit world, the spirits of men who once lived on the earth, desiring him to officiate for them in the Temple ordinances. This feeling is planted in the hearts of the people." He then went on to say, "The Lord has shown us that we must build temples in which to officiate for them. We have commenced to do so, and our fathers have already commenced to feel after us, manifesting themselves by dreams and visions, and in various ways to those most interested in their welfare."[684]

Wilford's message to the Saints regarding their responsibilities within the temples only intensified as the pressure on the Church and the Saints increased. His belief in the imminent return of the Savior added to the urgency of his plea to the Saints to increase their efforts. It also set the stage for his later decisions as President of the Church when the government threatened to confiscate the temples in an attempt to end the practice of polygamy.

~ 12 ~

Temples and Trials

The ten years that followed the death of Brigham Young were some of the most difficult for the Church and its members. Increasingly hostile federal legislation punishing those who practiced polygamy—and eventually even those who professed a belief in the doctrine of plural marriage—interfered with the Saints' ability to interact socially, carry out religious duties, and survive economically. Wilford viewed the opposition as a motivating factor for the Saints to focus on the things he considered critically important: their personal spiritual strength and the work to save the living and the dead in the temples. However, his single-mindedness was difficult to maintain in the face of his increasing responsibilities within the Church and the escalating crisis between the Church and the federal government.

FREEDOM OF RELIGION

In 1879 the United States Supreme Court denied the Church's First Amendment-based freedom of religion challenge to the Morrill Anti-Bigamy Law of 1862.[685] (This was the first of eighteen cases involving polygamy that the Supreme Court would rule on between 1879 and 1891; only three of their decisions were favorable to the Church.[686]) Members of the Church were shocked at the Court's decision. It meant that no member of the Church openly practicing polygamy, including Church leaders, was safe from prosecution under the law. But in order to prosecute a man for polygamy, the federal authorities had to prove that marriage ceremonies had taken place. Since temple sealings were not publicly recorded, it was almost impossible to prove multiple marriages had been solemnized.

The pressure on the Church increased in 1882 when Congress passed the Edmunds Act. This Act made plural marriage a felony, punishable by five years in prison and a $500 fine. "Unlawful cohabitation," defined simply as living with more than one woman, facilitated a lower standard of proof for conviction. As a misdemeanor, it also carried a lesser punishment: six months in prison and a $300 fine.[687] In addition, in an attempt to gather evidence for prosecution and take away the Church's ability to regulate marriages and divorces, the Edmunds Act included a provision that required all marriages—whether performed inside or outside the temple or Endowment House—to be publicly recorded.[688]

The government's various judicial appointees and changing tactics made life unpredictable for the Saints. Wilford and many others were periodically forced into hiding to avoid arrest by federal marshals, leaving their families to struggle without them.[689] This affected the ability of Church members to fulfill church responsibilities and interact with their families and communities. Not only were husbands and fathers in hiding or moving often to avoid arrest, but wives were forced to testify against their husbands, and those women who refused were jailed for contempt of court. Over 1,300 people were imprisoned for violation of these laws, or contempt of court. Most of the inmates were men, but some women were also imprisoned along with a few of their children.[690]

Utah Penitentiary prisoners serving sentences in 1885 for "unlawful cohabitation" including Francis and Moroni Brown, A. Milton Musser, Parley P. Pratt Jr., Rudger J. Clawson, and Job Pingree.[691]

The political power of the Church was dismantled piece by piece. Elected officials were replaced with government appointees. Polygamist men were prevented from holding public office or voting, and the voting rights of all Utah women—granted in 1870—were rescinded. In March 1887 the Edmunds-Tucker Act became law, resulting in the dissolution of the Church as a legal entity and the seizure of Church property.[692] Church real estate, offices, and even furniture, were put into receivership, and the Church was forced to pay rent in order to use them.[693] The dissolution of the Perpetual Emigration Fund and seizure of its accounts effectively ended the ability of most converts to gather with the Saints. Children born to polygamist marriages were ruled illegitimate and unable to inherit from their fathers. Church schools, and therefore the school's curriculum, were even placed under federal control.

FAMILIES UNDER FEDERAL LAW

Wilford's way of life during the 1880s was a microcosm of the Church as a whole during this same period of time. The federal persecution of the Saints interfered with his family relationships, prevented him from carrying out his Church responsibilities, and affected him physically and psychologically.

At one point in the 1860s, Wilford housed four generations of his family under one roof, including his father, four of his wives (Phebe, Sarah, Emma, and Delight) and their younger children. Wilford's married daughter Susan and her husband also lived with them in the "Valley House," along with their daughter Eugenia, the fourth generation.[694]

Woodruff residence built in 1851 in Salt Lake City (on the left) remodeled and converted to Valley House Hotel in 1879

Later, like many other men, Wilford housed his families separately. In 1871 he bought a ranch in Randolph, Utah, and moved his wife Sarah and her children there, along with his son Wilford Jr. and daughter-in-law Elizabeth. He settled his wife Delight and her children on a ten-acre farm in Salt Lake City in 1875. Mary Ann, who had divorced Wilford in 1848, was later resealed to him.[695] Nevertheless, they still did not reside in the same house. After their resealing, Mary Ann continued to live with their son James and daughter-in-law Fanny.[696] Eudora had moved with Wilford from St. George to Salt Lake City, but left him and Utah within a few years.[697]

Woodruff Farmhouse built in 1859 still stands at 1604 South 500 East (Wilford's daughter Emma Manella is on the porch holding her child)

After building separate houses for Phebe next door to the Valley House in downtown Salt Lake City and for Emma on his twenty-acre farm south of the city, Wilford moved out of the Valley House on January 1, 1879, and later leased it for use as a hotel.

THE ELEMENT OF OPPOSITION

If the economic and political interests of the Saints in the 1880s were put on one side of a scale and their spiritual interests on the other, Wilford found the burdensome weight of the temporal issues served to elevate the spiritual. Wilford nevertheless found a silver lining in the unbalanced situation. As he told the Saints in Nephi, Utah, "the element of opposition tends only to hasten the fulfillment of the purposes of God."[698]

Instead of continuing the effort to keep the Saints separated from the rest of the world or trying to force a balance between the temporal and spiritual sides, Wilford chose to help the Saints' focus on their personal spirituality. They could then live in the world without becoming "of" the world that was inevitably encroaching on Zion. His counsel to the Saints was not to spend their time on economic pursuits at the risk of neglecting temple ordinance work because "millions in the spirit world are watching over us with an interest and anxiety that have hardly entered into our hearts to conceive of."[699] He reminded them, "We have received something better than the love of gold, silver, houses and lands; we have received the promise of eternal life."[700]

In the midst of these challenges, Wilford continued his service in the Church and in the temple. On September 16, 1877, he had his first opportunity to speak to the Saints since his return from St. George. Reflecting on Brigham's funeral two weeks earlier, Wilford said Brigham left an unfinished work for the Saints to carry on. Specifically he told them, "[I]t is our duty to rise up and build these Temples . . . [as] the God of heaven requires."[701]

Wilford then spoke of some of his spiritual experiences in the St. George Temple, referring to both revelations and visions that had been experienced since January. He began by describing how the Lord had "stirred up" their minds and revealed many things "concerning the dead." "The dead will . . . seek after you as they have after us in St. George," he told the Saints. "They called upon us, knowing that we held the keys and power to redeem them." Identifying the spirits who gathered around him, he continued,

"These were the signers of the Declaration of Independence, and they waited on me for two days and two nights."[702] Acknowledging that those in the congregation who were not members of the Church might find his remarks strange, he testified that they would know he was speaking truth when they passed through the veil.

Declaring that the present efforts were only a beginning, he shared his conviction that during the Millennium, "a thousand years will be devoted to this work of redemption; and Temples will appear all over this land of Joseph,—North and South America—and also in Europe and elsewhere; and all of the descendants of Shem, Ham and Japheth who received not the Gospel in the flesh, must be officiated for in the Temples of God before the Savior can present the kingdom to the Father, saying, 'It is finished.'"[703]

HOUSES OF THE LORD

Wilford left the following day to participate in the cornerstone-laying ceremony of the Logan Temple with the other Apostles. The excavation of the foundation of the temple had begun in June. A sawmill and a lime kiln had been established in Logan Canyon and several quarries for the dark-grey siliceous limestone were developed. The work moved forward so quickly that on September 19, 1877, they were prepared to lay the cornerstones. An estimated 10,000 Saints gathered to witness the elaborate ceremony.[704] When Wilford addressed the crowd, he told them he believed there was also great rejoicing in the spirit world on this occasion. He wished the Saints' eyes could see the "hosts of spirits" gathered around them intently and anxiously witnessing the ceremony.[705]

The following month, five weeks after Brigham's death, a Solemn Assembly was held during the October

Church Conference to sustain the Twelve Apostles as the presiding authority of the Church with John Taylor as President of the Quorum.[706] On that day the sacrament was administered to 12,000 people.

In November Wilford met with other Church leaders in Manti and witnessed the blasting that began work on the foundation for the temple there. In his journal, he wrote that a trench had been dug into the side of the mountain and 375 pounds of powder were buried twenty-two feet down. "When it exploded it raised the pile of rocks and earth about 12 feet high. Then it fell broken in fragments, estimated at 3,000 yards, which was ready to be shoveled into wagons and removed."[707] The next day they decided to build the Manti Temple out of rock and paint it instead of covering bricks with plaster and whitewashing the exterior as they had done on the St. George Temple.[708]

While the three temples in northern Utah were under construction, the apostles determined that the Endowment House should be reopened. It was needed to facilitate the sealing of those who had been married in civil ceremonies during the previous year (when the Endowment House had been closed), as well as to provide a proper place to seal those unable to travel to St. George. They also decided that the endowment would only be administered there for "the very aged, sick or infirm" who could not make the trip to St. George and who would probably not live long enough to be endowed in the Manti, Logan, or Salt Lake temple when those were eventually completed.[709]

The first day that ordinances were administered, November 29, Wilford spent most of the day in the Endowment House helping to endow forty individuals and sealing five couples.[710] (The use of the Endowment House continued even after the Logan and Manti Temples were completed in 1884 and 1888 respectively. The building was razed in 1889.[711])

Endowment House in 1880s

A HARVEST ON BOTH SIDES OF THE VEIL[712]

After assisting in the settling of Brigham's estate, Wilford was finally able to return to St. George in January 1878 and work in the temple for two months.[713] He arrived on the 22nd and was happy to find the Saints had completed "a great deal of labor in the Temple in giving endowments" during his five-month absence.[714] The following day, after an inspection of the temple, he began officiating in ordinances. Wilford was again able to spend five days a week in the temple performing ordinances or working on preparing his family names for additional ordinances.

Record numbers of baptisms and endowments were completed while he was presiding. On Tuesday, February 5, 1878, he noted that 1,132 baptisms were performed, the most ever baptized in the temple in one day.[715] The following day he recorded endowments, ordinations, the sealing of couples, adoptions, sealings of children to parents, and second anointings. During February 1878, Wilford was also able to oversee the completion of the proxy endowments for the eminent men and women that had been started the week before Brigham's death.[716] In addition, he performed proxy ordinances for his own ancestors.

His seventy-first birthday on March 1, 1878, marked another special occasion in the temple. Of this experience he wrote, "One year ago today I spent in this St. George Temple and 154 sisters went into the Temple and got endowments for my dead. Today 214 came into the Temple and got endowments; 167 were for my dead, 56 men and 111 females. . . . The spirit of the Lord reigned in the House [of the Lord]."[717]

Two weeks later, on March 15, he found another "surprise party" waiting for him in the Temple."[718] Of the 173 endowments given that day, 134 were for his relatives. According to his record, of the 13,168 endowments given since the Temple was dedicated, 1,062 had been completed for his family members with the help of the local Saints.[719] He stayed in St. George for four more days in order to serve as proxy in the sealings of all his Hart relatives for whom endowments had been performed.

THE GREAT CAUSE OF SALVATION

After returning from his ten months in St. George in 1877, Wilford had admitted, "I feel to say little else to the Latter-day Saints wherever and whenever I have the opportunity of speaking to them, than to call upon them to build these Temples now under way, to hurry them up to completion."

In 1878, after only two months in St. George, Wilford arrived back in Salt Lake City on April 2. On April 6 when he spoke in the Church Conference, Wilford again reminded the Saints of their duty in the "interest of the great cause of salvation."[720] He told them that the St. George Temple was working at capacity, and the spirit of the work "does not lag." He then encouraged them to finish the temple in Salt Lake City, promising that the way would be opened before them. He emphasized that every minute was important and should be spent on those things of eternal significance. He went so far as to state: "Therefore, yours, as well as my eternal destiny, our future position throughout the ages of eternity, depend upon the few hours, the few days, the few weeks we spend in the flesh."[721]

Encouraging the Saints to focus their energies on their own spirituality and the work of salvation rather than on the increasing political and economic chaos in Utah, he emphasized their responsibility to attend to the "essentially necessary" work. "[F]or it takes just as much to save a dead man who never received the Gospel as a living man. And all those who have passed away without the Gospel have the right to expect somebody in the flesh to perform this work for them."[722] He promised that as the Saints turned their time and attention toward the temple, they would perceive its importance and magnitude.

AT WAR WITH PRIESTHOOD AND REVELATION[723]

On January 6, 1879, the Supreme Court upheld George Reynolds' conviction on polygamy, stating that although he was free to exercise his religious beliefs, laws could be passed by Congress prohibiting religious practices Congress considered detrimental to society.[724] With the "freedom of religion" defense eliminated, the federal government stepped up its efforts to prosecute polygamists.

Wilford left Salt Lake City for Southern Utah on January 3, 1879, the day after his wife Emma gave birth to Mary Alice, the last of his thirty-four children.[725] On his way south he went to Manti to see the progress on the temple there, and arrived in St. George on the January 20.[726] Wilford was able to officiate in the temple for only two weeks before learning that Marshal Stokes was in St. George looking for him.[727] He remained hidden in the temple for two days and on February 7 wrote, "For the first time in my life I have had to flee away from the enemies for the Gospel's sake. . . . They are now trying to arrest me on polygamy and, as I had to leave St. George, at 7 o'clock I got into a wagon from the temple with David H. Cannon and drove all night."[728]

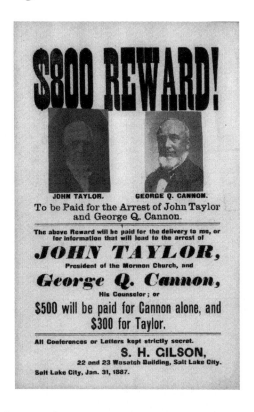

Wilford stayed in Bunkerville, Nevada, for about one week and then secretly returned to St. George. While secluded in his room in the temple, Wilford took the opportunity to compose a statement and testimony to be published to the Saints and "the whole world."[729] He condemned those who "made it a law of offense to obey one of the laws of our God."[730] Then he asked the question, "Now who shall we obey, God or man?" He stated his determination to obey God and added, "I will not desert my wives and my children and disobey the commandments of God for the sake of accommodating the public clamors of a generation steeped in sin and ripened for the damnation of Hell. I would rather [go] to prison and to death."⁷³¹ His message to the Saints throughout the world was: "[Be] faithful and true to your God, to your religion, to your families and to yourselves."⁷³²

Then, for the third year in a row, he was able to spend his birthday, March 1, in the St. George Temple completing ordinances for his relatives. When he entered the endowment room, he recorded that it was "a great surprise to the company" because they were not aware he had returned to St. George. In honor of his birthday, 148 men and women had come to the temple to serve as proxies for his ancestors. His greeting to those assembled was, "Glory Alleluia! God bless Zion. God bless the Saints. God bless those who are here."⁷³³ He spent the day officiating in additional ordinances, including having seventy-four women sealed to him by proxy and participating in the sealings of sixty-five couples from his Hart ancestry.⁷³⁴

In reviewing his record of temple ordinances several days later, Wilford concluded that 2,703 of his deceased relatives had been baptized and confirmed by proxy and 1,639 of them had been endowed by proxy.⁷³⁵ In addition, he had been able to seal over 400 couples in the Hart, Woodruff, and Thompson families.⁷³⁶ He was anxious to attend to their remaining ordinances, but was forced to leave St. George and the state of Utah on March 6, this time in the company of Erastus Snow.⁷³⁷ Although his immediate purpose in leaving Utah was to avoid arrest by federal marshals, while he was in Arizona and New Mexico, he was able to preach the gospel to the native Navajo and Moqui Indians. On one occasion, after speaking to a group of Navajos about the Bible and Book of Mormon, he shared with them the "experiences and revelations given [him] in the Temple."[738]

HOPE IN THE MILLENIAL REIGN

Wilford corresponded frequently with Church leaders and his families while he was in hiding from March 1878 to April 1880. He continued to preside over the work in the temple through letters, receiving updates from Erastus Snow, Moses Farnsworth, James Godson Bleak, and John D. T. McAllister, among others.[739] He also spent many hours pondering his future and the future of the Church. Wilford's belief that the Second Coming was imminent, and that God would destroy those who were working to destroy His Kingdom, is stated repeatedly in his journal. In fact, in 1879 he wrote that the Union would probably be broken up by 1890.[740] In a letter to A. Milton Musser written a few weeks later, Wilford conveyed his belief that if Ulysses S. Grant won the election, "he would be the last president, and the nation would go down on his hands."[741]

At the end of January 1880, in the same apocalyptic mindset, Wilford received what he titled the "Wilderness Revelation."[742] It not only contained details about the destruction of the enemies of the Church before Christ's Second Coming, it contained a confirmation of the patriarchal order of marriage and the need for the Saints to continue living a sanctified, separate existence in order to accomplish God's will. Specifically, God revealed to Wilford that their efforts to complete the temples would be rewarded.

Speaking to the Saints the following year Wilford repeated the idea that the stricter their adherence to the commandments, the more confident they could be that God would "contend for the rights of his Saints"[743] He promised, "[W]e shall be sustained from this time until he comes in the clouds of heaven, inasmuch as we shrink not from the performance of our duties. We have somebody to deal with besides man. The God of heaven holds our destiny; he holds the destiny of our nation and of all the nations, and he controls them." Wilford reminded them that persecution against the Church was not new; it began before the patriarchal order of marriage was revealed and was against the very principles of the gospel.

Temple Block in 1883 with Assembly Hall, Tabernacle, and partial temple
(Council House on the corner across South Temple Street)

He then gave the same response that John Taylor had given when asked about this topic, stating that in order to end the persecution, it would be necessary for the Saints to not only give up the practice of plural marriage, but all other principles of the gospel that led to persecution in the early days of the Church. He suggested that if the Saints were to renounce polygamy, they would need to renounce their belief in revelation, prophets, and then "do away with the idea and practice of building temples in which to administer ordinances for the exaltation of the living and the redemption of the dead; and at last we would have to renounce our Church organization, and mix up and mingle with the world, and become part of them." He instructed the Saints not to renounce a single principle or commandment, but to remain faithful.[744]

On February 29, 1880, Wilford received a letter from John Taylor asking him to come to Salt Lake City for April conference.[745] After fifteen months in hiding, Wilford was able to return home. When he met with the other apostles on April 4, 1880, he shared his Wilderness Revelation with them. They approved it as "the word of the Lord" and later carried out the revealed direction to wash their feet as a testament against those who had shed the blood of the prophets and persecuted the Saints.[746]

WE HAVE NO TIME TO LOSE[747]

Wilford's journals reflect his awareness that time was limited due to the impending Second Coming, and the work was made more urgent due to increasing oppression from outside forces. His discourses also stressed this theme and therefore the importance of redeeming the dead. The declining health and recent deaths of other Church leaders were reminders that he, too, was advancing in age. On June 6, Wilford spoke of those faithful members who had already "passed to the other side of the veil." Recognizing that many other early converts, like himself, would probably soon follow, he commented that when he got to the spirit world he did not want his relatives to say, "'You had the power to do a work for the redemption of the dead, but you have neglected these things.'"[748]

Wilford wanted the rising generation to recognize what they had been given by those who had established the Church, and to recognize their duties as a result. In August 1880, speaking of the importance of finishing the temple, he said, "If you knew and understood the feelings of the Prophet Joseph Smith, and those of his brethren associated with him . . . we would not tire, we would labor with all our might until the [temple] was finished and dedicated, and then we would labor for the redemption of our dead."[749] He expressed his wish that the veil would be lifted so the Saints could see and know the things of God as do those in the spirit world "who are laboring for the salvation of the human family." If the Saints could truly understand, he believed "their whole desires and labors would be directed to redeem their dead."[750]

On another occasion Wilford told the Saints, "I think many times some of us, perhaps all of us, more or less, fall short of comprehending and understanding the responsibilities which we are under to God. I believe there never was a dispensation or a generation of men in any age of the world that ever had a greater work to perform."[751] The work he outlined included preaching the gospel to the nations of the earth, gathering the Saints, and building temples. Emphasizing the importance of temple ordinance work, he said, "Our responsibilities are great; our work is great. . . . We have got to enter into those temples and redeem our dead—not only the dead of our own family, but the dead of the whole spirit world . . . and, if we do our duty, there is no power that can hinder this work, because the Lord is with us."[752]

~ 13 ~

Freedom of Religion

First Presidency in 1880: George Q. Cannon, John Taylor, and Joseph F. Smith

Three years after the death of Brigham Young, John Taylor was sustained as President of the Church on October 10, 1880.[753] As the next Apostle in seniority, Wilford became President of the Quorum of the Twelve at the age of seventy-three.[754] When given the opportunity to address the congregation, Wilford spoke of the effect that the sustaining of a new prophet would have on earth and in heaven. He then said, "[T]here is power with this people; there is power with the priesthood and in the ordinances of the house of God." Speaking directly to "the Elders of Israel," he reminded them that they were called of God and chosen to carry out His great purposes. Specifically, they were "called to bear the priesthood and to attend to the ordinances of the house of God . . . to redeem the living and the dead." He concluded, "It is a great calling, it is a great responsibility. . . . [As] servants of God . . . we should try in our minds to comprehend these things."[755]

GREAT AND MIGHTY THINGS[756]
With his new responsibilities as President of the Quorum of the Twelve, Wilford was not able to return to the St. George Temple until February 25, 1881. Once there, he "took up his abode" in the upper room that had been made into an apartment for him.[757] On his seventy-fourth birthday he wrote, "I wish to bear my testimony to all persons whomsoever may read this journal that the God of Israel has sustained me and watched over me by His power or agency from the hour of my birth up to the present hour."

Reflecting on the blessing of spending another birthday in the temple, he exclaimed, "This is one of the most glorious days of my life."[758] He knew there would be rejoicing in the spirit world because 110 men and women received endowments for his family members that day, bringing the total to 2,037. Over the next several days he acted as proxy in hundreds of sealings for his relatives and also spent time reviewing his records to make sure every name had been accurately recorded.[759]

Then Wilford headed north again on March 21, 1881, to participate in the General Church Conference and to attend to his other church and family responsibilities. With three temples under construction in Salt Lake City, Manti, and Logan, the dedication of the Saints was evident. When Wilford made a trip to Logan for the Stake Conference there, he was able to see for himself the progress that the Saints had made on the Logan Temple.[760]

Logan Temple construction in the 1880s

THE RIGHT OF HEIRSHIP

Wilford continued to preside over the St. George Temple, even as he assumed the increasing responsibilities of President of the Quorum of the Twelve. Forty-one years had passed since Joseph first taught the doctrine of proxy ordinances and explained the Saints' role in the redemption of the dead. The understanding of heirship, and the responsibility of the heirs to their own deceased relatives was a critical component of temple ordinances and the sealing power. In Phebe's first letter to Wilford regarding Joseph's instructions to the Saints in 1840, she had emphasized the role of the eldest convert in each family.[761] The method Joseph had outlined to ensure proper relationships and authority was still in place.

In 1873, Brigham Young reiterated that the first male convert to the Church within each family would be the designated heir, and if there was no male member of the Church, then the right of heirship would rest in the first female convert. The heir was important to temple work because he or she was not only the proper person to officiate in ordinances for his or her deceased relatives, but the person from whom authorization had to be obtained to perform a proxy ordinance. For example, Brigham Young taught if a man wanted to seal his parents by proxy, then his sister would be the proper heir to act as proxy for their mother. However, if the man had no sister but had a daughter old enough to officiate for her grandmother, his daughter—as a direct descendant and blood relative—would be the proper person to act as proxy. If the man had no daughter, his wife—although not a blood relative of his mother—could serve as proxy.[762]

One of the issues that arose following Wilford's public declaration of his work for the Signers of the Declaration of Independence in 1877 was the desire of some Saints to, in his words, "follow their whims" to perform ordinances for "any and everybody."[763] George Q. Cannon was concerned that some were gathering up "all the names of families whether they were related or not and perform ordinances for them." He stated his support of the effort to complete ordinances for everyone, as long as the "rights of heirship" were recognized. "We should do all we can for those for whom we have friendship or to whom we are attached in any way," he continued, "and who have no living representatives that we know of in the church."[764]

When Marriner W. Merrill, president of the Logan Temple, asked Wilford for direction on this subject, Wilford agreed that the Church leaders needed to enforce the rule regarding heirship more strictly stating, "[N]o man has the right, outside of his own kindred, to attend to ordinances for the dead without consultation and permission from the presiding authority in the Church." Wilford then explained to Marriner that he, as temple president, was "authorized to exercise a wise discretion in permitting persons to be baptized for friends," if they could show that the deceased individuals have no relative to act as proxy.[765]

This policy was later clarified by Lorenzo Snow, who was called to preside over the Salt Lake Temple after it was dedicated in April 1893. He explained, "In the performance of work for the dead the rights of heirship (blood relationship) should be sacredly regarded, when practicable. When an heir empowers another person to do the work in his or her stead, he or she should give the acting proxy a written authorization to that effect."[766] This is still part of Church policy today, though not as formal. The current Church Handbook states that members "should not request that temple ordinances be performed for any unrelated person without the approval of the person's closest living relative."[767]

THE LORD IS NOT TRIFLING WITH US[768]

As the number of Church members increased and their origins became more diverse, new converts and the rising generation had no direct connection to the Nauvoo-era experiences. In addition, as the number of temples increased, there was a need for uniformity in the administration of the ceremonies and a deeper understanding of the ordinances. The pattern established in the St. George Temple in 1877 became the standard. Many of the questions submitted to the First Presidency for clarification were answered by reference to the written record made under Brigham Young's supervision and the additional revelations Wilford received in St. George during 1877.[769]

Wilford recognized that understanding the significance of the ordinances was more important for the Saints than anything else. The ceremonies were only a vehicle to impart knowledge of God's plan for His children to them and help them realize their divine birthright. In December 1882, speaking to the "Elders of Israel," Wilford shared his belief that "very few of us fully comprehend our position, our calling, or relationship to God, our responsibility, or work the Lord requires at our hands." He told the men that the Lord had conferred upon them the priesthood so they would be able to administer in the ordinances of life and salvation. He then asked, "Do we comprehend these things? Do we comprehend that if we abide the laws of the Priesthood we shall become heirs of God and joint-heirs with Jesus Christ?"[770]

Wilford also wanted the Saints to understand that their responsibility extended beyond themselves. He continued his remarks by explaining that their duty was not just to build the temples, but to enter them and act as proxy for their deceased relatives so their relatives would be able to enjoy the same blessings as the Saints. Wilford reminded them that the work in the temples for those in the spirit world was equivalent to missionary work to those on earth who had not heard the gospel.[771]

Referring to Obadiah's prophecy, Wilford said, "These, brethren and sisters, are important works. They are works which we do for others that they cannot do for themselves. This is what Jesus Christ did when He laid down His life for our redemption, because we could not redeem ourselves. . . . Do what you can in this respect, so that when you pass to the other side of the veil your fathers, mothers, relatives and friends will bless you for what you have done, and inasmuch as you have been instruments in the hands of God in procuring their redemption, you will be recognized as Saviors upon Mount Zion."[772]

This responsibility, to exercise their priesthood within the temples and administer ordinances for both the living and the dead, only heightened their concern over the government's efforts to limit their interactions with their families and their ability to function in their leadership positions.

Wilford circa 1880s

THERE ARE MORE FOR US THAN AGAINST US[773]

On March 14, 1882, Wilford recorded in his journal: "Edmunds Act passed. The nation is taking a stand against God, against Christ, and against the Church, the Kingdom, and Zion of God on the Earth."[774] Wilford wanted the world to know that, in what was supposed to be a land of liberty, "the law is swiftly invoked to punish religion, but justice goes limping and blindfolded in pursuit of crime."[775]

Ten days later, Wilford met with the First Presidency to decide what to do. Their counsel to the Saints was for men to live with "only one wife under the same roof."[776] Nevertheless, when speaking in the Tabernacle in Salt Lake City several months later, Wilford declared to the world that God did in fact command Joseph Smith to introduce and practice the patriarchal order of marriage, including the plurality of wives. It was the same law given to Abraham, Isaac, and Jacob, and its purpose was so "holy men" might have their wives and children with them in their family organization after the resurrection and together they could inherit "kingdoms, thrones, principalities and powers in the presence of God throughout the endless ages of eternity."[777]

He also declared that the Saints were no more guilty of the crimes—such as adultery—that they were being accused of, than were Abraham, Isaac, and Jacob. Wilford then concluded, "What God has revealed unto us, and that which we know ourselves to be right and true, we cherish and revere; and the covenants that we have entered into in consequence of the revelations of God to us, we hold sacred. Our wives and children we love and respect, and we could no more deny them their claims upon us as husbands and fathers, than we could deny our God."[778] In George Q. Cannon's words, "Our crime has been: We married women instead of seducing them; we reared children instead of destroying them; we desired to exclude from the land prostitution, bastardy and infanticide."[779]

While the Saints were putting their trust in God's protection and defense, the Utah Commission filed its November 17, 1882, report on compliance with the Edmunds Act and stated its opinion that "the steady and continued enforcement of the law will place polygamy in a condition of gradual extinction."[780] Despite passage of the Edmunds Act, which made it possible to fine and imprison men for "unlawful cohabitation," the federal government was unable to carry out the threat until 1884. Unlawful cohabitation was a much easier charge to prove than polygamy because the government only had to show that a man publicly treated more than one woman as his wife. However, they did not have the personnel in place to arrest, indict, try, and convict those practicing polygamy.

In the meantime, Wilford and other Church leaders continued to openly function in their official capacities and interact socially.

Manti Temple construction in 1884

CALM BEFORE THE STORM

On May 17, 1884, Wilford participated in the dedication of Logan Temple.[781] This was the fulfillment of a promise he had made to the young people in Logan twenty-one years earlier. On August 22, 1863, he had prophesied, "You are to become men and women, fathers and mothers; yea, the day will come after your fathers and the prophets and apostles are dead and passed away into the spirit world, when you will have the privilege of going into the towers of a glorious temple, which will be built unto the name of the Most High . . . upon the Logan bench; and you will stand in the towers of that temple and your eyes survey this glorious valley, filled with cities and villages, occupied with tens of thousands of Latter-Day Saints."[782] Following Wilford's 1863 remarks, Brigham Young stood and stated, "All that Brother Woodruff has said is revelation and will be fulfilled."[783] The fact that Brigham did not live to see its fulfillment was also part of the prophecy.

Logan Temple (painted white to cover dark limestone)

Wilford estimated there were about 1,600 people present for the dedication of the Logan Temple as they stood together to give "a shout of Hosanna to God and the Lamb." He recorded in his journal that while attending the dedication he reflected on the many hours he had spent in prayer as a young man "calling upon God to permit [him] to live in the earth to see the Church of Christ established and a people raised up who would receive the Ancient Gospel and contend for the faith once delivered to the Saints." He wrote of the Lord's promise to him that he would live to find the people of God and have a place "within His House." He then concluded, "I today rejoice in having a name with His people and assist in the dedication of another temple to His most Holy name."[784]

Manti Temple construction on October 8, 1885

A STRANGE CHAPTER

Three months later, in August 1884, the systematic prosecution of polygamists began, which resulted in hundreds of convictions and prison sentences ranging from several months to over three years. Prisoners were housed in the penitentiary in Sugarhouse, as well as sent to prisons in other states. Once again, Church leaders went into hiding to avoid arrest.

After Wilford noticed someone watching his home on January 11, 1885, he hid in the Salt Lake Seventeenth Ward meetinghouse long enough to arrange his personal affairs before heading back to St. George on January 17.[785] He remained in the St. George area for ten months, moving between the temple and the homes of several different families in the area.[786] He used an assumed name, one of his childhood friends "Lewis Allen," to correspond with his family and others as he continued to preside over the temple. However, in 1885 he was only able to work in the temple for two weeks in January and June, and three days in May.

On November 1, Erastus Snow delivered a letter asking Wilford to return to Salt Lake City for a meeting of the apostles.[787] When he arrived home on November 5, he found his wife Phebe "severely low" as a result of a fall several weeks earlier. On November 9, realizing her serious condition, he "blessed her and anointed her for her burial."[788] His wife of more than forty-eight years died a few hours later.

Under these difficult circumstances, although he watched from the office window, he wrote, "I was not permitted to attend her funeral without being arrested for my religion, and imprisoned. . . . I am passing through a strange chapter in the history of my life. Persecution is raging against the Latter Day Saints. I am perfectly willing for my wife to lie down and go to sleep and be freed from any of the persecution from the wicked. I hope I may prove true and faithful unto the end that I may meet with her and our friends in the Celestial Kingdom of God."[789]

The next year, 1886, was a turning point for Wilford in many respects. He had vacated the home he had shared with Phebe across from the Temple Block and moved all his things to Emma's farmhouse located south of the city. From 1886 until the end of his life, although he maintained his family relationships with Sarah and Delight and their children, Emma was his public wife and her home his primary residence. Even so, to avoid arrest by federal Marshals, at times he had to stay with various friends in Salt Lake City and other parts of the state.[790] Wilford was not able to attend public meetings or officiate publicly in any Church functions for months at a time.[791]

In October he left Salt Lake City to once again take refuge in St. George. This time, however, he took Emma and his youngest child Mary Alice with him. They were able to go to the temple in St. George to perform vicarious ordinances, but did so at night to avoid attracting attention. On December 17, Emma and Wilford were sealed as proxies for thirty-four of their relatives. Wilford made special arrangements for Mary Alice to be baptized in the temple by William H. Thompson on January 4, 1887, two days after her eighth birthday. Temple president John D. T. McAllister confirmed her. A few days later Wilford and Emma returned to the temple to be sealed for another fifty-two individuals.

Phebe Woodruff (right) with her sisters Rhoda (left) and Sarah (center)

In his journal Wilford reminisced about his life of service in the Church following his baptism fifty-three years earlier. In summary he wrote, "I dedicated the St. George Temple in 1877 and have presided over that temple now for ten years and have held the keys for the redemption of my dead. And through the blessings of God and assistance of my friends, have redeemed almost three thousand of my dead friends, including the Woodruff, Hart and Thompson families."[792]

Perhaps the experiences of the previous ten years in particular, under the administrations of Brigham Young and John Taylor, led him to rethink the Church's approach to the increasing persecution of the Saints. Brigham Young's armed stance and John Taylor's open defiance had only served to entrench the two sides more deeply. Hiding from those tasked with enforcing the anti-polygamy laws was making it practically impossible for the Church to function. The Saints' repeated attempts to challenge the laws through the courts were failing. And the belief, that if they could only hold out until 1890 then the millennial reign would be ushered in and their persecutors would be destroyed, was waning as they got closer to that date without seeing the fulfillment of the necessary scriptural prerequisites.

The Saints' seventh attempt, and most concerted effort at statehood, culminated in the Constitutional Convention held in the summer of 1887. They hoped to regain the ability to vote in elections to choose their own governmental leaders, serve in public office, and educate their own children. But Congress rejected the petition for statehood, even though an article forbidding polygamy as "incompatible with a republican form of government" was included in the proposed state constitution.

Congress could not believe that Church leaders would actually adopt a constitution prohibiting polygamy and demanded that individuals charged with polygamy also take an oath in court to obey the laws against polygamy. In response, attorneys for the Church prepared a statement for the Quorum of the Twelve to consider having the Saints use in court. But the apostles concluded that "no Latter-day Saint could make such a promise and still be true to the covenants he had made with God and his brethren" at the time of his marriage sealing. Furthermore, they decided that if Congress was making the oath against polygamy a condition of granting statehood they could not accept it.[793]

Wilford in 1887

THE KINGDOM OF GOD IN OUR HANDS[794]

John Taylor had spent the last two years of his life in hiding and, as the two sides continued their struggle, died on July 25, 1887. Wilford was also in hiding from federal authorities when he learned of President Taylor's failing health. He left St. George for Salt Lake City on July 17 and was informed of John Taylor's death en route.[795] Wilford believed that John Taylor was "twice a martyr" because, when he was shot while confined in Carthage Jail in 1844, he "mingled his blood with the martyred Prophet;" and during his confinement in exile he died for continuing to practice plural marriage. As in the case of his wife's death two years earlier, Wilford could only watch John Taylor's funeral procession from a window due to the risk of arrest.[796]

John and Wilford were called to the apostleship on the same day and had served together for fifty years. Because he was older than John Taylor, Wilford had not expected to outlive him. To Wilford, John Taylor's death meant that the responsibility for and care of the Church was now on his shoulders. He wrote that it was a position he had "never looked for" during his life, but "in the providence of God" it was laid upon him.[797]

When the leadership of the Church passed to Wilford in 1887, he was eighty years old and the Church's continued existence was in jeopardy. Within days of John Taylor's funeral, the United States Attorney General confiscated all Church property valued above $50,000 and seized the money and assets of the Perpetual Emigration Fund. Frank Dyer was appointed Receiver and the Church leaders became tenants in their own offices with the federal government as landlord. Thus Wilford was immediately faced with the reality and difficulty of the Church's position.[798]

Wilford had adhered to prophetic direction his entire life and depended on revelation from God in conducting both his personal and his public affairs. This meant he not only embraced past revelations, but counted on continuing guidance through new revelation. As he demonstrated while presiding over the St. George Temple, following inspiration, he was open to changing Church practices and policies when those changes did not compromise the underlying principles and commandments. Yet, in spite of all that the Saints had endured and were still subject to, stopping the practice of polygamy was not an option. Wilford and the other Church leaders remained adamant in their stand.

The events that occurred between 1887 and 1890 would require Wilford to seek additional revelation and require the Saints to seek divine confirmation of the answers he received.

~ 14 ~

The Kingdom of God
or the Patriarchal Order

Wilford's decision to issue the 1890 Manifesto against further plural marriages tried the faith of many at the time, including his own.[799] The Manifesto was shocking to most people not only for what it said, but for what it didn't say, and because Wilford Woodruff was the one who said it.[800] Wilford, like John Taylor and Brigham Young before him, had been an outspoken defender of the doctrine and the practice of plural marriage. He had repeatedly stated his belief that God would save the Church from its enemies, the federal government among them, and that they would be allowed to live their religion—which included plural marriage—in peace. After forty-five years of refusals to give in or compromise, it was hard for those inside and outside of the Church to accept that the stand-off was over.

IT IS ENOUGH
Only a fraction of Church members practiced plural marriage, but all members suffered from the religious persecution against the practice.[801] Like Abraham when he laid his son Isaac on the altar, the Saints had been prepared to sacrifice whatever was required—personal freedoms, public status, civil rights, financial security—to do what God had commanded.[802] But the hoped-for "ram in the

thicket" as it was revealed in September 1890 was not what Wilford or the Saints had expected. Instead of the destruction of their persecutors and the long-awaited millennial theocracy providing vindication for their stance, God simply said, "It is enough." The timing of this divine deliverance appeared to be a brow-beaten capitulation to outside forces, rather than an answer to prayer.

The apostles had previously discussed the possibility of suspending polygamy until the Saints could "practice that principle of their religion unmolested."[803] On one occasion, Apostle Francis M. Lyman pointed to President Woodruff and said that in order to suspend polygamy, "it would take the word of the Lord through that man."[804]

The sacrifices of the Saints up to that point in 1889 had been personal, political, social, and financial, but not spiritual. The kingdom of God could move forward if the Saints were denied citizenship and the right to vote. Political unity could wait until Christ's return. Social standing and respect were not essential to salvation, and the Church as an organization would survive without legal status as a corporation. The Gathering to Zion would continue, however slowly, without the resources of the Perpetual Emigration Fund. All the Saints truly needed was the priesthood power to administer the saving ordinances and a place to perform those ordinances.

The oppression that had increased over the course of five decades did not reach a critical point for Wilford until September 1890. When it seemed that the government planned to put the priesthood leaders and temples "on the altar," Wilford's prayerful inquiry was simple: did the Lord want the Saints to continue practicing plural marriage "at the cost of the confiscation and loss of all the temples and the stopping of all the ordinances therein both for the living and the dead?"[805] The Lord's answer was "No." The vision

Wilford received in answer to his prayer on September 24, 1890, showed him what would happen if they continued to practice plural marriage. And if the priesthood holders were imprisoned, the temples were confiscated, and the ordinances ceased, then the kingdom of God could no longer offer salvation or exaltation, and God's work would be frustrated.

Wilford in the 1890s

Wilford was uniquely qualified to understand the sacrifices that would have to be made to keep the temples, and the greater sacrifices that would result should they continue to practice polygamy in spite of God's revealed instruction.[806] Few, if any, had a better understanding of the importance of temple work, or as much insight into the role of the living in the redemption of the dead. Of all the prophets, only Wilford participated in the building and completion of the Kirtland, Nauvoo, St. George, Logan, Manti, and Salt Lake temples. In addition, he was one of those to receive the "endowment of power" under Joseph Smith's direction in the Kirtland Temple. He was not only present at the first ordinance performed in the Nauvoo Temple in 1841, but helped Orson Hyde dedicate it in 1846 and was with the last group of Saints to perform work there before they were forced to abandon it. In Salt Lake City, he served and officiated in the Council House for years and in the Endowment House for decades. Brigham Young asked Wilford to assist in the 1877 dedication of the St. George Temple and to preside over the introduction of all of the ordinances there for the living and by proxy for the dead. In the 1880s Wilford witnessed the first ordinances in both the Logan and Manti temples and participated in dedicating them. He was involved in writing down all of the temple ceremonies for the first time in 1877, and later in harmonizing their administration. As a result, Wilford understood the vision from God in September 1890 and this precipitated his decision to issue the Manifesto.

EVERYTHING TO ENCOURAGE US

The critical events leading up to the Manifesto included adverse rulings by the Supreme Court and more targeted Congressional legislation. The three years between John Taylor's death in 1887 and the issuing of the Manifesto were especially difficult for the Saints and for Wilford personally. In the midst of their trials, he reminded the Saints of their blessings. Speaking in the 1889 Tooele Stake Conference he said, "We, as Latter-day Saints, have everything to encourage us. We have received the Gospel of Christ and the blessings thereof." He told them that he would do whatever was required to have his family with him "in the eternal worlds" and that blessing alone would compensate for all of the pain and suffering he had to endure in this world.[807]

Manti Temple dedication service
on May 21, 1888

On an earlier occasion he directed his remarks to "all men bearing the Holy Priesthood, as well as to all who have entered into covenant with God."[808] He told them "we can, as individuals and as a people, afford to maintain our integrity in this our day and generation, regardless of consequences. We can afford to be true and faithful to God; we can afford to carry out every principle and commandment which God has given unto us ... to meet the consequences, whatever they may be."[809] On the other hand, he continued, "there is not one soul of us who can afford to compromise one of the commandments which God has committed to our charge. No man can afford to do this who is called of God to build up this Kingdom." He then added that it was the kingdom of God or nothing for him.[810]

He wanted the Saints to be prepared for whatever the future held. The events which occurred following these remarks in 1881 through the pivotal year 1893 represented both the culmination of decades of work to build the kingdom—and the Salt Lake Temple—and the loss of almost everything they had struggled to establish and achieve.[811]

Among the most significant blessings the Saints enjoyed in the 1880s were the dedications of the Logan and Manti temples. Wilford had the privilege of presiding over the private dedication of the Manti Temple on May 17, 1888.[812] He noted that the beautiful temple—made of cream-colored oolitic limestone—was "the finest temple, best finished, and most costly of any building the Latter Day Saints have ever built since the organization of the Church."[813] It was on this occasion that he emphatically stated, "We are not going to stop the practice of plural marriage until the coming of the Son of Man."[814]

Wilford had received news that day that Frank Dyer, the receiver for the government, had already made a demand for all of the Church property in Logan including the temple, tabernacle, and tithing office.[815] Wilford's ongoing concern over the safety of all the temples was evident in his journal entry on May 17: "I felt to thank God that I had lived on the earth to once more have the privilege of dedicating another temple in the Rocky Mountains unto the Most High God and I pray God, my Eternal Father, that He will protect the Manti Temple and all other temples we have built . . . unto His holy name that they may never go into the hands of the Gentiles, our enemies, to be defiled by them."[816] Two years later, the answer to this prayer would directly conflict with his emphatic statement regarding plural marriage made earlier that day.

COMPROMISE FOR RELIGIOUS PURPOSES

Over the course of the next few months, Wilford records the numerous meetings with Church attorneys and other advisors as they worked out an agreement with the federal government's representatives to ensure the temples would not be confiscated.[817] The Edmunds-Tucker Act stipulated that buildings used solely for "religious purposes" would be exempt from the law escheating all Church property worth more than $50,000. The negotiations were specifically regarding the meeting houses, the temples in St. George, Logan, and Manti, and the tabernacle and partially completed temple in Salt Lake City.[818]

In the final agreement, which Wilford called "a hard piece of work," the temples remained under Church control.[819] The Utah Territorial Supreme Court approved the agreement and on October 8, 1888, directed Frank Dyer to return ownership of the Temple Block to the Church, which they had been renting from the federal government since its seizure.

During this same time, the reorganization of the First Presidency tested Wilford's patience and reconciliation skills.[820] The need for unity within the Quorum was critical and required extensive discussions, separation of personal and Church business, repentance, and forgiveness. At one point after the struggle to organize the new First Presidency had gone on for over a year and a half, Wilford told his secretary L. John Nuttall that he "would about as soon attend a funeral" as another Quorum meeting.[821] Wilford's diligent efforts and patience in allowing the apostles to work out their differences were rewarded when they finally came to a unanimous decision to move forward together with Wilford Woodruff as President and George Q. Cannon and Joseph F. Smith as his counselors in the First Presidency.[822]

Almost two years after the death of John Taylor, on Sunday, April 7, 1889, a Solemn Assembly was held sustaining Wilford Woodruff as prophet and President of the Church of Jesus Christ of Latter-day Saints.[823] He had wondered on many occasions why he outlived the younger Apostles, and how he would serve as a "conspicuous actor" in the kingdom as had been prophesied sixty years earlier.[824] The breadth of his experience gained over the course of those years of service in the Church and the nature of his personality were suited for the role he was called upon to play. Of this "most important day" he wrote, "This is the highest office ever conferred upon man in the flesh and what a responsibility it places upon me." He then recorded his prayer that God would protect him and give him power to magnify this calling "to the end of his days."[825]

The subsequent decade, the last ten years of Wilford's life, proved to be a time of reconciliation between the Church and the federal government. The Church leaders published a Political Declaration in 1889, and the Manifesto on polygamy followed in 1890. In 1893 the Salt Lake Temple was completed and a pardon was granted by President Harrison to those who had complied with federal laws after the Manifesto.[826] Confiscated Church properties were returned, and a general amnesty was granted by President Cleveland in 1894.[827] Utah's 1896 admission to the Union as a new state meant civil rights were restored to Church members throughout the West.[828] The key to this chain of events was the temples.

~ 15 ~

Temples and the Manifesto

B righam Young's plan to isolate the Saints long enough to allow them to regroup, reorganize, and recommit themselves to the gospel principles and the Church had worked for the most part. From the 1850s to the 1870s, Brigham Young established a clear line between the Saints and the Gentiles through rebaptism, the work of home missionaries, the reformation catechism, specific qualifications for temple recommends, and the United Order movements.

However, Wilford recognized that to truly accomplish God's plan of salvation for all mankind, the Saints must be "in the world." To fulfill the work of the ministry they could not continue to isolate themselves; and practically speaking, by the 1880s it was no longer physically possible to stop the world from moving into the Saints' communities. To influence the leaders of the country, to be represented in Congress, to change the laws and assert their freedom of religion, they had to emerge from their cocoon. To have a voice in their own destiny, they had to be able to participate in the election process which was a two-party system.

The Political Declaration issued by the apostles on December 12, 1889, stated emphatically that the Saints recognized civil authority, revered the Constitution, wanted to claim their right to vote, and would strictly adhere to separation between church and state functions.[829] This Declaration, and the official instruction to the Saints to join the national Democratic and Republican parties rather than the Mormon or People's Party, did not slow down the government's campaign against polygamy. By 1890 about 12,000 Utah citizens had been deprived of their right to vote. The Idaho legislature had disenfranchised all members of the Church who would not take an oath stating they did not belong to a church that believed in plural marriage. Candidates supported by the Church continued to lose elections and the Church lost control of the Territory's education system.

Wilford had expressed his frustration regarding decisions made by the Supreme Court and Congress.[830] His interpretation of the Supreme Court's decision was that the Saints could think whatever they wanted, but could not act. Wilford then asked if that was truly what the Founding Fathers had in mind when they drafted the Constitution. "If it was only intended that men should think and not act, why not say so in the instrument? Why should it be stated that 'Congress shall make no law respecting an establishment of religion, or prohibiting the free exercise thereof,' if men were not to be allowed to act?"[831] He concluded that Congress was overstepping the bounds of the Constitution to pass laws taking away the rights and privileges of any people because their religion "happens to differ from their neighbors."

Nevertheless, on May 19, 1890, in a 5-4 decision, the Supreme Court confirmed that the laws passed by Congress were Constitutional and the federal government therefore had the right to confiscate the Church's property.[832] At the same time, the Cullom-Struble Bill, which had been introduced in Congress in April 1890, threatened to disenfranchise all members of the Church in all territories of the United States. The Bill stated, in part, that no person who was a member of, or supported any organization which taught any person to "enter into bigamy, polygamy, or such patriarchal or plural marriage" would be allowed to vote, serve on a jury, or hold any civil office.

Wilford in the 1890s

Had the Cullom-Struble Bill passed, as similar legislation had in Idaho, it would have applied to all members of the Church whether or not they practiced plural marriage. It would also have applied to all persons who supported or contributed to the Church in any way, whether or not they were baptized members. The Edmunds-Tucker Act had taken civil rights away from those who continued to practice polygamy in spite of the laws passed by Congress; the new legislation would have punished those who had not even violated the law.

WE MUST SAVE OUR TEMPLES

Finally, in August 1890 a special commissioner was appointed to review Frank Dyer's actions in regard to the confiscated Church property. Among other things, Dyer was criticized for allowing the 1888 agreement between the Church and the government which exempted the temples from government seizure.[833] The purpose of the hearings was to determine if the Utah Territorial Supreme Court's acceptance of the agreement had been wrong. If so, then the newly appointed receiver and former Church member, Henry W. Lawrence, could begin actions to take the temples and other formerly exempt properties.[834]

Wilford believed that the Saints had received revelations not given to any former age or generation of the world, and the temple blessings were the pinnacle of the restoration. In 1843 the Lord had instructed Joseph that if the Saints did not complete the Nauvoo Temple, they "with their dead" would be rejected. To Wilford that meant their faith, works, and hopes would have been in vain.[835] Almost fifty years later, in 1890, the Saints had even more to lose. They had completed the St. George, Logan, and Manti temples, and the Salt Lake Temple was almost finished. On August 16, 1890, with the Territorial Court's decision looming, Wilford's declared, "We must do something to save our Temples."[836]

Wilford sought counsel from trusted advisors within and outside the Church. After the First Presidency met with the Church's lawyers, they left for California on September 3, 1890, to avoid being forced to testify in the upcoming proceedings. While in San Francisco they met with some of the political advisors that had previously advocated with the government on their behalf. The straightforward advice Wilford received was already obvious: the government would not restore the Saints' civil rights and their ability to self-govern as long as they continued to practice polygamy.

Manti Temple circa 1888

On September 14, 1890, the *Salt Lake Tribune* printed the most recent report of the federally-appointed Utah Commission. It included the claim that forty new plural marriages had been solemnized, and the report was perceived as the justification Congress needed to pass the proposed Cullom-Struble Bill. The First Presidency returned to Salt Lake City on September 21, facing the new accusations and the same dilemma. If they acted on their own to resolve the fight over the practice of plural marriage, the Saints might refuse to comply with whatever plan they proposed. They required divine intervention because they believed that, in George Q. Cannon's words, God gave the command to practice plural marriage and it would require the command of God to end it.[837] If Wilford Woodruff held the same authority Joseph Smith did when he received the revelation to institute plural marriage, "It required that same authority [for Wilford Woodruff] to say to us, 'It is enough. God has accepted your sacrifice.'"[838]

The First Presidency again met with the Church's attorney and other advisors on September 22, 1890. Then Wilford called a meeting of the apostles for September 24. In preparation for the meeting, Wilford spent that night in prayer. The divine intervention occurred through a vision. God revealed to him exactly what would take place if the practice of polygamy were not suspended. Wilford was shown that all the temples would be lost, all the ordinances therein would cease, the Church leaders and heads of family would be imprisoned, and the Saints' personal property would be confiscated, "all of which of themselves would stop the practice."

God also revealed the alternative. If the Saints stopped practicing polygamy, the "Prophets, Apostles and fathers" would remain at home where they could instruct the people and attend to their duties within the Church, and the temples would remain in the hands of the Saints, so they could "attend to the ordinances of the Gospel, both for the living and the dead."[839] He had his answer and recorded in his journal that he was "prepared to act."[840]

Among those who met on September 24, and heard Wilford explain the answer to his prayer and his decision to issue the Manifesto, was Apostle Marriner W. Merrill, President of the Logan Temple. Following their discussion, Marriner recorded in his journal that he agreed with Wilford's decision. He also believed the Manifesto was "the only way to retain the possession of our Temples and continue the ordinance work for the living and dead, which was considered more important than continuing the practice of plural marriage for the present."[841]

THE MANIFESTO

The apostles spent hours discussing the wording of the Manifesto so they did not say too much or too little. Nevertheless, Wilford believed their decisions were inspired and testified, "[W]hen the hour came . . . it was all clear to me. I went before the Lord, and I wrote what the Lord told me to write."[842] The following day the Manifesto, finalized in the form of a press release and signed only by Wilford Woodruff, was published in newspapers across the country.[843]

The government officials demanded more than just a declaration by the leader of the Church. They asked for a public acceptance of the Manifesto by the general Church membership. Therefore, ten days after the press release, the Manifesto was read in General Conference on October 6, 1890. Lorenzo

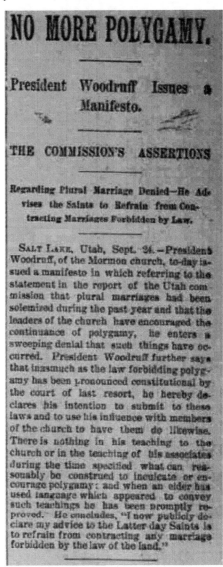

NO MORE POLYGAMY.

President Woodruff Issues a Manifesto.

THE COMMISSION'S ASSERTIONS

Regarding Plural Marriage Denied—He Advises the Saints to Refrain from Contracting Marriages Forbidden by Law.

SALT LAKE, Utah, Sept. 24.—President Woodruff, of the Mormon church, to-day issued a manifesto in which referring to the statement in the report of the Utah commission that plural marriages had been solemnized during the past year and that the leaders of the church have encouraged the continuance of polygamy, he enters a sweeping denial that such things have occurred. President Woodruff further says that inasmuch as the law forbidding polygamy has been pronounced constitutional by the court of last resort, he hereby declares his intention to submit to these laws and to use his influence with members of the church to have them do likewise. There is nothing in his teaching to the church or in the teaching of his associates during the time specified what can reasonably be construed to inculcate or encourage polygamy; and when an elder has used language which appeared to convey such teachings he has been promptly reproved. He concludes, "I now publicly declare my advice to the Latter day Saints is to refrain from contracting any marriage forbidden by the law of the land."

Salt Lake Herald, September 25, 1890

Snow, President of the Quorum of the Twelve Apostles, then called for a vote to accept as authoritative and binding President Woodruff's declaration concerning plural marriages. Some of those present abstained from voting, but the remainder sustained their prophet's decision.[844] George Q. Cannon then testified that the Manifesto was from God and was supported by the apostles. He added that at no time before then had the Spirit "seemed to indicate that this should be done. We have waited for the Lord to move in the matter."[845] Knowing there were those whose faith had been challenged by the announcement, he asked them to do as their leaders had done, and pray for their own confirmation that this was God's will.[846]

Wilford closed the Conference by restating his conviction: "I want to say to all Israel that the step which I have taken in issuing this manifesto has not been done without earnest prayer before the Lord. I am about to go into the spirit world, like other men of my age. I expect to meet the face of my heavenly Father . . . and for me to have taken a stand in anything which is not pleasing in the sight of God, or before the heavens, I would rather have gone out and been shot. . . . I am not ignorant of the feelings that have been engendered through the course I have pursued. But I have done my duty, and the nation of which we form a part must be responsible for that which has been done in relation to this principle."[847]

Many Saints felt betrayed and bewildered. Almost exactly one year before the Manifesto, in answer to Wilford's earlier prayerful request for guidance, God had instructed the apostles not to deny His word or His law.[848] The Saints wondered why they had fought so hard for so long if the Church leaders were going to capitulate after all.[849]

The apostles were accused of trading polygamy for statehood in direct contradiction of the statement made by them on November 27, 1882, that they "could not swap the Kingdom of God or any of its laws or principles for a state government."[850] Yet Wilford did not believe they had traded the doctrine of patriarchal marriage for statehood. The Manifesto did not deny that the patriarchal order of marriage was a doctrine revealed by God or an eternal law.[851] Nevertheless, claims that the Manifesto was written to facilitate statehood were reasonable.

For several years, under the leadership of Presidents Taylor and Woodruff, new plural marriages had been increasingly restricted.[852] The public announcement of this existing policy was strategic. The carefully chosen words in the Manifesto stated Wilford's intent to obey the laws of the land which was what the government insisted upon before it would consider acceptance of Utah's petition for statehood. Government officials said the Saints must obey the law, and in the Manifesto, Wilford stated, "I now publicly declare that my advice to the Latter-day Saints is to refrain from contracting any marriage forbidden by the law of the land."[853]

FAITH OR FEAR

Those who accused Wilford of issuing the Manifesto as an act of desperation were correct in a spiritual sense. Wilford had previously gone to God in prayer many times regarding plural marriage. However, in the fall of 1890, Wilford's query was different. His desperate prayer was for the temples and the sacred work that could only be carried on in places dedicated for that purpose. God's response was also different. God showed Wilford a vision, not of the apocalyptic end to the United States government he had expected, but of the end of all ordinances on both sides of the veil. Wilford said he did not know why the Manifesto was the answer, but he trusted that God knew.[854]

For the next few years Wilford found it necessary to defend and explain his decision to issue the Manifesto. This was in part due to the fact that Wilford, like his predecessor John Taylor, had stated emphatically and repeatedly for decades that the Church would not renounce polygamy. The same reasons Wilford had given earlier for not suspending or stopping the practice and for not renouncing or denying the principle of plural marriage, were now being thrown back at him.[855] He faced and endured the inevitable accusations from within the Church that he had lost the Spirit, betrayed those who had stood their ground for so many years, even apostatized.[856]

Wilford's response to the various accusations came from the very revelation he received on November 24, 1889, leading to the apostles' refusal to suspend polygamy a year earlier.[857] On that occasion the Lord had promised, "If the Saints will hearken unto my voice, and the counsel of my servants, the wicked shall not prevail. . . . I the Lord will deliver my Saints from the dominion of the wicked, in mine own due time and way."[858] It was not up to the dissenters within the Church, the persecutors outside the Church, the monogamist majority of Church membership, John Taylor, or Wilford Woodruff. "We did not reveal it," Wilford said, "—we cannot denounce or withdraw it."[859] Only God could command.

Wilford testified that the Lord's approach was different than his own, that 1890 was the time, and that the Manifesto was the way that God had chosen to deliver them from their enemies who sought not the end of polygamy, but the destruction of the kingdom of God. If he had to choose between pleasing God or man, he said would choose to do what God instructed.

Even Charles S. Varian, the attorney representing the United States government, understood that the change in

Church policy stated in the Manifesto was not because Church members decided to obey man's laws rather than the laws of God. He recognized that the Saints' decision was grounded in their belief that, as prophet, Wilford Woodruff spoke God's will. Furthermore, "though the practice of polygamy had ceased, the principle was undying."[860]

According to court testimony from October 28, 1891, Varian stated, "They are not obeying the laws of the land at all . . . but the counsel of the head of the church. The law of the land, with all its mighty power, and all the terrible pressure it was enabled to bring with its iron heel upon this people, crushing them to powder, was unable to bring about what this man did in an hour in the assembled Conference of this people. They were willing to go to prison; I doubt not some of them were willing to go to the gallows, to the tomb of the martyr, before they would have yielded one single iota."[861]

Each time Wilford spoke of the process he went through to arrive at that pivotal moment in Church history, his explanation was the same: God directed him to suspend the practice of plural marriage to save the temples and the priesthood, and thus continue the saving work for the living and dead. He also emphatically stated, "I would have let the temples go, gone to prison with the apostles and head of families, allowed the [Church] property to be taken, even suffered death if God had not commanded me to do what I did."[862] Wilford knew that salvation for the living was inextricably connected with salvation for the dead and both required the temples and the priesthood.

Wilford believed that God had commanded Joseph Smith to begin the practice and that God directed Wilford to suspend it. As the commandment was explained through the prophet Jacob 2,300 years earlier, "there shall not any man among you have save it be one wife" unless God commands His people to "raise up seed" unto Him.[863] The principle was not changed by the Manifesto. The Manifesto did not revoke the law of plural marriage or deny its re-vealed origins.[864] In fact, in their discussions regarding issuance of the Manifesto, the apostles had specifically agreed only to temporarily suspend the practice.[865] And Wilford firmly believed that the situation would only last for a short time . . . until Christ would come and they would not be subject to the laws of men, but of God.[866]

But Christ did not come in a short time and neither did statehood. Accordingly, Wilford had to shift in his planning and look for long-term solutions to the difficult problems the Church was facing. Not for himself, because he expected to be in the spirit world soon, but for the Church. His millennial expectations mellowed and he re-minded the Saints that they simply needed to do what was required.

He believed that through the Spirit all persons would be able to comprehend the positions they occupy on the earth. "You are held under great responsibility for the manner in which you do your duty and magnify your calling before the Lord," he told them, "and he is not trifling with us, nor with this generation."[867]

SACRED COVENANTS

The assumption that additional plural marriages would be solemnized after the Manifesto, and many husbands and fathers would maintain their polygamous family relation-ships, was echoed by those in and out of the Church. It took decades and the passing of a generation to change family dynamics, economics, and circumstances. The fact that they had made eternal covenants to each other was both a comfort and complication. Years earlier Wilford had expressed his feelings in these words, "The nature of our marriage covenant is sacred and binding both for time and eternity, and I would just as soon think of denying my God as to sever the relationship existing between me and my wives and children."[868] But, because of his age and the stage of life he and his families were in, Wilford was one of those who did not have to make the same difficult decisions other men and families did—such as which wife would be the "legal" wife, where the various wives and children would live, or how families would be cared for financially.

Wilford and Emma Woodruff in 1893

On November 1, 1891, while addressing the Cache Stake Conference in Logan, Wilford knew there were still many members of the Church "throughout Zion who are sorely tried in their hearts because of that Manifesto." His remarks drew their attention to the temple and the reason the Manifesto was issued. He told them they would have had "no use" for any of the men in the Logan Temple because all ordinances would have been stopped. He then reviewed the choices they had had and explained that he had followed the manifestations of the Lord, thus leaving the "Prophets, and Apostles, and fathers free men, and the temples in the hands of the people, so that the dead may be redeemed."[869]

It took many councils and courts to address the issues that arose from the Manifesto. In the meantime, federal persecution continued. The final anti-polygamy legislation was included in the Immigration Act of 1891, which denied polygamists admission into the United States. President Benjamin Harrison—who had met Wilford, visited Utah in 1891, and asked Church leaders to pray for his wife when she was seriously ill in 1892—granted a limited amnesty in January 1893 to those who had ceased practicing plural marriage when the Manifesto was issued. But Wilford believed it was of "little benefit."[870]

THE TEMPLE OF OUR GOD

Wilford's understanding of the significance of temple ordinances only increased his desire to complete the Salt Lake Temple and dedicate it on April 6, 1893. He had dreamed about, assisted in the construction of, and observed the progress on the Salt Lake Temple for over forty-six years.[871] Wilford, just as Brigham had with the St. George Temple, desired to live long enough to see the Salt Lake Temple finished.[872] So, in spite of the financial crisis the Church was facing, he called on the Saints to support the construction effort with their time and renew their commitment to its completion.

Salt Lake Temple capstone ceremony on April 6, 1892

In the presence of 50,000 people, Wilford laid the capstone on April 6, 1892. In his address to those assembled he said, "We want to finish the Temple as soon as we can so we can dedicate it to God so we can go to work therein and redeem the dead."[873] Lorenzo Snow then led the Saints in the Hosanna shout, "the most impressive scene of the day," as some 40,000 white handkerchiefs were waved by the Saints.[874] Francis M. Lyman followed Lorenzo Snow and repeated Wilford's stated desire to live to see the dedication of the temple. He asked for a pledge from the congregation individually and collectively to furnish the needed money and labor, so the dedication might take place on April 6, 1893, exactly forty years from the laying of the cornerstones. His challenge was accepted by the "uplifting of hands and a great shout."[875]

True to their pledge, one year later Wilford was able to dedicate the Salt Lake Temple.[876] In his dedicatory prayer he thanked God "with all the fervor of overflowing gratitude" that He had revealed the powers by which the hearts of the children are being turned to their fathers and the hearts of the fathers to the children. Wilford asked God to confirm upon the Saints the spirit of Elijah so "the sons of men in all their generations can be made partakers of the glories and joys of the kingdom of heaven." He continued, "We praise thee that our fathers from last to first, from now back to the beginning, can be united with us in indissoluble links by the holy Priesthood and that as one great family united in thee and cemented by thy power we shall together stand before thee and by the power of the atoning blood of thy Son be delivered from all evil be saved and sanctified exalted and glorified." To help the Saints in their efforts he asked if God would "permit holy messengers to visit us within these sacred walls and make known unto us with regard to the work we should perform in behalf of our dead."[877]

The following day, Wilford told the congregation that "the Heavenly Host" attended the first dedication service and if the eyes of the congregation could have been opened, they would have seen Joseph and Hyrum Smith, Brigham Young, John Taylor, and "all the good men who had lived in this dispensation assembled with us, as also Esaias, Jeremiah, and all the Holy Prophets and Apostles who had prophesied of the latter day work." He added, "They were rejoicing with us in this building which had been accepted of the Lord and [when] the [Hosanna] shout had reached the throne of the Almighty," they had joined with the Saints.[878]

As they celebrated the end of their forty-year struggle to build the temple in Salt Lake City, Wilford testified that

God had overcome Satan's designs to destroy the work and prevent the Saints from completing the magnificent temple. During the fourth session of the dedication services, Wilford referred to the vision he had which precipitated the 1890 Manifesto. He reminded them, "Yes, I saw by vision and revelation this Temple in the hands of the wicked. I saw our city in the hands of the wicked. I saw every temple in these valleys in the hands of the wicked. I saw great destruction among the people. All these things would have come to pass, as God Almighty lives, had not the Manifesto been given. Therefore, the Son of God felt disposed to have that thing presented to the Church and to the world for purposes in his own mind."[879]

Wilford then testified that the purpose God had in mind was the salvation of His children on both sides of the veil: "The Lord decreed the establishment of Zion. He had decreed the finishing of this temple. He had decreed that the salvation of the living and the dead should be given in these valleys of the mountains."[880]

RECONCILIATION AND RECOGNITION

In his summary of the year 1893 Wilford reviewed the great changes taking place with respect to the Church's relationship with the government and the nation: "A Bill for the admission of Utah into the Union as a State passed the House of Representatives with only five opposing votes. The Mormon choir took the second prize in the World's Fair in Chicago."[881] Wilford Woodruff, George Q. Cannon, and Joseph F. Smith, as the Presidency of the Church, were "received with open arms at the Chicago Fair by the leading men of the world."[882] "Even the Mayor and citizens of Jackson County entertained us and made us welcome. And all our opponents have laid down the weapons of war and ask for a state government."[883] He ended his annual summary with the simple statement: "Our temple is dedicated."[884]

On July 17, 1894, President Cleveland signed the Utah Enabling Act which would allow Utah to finally be admitted into the Union as a state. Wilford's journal entry reflects his relief, "This has been a hard struggle for years as it has seemed as though all earth and Hell had been combined against the Latter-day Saints having a state government. And now we have to give God the glory for our admission into the Union."[885] The Constitutional Convention was held in the spring of 1895 and the new constitution ratified on November 5.[886]

Two months later, on January 4, 1896, Wilford was at home working when Governor Wells came down with a group to congratulate him on the admission of Utah into the Union. They heard "a great noise in the city" that kept up for a long time with guns firing and bells ringing and he supposed the word of the President Cleveland's Proclamation had reached the city by telegraph. That night he recorded, "I felt to thank God that I had lived to see Utah admitted into the family of States. An event labored for for a generation."[887] It was "celebrated as no other day in Utah" on January 6, 1896.[888] The Saints decorated their homes, and for the parade Wilford and the First Presidency "occupied a place in front of the procession."[889]

HARMONIZING THE CEREMONIES
The significance of the Salt Lake Temple, its recognition now as a symbol of the Church throughout the world, is a testament to the Saints' commitment and dedication. At the time, however, its role in the development of temple doctrine and practices was not prominent. The procedures used in the St. George Temple and the pattern set there in 1877 was employed in subsequent temples.

Flag from celebration of Utah statehood hung on Salt Lake Temple

Following the dedication of the Salt Lake Temple, Wilford called all four temple presidents to Salt Lake City to harmonize "the different modes of ceremonies" being used.[890] Apostle Lorenzo Snow had been called to serve as President of the Salt Lake Temple and Apostle Marriner W. Merrill was presiding over the Logan Temple. Wilford's former counselors in the St. George Temple presidency, David H. Cannon and John D. T. McAllister, were presiding over the St. George and Manti Temples respectively. On October 17, 1893, the First Presidency met with them to discuss the changes that needed to be made to ensure the ceremonies were correctly uniform.

Over the course of the sixteen years following the written record of temple ceremonies compiled in St. George in 1877, the presentation of the ordinances in the various temples had only diverged slightly. For example, in one temple the word "forefinger" was used instead of "index finger" and in another temple the word "representing" was inserted after the phrase "this man."

The following year the First Presidency sent a letter outlining the necessary changes in not only the words used in, but the manner of presenting the ceremonies.[891] Wilford attended the first endowment ceremony in the Salt Lake Temple on April 18, 1894.[892] The procedures and ceremonies were conducted based on the records he had helped make under the direction of Brigham Young seventeen years earlier.

TEMPLE ATTIRE

The dedication of the Salt Lake Temple also presented an opportunity to ensure that temple clothing was uniformly made and the symbols used were correct. Dressing in white clothing while officiating or participating in temple ordinances is required in modern temples. Likewise, the symbolic nature of the white underclothing known officially as "the garment of the holy priesthood" or the temple garment is now an accepted part of temple worship.[893] However, these important aspects of temple worship also had to be addressed periodically.

The garment and ceremonial temple clothing were introduced by Joseph Smith to those who participated in the first endowment ceremony in May 1842. The garment was worn beneath regular clothing.[894] Regular clothing was worn along with ceremonial clothing to participate in the ordinances in the various locations in Nauvoo and later inside the temple. However, by December 1845, when the Nauvoo Temple was dedicated, Brigham Young commented that there were "scarcely two aprons alike nor two garments cut or marked right."[895] To restore order in this, Brigham Young asked that all the cloth the Saints intended to use to sew their temple clothing and garments be brought to the temple. He wanted the garments and clothing to be made correctly under the supervision of those who knew how to do it right.

On December 16, 1846, Brigham Young observed that Elizabeth Whitney and Vilate Kimball were busy instructing the sisters in cutting and making temple robes and garments. The following week Brigham announced that in order to keep up with the number of individuals receiving their endowments, it was not necessary for the Saints to wait to get linen or bleached cotton to make the temple garments.[896] "Shirting or sheeting will do for garments," Brigham told them, "The women can cut theirs from the cuts on their husbands."[897]

In 1893, almost fifty years after Brigham Young's instruction in the Nauvoo Temple, individuals still sewed their own garments and temple clothing. Although the garment was originally made of muslin, over the course of the nineteenth century garments were made with a variety of colors and materials, including linen, cotton, and wool. In December 1893, the First Presidency and Twelve Apostles instructed the Saints that all garments should be white. "Colored garments should not be used."[898]

The temple garment represents the covenants made during the endowment ceremony.[899] The marks on the garment—symbolic of the gospel principles of discipleship, truth, direction, and obedience—were originally cut into the garment through the outer clothing during the first part of the endowment ceremony. After returning home from the ceremony, the endowed individuals would then sew the marks that had been cut into their clothing and garment. In 1894, Wilford and his counselors issued instructions that it was unnecessary to mark the outer clothing; marking the garments with the symbols was sufficient.[900] Later the Church began manufacturing the garments with the marks already sewn in.[901]

What had been customary in the past, regarding apparel worn during the ceremonies, became a requirement under the presidency of Wilford Woodruff. In 1877, Wilford, as President of the St. George Temple, and Lucy Bigelow Young, as the head of the female temple workers there, were the first to dress in all-white clothing to officiate in the temple. In the 1890s, all those who officiated in the temples as well as those attending the temple to participate in ordinances for themselves or others were required to dress in all-white clothing.

Oxen cast and painted for Salt Lake Temple baptismal font

WELL-TRIED AND PROVED

By the 1890s, the growth of the Church also precipitated another change in the preparation for attending the temple. Up until 1891, although bishops or stake presidents could recommend someone as worthy to participate in temple ordinances, each person still needed the endorsement of the President of the Church.[902] After Wilford was sustained as President of the Church, he signed 3,944 recommends in 1889, 3,992 in 1890, and 3,898 in 1891. Sometimes he had to sign more than eighty a day and, as a practical matter, it became too burdensome.[903] More importantly, as Church membership increased, Wilford no longer felt it appropriate for him to verify the worthiness of individuals he did not know, and placed that responsibility on their bishops and stake or mission presidents.

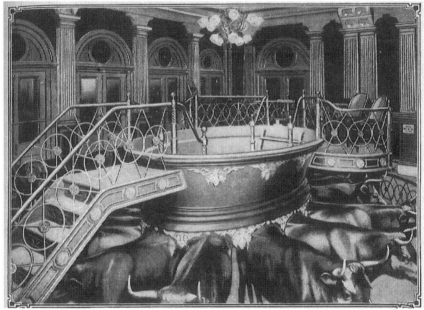

Salt Lake Temple baptismal font set on oxen cast by Silver Brothers

The only ordinance for which Wilford's signature as President of the Church was still required after 1891 was second anointings.[904] The recommendations for second anointings were limited further based on age and experience.[905] When responding to a request to administer the second anointing by proxy in 1888, Wilford explained that he felt it improper to administer this ordinance to young men, either living or dead. He continued his letter by explaining, "In the days of the Prophet Joseph and Brigham this ordinance was not sought for and would not have been administered to any who did seek for it. It was administered only to aged people . . . who were well tried and proved."[906] The Saints were reminded many times that this was not an ordinance that should be requested for oneself or a deceased family member. Wilford explained that individuals should instead be recommended by their bishop, stake president, or the president of a temple.[907]

Similarly, the idea that converts needed to mature in the gospel and have an opportunity to "summer and winter" in the Church before receiving their endowments in the temple became a part of Church practice beginning in the 1880s. This has now been formalized, and in the Church today individuals are required to prepare for one year after their baptism before receiving their temple endowments.

SETTING THE STAGE

The dedication of the Salt Lake Temple stands out as a crowning achievement in Wilford's life. Finally with priesthood power to officiate in the ordinances, four temples built where the ordinances could be administered, and generations of Saints to serve in the temples, Wilford believed the work could move forward rapidly. However, there were several things that still concerned him. Accordingly, Wilford made some significant changes in temple ordinances and practices that he believed were necessary to fulfill "the promises made to the fathers" consistent with Elijah's mission.[908] The most important of these changes was to replace priesthood adoptions with multigenerational family sealings. The revelation he received in 1894 transformed temple work and defined it for subsequent generations.

~ 16 ~

Sealing and the Law of Adoption

Wilford in his office on December 10, 1894

U NLOCKING THE HEAVENS
Wilford believed revelation from God was essential
and that through His prophets God would unlock the
mysteries of heaven. Before he heard the restored gospel in
1833, like many in his generation, he wondered why there
were "no Prophets, no Apostles, . . . no visions, no angels,
no revelations, no voice of God."[909] He longed for direction
from prophets, believing they would, as he put it, "pour

forth that Gospel light, knowledge, and truth, of which the heavens are full, and which has been poured out in every generation when Prophets appeared among the children of men."[910]

Wilford met Joseph Smith in 1834 and over the course of their eleven-year association he gained an unshakable testimony of Joseph's role as a prophet who communicated revealed truths.[911] From 1834 to 1844 Wilford was a witness to the doctrines revealed to Joseph that moved the Saints forward in their understanding of God's plan. He could not have imagined that forty-five years after Joseph's death he would stand as the prophet of a new generation with the keys to unlock the heavens.

As prophet, Wilford relied on continuing revelation. Staying true to the purity of the restored gospel while being open to continual refinements and even corrections was a responsibility he understood well. He had witnessed Joseph's adaptation to circumstances, such as the revelation on baptism for the dead. The initial revelation did not include practical details. The instructions on whether baptisms could be performed in the local river and streams changed once the temple font was prepared. The necessity of proper record keeping and the importance of witnesses were subsequently revealed, as was the need for women to act as proxies for women, and men for men.[912] In 1857 Wilford reflected on these events and explained, "All was not revealed at once, but the Lord showed the Prophet a principle, and the people acted upon it according to the light which they had."[913]

REPENTANCE AND REBAPTISM
Wilford approached changes in temple practices in the 1890s with the same matter-of-fact acknowledgment that the Saints were doing the best they could with the infor-

mation they had at the time. For example, rebaptism for the remission of sins was an accepted practice in the 1840s, and Joseph Smith had encouraged the Saints to be rebaptized. Fifty years later, rather than symbolizing the renewal of their commitment to the principles of the gospel, rebaptism led some Saints to question the significance of their original baptism into the Church. Moreover, some had come to believe that rebaptism could be a substitute for true repentance, particularly in cases that might merit church discipline or excommunication.[914]

This led to the official change in Church policy regarding the practice.[915] In 1892, the First Presidency met with members of the Quorum of the Twelve to discuss the various forms of baptism, and to determine the correct way of administering the ordinance.[916] President Woodruff stated his position that the wording should follow what was outlined in the scriptures, except in the case of baptisms for health.

Recommend to attend dedication of Salt Lake Temple

Then, in March 1893, the First Presidency determined that rebaptism would not be required to qualify for a recommend to attend the dedication of the Salt Lake

Temple.[917] All "who had a standing in the Church" would be allowed to attend if they would "confess their sins and make reconciliation one with another before they go."[918] Later that year the First Presidency announced that, in fact, "frequent baptisms" would no longer be allowed because the sacred ordinance was "becoming too common."[919] This message was reiterated by Church leaders in Stake and General Conferences for several more years.[920]

The practical limitations on the baptismal fonts in the temples contributed to the waxing and waning of the practice of rebaptism; rebaptisms increased after the respective dedications of the St. George, Logan, and Manti Temples and then decreased over time.[921] As the Saints' understanding of temple ordinances developed and the number of proxy baptisms grew exponentially, the availability of the temple fonts for other baptisms was necessarily limited.[922]

Nevertheless, ending the fifty-year-old practice took time. On October 26, 1895, Wilford recorded in his journal that the Quorum of the Twelve met with him in the temple to discuss the "subject of rebaptizing people for wrong doings, etc."[923] In their meeting held May 17, 1896, the apostles decided to remove the phrase "for the remission of your sins," which had been inserted into the baptism ordinances administered in the temples, so that all forms of baptism followed the revealed wording in Doctrine and Covenants 20:73.[924]

In the October 1897 Church Conference, the Saints were reminded again that "the First Presidency and the Twelve have felt that so much rebaptism ought to be stopped. Men, when they commit sin, think if they can only get the Bishop to re-baptize them, they are all right and their sins are condoned. It is a fallacy; it will lead to destruction. There is no such thing in the Gospel of the Lord Jesus Christ. It is repentance from sin that will save you, not re-baptism."[925] Temple records show that from 1887 to 1897 the number of rebaptisms for remission of sins or renewal of covenants decreased from over 1,000 a year to less than 140, and 122 of those were performed in the Logan Temple alone.[926]

ENDING REBAPTISMS FOR HEALTH

The meeting of the apostles on May 7, 1896, which included a discussion of the various forms of baptism, resulted in instruction on the differences between baptism into the Church, baptism for the dead, and rebaptisms for health or the renewal of covenants.[927] In a letter sent to temple presidents two weeks later, the First Presidency stated, "We have had this matter under consideration from time to time, and supposed that our views had been made known."[928] But clarification was apparently still needed. They continued their instruction by delineating the exact language that should be used in first baptisms and in baptisms for the dead and differentiated those types of baptisms from rebaptisms. They noted that there is a clear distinction between baptism for the restoration of health and "the form of baptism which the Lord requires His children to obey to become members of His Church." Baptism is an ordinance of salvation, and baptism for health and healing, "while it may be termed an ordinance, is not imperative on the members of the Church."[929]

Later the Saints were encouraged not to go to the temple to be baptized or anointed for their health, but to seek priesthood anointings and blessings for health within their own homes.[930] The concern was that some members believed going to the temple for the administration of a blessing was superior to an ordinance given by the power of the priesthood outside the temple. As was the case with rebaptism for the remission of sins, the practice of baptism for the restoration of health detracted from the significance of the original ordinance of baptism, as well as from the principle of faith in the power of priesthood blessings.[931]

The end of rebaptism was designed to help the Saints return to the fundamental gospel principles: the need for sincere repentance, the saving ordinance of baptism, the necessity of reliance on the Spirit, and the importance of faith in the power of the priesthood to heal. The current practice of personal recommitment and renewal through partaking of the sacrament is a weekly reminder of these principles.

DO EXACTLY WHAT GOD SAID

Wilford described his perspective on the unfolding of gospel principles and doctrines this way: "When a boy begins his education at school he begins at the first rudiments, and continues to progress step by step. It is so with the student in the study of the everlasting Gospel. There were not many principles revealed to us when we first received it, but they were developed to us as fast as we were capable of making use of them."[932]

Although Joseph Smith had been taught about Elijah's mission in 1823 and began sealing couples in the 1840s, fifty years passed before the Saints had the experience necessary to understand the next step. It took time for them to raise or convert families who were prepared to enter the temples, and for those Saints to then vicariously baptize, ordain, and endow generations on the other side of the veil. The multigenerational growth of the Church was the final element needed to fulfill the instruction Joseph Smith had received seventy-one years earlier.

In April 1894 Wilford received the revelation on the law of adoption which led to a complete restructuring of the sealing ordinances. During the General Church

Conference he shared the revelation with the Saints. Rather than adoption into the priesthood lineage of Church leaders, Wilford told the Saints to seal children to parents, and parents to grandparents. "Then," he explained, "you will do exactly what God said when He declared He would send Elijah the prophet in the last days."[933] With this pronouncement, Wilford expanded and extended the scope of temple ordinance work and changed the sealing practices that had been taught in the Church since the Nauvoo period.

Wilford with daughter Phebe Amelia, grandson Orion Snow, and great-grandson Orion Jr.

Wilford received this revelation almost twenty-two hundred years after Malachi recorded his prophecy regarding the sealing powers of Elijah and seventy years after Elijah's mission to connect the generations of the children of God was explained to Joseph Smith. However, the concepts that Joseph had introduced in the months before his death were subsequently interpreted and instituted by

Brigham Young and John Taylor according to the understanding they had at the time. Wilford told the Saints that he, Brigham Young, and John Taylor felt "there was more to be revealed on the subject."[934]

For the fifty years preceding Wilford's 1894 revelation, there had been three types of sealing ordinances: the sealing of couples, the sealing of children to their parents, and sealings into another man's priesthood lineage, known as adoptions. Wilford's concerns and inquiries regarding these practices led to the revelation in 1894 and the changes he understood were necessary to correctly implement God's will. Only then could family units be created generation upon generation through the sealing power, and links in the eternal family chain be properly connected. When Wilford acknowledged in 1857 that the "full particulars of this order" were not revealed until after the days of Joseph Smith, he told the Saints this showed an advance in building the kingdom and proved the importance of continuing revelation.[935] His statement foreshadowed the fact that he was not only a witness to the incremental development of temple ordinances and practices over the course of nineteenth-century Church history, he was also the instrument through which many revealed changes were made.[936]

Understanding the development of Church doctrine and practices regarding the sealing ordinances from 1844 to 1894 is key to comprehending the impact of the revelation Wilford received. During Joseph Smith's lifetime, although he taught the concept of an unbroken patriarchal priesthood chain spanning the dispensations and discussed the need for children to be sealed to their parents, he only officiated in the ordinance of sealing men and women as couples.[937] There are no records of any priesthood adoptions or child-to-parent sealings before he was killed in June 1844. It was only after Joseph's death, when the Nauvoo

Temple was sufficiently completed in 1845, that Brigham Young began sealing children to parents and initiated the first adoptions of men into the priesthood lineage of other men.

When the Endowment House was constructed in Salt Lake City in 1855, only endowments and marriage sealings were performed there; priesthood sealings or adoptions and the sealing of children to parents would not be allowed until the St. George Temple was dedicated.[938] In January 1856, Brigham gave what some considered "one of the greatest sermons he had ever delivered on earth."[939] Wilford recorded Brigham's counsel on families, Elijah's mission, ordinances, and covenants, among other things. In his discourse Brigham called priesthood adoptions "the highest ordinance," and "the last ordinance of the Kingdom of God on the earth."[940] He told the Saints that priesthood adoptions represent a final sealing and were "above all the endowments that can be given you."[941]

Yet, in 1862, Brigham referred to adoption as the "principle that has not been named by me in years." He told the Saints that although priesthood adoption was a glorious doctrine, and they needed to complete the unbroken chain of the priesthood from Adam to the latest generation, the Saints were not ready for it.[942] He then explained he had received revelation on "how to organize this people so that they can live like the family of heaven," but could not carry it out "while so much selfishness and wickedness reign in the Elders of Israel."[943] His reluctance was due to the unsuccessful attempt to use priesthood adoption as an organizational tool in the exodus from Nauvoo.

Five years later, in Brigham Young's remarks to the Saints gathered in the Tabernacle, he wondered out loud, "Will the time ever come that we can commence and or-

ganize this people as a family? It will. Do we know how?
Yes; what was lacking in these revelations from Joseph to
enable us to do so was revealed to me. Do you think we
will ever be one? When we get home to our Father and
God will we not wish to be in the family? Will it not be our
highest ambition and desire to be reckoned as the sons of
the living God, as the daughters of the Almighty . . . ?"[944]

Accordingly, as the construction of the temple progressed in St. George, Church leaders began to encourage
the Saints to prepare themselves for the ordinances of
sealing and adoption that they would finally be able to
administer.[945] Wilford's discourses through the years maintained this central theme: that God had raised them up in
the last dispensation to carry on His work; His work would
be accomplished through the priesthood; and God had
given the Saints "the kingdom and the keys thereof."[946] He
pleaded with the Saints not to disappoint God or neglect
the things of eternal life for earthly pursuits. He then told
the men that one thing—making it possible for their wives
and children to dwell with them in the presence of God—
would amply pay them for "the labors of a thousand years."
Finally he asked, "What is anything we can do or suffer, to
be compared with the multiplicity of kingdoms, thrones and
principalities that God has revealed to us?"[947]

ADOPTIONS IN THE ST. GEORGE TEMPLE

After the completion of the St. George Temple in 1877, the
ordinance of adoption was reintroduced and practiced in
conjunction with sealings of husbands to wives, and children to parents, for both the living and dead. Wilford
performed the first adoption in the St. George Temple on
March 22, 1877, and began having others adopted to him
shortly thereafter.[948] By 1885 his journal record shows that
forty-five persons had been adopted to him. Between 1877

and 1894 he officiated in the adoptions of ninety-six men to other priesthood holders.[949]

St. George Temple

Sealing the marriages of deceased husbands and wives was also done in the St. George Temple. However, widows who had been married to non-members or "unworthy" husbands were counseled to be sealed to living priesthood holders, rather than take the risk that their deceased husbands might not accept the gospel or be valiant in the spirit world.[950] Depending on their ages and temporal needs, the sealings were either considered adoption into a man's priesthood line or resulted in plural marriage relationships.

The children, if any, were sealed rather than adopted to the new husband, and the deceased spouse was then adopted as a child as well, in order to ensure his connection to the family's priesthood line.[951]

BORN UNDER THE COVENANT

Because adoption was a sealing ordinance, the two terms were used almost interchangeably. The difference was determined by biological relationships in some cases, and the distinction was made based on when parents were endowed and sealed. In answer to the question, "How many children are entitled to the blessings of Abraham?" Wilford recorded Brigham's counsel. Brigham had explained that all children who are born after their parents have been endowed and sealed are entitled to those blessings. Children born before their parents' sealing would need to be adopted to their parents. He encouraged all who want the blessings of Abraham, Isaac, and Jacob, to get their endowments before getting married. "Then," he assured them, "all your children will be heirs to the Priesthood."[952]

After waiting for thirty-one years, children—born before their parents' marriage was sealed—could be sealed to their parents in the St. George Temple. Wilford and Phebe's first child Sarah, who died as a child prior to their sealing in 1843, was sealed to them by proxy on November 9, 1881.[953] Children whose deceased parents were not members of the Church were adopted to a priesthood holder. This alleviated the concern over the worthiness of deceased parents, particularly those who had been adamantly opposed to their child's affiliation to the Church when they were alive. For this reason, the practice of adoption to living and deceased Church leaders—rather than parents for whom ordinances had been performed by proxy—continued.

SEALING AND ADOPTIONS

By 1893 approximately 16,000 proxy sealings had been performed and over 13,000 proxy adoptions.[954] Those sealed were usually children and infants who had died, while those who were adopted were usually the siblings, parents, and other relatives of the Saints that had not become members of the Church. Proxy adoptions to Church leaders decreased as the number of endowed and sealed Church members increased.

Wilford had his deceased sister Eunice sealed to him, as her priesthood leader. Perhaps he felt that because she and her husband Dwight Webster had not followed the Quorum of the Twelve Apostles after the death of Joseph Smith, therefore Dwight was not a worthy priesthood holder. Wilford also had Rebecca Brown sealed to him. (Rebecca had died, along with her father Captain Charles Brown, as their family traveled with the Woodruffs from Maine to join the Saints in Illinois.[955]) That same day Phebe and Wilford acted as proxies in the sealing of Wilford's father Aphek to Wilford's mother Beulah and to his stepmother Azubah.

By contrast, between 1877 and 1893, over 19,000 living persons were sealed to their biological parents, while only 1,200 living persons were adopted.[956] Many of those sealed to their parents were children under the age of eighteen, and the rest were adult children of Church members. In almost all cases, those adults who requested adoption to a Church leader were those whose parents were not members of the Church. This reflected their need to still be connected to the family of God and receive the sealing blessings.

A difficult question regarding the proxy sealing of children was posed this way: "Shall children born outside of the marriage relation, and who are dead, be sealed to their

Wilford Woodruff's Witness

father, or to their mother?" Brigham's answer was they should be sealed to "the one who has received the Gospel and lived it."[957] John D. T. McAllister, counselor to Wilford in the temple presidency, sought additional clarification on this using his own situation as the example. His father had not joined the Church, but his mother "embraced the Gospel, gathered with the Church, received her endowments, and lived the Gospel."[958] John was baptized on behalf of his father, and his mother was then sealed to his father. He wondered if that meant he should be sealed to his mother, not his father. The counsel was that his mother would have to "be sealed to a man in the Priesthood, faithful in the Church," and John and his siblings must then be adopted to their mother and the faithful man.[959] Accordingly, on April 10, 1877, John D. T. McAllister, his mother and his family were adopted to Brigham Young.[960]

This instruction was difficult for some, including Wilford, to understand. Some Saints did not pursue sealings for this reason.[961] On January 3, 1857, Wilford recorded a conversation with Heber C. Kimball in his journal. He wrote that Heber "taught us good doctrine. He said that he did not believe in this custom of adoption that had been practiced in this Church. No man should give his birthright to another but should keep his birthright in the lineage of his fathers and go to and unite the link through the whole lineage of their fathers until they come up to a man in the lineage who held the priesthood. Now, unless a man is a poor cuss, he should keep his priesthood and unite it with his fathers, and not give it to another."[962]

MORE TO BE REVEALED

Even though the practice of priesthood adoption continued under Wilford's leadership as President of the St. George Temple, it was something that concerned him. Wilford's

280

own reticence is evidenced by the fact that he waited eighteen years after the reintroduction of the adoption ordinance in 1877 to have members of his family adopted to Joseph Smith.[963] When the Logan and Manti temples began operating in the 1880s and the Salt Lake Temple was finally completed in 1893, the implications of the practice became more troublesome to Wilford as President of the Church. Those, including Wilford, who had traced their family history back many generations wanted to seal or adopt their family members so their place in the family of God would be secured.

In 1891 Edward Bunker Sr., a good friend of Wilford's and a former Bishop in the St. George Stake, wrote a letter detailing his concerns regarding the practice of adoption (among other things) to the Stake leadership. Edward did not believe there was a man on earth that thoroughly understood the principle of adoption, or at least he had never been taught it in a way he could understand. He wrote, "I believe it is permitted more to satisfy the minds of the people for the present until the Lord reveals more fully on the principle."[964]

Edward Bunker's sentiments echoed those of Brigham Young spoken in 1846, almost fifty years earlier. At that time Brigham had explained that the law of adoption was "a schoolmaster to bring them back into the covenant of the Priesthood" and he was aware that it was "not clearly understood by many" at that time. Brigham then confessed that even he "had only a smattering of those things," but was sure that more would be revealed.[965]

Based on Wilford's own concerns, and perhaps those expressed by others through the years, he sought additional revelation on the sealing ordinances. In his April 1894 Conference address, Wilford confirmed Brigham's statement. He told the Saints that, although they had been acting according to all the light and knowledge they had, "I have not felt satisfied, neither did President Taylor, neither has any man since the Prophet Joseph who has attended to the ordinance of adoption in the temples of our God. We have felt that there was more to be revealed upon the subject than we had received."[966] Wilford explained that he and his counselors had prayed over the matter, and he had indeed received revelation outlining the changes that must be made "in order to satisfy our Heavenly Father, satisfy our dead and ourselves."[967]

He then announced that it was the will of the Lord for the Saints "from this time to trace their genealogies as far as they can, and to be sealed to their fathers and mothers."[968] He also said that the Saints should have children sealed to their parents, and "run this chain through as far as you can get it."[969] This meant they would be connecting the generations by strengthening natural ties instead of creating convoluted links.

Recognizing the simplicity of the revelation, Wilford reflected on the commencement of the practice of adoption in Nauvoo. Referring to the fact that some men campaigned in an effort to enlarge their "kingdoms," he acknowledged that "there was a spirit manifested by some in that work that was not of God." Hundreds of men and women were adopted to men "not of their lineage." He told the Saints that when he prayed to know who he should be adopted to, "the Spirit of God said to me, 'Have you not a father, who begot you?' 'Yes, I have.' 'Then why not honor him? Why not be adopted to him?' 'Yes,' said I, 'that is right.'"[970]

In his remarks, Wilford also included special instructions to the women of the Church whose husbands had died without hearing the gospel. In the past, he said, the request of a woman in this situation who wanted to be sealed to her husband was denied and she was told she could not be sealed to him.[971] He continued, "Many a woman's heart has ached because of this, and as a servant of God I have broken that chain."[972] He did not think it right to deprive a woman of being sealed to her husband because, he queried, "What do any of us know with regard to him? Will he not hear the gospel and embrace it in the spirit worlds?"[973]

Aphek Woodruff, Wilford's father, age 83

ONE STEP IN ADVANCE

Wilford emphasized that this change in practice was not a new doctrine, but actually based on what had been revealed to Joseph Smith regarding the mission of Elijah. He referred to Joseph's 1842 letter to the Saints when Joseph first said there must be a welding link between the fathers and the children.⁹⁷⁴ Wilford went on to explain, "I was adopted to my father, and should have had my father sealed to his father, and so on back; and the duty that I want every man who presides over a temple to see performed from this day henceforth and forever, unless the Lord Almighty commands otherwise, is, let every man be adopted to his father. When a man receives the endowments, adopt him to his father; not to Wilford Woodruff, nor to any other man outside the lineage of his fathers. That is the will of God to this people. . . . [L]et every man be adopted to his father; and then you will do exactly what God said when he declared he would send Elijah the prophet in the last days. . . . [T]hen we will make one step in advance of what we have had before. This is the will of the Lord to this people, and I think when you come to reflect upon it you will find it to be true."⁹⁷⁵

The Saints had initially worried that being sealed to those who had not accepted the gospel on earth, including their own parents, might put their salvation in jeopardy if those individuals did not accept the gospel in the spirit world. Wilford's response to this concern was three-fold. First he reminded them that "God is no respecter of persons; he will not give privileges to one generation and withhold them from another; and the whole human family, from father Adam down to our day, have got to have the privilege, somewhere, of hearing the Gospel of Christ; and the generations that have passed and gone without hearing that Gospel in its fullness, power and glory, will never be held responsible by God for not obeying it, neither will he bring them under condemnation for rejecting a law they never saw or understood; and if they live up to the light they had they are justified so far, and they have to be preached to in the spirit world."⁹⁷⁶

Wilford with his son Wilford Jr. (left), grandson Wilford S. (right),
and great-grandson Charles Wilford on August 16, 1897

Second, he wanted the Saints to understand it was not
the responsibility of the living to judge, but to do their part
in offering the choice by performing the saving ordinances
by proxy for every member of the human family regardless
of their perceived worthiness. To those who asked, "What
if these people do not receive the Gospel?" he answered,

"That will be their fault, not mine. This is a duty that rests upon all Israel, that they shall attend to this work, as far as they have the opportunity here on the earth."[977] This, in Wilford's view, was what was required of the Saints. The knowledge that all of the temple ordinances would eventually be performed for all God's children changed the Saints' perspective on the perceived need to be sealed to one of the leaders of the Church instead of their own fathers and mothers

Finally, Wilford assured them that, "There will be very few, if any, who will not accept the Gospel."[978] Confusion regarding the status of adoptions to leaders or relatives who subsequently left the Church was replaced with the understanding that, regardless of their perceived worthiness or faithfulness on earth, all God's children should be given the benefit of the doubt and be included as a link in the eternal family. Furthermore, the sealing blessings would still be applicable to each individual who remained worthy of their sealing covenants regardless of the choices made by others.

Wilford concluded his remarks by saying, "It is my duty to honor my father who begot me in the flesh. It is your duty to do the same. When you do this, the Spirit of God will be with you. And we shall continue this work, the Lord adding light to that which we have already received. . . . Go and be adopted to your fathers, and save your fathers, and stand at the head of your father's house, as saviors upon Mount Zion, and God will bless you in this." "This is," he continued, "what I want carried out in our temples. I have had a great anxiety over this matter. I have had a great desire that I might live to deliver these principles to the Latter-day Saints, for they are true. They are one step forward in the work of the ministry and in the work of the endowments in these temples of our God."[979]

When he reflected on the history of the Church and the development of his own understanding, he simply said, "There will be no end to this work until it is perfected."[980]

George Q. Cannon—his first counselor in the First Presidency—spoke next and added his testimony in support of the revealed changes. "[Y]ou can see the advantage of pursuing now the course that is pointed out by the word of God to us," he said, "It will make everyone careful to obtain the connection and to get the names properly of the sons and daughters of men to have them sealed to their parents. It will draw the line fairly; it will define lineage clearly."[981]

First Presidency on March 2, 1894
Left to right: George Q. Cannon, Wilford Woodruff and Joseph F. Smith

THE FAMILY OF GOD

These principles are still practiced and believed by Church members: the fulfillment of the mission of Elijah is to bind families together, to link the generations, to seal the children to their fathers and the fathers to their God. All other priesthood ordinances are designed to lead members step by step toward this ultimate goal of eternal families.

Wilford's announcement rewrote the nature of temple ordinances and changed the perspective of the Saints not only regarding their own parents and grandparents but with regard to the need to return to the temple again and again. For fifty years, following the introduction of proxy temple sealings, the Saints were only able to seal children to parents if the father was ordained to the priesthood. Therefore, sealings to deceased parents were limited to those who had accepted the gospel in mortality until proxy ordination began in 1877 in the St. George Temple. Even then, proxy sealings were only performed for one deceased generation. Although Church members had collected names of relatives in order to act as proxy in their baptisms and endowments, they were not able to organize these relatives into individual family units and perform sealings generation upon generation.

With the reassurance that most, if not all, of their family members would accept the gospel in the spirit world, the Saints were able to move forward. Rather than only performing ordinances for those they judged worthy or sealing to those they presumed would accept the gospel, they would leave judgment to God. Following Wilford's announcement in 1894, those who had previously sealed fathers to non-relatives or mothers and their children to priesthood leaders could now make natural family connections, sealing children to parents through every generation. By 1897, in the Salt Lake Temple alone, 21,288 couples were sealed by proxy and 17,936 children were sealed to their parents.[982]

Naturally the Saints wondered about the validity of the more than 13,000 sealings and adoptions previously performed between unrelated individuals. The counsel given was to focus on organizing and sealing generational families, not to worry about undoing ordinance work previously completed.[983] This also remains the standard in Church practice regarding proxy ordinance work. The Saints are counseled to do their best research and record keeping and rest assured that the validity of all ordinances will be determined "beyond the veil."[984] Ultimately it is up to each individual, because all must "qualify themselves" for and accept the saving and exalting ordinances performed in their behalf.[985]

THEY SHALL LEARN WISDOM
Throughout the history of the Church, whenever changes occurred in the temple ordinances or the Church organization, some questioned why these things were not perfected in the beginning. To those who wondered, and those who still wonder, the Lord responds: "I will give unto the children of men line upon line, precept upon precept, here a little and there a little; and blessed are those who hearken unto my precepts, and lend an ear unto my counsel, for they shall learn wisdom; for unto him that receiveth I will give more; and from them that shall say, We have enough, from them shall be taken away even that which they have."[986]

In Wilford's May 1894 address he made it clear that God would continue to guide the work of the Church, particularly in relation to the temples: "I want to say, as the president of the Church of Jesus Christ of Latter-day Saints, that we should now go on and progress. We have not gotten through with revelation. We have not gotten through with the work of God. But at this period we want to go on and fulfill this commandment of God given through Malachi—that the Lord should send Elijah the prophet."[987] Wilford explained that although Brigham Young accomplished all that God required at his hands, he did not receive all the revelations that belong to this work; neither did John Taylor nor had Wilford as prophet. Wilford then concluded, "There will be no end to this work until it is perfected."[988]

Thus he reminded the Saints that prophets and revelation were still a vital part of the progress of God's work, that although Joseph Smith had been inspired to lay a firm foundation before his death in 1844, God would work through His subsequent prophets to continue perfecting the Church structure built on that foundation. Wilford's devotion to Joseph and deference to his predecessors did not prevent him from believing that God had yet to reveal many great and important things pertaining to His Kingdom.[989]

GREAT WORK OF THE LAST DISPENSATION[990]
Seven months after his revelation on the sealing ordinances, Wilford and the First Presidency directed the establishment of the Genealogical Society of Utah. The Society was organized to help the Saints complete the family research necessary to make generational sealings possible. Wilford had noted earlier that it seemed as if "every avenue has been closed to obtaining such records," but felt that the Lord was influencing the nation. As a result, thousands were "laboring to trace the genealogical descent" of their ancestors and the Church would be able to gather the research and information that had recently come to light and make it accessible to those who wanted to research

their family histories.[991] The hope was that cooperation in research and recording would minimize cost and eliminate duplication of efforts and ordinances.

In his dedicatory prayer for the Salt Lake Temple Wilford had asked God to bless the Saints in their efforts to redeem the dead. He also prayed for those outside the Church to be assisted in their genealogical work: "And, as thou hast inclined the hearts of many who have not yet entered into covenant with thee to search out their progenitors, ... we pray thee that thou wilt increase this desire in their bosoms, that they may in this way aid in the accomplishment of thy work. Bless them, we pray thee, in their labors, ... open before them new avenues of information, and place in their hands the records of the past, that their work may not only be correct but complete also."[992]

Church Historian's Office

The expressed two-fold duty of the Genealogical Society was: "To spread among the people the knowledge of the doctrine of salvation for the dead, and to advance the work of gathering genealogical records for use in the temple work for the dead."[993] The first Genealogical Society Library was housed in the Church Historian's Office in Salt Lake City.[994] Membership in the new organization was not restricted; all those interested in pursuing genealogical research were welcome. The floodgates were opened.

The Society, now known as the Family History Department of the Church, is the largest genealogical organization in the world. The Family History Library in Salt Lake City houses information on more than three billion people from over 100 countries. Tens of thousands visit each year, fulfilling the prophecy of Malachi as they turn their hearts to their ancestral fathers.

~ 17 ~

Promises Made to the Fathers

Wilford in 1897

I HELD THE KEYS OF THEIR SALVATION[995]
Wilford taught the Saints of their unique role in the final
dispensation, "The Lord . . . will hold us responsible for the
use we make of the holy Priesthood, the ordinances of this

house and the power that is put into our hands to accomplish the work of God, and to build Temples to his name."[996] In 1896 he reminded the Saints that they had an opportunity that few, if any, had had before them. "Who besides the Latter-day Saints, since the days of Christ and His Apostles, have ever taught the principle of the redemption of the dead?" he asked. "Here we have four temples reared in this State by the Latter-day Saints, and tens of thousands of the dead have been redeemed by the administration of the Gospel of Christ to their posterity or friends. This is one of the evidences of the fulfillment of the Gospel of Jesus Christ. The prophet says, 'saviors shall come upon mount Zion . . . and the kingdom shall be the Lord's.' If we were not the Saints of God, we could not do this."[997]

In 1897, not wanting the Saints to ignore their responsibilities or forfeit the blessings that would come from fulfilling them, Wilford asked, "What is there in this life that will pay us to lose all those blessings which belong to the first resurrection and to the kingdom of heaven? It is within our power, by keeping the commandments of God, to come forth out of our graves, clothed in immortal, celestial bodies, with our wives, our children, our fathers, our mothers, our relatives, and our friends, and occupy high and exalted positions in the presence of God and the Lamb, and dwell with them forever and forever."[998]

Wilford often shared his feelings of joy in the privilege of completing ordinances for over four thousand of his own family members as well as many others. It was a blessing and privilege he believed "the fulness and glory of which we will never know until the veil is opened."[999] He expected the reunions that would occur on the other side of the veil would be happy ones unless the Saints ignored or neglected their responsibilities to their own deceased family members. Using himself as an example, he asked: "How would I feel, after living as long as I have, with the privileges I have had of going into these temples, to go into the spirit world without having done this work?"[1000] He did not want to meet his progenitors and have one say, "You held in your hand the power to go forth and redeem me, and you have not done it."[1001] He did not want the Saints to face that prospect either.

Cache Valley and Logan Temple

Wilford believed the Lord has held responsible and will hold responsible—in time and in eternity—every man and every people into whose hands the Holy Priesthood and the keys of the kingdom of God have been committed, for how they use the gifts, blessings, and promises given to them.[1002] In fact, he stated that this was the difference between those who keep the celestial law and those who do not.[1003] "For," he said, "all men know what laws they keep, and the laws which men keep here will determine their position hereafter; they will be preserved by those laws and receive the blessings which belong to them."[1004] Knowing members of the Church will have to give an account to

God for the priesthood and the keys of the kingdom with which God has entrusted them, Wilford reminded the Saints to make use of the "blessings, privileges and powers which we enjoy in connection therewith."[1005]

At the same time he stressed that the responsibility of temple ordinance work was not meant to be a burden. Wilford felt it was not only a blessing for those on the other side of the veil, but a blessing for the Saints as well.[1006] He explained, "This is the work of our lives, and it makes life of some consequence to us."[1007] After decades of witnessing the impact of temple worship on the Saints, Wilford knew that serving as proxies in the temples also allowed the Saints to review and renew their own covenants: obedience to God's commands, discipleship to the Savior, seeking truth, and being willing to sacrifice their time and talents to building the kingdom of God.

The Saints had made incredible sacrifices to build six temples, fulfilling what Wilford considered one of their most important obligations in the dispensation of the fulness of times. With four temples in Utah dedicated to the work of universal salvation, thousands of ordinances were being performed for the living and by proxy for the deceased every year.[1008] Comparing the value of salvation to worldly wealth, Wilford said riches "perish with the using." On the other hand, he continued, "To be saved ourselves, and to save our fellowmen, what a glorious thing!"[1009] There was "hardly any principle the Lord had revealed" that he had rejoiced in more.[1010] "These are grand principles," he testified, "They are worth every sacrifice."[1011]

WE AIM AT CELESTIAL GLORY[1012]
When Wilford embraced the restored gospel, he did so because, although he felt he had great faith and gospel knowledge, he wanted more. He prayed that God would

enable him to be faithful because the object of his life was salvation. His expressed goal was eternal life, and he said this was the principle that sustained him from the time he entered the Church as the kingdom of God on the earth.[1013] In 1833, at the age of twenty-six, Wilford joined a church of 3,100 converts that had existed for only three years. At the age of eighty, he became the leader of that same church with a membership of 180,000 members. At the time of his death in 1898, the Church had expanded throughout the world and Church membership had surpassed 280,000.

Sanpete Valley and Manti Temple

Wilford spent the first ten years after he joined the Church preaching the gospel to redeem the living.[1014] He then spent fifty years working to perfect the Saints. To him perfecting the Saints meant redeeming the dead, for he wholeheartedly believed that we without them cannot be made perfect.[1015] Moroni's message to Joseph Smith in 1823 signaled that every living member of Christ's church was required to participate in God's plan of salvation for themselves and their forefathers. Wilford understood that accomplishing God's purpose "to bring to pass the immortality and eternal life of man" was contingent on the children remembering the promises made to their fathers and redeeming them.[1016] God had revealed that if the promises to the fathers were not kept, man's mortal existence would be wasted; the work of God would fail.[1017] Wilford not only taught the message of universal redemption with clarity, he expanded the effort to offer salvation and eternal life to all.

NOTHING THAT IS EQUAL TO IT

Wilford is regarded as one of the greatest missionaries in the history of the Church. For him, however, the missionary effort to share the gospel with the living on earth was equal to the need to redeem the living in heaven.[1018] Wilford encouraged the Saints in their efforts, saying, "What greater calling can any man have on the face of the earth than to hold in his hands power and authority to go forth and administer in the ordinances of salvation? Do we prize these things in their fulness? . . . Certainly there has been nothing in this work that I have had greater consolation in than in preaching the Gospel to my fellowmen and in administering unto them the ordinances of the house of God, both for the living and the dead. . . . You give unto any soul the principles of life and salvation and administer these ordinances to him, and you become an instrument in the hands of God in the salvation of that soul. There is nothing given to the children of men that is equal to it."[1019]

On March 19, 1897, Wilford made the only known recording of his voice, immortalizing his testimony of Joseph Smith's inspired restoration of the gospel principles and priesthood ordinances. On this occasion, he testified that Joseph "was the author of the endowments as received by the Latter-day Saints. I received my own endowments under his hands and direction, and I know they are true principles. . . . The Prophet Joseph laid down his life for the word of God and testimony of Jesus Christ, and he will be crowned as a martyr in the presence of God and the Lamb. In all his testimonies to us the power of God was visibly manifest with the Prophet Joseph."[1020]

Later that year, Wilford asked the Saints if there was any other individual or church on the earth with the power to "redeem their dead." He then testified, "There never was a soul anywhere that could do this until God organized His Church upon the earth."[1021] Then, in April 1898, he reminded the Saints of his experience in the St. George Temple with the Signers of the Declaration of Independence.[1022] The nobility of their spirits was evident to him because they recognized that Wilford, "as an Elder in Israel," held the priesthood authority and had the ability to perform the temple ordinances in their behalf.[1023]

Wilford dedicating Pioneer Park on July 24, 1898

Because the Saints possess the restored Priesthood, he declared, "We have no excuse ... for the blessings are given to us; they are within our reach, and it is your privilege and mine to enjoy them."[1024] He simply wanted to remain faithful so, at the close of his earthly probation, he would know he had done the best he could and, acting up to the best light he had, be welcomed into the kingdom of God.[1025] "I want to live as long as I can do good; but not an hour longer than I can live in fellowship with the Holy Spirit, with my Father in heaven, my Savior, and with the faithful Latter-day Saints. To live any longer than this, would be torment and misery to me. When my work is done I am ready to go."[1026]

Wilford's funeral service on September 8, 1898

Wilford delivered his final conference address on April 10, 1898. He had celebrated the fiftieth anniversary of the Saints' arrival in the Salt Lake Valley the previous year, and his final public appearance on July 24, 1898, was at the dedication of Pioneer Park, the site of the fort he helped build in 1847.[1027] At the age of 91, six weeks after the dedication, he died in San Francisco, California. His passing was mourned by his three wives, twenty children, 103 grandchildren, sixteen great-grandchildren, and hundreds of thousands of Saints.[1028]

Wilford's funeral cortege on September 8, 1898

WE HAVE A GREAT WORK BEFORE US

Wilford believed that before the Savior's death He organized His earthly followers, the Apostles, to preach the gospel to the living.[1029] As Peter did in his epistle to the early Saints, Wilford taught that between the Savior's death and resurrection, Christ also began the process of sharing "the light of the Gospel to them that were in darkness" in the spirit world.[1030] Furthermore, Christ's efforts in the spirit world were in preparation for His command to the Latter-day Saints to act as proxies for those who live "according to God in the spirit" but must be judged "according to men in the flesh."[1031] To Wilford, the Saints' participation in the redemption of the dead was proof of their belief in Christ's infinite Atonement and a universal resurrection: that truly "in Christ shall all be made alive."[1032]

He testified of Christ's Second Coming and what He expects from the Latter-day Saints in regard to the salvation of all the children of God before His return. Encouraging the Saints to take these things to heart, he asked them to continue filling up their family records "righteously before the Lord." He also promised them that the blessings of God would be with them, and those who are redeemed will bless them in days to come. "If we do attend to this," he explained, "then when we come to meet our friends in the celestial kingdom, they will say, 'You have been our saviors, because you had power to do it. You have attended to these ordinances that God has required.'" Alternatively, he said, "If we do not do what is required of us in this thing, we are under condemnation."[1033]

His prayer was that the Saints' eyes would be opened to see and their hearts would understand the great work that rested upon their shoulders because, he believed, it was far more important than they realized or comprehended.[1034]

HAVE WE FAITH IN OUR OWN RELIGION?[1035]
Wilford understood the Saints' unique position in God's plan for the redemption of His children. Yet his efforts to further the work were simply an extension of what was begun by the prophets who preceded him, and the development of temple ordinances and practices continued after his death.

Spoken by him more than a century ago when only four temples had been built, Wilford's earnest plea is even more applicable to a generation of Saints with access to almost 150 temples: "You have had power to . . . redeem your dead. A great many of you have done this, and I hope all of you will continue as long as you have any dead to redeem. Never cease that work while you have the power to enter into the Temple."[1036]

"Portrait of the Prophets" by Doc Christenson

So, what will this generation do with all they have received? In Wilford's words, "Are we living up to our privileges? Are we performing the work required at our hands?"[1037]

NOTES

ACKNOWLEDGMENTS

1. Agnes de Mille, *Martha: The Life and Work of Martha Graham*. (New York City: Random House, 1991).

AUTHOR'S INTRODUCTION

2. N. B. Lundwall, *Temples of the Most High* (Salt Lake City: Press of Zion's Printing & Publishing Co., 1943), 122.

3. Alma 32:26–27.

CHAPTER 1

4. "History of Wilford Woodruff (From His Own Pen)," *Latter-day Saints' Millennial Star* (Liverpool, England: April 1842 – March 3, 1932), 27:23 (June 17, 1865), 374–76; 27:25 (June 24, 1865), 391–92. http://lib.byu.edu/digital/mpntc/az/M.php#latter-star.

5. *Wilford Woodruff's Journal, 1833–1898, Typescript*, edited by Scott G. Kenney, 9 vols. (Midvale, Utah: Signature Books, 1983–1984), 4:414–15, April 28, 1856. Spelling is modernized, and punctuation, capitalization, and paragraphing are sometimes altered for clarity.

6. "History of Wilford Woodruff. {From His Own Pen.)," *Millennial Star* 27:24 (June 17, 1865), 374–75.

7. Throughout this book, "the Church" refers to The Church of Jesus Christ of Latter-day Saints that has been known by various names since it was officially organized on April 6, 1830. See The Book of Mormon 3 Nephi 27; Doctrine and Covenants 115:4; and Joseph Smith and B. H. Roberts, *History of the Church of Jesus Christ of Latter-day Saints* (Salt Lake City: Deseret Book Co., 1970), 2:22, 2:28, 2:62–63.

8. "History of Wilford Woodruff. (From His Own Pen.)," *Millennial Star,* 27:11 (March 11, 1865), 167. "My father, Aphek Woodruff, was born in Farmington, Nov. 11, 1778; he married Beulah Thompson, who was born in 1782, Nov. 29, 1801. She bore three sons–namely, Azmon, born Nov. 29, 1802; Ozem Thompson, born Dec. 22, 1804; myself born March 1, 1807. My mother died with the spotted fever, June 11, 1808, aged 26 years, leaving me fifteen months old. My father's second wife, Azubah Hart, was born July 31, 1792; they were married Nov. 9, 1810; they had six children–viz., Philo, born Nov. 29, 1811, and died by poison adminis-

tered by a physician Nov. 25, 1827; Asahel Hart, born April 11, 1814, and died in Terrehaute [Terre Haute, Indiana], Oct. 18, 1838; Franklin, born March 12, 1816, and died June 1; Newton, born June 19, 1818, drowned Sept. 1820; Julius, born April 22, 1820, and died in infancy; Eunice, born June 19, 1821." Aphek and Beulah's three sons, Azmon, Thompson, and Wilford lived to be 87, 90, and 91 respectively. Four of Aphek and Azubah's sons died before the age of 17. The fifth son, Asahel, died at age 24. Eunice, their only daughter, married Dwight Webster, but did not bear children and died at the age of 33.

9. "History of Wilford Woodruff. (From His Own Pen.)," *Millennial Star* 27:23 (June 10, 1865), 359–60.

10. Matthias F. Cowley, *Wilford Woodruff: History of His Life and Labors As Recorded in His Daily Journals* (Salt Lake City: Bookcraft, 1964), 6. http://books.google.com/books/about/Wilford_Woodruff.html?id=UsoEAAAAYAAJ.

11. "History of Wilford Woodruff. (From His Own Pen.)," *Millennial Star* 27:23 (June 10, 1865), 359–60.

12. Cowley, *Life and Labors*, 6.

13. Ibid., 7–8.

14. "History of Wilford Woodruff. (From His Own Pen.)," *Millennial Star* 27:23 (June 10, 1865), 359.

15. Zion's Camp was an armed expedition from Ohio to Missouri between May and June 1834. The Saints had been driven out of Jackson County, Missouri, in November 1833 and Zion's Camp was formed to provide supplies and support to help protect the Saints and return them to their homes. Wilford Woodruff was one of those who responded to the call for volunteers (see Doctrine and Covenants 103 for revelation received February 24, 1834) when Parley P. Pratt came to his New York home. *Wilford Woodruff's Journal*, 1:7, April 1, 1834. For more information, see Thomas G. Alexander's article, "Wilford Woodruff and Zion's Camp: Baptism by Fire and the Spiritual Confirmation of a Future Prophet," *BYU Studies* 39, no. 1 (2000):130–46. https://ojs.lib.byu.edu/spc/index.php/BYUStudies/.

16. *Wilford Woodruff's Journal*, 2:128, September 25, 1841; 3:361, August 4, 1848.

17. Wilford Woodruff, *Leaves from My Journal* (Salt Lake City: Juvenile Instructor Office, 1882), 20. See also *Wilford Woodruff's Journal*, 1:48, November 15, 1835.

18. See *Wilford Woodruff's Journal*, 1:146, May 5, 1837; and 1:324, April 3, 1839.

19. Ibid., 2:230, May 14, 1843.

20. Ibid., 2:185–86, August 10, 1842.

21. Ibid., 3:93–94, October 15, 1846.

22. "History of Wilford Woodruff. (From His Own Pen.)," *Millennial Star* 27:25 (June 24, 1865), 392.

23. *Wilford Woodruff's Journal*, 3:94, November 4, 1846.

24. Ibid., 3:96, November 24, 1846.

25. Ibid., 3:95, November 12, 1846.

26. Ibid., 3:97, December 10, 1846.

27. Ibid., 4:416, April 28, 1856.

28. Ibid., 5:392, October 26, 1859.

29. Ibid., 5:393, October 28, 1859.

30. Ibid., 7:156, September 25, 1873.

31. Ibid., 8:403, September 13, 1886.

32. Bilious colic was the term given to any severe, sporadic abdominal pain that caused the afflicted person to vomit bile. It was the result of an obstruction or spasm in the intestines; or referred to appendicitis, the passage of gallstones, or other acute conditions.

33. *Wilford Woodruff's Journal*, 7:482, May 4, 1879.

34. Ibid., 9:249, June 1, 1893.

35. "The Temple Workers' Excursion," *Young Woman's Journal*, 5, no. 11 (August 1894): 513. http://contentdm.lib.byu.edu/cdm/compoundobject/collection/YWJ/id/27574/rec/5.

36. *Wilford Woodruff's Journal*, 1:34, June 28, 1835. See also Ibid., 1:16, December 31, 1834. "Be it known that I, Willford Woodruff, do freely covenant with my God that I freely consecrate and dedicate myself, together with all my properties and effects, unto the Lord for the purpose of building up His Kingdom, even Zion, on the earth; that I may keep His law and lay all things before the bishop of His Church, that I may be a lawful heir to the Kingdom of God, even the Celestial Kingdom.

The following is an inventory of my property:	$ cts
One due bill payable in one year	20.00
One trunk and its contents principally books	18.00
Hat, boots and clothing	23.00
One valise	2.50
One English watch	8.00
One rifle and equipments	9.00
One sword	5.00
One pistol	1.50
Also sundry articles	3.00
And notes which are doubtful and uncertain	150.00
Total	$240.00"

37. See Ibid., 8:366–69, Synopsis of Travels and Labors from 1834–1885; and 9:407–8, 440, Synopsis of Wilford Woodruff Travels in the Ministry 1834–1895.

38. Ibid., 7:55, January 20, 1872. On August 21, 1860, Church Historian George A. Smith said that he [Wilford Woodruff] "had done more to preserve the history of this Church than any man on the earth." Ibid., 5:484.

39. *Journal of Discourses*, 26 vols. (Liverpool and London: F. D. and S. W. Richards, 1854–86), 7:98–99, January 10, 1858.

40. "History of Wilford Woodruff," *Millennial Star* 27:25 (June 24, 1865), 39. See also *Wilford Woodruff's Journal*, 9:187, March 1, 1892.

41. *Wilford Woodruff's Journal*, 9:449, March 1, 1897. See "President Woodruff's Birthday," *Deseret Weekly*, March 6, 1897, 371. http://lib.byu.edu/digital/deseret_news/. See also *Wilford Woodruff's Journal*, 9:490, July 9, 1897. This was his favorite hymn, and was sung at his funeral.

42. "Discourse by President Wilford Woodruff," *Millennial Star* 58:20 (May 14, 1896), 307–9. http://contentdm.lib.byu.edu/cdm/compoundobject/collection/

MStar/id/36073/rec/58.

43. Cowley, *Life and Labors,* 423 (referring to *Wilford Woodruff's Journal,* 6:18–25, February 12, 1862).

CHAPTER 2

44. "President Woodruff's Birthday," *Deseret Weekly,* March 6, 1897, 370. http://lib.byu.edu/digital/deseret_news/.

45. Matthias F. Cowley, *Wilford Woodruff: History of His Life and Labors As Recorded in His Daily Journals* (Salt Lake City: Bookcraft, 1964), 33. http://books.google.com/books/about/Wilford_Woodruff.html?id=UsoEAAAAYAAJ.

46. See *Journal of Discourses,* 26 vols. (Liverpool: F. D. and S. W. Richards, 1854–86), 4:100, October 6, 1856.

47. "Discourse by President Wilford Woodruff," *Latter-day Saints' Millennial Star* 58:20 (May 14, 1896), 309. http://contentdm.lib.byu.edu/cdm/compoundobject/collection/MStar/id/36073/rec/58.

48. *Diaries of Reverend Rufus Hawley 1756–1826,* Avon Historical Society. Copy sent to author. Courtesy of Nora Oakes Howard. See Nora's book *Catch'd on Fire: The Journals of Reverend Rufus Hawley, Avon, Connecticut* (The History Press, 2011).

49. "History of Wilford Woodruff," *Millennial Star* 27:11 (March 18, 1865), 168.

50. Wilford Woodruff, *Leaves from My Journal* (Salt Lake City: Juvenile Instructor Office, 1882), 1. *Journal of Discourses,* 11:61, January 22, 1865.

51. *Leaves from My Journal,* 1.

52. *Wilford Woodruff's Journal, 1833–1898, Typescript,* edited by Scott G. Kenney, 9 vols. (Midvale, Utah: Signature Books, 1983–1984), 1:215. Preface to year 1838. Spelling is modernized, and punctuation, capitalization, and paragraphing are sometimes altered for clarity.

53. "Discourse delivered by President Wilford Woodruff at Springville, Tuesday Morning, March 5th, 1889." *Deseret Weekly,* April 6, 1889, 449. http://lib.byu.edu/digital/deseret_news/.

54. *Journal of Discourses,* 18:40, June 24, 1875.

55. Ibid., 13:165–66, December 12, 1869.

56. Ibid., 24:241, July 20, 1884.

57. Ibid., 13:165–66, December 12, 1869.

58. Ibid., 13:321–22, September 5, 1869.

59. *Leaves from My Journal,* 1.

60. Ibid., 1–2. See also *Journal of Discourses,* 18:117, September 12, 1875.

61. Cowley, *Life and Labors,* 22.

62. "Discourse delivered by President Wilford Woodruff at Springville, Tuesday Morning, March 5, 1889," *Deseret Weekly,* April 6, 1889, 450. http://lib.byu.edu/digital/deseret_news/.

63. Ibid.

64. Cowley, *Life and Labors,* 15.

65. *Journal of Discourses,* 11:62, January 22, 1865.

66. Ibid., 8:268–69, August 26, 1860.

67. Cowley, *Life and Labors*, 27.

68. *Leaves from My Journal*, 4.

69. Although Wilford relates this experience in *Leaves from My Journal*, at this point in the narrative most secondary sources include an additional phrase, found only in Matthias F. Cowley's biography of Wilford Woodruff. The additional phrase gives the impression that Robert Mason would benefit from vicarious ordinances after his death: "You will be blest of the Lord after death because you have followed the dictation of my Spirit in this life." See Cowley, *Life and Labors*, 17. Cowley does not cite a source for this additional information.

70. *Leaves from My Journal*, 3. See also *Journal of Discourses*, 4:99, October 6, 1856.

71. That year the Collins Axe Company "paid a premium to bring in the best men in each branch of the business." "Memorandums of Sam Collins 1826–1867," History—Collins Axe Company, http://www.visitcollinsville.com/samcollins.pdf.

72. *Journal of Discourses*, 18:40, June 27, 1875.

73. Cowley, *Life and Labors*, 28.

74. Ibid., 28–29. See also "The Gospel of Jesus Christ," *Millennial Star* 38:30 (July 24, 1876), 467–71.

75. *Journal of Discourses*, 23:126, May 14, 1882.

76. Cowley, *Life and Labors*, 29.

77. George Phippen, Letter to Wilford Woodruff, January 7, 1831, 5, MS 1352, Church History Library, Salt Lake City.

78. Cowley, *Life and Labors*, 29.

79. See endnote 6 above regarding the changing names of the Church of Jesus Christ organized in 1830.

80. I. W. T., "Mormonism in the East." *Boston Investigator*, May 11, 1832. Boston Public Library, Boston, Massachusetts, Microfilm AN2.M4B6414.

81. "History of Wilford Woodruff (From His Own Pen)," *Millennial Star* 27:12 (March 25, 1865), 182. http://contentdm.lib.byu.edu/cdm/compoundobject/collection/MStar/id/8615/rec/27.

82. Ibid.

83. Doctrine and Covenants 75:13.

84. "History of Wilford Woodruff (From His Own Pen)," *Millennial Star* 27:12 (March 25, 1865), 182. http://contentdm.lib.byu.edu/cdm/compoundobject/collection/MStar/id/8615/rec/27.

85. The land purchased by Wilford and his two brothers, Ozem and Azmon, was located on Grindstone Creek. The deeds signed May 3 and June 15, 1832, indicate their property included lots 57 and 70 and comprised a total of 117.34 acres.

86. *Typescript of Autobiography of Zera Pulsipher (1789–1872)*, L. Tom Perry Special Collections, Harold B. Lee Library, Brigham Young University, 7 (hereafter Perry Special Collections).

87. Elijah Cheney and Zerah Pulsipher were both converted to the Gospel in January 1832 through the preaching of Jared Carter. *Typescript of Autobiography of John Pulsipher (1827–1891)*, Perry Special Collections., 1. They and their families were part of what became known as the "Mormon Exodus." See George Knapp Collins,

Spafford, Onondaga County, New York, (Onondaga Historical Association, 1917), 47–48. http://archive.org/details/spaffordonondaga01coll .

88. "President Woodruff's Birthday." *Deseret Weekly*, March 6, 1897, 370. http://lib.byu.edu/digital/deseret_news/.

89. Cowley, *Life and Labors*, 33.

90. Ibid.

91. *Wilford Woodruff's Journal*, 1:6.

92. Doctrine and Covenants 22:1–4.

93. Cowley, *Life and Labors*, 35.

94. Azmon Woodruff and Noah Holton were ordained Elders to lead the new branch of the Church established by Zerah Pulsipher in Richland Township, New York. The church congregations were organized geographically into wards (for larger congregations, led by a bishop) or branches (for smaller congregations, led by a branch president). Initially, there were twelve members in the Richland Branch, including Wilford. *Wilford Woodruff's Journal*, 1:6–7, January 2, 1834.

95. Cowley, *Life and Labors*, 36.

96. The printing press and other copies of the *Book of Commandments* were destroyed by a mob in 1833. Wilford Woodruff's handwritten notes in his own copy of the *Book of Commandments* preserved the unpublished portion of Section 65. *Wilford Woodruff's Journal*, 1:43, September 23–24, 1835.

97. *Leaves from My Journal*, 4.

98. Ibid., 3.

99. Ephesians 2:19.

100. Doctrine and Covenants 22:1. The fullness of the Gospel of Jesus Christ is "the new and everlasting covenant" and it includes individual covenants such as baptism and marriage. See Doctrine and Covenants 66:2, 45:9, 131:2.

CHAPTER 3

101. *Journal of Discourses*, 26 vols. (Liverpool and London: F. D. and S. W. Richards, 1854–86), 5:84, April 9, 1857.

102. "Discourse Delivered by President Wilford Woodruff ... April 6, 1890," *Deseret Weekly*, April 19, 1890, 562. http://contentdm.lib.byu.edu/cdm/compoundobject/collection/desnews4/id/12693/rec/5.

103. *Pearl of Great Price*, Joseph Smith—History 1:54. The four parts of the *Pearl of Great Price* were first published together in 1851, however, the Joseph Smith—History portion was published serially in the *Times and Seasons* in 1842. The account of Moroni's 1823 appearance and his instructions regarding Elijah were included in the April 15, 1842 edition of the *Times and Seasons*, 3: 753–54.

104. *Pearl of Great Price*, Joseph Smith—History, 1:29–39. September 21, 1823.

105. Compare Malachi 4:5–6; Doctrine and Covenants 2; 3 Nephi 24:1. See also Doctrine and Covenants 128:17, 133:64, and 138:46–48.

106. *Wilford Woodruff's Journal, 1833–1898, Typescript*, edited by Scott G. Kenney, 9 vols. (Midvale, Utah: Signature Books, 1983–1984), 2:362–65, March 10, 1844. Spelling is modernized, and punctuation, capitalization, and paragraphing are sometimes altered for clarity.

107. 1 Peter 3:18–19 and Doctrine and Covenants 76:72–73.

108. See Doctrine and Covenants 137, January 21, 1836. See also Ibid., 76:50–70 (February 16, 1832) and *Journal of Discourses,* 22:146–47.

109. Doctrine and Covenants 137:7–9, January 21, 1836.

110. Smith, Joseph, and B. H. Roberts, *History of the Church of Jesus Christ of Latter-day Saints* (Salt Lake City: Deseret Book Co., 1970), 5:425–26.

111. *Journal of Discourses,* 8:266, April 22, 1860.

112. Ibid., 5:84, April 9, 1857. See Doctrine and Covenants 76:50–112 and 1 Corinthians 15:40–42.

113. Prior to this, the ritual of washing the feet of those participating in the School of the Prophets was begun with the first meeting held on January 23, 1833. This was done as directed by the revelation recorded in Doctrine and Covenants 88:138–40. Minutes, January 22–23, 1833, 2–3, The Joseph Smith Papers. Accessed January 19, 2014, http://josephsmithpapers.org/paperSummary/minutes-22-23-january-1833. See also *History of the Church,* 1:323.

114. Exodus 29:4,7; 30:17–37; 40:12–15. Leviticus 8:6, 12. See also John 13:1–16.

115. The first School of the Prophets in Kirtland met from January to April 1833, and priesthood members were instructed on doctrine to prepare them for their eventual missionary work. The second School of the Prophets met in Kirtland during the winter of 1834–1835, and a third met during the winter of 1835–1836. These subsequent Schools were expanded from doctrinal discussions to include additional subjects such as geography, history, philosophy, and languages in accordance with Doctrine and Covenants 88:77–80. (The classes were larger and the washing of feet was not observed as before.) The curriculum of the second School of the Prophets was later included in the Doctrine and Covenants under the heading "Lectures on Faith."

116. Joseph Smith's Journal 1835–1836, January 21–22, 1836, 135–37, The Joseph Smith Papers. Accessed January 28, 2014, http://josephsmithpapers.org/paperSummary/journal-1835-1836?p=135. See also *History of the Church,* 2:379–80. A similar meeting was held on January 28, 1836. See Journal 1835–1836, January 28, 1836, 145–46, The Joseph Smith Papers. Accessed January 19, 2014, http://josephsmithpapers.org/paperSummary/journal-1835-1836?p=145.

117. Journal 1835–1836, February 6, 1836, 152, The Joseph Smith Papers. Accessed January 19, 2014, http://josephsmithpapers.org/paperSummary/journal-1835-1836?p=152. See also *History of the Church,* 2:391.

118. Doctrine and Covenants 97:13–14.

119. Ibid., 105:10–12. See also Ibid., 103.

120. Ibid., 95:8; 105:33.

121. Ibid., 109:36. See also *Journal of Discourses,* 22:332–33, October 8, 1881, for Wilford's description of the remarkable vision he received of the resurrection of the dead after receiving Joseph's letter.

122. *Wilford Woodruff's Journal,* 1:67, April 19, 1836. See Doctrine and Covenants 84:18–23.

123. Richard Lyman Bushman and Jed Woodworth, *Joseph Smith: Rough Stone Rolling* (New York: Alfred A. Knopf, 2005), 319–21.

124. See Doctrine and Covenants 84:18–23.

125. Matthew 17:3.

126. See *Pearl of Great Price*, Abraham 2:9–11; and Doctrine and Covenants 110:11–13. Although these experiences were recorded in Joseph Smith's journal by Warren Cowdery in April 1836 and incorporated into the *Manuscript History of the Church* by Willard Richards in 1843, they were not published publicly until November 6, 1852 in the *Deseret News* and in the November 12, 1853 edition of the *Millennial Star*. The current Section 110 was not included in the 1844 edition of the Doctrine and Covenants, but was incorporated into the next edition of the Doctrine and Covenants which was published in 1876 (and accepted as scripture in the October 1880 General Conference).

127. *Pearl of Great Price*, Joseph Smith—History 1:38. See Doctrine and Covenants 110:14–16.

128. What Joseph Smith understood regarding the connection between the sealing power and the mission of Elijah at the time of Elijah's appearance in 1836 is not clear. The dedicatory prayer on the Kirtland Temple (Doctrine and Covenants 109:35, 38, 46) includes references to "sealing the law" and sealing anointings with power from on high, even before Elijah came. In 1838 David W. Patten included Elijah—along with Moroni, Elias, and John the Baptist—in the list of those who had bestowed upon Joseph Smith "the keys of the dispensation of the fulness of times." See "To the Saints Scattered Abroad," *Elders' Journal of the Church of Jesus Christ of Latter-Day Saints*, 1, no. 3 (July 1838), 42. The best description of Joseph Smith's mindset at the time of the appearance of Elijah, Elias, Moses, and Jesus Christ in the Kirtland Temple is by Richard Bushman in *Rough Stone Rolling*, 319–21. See also *Wilford Woodruff's Journal*, 8:5, 8:154.

129. It was not until September 6, 1842, that Joseph Smith wrote a letter to the Saints explaining for the first time the connection between sealing keys and Elijah's mission to link the generations together. Doctrine and Covenants 128:14–18.

130. Spencer W. Kimball, "A Report of My Stewardship," *The Ensign of The Church of Jesus Christ of Latter-day Saints* (May 1981), 5. Ephesians 4:12–13.

131. Matthew 28:19–20.

132. Moroni 6.

133. Doctrine and Covenants 110:1–10.

134. See explanation of the priesthood by Joseph Smith in *Wilford Woodruff's Journal*, 2:365, March 10, 1844.

135. Ibid., 1:106, November 25, 1836.

136. Ibid., 1:106–8, November 25, 1836.

137. Ibid., 1:118, 216. To be "called" to an assignment or position of service in the Church means one is asked by a Church leader, such as one's Bishop or Stake President, to accomplish a task or to complete specific duties. One serves until officially released by the Church leader.

138. *Wilford Woodruff's Journal*, 1:111–41, December 5, 1836, to April 1837.

139. Ibid., 1:128, April 3, 1837. See also Exodus 30 and 40.

140. Doctrine and Covenants 38:32, 38:38.

141. *Wilford Woodruff's Journal*, 1:128-29, April 3, 1837. On this occasion, the Elders first washed "from head to foot" with soap and water, second with "clear

water," and then with "perfumed spirits." (See also Doctrine and Covenants 89:7 for reference to practice.) On other occasions only water was used for washing and perfumed oil was used for anointing.

142. "Penny" is a reference to the parable of the laborers in the vineyard found in Matthew 20:1–16.

143. *Wilford Woodruff's Journal,* 1:129–30, April 4, 1837. The School of the Prophets was first reestablished in Salt Lake City by Brigham Young in December 1866. Ibid., 6:377, 381. When the School of the Prophets was reinstituted on October 12, 1883, President John Taylor washed the feet of Zebedee Coltrin "as it was done in Kirtland 47 years ago by the Prophet Joseph Smith as an Initiatory ordinance into the School of the Prophets . . . as [Zebedee Coltrin] was the only man living that was in the first School of the Prophets organized by Joseph Smith in Kirtland." Ibid., 8:201.

144. Ibid., 1:131, April 6, 1837.

145. "Mystery of Godliness," *Times and Seasons,* September 15, 1843, 329. http://contentdm.lib.byu.edu/cdm/ref/collection/NCMP1820-1846/id/8618. The endowment as developed in Nauvoo would serve to figuratively bring the Saints into the presence of God to help them prepare for and be worthy of eventually actually being in God's presence.

146. *Wilford Woodruff's Journal,* 1:133, April 6, 1837.

147. Ibid.

148. Ibid., 1:136, April 6, 1837.

149. Ibid., 1:142–43, April 13, 1837.

150. "Discourse Delivered . . . October 19th, 1896, by Pres[iden]t Wilford Woodruff," *Deseret Weekly,* November 7, 1896, 1. http://contentdm.lib.byu.edu/cdm/compoundobject/collection/desnews5/id/26285/rec/8.

151. *Wilford Woodruff's Journal,* 1:276–77, August 9, 1838.

152. Wilford Woodruff, Letter to Asahel Woodruff, dated August 29, 1838, in Robert H. Slover, "A Newly Discovered Wilford Woodruff Letter," *BYU Studies* 15, no. 3 (Spring 1975): 355.

153. *Wilford Woodruff's Journal,* 1:267, July 1, 1838.

CHAPTER 4

154. *Wilford Woodruff's Journal, 1833–1898, Typescript,* edited by Scott G. Kenney, 9 vols. (Midvale, Utah: Signature Books, 1983–1984), 2:165, March 27, 1842. Spelling is modernized, and punctuation, capitalization, and paragraphing are sometimes altered for clarity.

155. "Minutes of a Conference . . . Commencing October 1st, 1841," *Times and Seasons,* October 15, 1841, 576–78. http://contentdm.lib.byu.edu/cdm/ref/collection/NCMP1820-1846/id/9099. See also Joseph Smith and B. H. Roberts, *History of the Church of Jesus Christ of Latter-day Saints* (Salt Lake City: Deseret Book Co., 1970), 4:425.

156. Letter, Phebe Woodruff to Wilford Woodruff, October 6, 1840. Holograph in MS 19509, Church History Library, Salt Lake City.

157. Ibid.

158. See *Journal of Discourses,* 5:85, April 9, 1857. The first documented proxy baptism was on September 12, 1840, when Jane Neyman was baptized by Harvey Olmstead for her deceased son Cyrus. See Alexander L. Baugh, "'For This Ordinance Belongeth to My House': The Practice of Baptism for the Dead Outside the Nauvoo Temple," *Mormon Historical Studies* 1 (Spring 2002): 48. http://mormon historicsites.org/wp-content/uploads/2013/05/MHS3.1Spring2002Baugh.pdf.

159. Documents, Letter to the Council of the Twelve, December 15, 1840, 6, The Joseph Smith Papers. Accessed January 19, 2014, http://josephsmithpapers. org/paperSummary/letter-to-the-council-of-the-twelve-15-december-1840?p=6. See also *History of the Church,* 4:226–32. October 19, 1840.

160. See also *Wilford Woodruff's Journal,* 2:165, 240; Letter Phebe Woodruff to Wilford Woodruff, October 6, 1840. Holograph in MS 19509, Church History Library, Salt Lake City.

161. *Wilford Woodruff's Journal,* 2:165, 240. See also *History of the Church,* 4:231.

162. *Journal of Discourses,* 5:84, April 9, 1857.

163. "Remarks Made at the Salt Lake Stake Conference, Sunday, December 29, 1897 by President Wilford Woodruff," *Deseret Weekly,* December 25, 1897, 34. http://contentdm.lib.byu.edu/cdm/compoundobject/collection/desnews5/id/213 80/rec/20.

164. *Journal of Discourses,* 5:84–85, April 9, 1857.

165. "General Conference," *Latter-day Saints' Millennial Star* (Liverpool, England: April 1842 – March 3, 1932), 49:47 (November 21, 1887), 742–43. http:// contentdm.lib.byu.edu/cdm/compoundobject/collection/MStar/id/32536/rec/49.

166. See John 3:3–5, Article of Faith 4, and Doctrine and Covenants 20:37, 68–74.

167. *Journal of Discourses,* 18:191, April 6, 1876.

168. In explaining Christ's use of the term "paradise" on the cross (Luke 23:43), and the biblical use of "spirits in prison" (1 Peter 3:19), Joseph Smith said, "But what is paradise? . . . What is hell? . . . It is taken from Hades, the Greek, or Sheol, the Hebrew, and the true signification is a world of spirits. Hades, Sheol, paradise, spirits in prison, is all one: it is a world of spirits." *Wilford Woodruff's Journal,* 2:41, June 11, 1843.

169. "The Law of Adoption," *Deseret Weekly,* April 21, 1894, 542. http:// contentdm.lib.byu.edu/cdm/compoundobject/collection/desnews7/id/7443 rec/16.

170. "Discourse by Elder Wilford Woodruff Delivered . . . April 6, 1878," *Deseret Weekly,* May 15, 1878, 226. http://contentdm.lib.byu.edu/cdm/compound object/collection/desnews3/id/2221053/rec/4.

171. "History of Joseph Smith," *Millennial Star* 23:31 (August 3, 1861), 487. (Discourse delivered May 12, 1844.) http://contentdm.lib.byu.edu/cdm/ref/ collection/MStar/id/22276. See also *History of the Church,* 6:366; *Journal of Discourses,* 16:188, http://lib.byu.edu/digital/mpntc/az/J.php#journal-discourses; and February 29, 2012, Letter from the First Presidency restating that the Saints' "preeminent obligation is to seek out and identify [their] own ancestors." "Names Submitted for Temple Ordinances." *Church News and Events.* The Church of Jesus Christ of Latter-day Saints, March 1, 2012. http://www.lds.org/church/news/

names-submitted-for-temple-ordinances.

172. "History of Joseph Smith," *Millennial Star* 23:31, (August 3, 1861), 486. http://contentdm.lib.byu.edu/cdm/ref/collection/MStar/id/22276. See also *History of the Church*, 6:365.

173. According to Susan Easton Black, 97% of proxy baptisms were performed for family members, 203 or 2.98% for friends, and 89 or 1.31% undetermined. "A Voice of Gladness for the Living and the Dead," Presented at Family History Fireside, Brigham Young University, Provo, Utah, February 21, 2003. http://familyhistory.byu.edu/resources/firesides/2003-02-21.pdf.

174. *Nauvoo Baptisms for the Dead, Book A*, 1841, Salt Lake Temple Record, Microfilm No. 183379. Family History Library, Salt Lake City.

175. *Wilford Woodruff's Journal*, 2:455, August 26, 1844.

176. *Journal of Discourses*, 5:84, April 9, 1857.

177. "The Law of Adoption," *Deseret Weekly*, April 21, 1894, 542. http://contentdm.lib.byu.edu/cdm/compoundobject/collection/desnews7/id/7443/rec/16.

178. Doctrine and Covenants 127:6–8.

179. See "Speech Delivered by President B. Young . . . April 6th, 1845," *Times and Seasons*, July 1, 1845, 954–55. http://contentdm.lib.byu.edu/cdm/ref/collection/NCMP1820-1846/id/9684. "I have said that a man cannot be baptized for a woman, nor a woman for a man, and it be valid. I have not used any argument as yet; I want now to use an argument upon this subject."

180. *Journal of Discourses*, 5:84, April 9, 1857.

181. *Wilford Woodruff's Journal*, 7:111, 2:177, 2:204–5, May 29 and August 25, 1842.

182. Ibid., 2:455, August 25, 1844.

183. *Journal of Discourses*, 16:166, August 31, 1873.

184. First Presidency, "To The Saints Scattered Abroad," September 15, 1840; *Times and Seasons*, October 1840, 177–79. http://contentdm.lib.byu.edu/cdm/ref/collection/NCMP1820-1846/id/9373.

185. Account of Joseph Smith's discourse given June 11, 1843, in *Wilford Woodruff's Journal*, 2:240, and quoted in *History of the Church*, 5:423.

186. Doctrine and Covenants 124:29–32.

187. First Presidency, "A Proclamation to the Saints Scattered Abroad," *Millennial Star* 1:11(March 1841), 271, January 15, 1841. http://contentdm.lib.byu.edu/cdm/compoundobject/collection/MStar/id/150/rec/1.

188. In 1840 the population of Nauvoo, Illinois, was only 2,900 and 4,470 in Chicago. The population of Hancock County, Illinois, was 9,946. See United States Census Bureau statistics at http://www.census.gov. Membership of the Church at the end of 1840 was 16,865, with approximately 5,814 still residing in the British Isles. See History 1838–1856, vol. C-1, April 6, 1841, 358–59, The Joseph Smith Papers. Accessed January 19, 2014, http://josephsmithpapers.org/paperSummary/history-1838-1856-volume-c-1-2-november-1838-31-july-1842?p=358.

189. 1 Kings 7:23–25.

190. *Wilford Woodruff's Journal*, 1:348, July 22, 1839.

191. Obadiah 1:21; see also Doctrine and Covenants 103:9–10.

192. "History of Joseph Smith," *Millennial Star* 18:44 (November 1, 1856), 694. Discourse given by Joseph Smith at Church Conference in Nauvoo on October 2, 1841. http://contentdm.lib.byu.edu/cdm/compoundobject/collection/MStar/id/22946/rec/18.

193. Ibid.

194. Doctrine and Covenants 124:28–34. "Minutes of a Conference of The Church of Jesus Christ of Latter-day Saints . . . October 1, 1841," *Times and Seasons,* October 15, 1841, 578. http://contentdm.lib.byu.edu/cdm/ref/collection/NCMP 1820-1846/id/9200. See also *History of the Church,* 4:426.

195. *Wilford Woodruff's Journal,* 2:138, November 21, 1841.

196. "History of Joseph Smith," *Millennial Star* 18:44 (November 1, 1856), 694. http://contentdm.lib.byu.edu/cdm/compoundobject/collection/MStar/id/22946/rec/18.

197. *History of the Church,* 7:282, 292–93.

198. See infra pages 268–72 for information on the eventual reversal of this practice.

199. *Wilford Woodruff's Journal,* 2: 175, May 7, 1842.

200. 2 Kings 5:9–14; John 9:1–7. *Wilford Woodruff's Journal,* 2:165, March 27, 1842.

201. John 5:2–13.

202. "An Epistle of the Twelve, Nauvoo, October 12, 1841," *Times and Seasons,* October 15, 1841, 569. http://contentdm.lib.byu.edu/cdm/ref/collection/NCMP1820-1846/id/9200. See also "An Epistle of the Twelve, To the brethren scattered abroad on the Continent of America," *Millennial Star* 2:8 (December 8, 1841), 122.

203. *Manchester Mormons: the Journal of William Clayton, 1840 to 1842,* edited by James B. Allen and Thomas G. Alexander (Salt Lake City and Santa Barbara: Peregrine Smith, 1974), 212.

204. For a thorough examination of this subject see Jonathan A. Stapley and Kristine L. Wright, "'They Shall Be Made Whole': A History of Baptism for Health," *Journal of Mormon History,* 34, no. 4 (Fall 2008):69–112.

205. *Manchester Mormons,* 209, 212, April 8 and 11, 1841.

206. *Journal of Jared Carter,* 1831–1833, 66–67, May 7, 1832, MS 1441, Church History Library, Salt Lake City.

207. 2 Nephi 31:17–20.

208. *Wilford Woodruff's Journal,* 2:164, March 20, 1842. Wilford also recorded rebaptisms in outlying areas of the Church. For example, see Ibid., 2:413, June 27, 1844.

209. Ibid., 2:165.

210. Ibid., 2:165, March 27, 1842.

211. "Conference Minutes," *Times and Seasons,* April 15, 1842, 763. http://contentdm.lib.byu.edu/cdm/ref/collection/NCMP1820-1846/id/9200.

212. Brigham Young was last rebaptized in July 1875, just two years before his death, along with Wilford Woodruff and other members of the Quorum of the Twelve. See *Wilford Woodruff's Journal,* 7:234.

213. Romans 9:3–8

214. "The Law of Adoption," *Millennial Star* 4:2 (June 1843), 17. http://contentdm.lib.byu.edu/cdm/compoundobject/collection/MStar/id/277/rec/4.

215. Parley P. Pratt, *"A Voice of Warning and Instruction to All People: Or an Introduction to the Faith and Doctrine of the Church of Jesus Christ of Latter-Day Saints, commonly called Mormons"* (New York: W. Sanford, 1837), 99.

216. Ibid., 92.

217. Ibid.

218. "The Law of Adoption," *Millennial Star* 4:2 (June 1843), 19. http://contentdm.lib.byu.edu/cdm/compoundobject/collection/MStar/id/277/rec/4. Romans 8:15–17, 9:3–8; Galatians 4:5–7; Ephesians 1:5.

219. Hebrews 11:40. Doctrine and Covenants 128:18, September 6, 1842. See also *History of the Church*, 5:148–53.

220. Doctrine and Covenants 128:18.

221. Ibid., 128:14.

222. John 3:1–5.

223. "Remarks Made at the Salt Lake Stake Conference, Sunday, December 29, 1897 by President Wilford Woodruff," *Deseret Weekly,* December 25, 1897, 34. http://contentdm.lib.byu.edu/cdm/compoundobject/collection/desnews5/id/21380/rec/20. Wilford spoke of the time when he finally had the opportunity to have his mother sealed to his father. He said, knowing that she "will have a part in the first resurrection . . . this alone would pay me for all the labors of my life." "Talks to the Sisters," Ibid., February 24, 1894, 288. http://contentdm.lib.byu.edu/cdm/compoundobject/collection/desnews7/id/6522/rec/8. See also "The Law of Adoption," Ibid., April 21, 1894, 541, 544. http://contentdm.lib.byu.edu/cdm/compoundobject/collection/desnews7/id/7443/rec/16.

224. *Wilford Woodruff's Journal,* 2:171, 177, April 21 and May 29, 1842.

225. M. Guy Bishop estimates 6,818 proxy baptisms were performed in 1841; no data for 1842; 1,329 in partial records from 1843; and 3,359 in 1844. See "'What Has Become of Our Fathers?': Baptism for the Dead at Nauvoo," *Dialogue* 23, no. 2 (Summer 1990): 88–89, 95. Susan Easton Black, "A Voice of Gladness," *The Ensign of The Church of Jesus Christ of Latter-day Saints,* (February 2004): 35.

CHAPTER 5

226. Journals, The Joseph Smith Papers, 192, March 30, 1836, The Joseph Smith Papers. Accessed January 19, 2014, http://josephsmithpapers.org/paperSummary/journal-1835-1836?p=192.

227. Doctrine and Covenants 124:39–42.

228. 2 Nephi 31:17–20.

229. Doctrine and Covenants 131, May 16–17, 1843.

230. *Wilford Woodruff's Journal, 1833–1898, Typescript,* edited by Scott G. Kenney, 9 vols. (Midvale, Utah: Signature Books, 1983–1984), 2:155, February 19, 1842. Spelling is modernized, and punctuation, capitalization, and paragraphing are sometimes altered for clarity.

231. Ibid., 2:151, January 1, 1842.

232. The *Times and Seasons* newspaper was established in 1839 by Don Carlos Smith and Ebenezer Robinson to publish information about the Church and a variety of general subjects. Wilford Woodruff and John Taylor edited the newspaper from 1842 until April 1844. The *Times and Seasons* was published until February 15, 1846, when the Saints left Nauvoo.

233. The Book of Moses is an extract from Joseph Smith's translation of the Bible, which he began in 1830. Excerpts were first published in 1832. The Book of Abraham contains details about Abraham's life and the creation of the world, similar to the account in Genesis. It originated from the Egyptian papyri purchased by Church members in 1835, and portions of it were published in the *Times and Seasons* in 1842. Both books were included in the 1878 edition of the *Pearl of Great Price*, and then accepted as scripture by the Church membership in 1880.

234. When Joseph Smith was translating the Book of Abraham, he wrote explanations for the illustrations that accompanied his translation. For example, in Facsimile 2 he indicated that figures 3 and 7 represented, in part, "the grand Key words of the Holy Priesthood." *Times and Seasons*, March 15, 1842, 719–21. http://contentdm.lib.byu.edu/cdm/ref/collection/NCMP1820-846/id/9200. These explanations were shared with individuals as early as 1841 and published in the *Times and Seasons*, March 1, 1842, 703–6; and May 16, 1842, 783–84.

235. *Wilford Woodruff's Journal*, 2:155, February 19, 1842.

236. Doctrine and Covenants 138:53–56.

237. Sidney Rigdon and John C. Bennett were among other Church leaders who either caused problems within the Church or left the Church and aided persecution from without, because of the practices of "spiritual wifery" and "plural marriage." April 28, 1842, address to the Nauvoo Relief Society. Andrew F. Ehat and Lyndon W. Cook, *The Words of Joseph Smith: The Contemporary Accounts of the Nauvoo Discourses of the Prophet Joseph* (Provo: Religious Studies Center, Brigham Young University, 1980), 116–17.

238. Ehat and Cook, *Words of Joseph Smith*, 120n5, May 1, 1842.

239. Lucius N. Scovil, "The Higher Ordinances," *Deseret News*, February 20, 1884, 6. http://lib.byu.edu/digital/deseret_news/.

240. Congregations of the Church are organized geographically into wards and branches. A ward is a larger congregation led by a Bishop (similar in responsibilities to a priest or rabbi), and a branch is a smaller congregation led by a Branch President.

241. Ehat and Cook, *Words of Joseph Smith*, 116–17, May 4, 1842. See also Joseph Smith and B. H. Roberts, *History of the Church of Jesus Christ of Latter-day Saints*, 7 vols. (Salt Lake City: Deseret Book Co., 1970), 5:1–2.

242. Joseph Smith Jr., *The Journal of Joseph: The Personal History of a Modern Prophet*, edited by Leland R. Nelson (Provo: Council Press, 1979), 191.

243. Examinations of these parallels can be found in Matthew B. Brown, *Exploring the Connection Between Mormons and Masons* (American Fork, Utah: Covenant Communications, 2009); Anthony W. Ivins, *The Relationship of "Mormonism" and Freemasonry* (Salt Lake City: Deseret News Press, 1934); E. Cecil McGavin, *Mormonism and Masonry*, (Salt Lake City: Bookcraft, 1956).

244. See Exodus 29, 30, 40:12–15. See also Marcus von Wellnitz, "The Catholic Liturgy and the Mormon Temple," *BYU Studies* 21, no. 1 (Winter 1981]: 3–36.

245. See, for example, Andrew F. Ehat, "'They Might Have Known That He Was Not a Fallen Prophet'—The Nauvoo Journal of Joseph Fielding," *BYU Studies* 19, no. 2 (Winter 1979), 145, 147; Heber C. Kimball, Letter to Parley P. Pratt, June 17, 1842, MS Parley P. Pratt Papers, Church History Library, Salt Lake City; Stan Larson, ed., *A Ministry of Meetings: The Apostolic Diaries of Rudger Clawson* (Salt Lake City: Signature Books, 1993), 42.

246. *Wilford Woodruff's Journal*, 2:158–59, 2:170, 2:176, 2:179, 2:180, 2:185, 2:192, 2:245, 2:359, 2:373, 2:539, 2:545; 5:418, 5:482–4. In his handwritten "History of Masonry," Wilford does not draw parallels from Masonic traditions to the temple ordinances or practices. (See reference Ibid., 2:545, May 9, 1845.) His "History of Masonry" is simply a transcription of portions of George Oliver's book, *The Antiquities of Free-masonry: Comprising Illustration of the Five Grand Periods of Masonry, from the Creation of the World to the Dedication of King Solomon's Temple*. (See "History of Masonry," MS 5506, Church History Library, Salt Lake City.)

247. Ibid., 1:131, April 6, 1837.

248. Doctrine and Covenants 110:2–8, April 3, 1836; 76:19–23, February 16, 1832; Joseph Smith—History 1:17, 1820.

249. Bushman, *Joseph Smith: Rough Stone Rolling*, 449–52.

250. Doctrine and Covenants 131:2, May 16, 1843.

251. Ibid., 132:15–17.

252. 1 Corinthians 11:11.

253. On May 29, 1843, Church Patriarch Hyrum Smith was sealed to Mary Fielding and by proxy to his deceased wife Jerusha Barden. That same day Apostle Brigham Young was sealed to Mary Ann Angell and by proxy to his deceased wife Miriam Works; and Apostle Willard Richards was sealed to Jennetta Richards. Other members of the Quorum of the Twelve Apostles who were sealed to their wives: Heber C. Kimball and Vilate Murray in 1841; Orson Hyde and Marinda Johnson in 1845 (also in April 1842 Marinda was sealed to Joseph Smith); Parley P. Pratt to Mary Ann Frost on June 23, 1843, and to his deceased wife Thankful Halsey by proxy on July 24, 1843; Orson Pratt and Sarah Marinda Bates on November 22, 1844; John Taylor and Lenora Cannon on January 30, 1844; Wilford Woodruff and Phebe W. Carter on November 11, 1843; George A. Smith and Bathsheba Bigler on January 20, 1844; William Marks and Rosannah Robinson on October 1, 1843; Lyman Wight and Harriet Benton in May 1844?; Amasa Lyman and Maria Tanner on December 22, 1844?; and William Smith may have been sealed to several women in 1845. Members of the First Presidency, William Law and Sidney Rigdon, and Apostle John E. Page were not sealed to their wives.

254. "Plural marriage" was a term used by the Saints to describe the sealing of one man to more than one woman at the same time. Polygamy is the term generally used to describe this practice and, in this book, the two terms are used interchangeably. Joseph Smith may have been sealed to Fanny Alger in the 1830s in Kirtland, and to Louisa Beaman in 1841 in Nauvoo. Historians disagree on the interpretation of the existing second- and third-hand accounts from those who witnessed or heard about the sealings of Fanny or Louisa to Joseph Smith. See Richard Lyman Bush-

man and Jed Woodworth, *Joseph Smith: Rough Stone Rolling* (New York: Alfred A. Knopf, 2005), 323–27, 437–39; and "Plural Marriage in Kirtland and Nauvoo," October 27, 2014, https://www.lds.org/topics/plural-marriage-in-kirtland-and-nauvoo?lang=eng#19.

255. Doctrine and Covenants 132:18–19.

256. "P. P. Pratt's Proclamation," *Latter-day Saints' Millennial Star* (Liverpool, England: April 1842 – March 3, 1932), 5:10, (March 10, 1845), 151.

257. *Journal of Discourses*, 26 vols. (Liverpool and London: F. D. and S. W. Richards, 1854–86), 18:113, September 12, 1875.

258. Doctrine and Covenants 128:9–10 referring to Matthew 16:18–19.

259. See Matthew 16:19 and 18:18. See also Helaman 10:7.

260. Doctrine and Covenants 109:35; 124:21. See also 2 Corinthians 1:21–22.

261. On October 25, 1831, Joseph explained, "The order of the High-priesthood is that they have power given them to seal up the Saints unto eternal life." See Minutes, October 25–26, 1831, The Joseph Smith Papers. Accessed January 19, 2014, http://josephsmithpapers.org/paperSummary/minutes-25-26-october-1831?p=2. See also Romans 4:11; 2 Corinthians 1:22; Ephesians 1:13–14 and 4:30; Doctrine and Covenants 1:8–10 and 68:12. See also Doctrine and Covenants 77:8, 11–13 regarding power to seal up to eternal life received in 1832 and 76:50–70 that describes those who will inherit the celestial kingdom, as "sealed by the Holy Spirit of promise."

262. *Journal of Discourses*, 24:243–44, July 20, 1883.

263. *Wilford Woodruff's Journal*, 2:326–27, November 11, 1843.

264. Wilford was apparently the first to record the use of the term "seal" in reference to individuals rather than ordinances or covenants. Ibid., 2:340, January 21, 1844.

265. Ibid., 2:326–27, November 11, 1843.

266. Doctrine and Covenants 132:36.

267. Ibid., 132:37, 39, 52.

268. Jacob 2:27–35.

269. Doctrine and Covenants 132:36.

270. Ibid., 42:22 and 49:16. *See also* the original section 101 in the 1835 edition of the Book of Doctrine and Covenants as reprinted under the title: "On Marriage," in *Times and Seasons*, October 1, 1842, 939–40. http://content dm.lib.byu.edu/cdm/ref/collection/NCMP1820-1846/id/9200. Section 101 was removed in the 1876 edition of the Doctrine and Covenants when Section 132 was added.

271. The inclusion of washing and anointing ordinances and the clothing described in Exodus 28–30 and 39–40 was also part of the "restoration of all things."

272. According to George D. Smith, at the time of Joseph Smith's death in 1844, thirty men had married additional wives. By the time the Saints left Nauvoo in 1846, 153 men had been sealed to a total of 587 wives. When the Manifesto was issued in 1890, he estimates approximately 2,450 husbands were plurally married to 6,200 wives. See "Nauvoo Roots of Mormon Polygamy, 1841–46: A Preliminary Demographic Report," *Dialogue: A Journal of Mormon Thought*, 27, no. 1 (Spring 1994), 1–72. Stanley Ivins' study of polygamy in Utah concluded that of 1,784 polygamist men, 66% married one plural wife, 21.3% married two plural wives,

6.7% married three plural wives, 3% married four, and less than 3% married five or more plural wives. See "Notes on Mormon Polygamy," *Utah Historical Quarterly* 35, no. 4 (Fall 1967): 313–14, 316.

273. The practice of plural marriage was not publicly acknowledged until Orson Pratt's speech in Salt Lake City on August 29, 1852. See *Journal of Discourses*, 1:58. Doctrine and Covenants 132 was not included in the Doctrine and Covenants until a new edition was printed in 1876.

274. "Autobiography of Phebe Carter Woodruff," Edward W. Tullidge, *The Women of Mormondom* (Salt Lake City: Tullidge and Crandall, 1887), 399–400.

275. From a speech Phebe Woodruff gave at a meeting of 3,000 women held January 13, 1870, in Salt Lake City, Utah. "The Great Indignation Meeting of the Ladies of Salt Lake City to Protest Against the Passage of Cullom's Bill," *Deseret Evening News*, 554, January 19, 1870. http://contentdm.lib.byu.edu/cdm/compound object/collection/desnews2/id/41816/rec/1.

276. *Journal of Discourses*, 24:244, July 20, 1883.

277. Ibid.

278. Ibid., 12:389–90, May 19, 1867.

279. Ibid., 13:168, December 12, 1869.

280. Ibid., 24:244, July 20, 1883.

281. *Wilford Woodruff's Journal*, 2:308–9, September 17–18, 1843. Rhoda Foss was sealed as Willard Richards's sixth wife in 1851. Willard died in 1854 and in 1857 Rhoda was sealed to Franklin D. Richards (Willard's nephew) as his seventh wife.

282. Historians disagree on whether Sarah Elinor Brown and Mary Caroline Barton were sealed to Wilford on August 2, 1846. His journal record does not specifically state that a marriage/sealing ceremony was performed at the meeting held that day with Brigham Young. See *Wilford Woodruff's Journal*, 3: 64–65. However, less than four weeks later, after Wilford had warned them not to continue going out at night with young men in the camp, a second meeting with Brigham Young was held. Sarah and Mary were given the option of leaving Wilford's family at that time, and both chose to do so. The fact that Willard Richards prophesied to them that in the future they would "be willing to have their right arm severed from their body if that would restore them to the place and station they were now losing" is the best evidence that they had been sealed to Wilford rather than simply affiliating with the group over which he had stewardship or that they had only been unofficially "adopted" into his family. See Ibid., 3:71–73, August 26 and 29, 1846.

283. According to Mike Quinn, Wilford asked Brigham Young's permission to marry Leonard Hardy's daughter Clarissa in 1852. D. Michael Quinn, *The Mormon Hierarchy: Origins of Power* (Salt Lake City: Signature Books, 1994), 605. I found no evidence that Clarissa and Wilford were ever married/sealed. (Clarissa became Alonzo H. Russell's third plural wife on December 11, 1853.) On January 23, 1857, Wilford sought permission to be sealed to Lydia Maxline, but I found no evidence that Wilford and Lydia were subsequently married/sealed. See Ibid., 5:11.

284. Ibid., 7:407. Some historians believe Wilford's last plural marriage was to Lydia Mary Olive Mamreoff von Finkelstein Mountford ("Madame Mountford") on September 20, 1897, aboard a ship off the coast of California. Thomas G. Alexander's research proves this was physically impossible because Madame

Mountford was presenting lectures in San Francisco on the 20th and 21st, while Wilford was onboard the ship from September 20th to 22nd traveling between San Francisco, California and Astoria, Oregon. See Thomas G. Alexander, *Things in Heaven and Earth: The Life and Times of Wilford Woodruff, a Mormon Prophet* (Salt Lake City, Signature Book, 1993), 327–29. Madame Mountford died March 22, 1917, and was posthumously sealed to Wilford Woodruff on November 20, 1920.

285. Wilford Woodruff, Letter to Blanche Woodruff, September 16, 1894, *Emma S. Woodruff Collection 1832–1919*, MS 2081, Reel 1 Folder 5, Church History Library, Salt Lake City.

286. "Remarks by President Wilford Woodruff . . . May 19 and 20, 1889," *Deseret Weekly*, June 22, 1889, 823. http://lib.byu.edu/digital/deseret_news/.

287. *Journal of Discourses*, 15:346–47, February 23, 1873.

288. Prayer circles were part of religious practice anciently and in nineteenth-century Protestant gatherings, and are mentioned in Church historical documents as early as the 1833 School of the Prophets in Kirtland, Ohio. Joseph Smith may have introduced the prayer circle as part of the temple ceremonies when he first administered the endowment on May 4, 1842. The first full prayer circle, with both women and men, was formed on September 28, 1843, the day the washing, anointing, and endowment of women began. Prayer circles continued in Nauvoo between 1843 and 1846 and during the exodus to Utah (see, for example, *Wilford Woodruff's Journal*, 3:191, May 30, 1847). Prayer circles were recommenced formally in Salt Lake City in 1851 (Ibid., 4:43). At the direction of Brigham Young, Wilford and the other apostles established separate prayer circles in 1858 (Ibid., 5:202). Wilford records meeting in 45 prayer circles in 1857; 36 with the Quorum of the Twelve in 1858; 33 with the apostles and 32 with his own circle in 1859; 30 with the apostles and 32 with his own circle in 1860; 45 in 1861; 78 in 1862; 66 in 1863; 66 in 1864, etc. Prayer circles continued within the Church, both separate from temple worship and as part of the temple endowment ceremony, until 1978 when the First Presidency directed that all prayer circles outside the temple be discontinued. See George Tate, "Prayer Circle," *Encyclopedia of Mormonism*, ed. Daniel H. Ludlow, 4 vols. (New York: Macmillan, 1992), 3:1120–121; Hugh Nibley, "The Early Christian Prayer Circle," *BYU Studies* 19, no. 1(Fall 1978): 41–78; D. Michael Quinn, "Latter-day Saint Prayer Circles," Ibid., 79–105.

289. *Wilford Woodruff's Journal*, 2:329, December 2, 1843.

290. Ibid., 2:332.

291. *Journal of Discourses*, 23:131, May 14, 1882.

292. *Wilford Woodruff's Journal*, 2:271. See also Revelation 1:5–6.

293. Doctrine and Covenants 76:55-59, February 16, 1832 and 132:19–20, May 14, 1843. See also *Journal of Discourses*, 5:50.

294. *Wilford Woodruff's Journal*, 2:329, December 2, 1843. Wilford writes about receiving his "anointing preparatory to further blessings," indicating receipt of the initiatory anointings. "History of Brigham Young," *Millennial Star* 26:17 (April 23, 1864), 263. http://contentdm.lib.byu.edu/cdm/compoundobject/collection/MStar/id/27922/rec/26. See also *History of the Church*, 5:527.

295. Daniel Tyler, "Temples," *Juvenile Instructor*, 15, no. 10 (May 15, 1880): 111.

296. Doctrine and Covenants 131:5, 2 Peter 1:10–11.

297. History 1838–1856, vol. C-1, Addenda June 27, 1839, The Joseph Smith Papers. Accessed January 19, 2014, http://josephsmithpapers.org/paperSummary/history-1838-1856-volume-c-1-2-november-1838-31-july-1842?p=543. Joseph Smith references Ephesians 1:13:14 and John 14:12-27. See also Doctrine and Covenants 77: 11 and Revelation 14:1, 22:4; 2 Peter 1:10–11; Doctrine and Covenants 84:33–39; and Andrew F. Ehat, "Joseph Smith's Introduction of Temple Ordinances and the 1844 Mormon Succession Question," (Master's thesis, Brigham Young University, 1982), 47–48, www.scribd.com/doc/35205295/.

298. 2 Peter 1:3–10, 16–19. Note that Peter linked one's calling and election to "the more sure word of prophecy" which Joseph Smith defined as "a man's knowing that he is sealed up unto eternal life, by revelation and the spirit of prophecy, through the power of the Holy Priesthood." Doctrine and Covenants 131:5. See also John 14:12–27.

299. Doctrine and Covenants 131:2–3; 132:19–20. However, Joseph Smith also made it clear that simply participating in an ordinance was not the only requirement; each person would need to prove to the Lord that he or she is willing "to serve Him at all hazard." Joseph Smith, Discourse, ca. June 1839, *Willard Richards Pocket Companion*, 19; The Joseph Smith Papers. http://josephsmithpapers.org/paperSummary/report-of-instructions-circa-june-1839-as-reported-by-willard-richards. See also *History of the Church*, 3:379–81; Abraham 3:25; and Doctrine and Covenants 98:12–15, 101:4–5. Joseph Smith apparently proved himself, and his exaltation was "sealed upon him" prior to his death. See Doctrine and Covenants 132:49–50.

300. From Willard Richards' notes, *History of the Church*, 5:554–55, August 27, 1843. See also Ehat and Cook, *Words of Joseph Smith*, 243–47.

301. *Pearl of Great Price*, Abraham 3:24–25.

302. Ibid.

303. *Journal of Discourses*, 22:209, January 9, 1881.

304. On September 28, 1843, Joseph Smith "was by common consent and unanimous voice chosen President of the quorum and anointed and ord[ained] to the highest and holiest order of the priesthood (and companion [Emma])." See Ehat, "Joseph Smith's Introduction of Temple Ordinances," 55, quoting Joseph Smith's diary. The narrative in *History of the Church*, 6:39, reads "By the common consent and unanimous voice of the council, [Joseph Smith] was chosen president of the special council." At least sixty-six men and women received their second anointings during Joseph's lifetime. In addition, Brigham Young administered second anointings to twenty-four individuals in the Nauvoo Temple.

305. Hyrum and Mary (Fielding) Smith received their second anointings on October 8, 1843; William and Rosannah (Robinson) Marks on October 22, 1843; Newel K. and Elizabeth Ann (Smith) Whitney on October 27, 1843; Joseph Smith Sr. (by proxy) and Lucy (Mack) Smith on November 12, 1843; Alpheus and Lois (Lathrop) Cutler on November 15, 1843; Reynolds and Thirza (Stiles) Cahoon on November 12, 1843. See George A. Smith, "Christmas Assembly in St. George," *Millennial Star* 37:5 (February 2, 1875), 66. Discourse on December 25, 1874.

306. Heber C. and Vilate (Murray) Kimball received their second anointings on January 20, 1844; Parley P. and by proxy Thankful (Halsey) Pratt on January 21,

1844; Orson Hyde on January 25, 1844; Orson Pratt on January 26, 1844; Willard and Jennetta (Richards) Richards on January 27, 1844; Wilford and Phebe W. (Carter) Woodruff on January 28, 1844; John and Leonora (Cannon) Taylor on January 30, 1844; George A. and Bathsheba W. (Bigler) Smith on January 31, 1844.

307. *Wilford Woodruff's Journal,* 2:344–45.

308. Ibid., 2:393. See also Ibid., 6:306–7, December 26, 1866, regarding the manner in which the ceremony should be performed. The first post-Nauvoo second anointings were administered on December 31, 1866. See Ibid., 6:310.

309. Nauvoo Relief Society Minute Book, March 30, 1842, 19, The Joseph Smith Papers. Accessed January 19, 2014, http://josephsmithpapers.org/paper Summary/nauvoo-relief-society-minute-book?p=19. The Female Relief Society was officially organized on March 17, 1842, with its leadership ordained to preside over the society, Ibid, 3. On March 30, 1842, 'Prest. J. Smith arose—spoke of the organization of the Society—said he was deeply interested that it might be built up to the Most High in an acceptable manner . . . that the Society should move according to the ancient Priesthood. . . . Said he was going to make of this Society a kingdom of priests as in Enoch's day," Ibid, 19. Compare with synopsis of Joseph's remarks in *History of the Church,* 4:570. "Spoke of the organization of the Female Relief Society; said he was deeply interested that it might be built up to the Most High in an acceptable manner; . . . [a]ll . . . should move according to the ancient Priesthood. . . . The Lord was going to make of the Church of Jesus Christ a kingdom of Priests, a holy people, a chosen generation, as in Enoch's day."

310. Exodus 19:6.

311. History 1838–1856, vol. C-1, April 28, 1842, 500, The Joseph Smith Papers. Accessed January 19, 2014, http://josephsmithpapers.org/paperSummary/history-1838-1856-volume-c-1-2-november-1838-31-july-1842?p=500. See also Andrew F. Ehat and Lyndon W. Cook, *The Words of Joseph Smith: The Contemporary Accounts of the Nauvoo Discourses of the Prophet Joseph* (Provo,: Religious Studies Center, Brigham Young University, 1980), 119. See also *History of the Church,* 4:602.

312. Nauvoo Relief Society Minute Book, 37–38. He [Joseph] spoke of delivering the keys to this Society and to the church . . . that the keys of the kingdom are about to be given to them . . . as well as to the Elders." Minutes also in *Wilford Woodruff's Journal,* 2:199. Compare with *History of the Church,* 4:604–5: "He spoke of delivering the keys of the Priesthood to the Church, and said that the faithful members of the Relief Society should receive them in connection with their husbands." According to the Nauvoo Relief Society Minutes, it was Newel K. Whitney who made the following statement to the Relief Society on May 28, 1842: "In the beginning God created man male and female and bestow'd upon man certain blessings peculiar to a man of God, of which woman partook, so that without the female all things cannot be restor'd to the earth it takes all to restore the Priesthood. It is the intent of the Society, by humility and faithfulness; in connexion (sic) with those husbands that are found worthy." Nauvoo Relief Society Minute Book, 58. The Joseph Smith Papers. Accessed January 19, 2014. http://josephsmith papers.org/.

313. On September 21, 1883, Wilford Woodruff recalled: "During December 1843 and January, February, and March, 1844, Joseph Smith gave the Twelve

Apostles their Endowments, their First and Second Anointings, and taught them many things appertaining to the Kingdom of God." "Testimony of Wilford Woodruff, Concerning Remarks by Joseph Smith to the Twelve Apostles and Others," quoted in Alexander L. Baugh and Susan Easton Black, eds., *Banner of the Gospel: Wilford Woodruff* (Provo: Religious Studies Center, Brigham Young University; Salt Lake City: Deseret Book, 2010), 361n45.

314. Doctrine and Covenants 132:19–20. See account of Joseph Smith's discourse given June 11, 1843, in *Wilford Woodruff's Journal*, 2:240.

315. Joseph Smith's discourse given April 8, 1844. This phrase is in the accounts recorded in the diaries of Joseph Smith and William Clayton. See Ehat and Cook, *Words of Joseph Smith*, 362–65. For the version recorded by Wilford Woodruff, see *Wilford Woodruff's Journal*, 2:388–89. See also the amalgamated version in *History of the Church*, 6:319.

316. See for example, *Wilford Woodruff's Journal*, 2:340–52, January 20–February 28, 1844. The notable exceptions were Orson Hyde and Orson Pratt who received their second anointings singly, before their wives. (See Ibid., 2:343, January 25–26, 1844.)

CHAPTER 6

317. "General Conference," *Latter-day Saints' Millennial Star* (Liverpool, England: April 1842 – March 3, 1932), 53:26 (June 29, 1891), 403. http://contentdm. lib.byu.edu/cdm/compoundobject/collection/MStar/id/31248/rec/53.

318. *Journal of Discourses*, 26 vols. (Liverpool and London: F. D. and S. W. Richards, 1854–86),13:164–65, December 12, 1869.

319. Doctrine and Covenants 128:18. *Wilford Woodruff's Journal, 1833–1898, Typescript*, edited by Scott G. Kenney, 9 vols. (Midvale, Utah: Signature Books, 1983–1984), 3:131, February 16, 1847.

320. "Minutes of a Conference . . . Commencing October 1st, 1841," *Times and Seasons*, October 15, 1841, 576–78. http://contentdm.lib.byu.edu/cdm/ref/collection/NCMP1820-1846/id/9099.

321. "Baptism for the Dead," *Times and Seasons*, April 15, 1842, 761. See also Joseph Smith and B. H. Roberts, *History of the Church of Jesus Christ of Latter-day Saints* (Salt Lake City: Deseret Book Co., 1970), 4:599.

322. Joseph Smith, discourse given April 8, 1844, recorded in accounts by William Clayton and Thomas Bullock. See Andrew F. Ehat and Lyndon W. Cook, *The Words of Joseph Smith: The Contemporary Accounts of the Nauvoo Discourses of the Prophet Joseph* (Provo,: Religious Studies Center, Brigham Young University, 1980), 362–65. Compare version in *Wilford Woodruff's Journal*, 2:388-89 and that recorded by Willard Richards, "History of Joseph Smith," *Millennial Star* 23:18 (May 4, 1861), 280. http://contentdm.lib.byu.edu/cdm/compoundobject/collection/MStar/id/22276/rec/23. See also *History of the Church*, 6:319.

323. *Wilford Woodruff's Journal*, 2:341–42, January 21, 1844. See also *History of the Church*, 6:184.

324. The phrase "plan of salvation" was used by Joseph Smith as early as June 1830 when he began his revision of the Bible. See *Pearl of Great Price*, Moses 6:62.

See transcription of original revelation in Revelations and Translations, Old Testament Revision 1, 15, The Joseph Smith Papers. Accessed January 19, 2014, http://josephsmithpapers.org/paperSummary/old-testament-revision-1?p=15. The phrase is explained in a letter dated January 22, 1834, published under the heading "The Elders of the Church in Kirtland, to Their Brethren Abroad" in *The Evening and Morning Star*, April 1834, 152. "The great plan of salvation is a theme which ought to occupy our strict attention, and be regarded as one of heaven's best gifts to mankind." http://contentdm.lib.byu.edu/cdm/compoundobject/collection/NCMP1820-1846/id/28104/rec/89. See also *History of the Church*, 2:23.

325. Doctrine and Covenants 132:45–48.

326. *Wilford Woodruff's Journal*, 2:359–66, March 10, 1844.

327. Ibid., 2:362, March 10, 1844. See also *History of the Church*, 6:251.

328. Ibid., 2:362. See also *History of the Church*, 6:251–52.

329. Ibid., 2:364, March 10, 1844.

330. "Baptism for the Dead," *Times and Seasons*, April 15, 1842, 759–61. http://contentdm.lib.byu.edu/cdm/ref/collection/NCMP1820-1846/id/9200. See also *History of the Church*, 4:595–99.

331. *Wilford Woodruff's Journal*, 2:359–66. See also *History of the Church*, 6:313. April 7, 1844.

332. Ehat and Cook, *Words of Joseph Smith*, 241, August 13, 1843, discourse regarding the death of Elias Higbee. See also *History of the Church*, 5:530.

333. "The Law of Adoption," *Deseret Weekly*, April 21, 1894, 541–44. http://contentdm.lib.byu.edu/cdm/compoundobject/collection/desnews7/id/7443/rec/16.

334. Ibid.

335. Some of the couples who had their children sealed to them were George A. and Bathsheba Smith, Newel K. and Elizabeth Whitney, Willard and Jennetta (by proxy) Richards, Orson and Sarah Pratt, Amasa and Maria Lyman, George and Mary Miller, Howard and Martha Coray, Orson and Marinda Hyde, Heber and Vilate Kimball, David and Mary Candland, Orson and Catherine Spencer, as well as Hyrum and Jerusha Smith (by proxy). See Nauvoo Sealings and Adoptions, 1846–1857, Family History Library Special Collections, Salt Lake City, Microfilm No. 183374, Book A, 227, 283, 377, 385, 389, 415, 561.

336. Brigham Young, *Journal of Discourses*, 16:186, September 4, 1873.

337. Editor, "The Law of Adoption," *Millennial Star* 5:12 (May 1844), 194; Romans 9:3–8. For other reviews of the introduction of temple ordinances in Nauvoo, see Andrew F. Ehat, "Joseph Smith's Introduction of Temple Ordinances and the 1844 Mormon Succession Question," (Master's Thesis, Brigham Young University, 1982). http://www.scribd.com/doc/35205295/Joseph-Smith-s-Introduction-of-Temple-Ordinances-and-the-1844-Mormon-Succession-Question-by-Andrew-Ehat; and Devery S. Anderson and Gary James Bergera, *Joseph Smith's Quorum of the Anointed, 1842–1845: A Documentary History* (Salt Lake City: Signature Books, 2005).

338. Doctrine and Covenants 84:33, 38.

339. *Journal of Discourses*, 18:128, October 8, 1875.

340. Exodus 19:5–6.

341. August 13, 1843, discourse regarding the death of Elias Higbee as record-ed by Willard Richards. See Ehat and Cook, *Words of Joseph Smith*, 241, 300; compare *History of the Church*, 5:530–31.

342. See also Joseph Smith Translation Hebrews 7:3.

343. Doctrine and Covenants 84:33–34.

344. *History of the Church*, 5:555, August 27, 1843.

345. Several of the women sealed to Joseph Smith for eternity only were mar-ried to men who did not join the Church: 1) Ruth Vose Sayers, 2) Mary Elizabeth Rollins Lightner, and perhaps 3) Sarah Kingsley Howe Cleveland. Prescindia Lathrop Huntington Buell's husband had been baptized but was no longer partici-pating in the Church, and Sylvia Sessions Lyon's husband was excommunicated from the Church from 1842 to 1846. Four women had husbands who were faithful members of the Church: 1) Patty Bartlett Sessions, 2) Marinda Nancy Johnson Hyde, 3) Elvira Annie Cowles Holmes, and 4) Zina Diantha Huntington Jacobs. Mary, Prescindia, and Zina were resealed to Joseph Smith for eternity and to Brigham Young for mortality; Sylvia was resealed to Joseph for eternity and to Heber C. Kimball for mortality; and Elvira was resealed to Joseph for eternity and her husband Jonathan for mortality in the Nauvoo Temple in 1846 (see infra endnote 391). Patty was resealed to Joseph Smith for time and eternity in 1867.

346. Joseph Smith made this statement March 4, 1844, when meeting with the First Presidency, members of the Twelve, the Nauvoo Temple committee, and others to discuss how to allocate the Church's resources at the time. His decision was to "put all our forces on the Temple." "History of Joseph Smith," *Millennial Star* 23:1 (January 5, 1861), 6. http://contentdm.lib.byu.edu/cdm/compoundobject /collection/MStar/id/22276/rec/23. See also *History of the Church*, 6:230.

347. Plural marriage led to internal dissension within the Church. As a result, William Law—Joseph Smith's former counselor in the First Presidency who was excommunicated in April 1844—filed a lawsuit in Hancock County in May 1844 accusing Joseph of adultery. Then in June, William along with several others, published the first and only issue of the *Nauvoo Expositor* in an effort to expose the practice of polygamy. Their printing press was destroyed by the June 10 order of the Nauvoo City Council and Mayor Joseph Smith. Joseph and Hyrum Smith were charged with inciting a riot and they surrendered to the authorities after Governor Ford promised they would be protected. They were incarcerated in Carthage Jail on June 25, 1844, to await trial on charges of treason, and killed on June 27.

348. E. Cecil McGavin, *Nauvoo Temple* (Salt Lake City: Deseret Book Compa-ny, 1962), 56. See also "Discourse by Elder Wilford Woodruff Delivered . . . April 6, 1878," *Deseret Weekly*, May 15, 1878, 226. http://contentdm.lib.byu.edu/cdm/ compoundobject/collection/desnews3/id/2221053/rec/4.

349. *Wilford Woodruff's Journal*, 2:419, July 9, 1844.

350. Ibid., 2:433–40.

351. For detailed analysis of the succession issues, see Ehat, "Joseph Smith's Introduction of Temple Ordinances," 108–40; Ronald Esplin, "Joseph, Brigham and the Twelve: a Succession of Continuity," *BYU Studies* 21, no. 3 (Summer 1981): 301–41.

352. For an analysis of the strength of their claims, and the standing of others such as Lyman Wight and William Smith, see D. Michael Quinn, "The Mormon Succession Crisis of 1844," *BYU Studies* 16, no. 2 (Winter 1976): 187–233.

353. "The Temple Workers' Excursion," *Young Woman's Journal* 5, no. 11 (August, 1894): 513. See also *Wilford Woodruff's Journal*, 8:5–6, January 16, 1881.

354. "History of Joseph Smith," *Millennial Star* 25:15 (April 11, 1863), 231. http://contentdm.lib.byu.edu/cdm/compoundobject/collection/MStar/id/7990/rec/25. See also *History of the Church*, 7:233.

355. "W. Woodruff's Address to The Church of Jesus Christ of Latter-day Saints," *Millennial Star* 5:7 (December 1844), 109–10. http://contentdm.lib.byu.edu/cdm/compoundobject/collection/MStar/id/390/rec/5.

356. Ibid., 111.

357. *Journal of Discourses*, 17:191–92, October 7, 1874.

358. "An epistle of the Twelve, to the Church of Jesus Christ of Latter-day Saints in all the world," *Times and Seasons,* January 15, 1845, 779. http://contentdm.lib.byu.edu/cdm/ref/collection/NCMP1820-1846/id/9684.

359. *Wilford Woodruff's Journal*, 2:444, August 18, 1844, is quoted in *History of the Church*, 7:255.

360. Ibid., 2:444, 2:447 is quoted in *History of the Church*, 7:256, 259.

361. *Wilford Woodruff's Journal*, 2:440, August 9, 1844.

362. *Journal of Discourses*, 4:229, February 22, 1857.

363. *Wilford Woodruff's Journal,* 2:454–55, August 25, 1844.

364. When Brigham was asked if the Saints should resume officiating in baptisms for the dead, he replied that he "had no counsel to give upon that subject at present, but thought it best to attend to other matters in the meantime." From "Manuscript History of Brigham Young" in *History of the Church*, 7:254.

365. *Journal of Discourses*, 16:269, October 8, 1873.

366. *Wilford Woodruff's Journal*, 3:252–53, August 8, 1847.

367. *History of the Church*, 7:261.

368. *Wilford Woodruff's Journal*, 2:455, August 25, 1844. Wilford and Phebe had previously been baptized by George A. Smith on May 29, 1842 (Ibid., 2:177), and August 25, 1842 (Ibid., 2:204–5), for these same relatives, but they were repeating the ordinances "In consequence of there being no [official] record kept in the above baptisms, we [had] to be baptized again, and women were baptized for men which is not legal." Ibid., 7:111.

369. Ibid., 2:458, August 28, 1844.

370. "Extract from President Young's Letter [dated June 27, 1845]," *Millennial Star* 6:6 (September 1, 1845), 91. http://contentdm.lib.byu.edu/cdm/compound object/collection/MStar/id/1387/rec/6.

371. "Manuscript History of Brigham Young" in *History of the Church*, 7:534.

372. Stanley B. Kimball, ed., *On the Potter's Wheel: The Diaries of Heber C. Kimball*, (Salt Lake City: Signature Books in association with Smith Research Associates, 1987), 168. http://signaturebookslibrary.org/?p=1790.

373. "Manuscript History of Brigham Young" in *History of the Church*, 7:543.

374. See daily totals for December 10–31, 1845, in Ibid., 7:542–58.

375. Ibid., 7:553, December 26, 1845.

376. Ibid., 7:566.

377. Polygamy is defined as having more than one spouse at the same time and includes both polygyny, a man having more than one wife, and polyandry, a woman having more than one husband. Historians disagree regarding the use of the term "polyandry" in describing Joseph Smith's sealings to married women due to the fact that the extant records do not definitively state whether the women were sealed to him in a ceremonial or priesthood sense only or were also married to him in a physical, sexual, financial, and/or social sense. Relationships formed by these women through marriage to their first spouse ("for time" or life on earth) and sealing to Joseph Smith "for eternity" only—with the sealing have no effect until the life hereafter—would be considered consecutive, not polyandrous marriages. However, the term polyandry is applicable to those women who left but did not divorce the husbands they had been married to civilly, and became the physical wives of men to whom they had been or were later sealed.

378. Governor Thomas Ford, Letter to Hancock County Sheriff Jacob Backenstos, December 29, 1845, MS 6057, "Thomas Ford Letters to J. B. Backenstos, 1845." Church History Library, Salt Lake City. See also *History of the Church*, 7:562–64, January 4, 1846.

379. "Manuscript History of Brigham Young" in *History of the Church*, 7:567.

380. On July 24, 1846, eleven members of the Quorum of Twelve met together regarding the administration of the sealing ordinance. They agreed that "no man has a right to attend to the ordinance of sealing except the President of the Church or those who are directed by him so to do." *Wilford Woodruff's Journal*, 3:62. In his October 8, 1866 Conference address, Brigham Young stated that Joseph Smith's instructions were, should he die, no one had authority to seal except Brigham, the President of the Quorum of the Twelve. *Wilford Woodruff's Journal*, 6:300.

381. Ibid., 3:130–32, February 16, 1847.

382. Ibid., 6:553, June 18, 1870. See also *Journal of Discourses*, 16:186, September 4, 1873.

383. *Journal of Discourses*, 24:52, January 27, 1883.

384. *Wilford Woodruff's Journal*, 6:553.

385. Parley P. Pratt, *"A Voice of Warning and Instruction to All People: Or an Introduction to the Faith and Doctrine of the Church of Jesus Christ of Latter-Day Saints, commonly called Mormons"* (New York: W. Sanford, 1837), 99. Another perspective on the Church practice of adoption through baptism comes from the observations of surveyor John Williams Gunnison, who wrote the following to his commanding officer, Captain Howard Stansbury: "The Book of [Doctrine and] Covenants teaches that baptism is duly administered by being fully immersed in the water. . . . The further peculiarity of the subject consists in a vicarious immersion of living persons for their dead friends, who have never had the opportunity, or neglected it when living. This is called 'Baptism for the Dead.' . . . All those who are thus admitted to salvation will be added to the household of the baptized person at the resurrection, who will then . . . do as our Lord did at the grave of Lazarus, and call them forth in the name of Jesus." Lieut. J. W. Gunnison, *The Mormons, or, Latter-day Saints, in the Valley of the Great Salt Lake*, (Philadelphia: J. B. Lippincott & Co., 1852), 45–46. https://books.google.com/books?isbn= 142901931X.

386. On June 15, 1892, Wilford had thirty-six members of his family adopted to Joseph Smith, beginning with his own father Aphek Woodruff. See *Wilford Woodruff's Journal,* 9:204.

387. In fact, the practice would later be modified to allow a woman, after being sealed as the spiritual wife of a priesthood leader, to have her earthly husband adopted into the newly created priesthood family. See *Wilford Woodruff's Journal,* 7:401, March 1, 1878. See also Daniel H. Wells to Wilford Woodruff, May 26, 1890, in Devery S. Anderson, ed., *The Development of LDS Temple Worship 1846–2000: A Documentary History* (Salt Lake City: Signature Books, 2011), 86.

388. "Manuscript History of Brigham Young" in *History of the Church,* 7:566, January 7, 1846.

389. Sealings of children were both to living and deceased parents. See "Temple Ordinance Chronology," 1975 Church Almanac, F5–F6; and *Nauvoo Sealings and Adoptions, 1846–1857,* FHL Special Collections, Microfilm No. 183374, Book A, 227, 283, 377, 385, 389, 415, 561.

390. See Devery S. Anderson and Gary James Bergera, eds., *The Nauvoo Endowment Companies 1845–1846* (Salt Lake City: Signature Books, 2005), 551, 565–66, 581–87, 609; Gordon Irving, "The Law of Adoption: One Phase of the Development of the Mormon Concept of Salvation," 1830–1900, *BYU Studies* 14, no. 3 (Spring 1974): 294; Jonathan A. Stapley and Kristine L. Wright, "Adoption Sealing Ritual in Mormonism," *Journal of Mormon History,* 37, no. 3 (Summer 2011): 53–117.

391. The five married women who chose to be sealed to Joseph Smith (by proxy) for eternity and their husbands for mortality in the Nauvoo Temple were: Jane Tibbetts Luddington, Phoebe Watrous Woodworth, Cordelia Calista Morley Cox, Elvira Anne Cowles Holmes, and Lucinda Pendleton Harris. See Anderson and Bergera, eds., *The Nauvoo Endowment Companies 1845–1846,* 423, 464, 505, 581.

392. Ibid., 566. Other posthumous adoptions to Joseph Smith's priesthood lineage as the head of the final dispensation did not take place until the St. George Temple was completed in 1877, thirty-one years later. See *Wilford Woodruff's Journal,* 7:340–41.

393. Joseph Smith's mother Lucy Mack Smith did participate in ordinances in the Nauvoo Temple, renewing all the ordinances she had received during Joseph Smith's lifetime. Those who would later officiate in the ordinances in the Nauvoo Temple repeated their endowment on December 10, 1845, and Lucy Mack Smith joined them on December 11, 1845. See *History of the Church,* 7:543–44.

394. See, for example, *Wilford Woodruff's Journal,* 7:144–45, July 1, 1873.

395. Brigham Young, *The Journal of Brigham: Brigham Young's Own Story in His Own Words,* edited by Leland R. Nelson (Provo: Council Press, 1980), 128, February 3, 1846. See also *History of the Church,* 7:579, February 3, 1846.

396. Based on Church Historian George A. Smith's calculations in the 1850s, the figure was 5,634. In 1995 the total number of endowments reported was 5,615. See "No Sacrifice Too Great," *Church News,* December 2, 1995. http://www.lds churchnews.com/articles/26617/No-sacrifice-too-great.html#. For daily figures see "Manuscript History of Brigham Young," January 1 to February 7, 1846, in *History of the Church,* 7:560–80. In addition to endowments, at least 594 people—172 men and 422 women—received their second anointing, including nine men by proxy.

The number of marriage sealings (monogamous and plural) performed between 1842 and 1846 was 1,303 (206 by proxy). Adoptions (children sealed to their parents; and men, with their families, sealed to other men) numbered 294, of which 202 were non-biological adoptions to church leaders. See *Nauvoo Sealings, Adoptions, and Anointings: A Comprehensive Register of Persons Receiving LDS Temple Ordinances, 1841–1846* (Salt Lake City: The Smith-Pettit Foundation, 2005), Appendix I; and Richard O. Cowan, *Temple Building Ancient and Modern,* (Provo: Brigham Young University Press, 1971), 29.

397. Ogden Kraut, comp., *L. John Nuttall Diary Excerpts* (Salt Lake City: Pioneer Press, 1994), 14, February 7, 1877.

398. *Wilford Woodruff's Journal,* 6:245–47, September 17, 1865.

399. See infra endnote 913.

400. *Journal of Discourses,* 19:12, May 12, 1877.

401. Kraut, *Nuttall Diary,* 14, February 7, 1877.

402. *Wilford Woodruff's Journal,* 6:247, September 17, 1865.

CHAPTER 7

403. "Special Conference in Manchester, December 14th, and 15th, 1845," *Latter-day Saints' Millennial Star* 7:1, (Liverpool, England: April 1842 – March 3, 1932), (January 1, 1846), 4.

404. "Special General Conference," *Millennial Star* 7:1, (January 1, 1846), 1–2. http://contentdm.lib.byu.edu/utils/getfile/collection/MStar/id/1392/filename/1393.pdf.

405. *Wilford Woodruff's Journal, 1833–1898, Typescript,* edited by Scott G. Kenney, 9 vols. (Midvale, Utah: Signature Books, 1983–1984), 3:254–55, Aug 8, 1847.

406. *Wilford Woodruff's Journal,* 3:38–39, April 14, 1846.

407. Ibid., 3:39.

408. Ibid., 3:39, April 30, 1846.

409. Doctrine and Covenants 124:32.

410. *Wilford Woodruff's Journal,* 3:41, April 30, 1846. For information on the Hosanna Shout see http://eom.byu.edu/index.php/Hosanna_Shout.

411. Ibid., 3:46. A public dedication of the Nauvoo Temple was held on May 1, 1846. Wilford opened the meeting and Orson Hyde offered the dedicatory prayer.

412. Ibid., 3:41–48.

413. Ibid., 3:132, February 16, 1847.

414. See Doctrine and Covenants 136 and *Wilford Woodruff's Journal,* 3: 116–17, January 14–15, 1847.

415. See for example, Elden J. Watson, ed., *Manuscript History of Brigham Young, 1846–1847* (Salt Lake City, 1971), 493, January 6, 1847. A record of those who wanted to be adopted into the families of various church leaders was kept. For example, a list of 275 individuals requesting adoption into Brigham Young's family can be found in *Nauvoo Sealings and Adoptions, 1846–1857*, Microfilm No. 183374, Book A, 787–94, Family History Library (hereafter FHL), Special Collections, Salt Lake City.

416. *Wilford Woodruff's Journal*, 3:118. See also Doctrine and Covenants 136:4.

417. Ibid., 3:119.

418. Ibid.

419. Ibid., 3:130, February 16, 1847.

420. Brigham Young, *Journal of Discourses*, 26 vols. (Liverpool and London: F. D. and S. W. Richards, 1854–86), 2:314, July 8, 1855.

421. Ibid.

422. It is interesting to note that Brigham Young sought doctrinal clarification from Joseph Smith rather than praying to God for further revelation, and Joseph's advice was to follow the direction of the Spirit. See another reference to Joseph Smith's instruction in *Wilford Woodruff's Journal*, 4:391, January 13, 1856.

423. Brigham Young, *The Journal of Brigham: Brigham Young's Own Story in His Own Words*, edited by Leland R. Nelson, (Provo: Council Press, 1980), 209, February 23, 1847.

424. Ibid.

425. Ibid.

426. Ibid.

427. *Wilford Woodruff's Journal*, 3:260.

428. Ibid., 3:132–33, February 16, 1847.

429. Brigham Young, *Journal of Discourses*, 6:307–8, April 8, 1853.

430. *Wilford Woodruff's Journal*, 3:250, August 7, 1847.

431. Emphasis in original. *Journal of Discourses*, 6:306–8, April 8, 1853.

432. *Wilford Woodruff's Journal*, 3:234, July 24, 1847. See also Wilford Woodruff, "The Pioneers," *The Contributor* (August 1880), 253. https://archive.org/stream/contributor0111eng#page/252/mode/2up/search/wilford+woodruff.

433. "Discourse Delivered by President Wilford Woodruff at the General Conference . . . April 6, 1891," *Deseret Weekly*, April 25, 1891, 554. http://content dm.lib.byu.edu/cdm/compoundobject/collection/desnews4/id/18928/rec/33. See also Wilford Woodruff's speech on July 24, 1898: "Pioneer Park Dedicated," *Deseret Evening News*, July 25, 1898, 1. http://chroniclingamerica.loc.gov/lccn/sn83045555/1898-07-25/ed-1/seq-1/.

434. The "Old Fort" was located three blocks south and three blocks west of the temple block. Two additions to the fort, the North Fort and the South Fort were later added to accommodate expected arrivals. The total area after the additions was 660' x 1980', and incorporated a bowery in the old section and two corrals, one in the north end and one in the south.

435. *Wilford Woodruff's Journal*, 3:249, August 6, 1847.

436. Ibid.

437. Ibid., 3:250–51, August 8, 1847.

438. *Journal of Discourses*, 1:324.

439. Ibid., 2:8–9, October 23, 1853.

440. *Wilford Woodruff's Journal*, 3:249, August 6, 1847. Ogden Kraut, "Rebaptism," 23. http://www.ogdenkraut.com/REBAPTISM.htm.

441. James Jackson Woodruff, "A Brief Sketch of the Life of James Jackson Woodruff, Pioneer of 1847," July 24, 1926, in *Chronicles of Courage*, 8 vols. (Salt Lake

City: Daughters of Utah Pioneers, 1990–97), 2:127–29. *Wilford Woodruff's Journal*, 3:267, September 5, 1847.

442. *Wilford Woodruff's Journal*, 6:72, August 23, 1862.

443. Ibid., 3:283, October 12, 1847.

444. Ibid., 3:288.

445. Ibid., 3:294–95.

446. Ibid., 3:301–2.

447. Ibid., 3:353.

448. Ibid., 3:358–59, July 18–22, 1848. "Shuah C. Woodruff October 28, 1847–July 22, 1848. (8 months and 25 days.)"

449. Ibid., 3:433–34.

450. Ibid., 3:577.

451. Ibid., 3:577–78, October 14, 1850. (Five days after arriving in the Valley, Wilford moved his two cabins from the Pioneer Fort, located at about 300 South and 300 West, to his lot adjacent to the Temple Block on the corner of what are now called South Temple and West Temple streets.) Fewer than 150 people had traveled from Winter Quarters to the Salt Lake Valley with Wilford Woodruff and the other pioneers in the summer of 1847. When Wilford returned with his family in 1850, the population of Salt Lake City numbered over 6,100.

452. *Journal of Discourses*, 6:120, December 6, 1857.

453. Ibid., 6:140, 142, December 27, 1857.

454. The Mormon Battalion was a force of 497 volunteers, the only religiously based unit in the history of the United States military. The Battalion was mustered out to serve in the Mexican-American War (1846–1848), but did not fight in any battles. However, their service helped both the Church and the United States by proving the loyalty of the Saints to the United States and by helping to literally clear the way for settlement in the West by building a wagon road from Santa Fe, New Mexico, to San Diego, California.

455. *Wilford Woodruff's Journal*, 3:336. Other authors have stated that Wilford performed nine baptisms for the dead on this occasion; however his journal record states he only performed one proxy baptism. He rebaptized one woman for remission of sins, then baptized her as proxy for her daughter and also baptized eight others including Samuel H. Smith's son (who was ten years old). According to Alexander L. Baugh, the only other proxy baptism recorded before the font was completed adjacent to the Endowment House in 1856 was performed in City Creek on August 21, 1855. On that occasion Margaret E. Moffatt was baptized for Lyrena E. Moffatt by Ezra T. Benson. See "'For This Ordinance Belongeth to My House': The Practice of Baptism for the Dead Outside the Nauvoo Temple," *Mormon Historical Studies* 3 (Spring 2002): 54. http://mormonhistoricsites.org/wp-content/uploads/2013/05/MHS3.1Spring2002Baugh.pdf. See also Microfilm No. 183382, Family History Library, Salt Lake City, Utah.

456. See B. H. Roberts, *A Comprehensive History of the Church of Jesus Christ of Latter-day Saints*, 6 vols. (Salt Lake City, Deseret News Press, 1930), 3:386n10. This is the first recorded endowment following the cessation of ordinances in the Nauvoo Temple in April 1846. It was presumably administered according to Joseph Smith's instructions, given May 1, 1842, that the rich must receive the keys of the kingdom

in the temple, but "the poor may get them on the mountain top as did Moses." Andrew F. Ehat and Lyndon W. Cook, *The Words of Joseph Smith: The Contemporary Accounts of the Nauvoo Discourses of the Prophet Joseph* (Provo: Religious Studies Center, Brigham Young University, 1980), 119–20. See also *History of the Church*, 4:608.

457. *Wilford Woodruff's Journal*, 5:13, February 1, 1857.

458. The Council House was originally constructed to house the government of the State of Deseret, organized in 1849. However, the State of Deseret was not recognized by the United States government, and by the time the building was completed in 1851, the Territory of Utah had been established. The Territorial Legislature met in the Council House from 1851 to 1855.

459. *Wilford Woodruff's Journal*, 4:14. February 20, 1851. See also *Endowment House Records, 1851–1854*, Microfilm No. 183390 and No. 183393, Family History Library, Special Collections, Salt Lake City.

460. In 1851, 469 (211 men and 258 women) were endowed. During the year 1852 there were 522 men and 696 women who received their endowment, a total of 1,218. In 1854, 535, (233 men and 302 women) were endowed. See Gilbert Bradshaw, "The Council House as a House for Sacred Ordinances in the Early Church," 3–4.

461. *Wilford Woodruff's Journal*, 4:47, 4:90, 4:211, 4:250–51, 4:256, 4:298.

462. Ibid., 4:211. Wilford and Phebe were originally sealed by Hyrum Smith in Nauvoo on November 11, 1843, but because it was not officially recorded, they were resealed by Brigham Young in the Council House.

463. Brigham Young, *Journal of Discourses*, 16:186, September 4, 1873.

464. *Wilford Woodruff's Journal*, 2:240, and quoted in *History of the Church*, 5:423.

CHAPTER 8

465. Wilford Woodruff, *Journal of Discourses*, 26 vols. (Liverpool and London: F. D. and S. W. Richards, 1854–86), 9:223, July 15, 1855.

466. *Wilford Woodruff's Journal, 1833–1898, Typescript*, edited by Scott G. Kenney, 9 vols. (Midvale, Utah: Signature Books, 1983–1984), 3:259, August 15, 1847. "As soon as we get up some [adobe] Houses for our families we shall go to work to build another Temple & as soon as a place is prepared we shall commence the Endowments long before the Temple is built & we shall take time & each step the Saints take let them take time enough about it to understand it. Every thing (sic) at Nauvoo went with a rush."

467. For more information on the Endowment House, see James Dwight Tingen, "The Endowment House, 1855–1889," Senior History Research Paper, L. Tom Perry Special Collections, Harold B. Lee Library, Brigham Young University, Provo, Utah, 1974; and Lisle Brown, "'Temple Pro Tempore': The Salt Lake City Endowment House," *Journal of Mormon History*, 34, no. 4 (Fall 2008): 1–68.

468. *Wilford Woodruff's Journal*, 4:316, May 5, 1855.

469. Ibid., 4:407–8, March 18, 1856. In his journal Wilford states he spent the day in the Council House, so it is not clear whether the Council House was still being used at this time for temple ordinances, or if his children were endowed in the Endowment House and he also spent time in the Council House that day.

470. *Wilford Woodruff's Journal*, 5:27–28. Mary Carter was born March 22, 1814, and died September 8, 1851. The fact that Wilford was not resealed to Mary Meek Giles Webster on this occasion is noteworthy due to the fact that they were sealed for time and eternity in 1852.

471. Brigham Young, *Journal of Discourses*, 16:187, September 4, 1873.

472. Discourse of Parley P. Pratt delivered at Quarterly Conference in Farmington, Utah, *Wilford Woodruff's Journal*, 4:342. October 20, 1855.

473. Ibid., 4:407, March 17, 1856.

474. Brigham Young, Heber C. Kimball, and Wilford Woodruff visited the workshop on Temple Square where masons were preparing the font. Ibid., 440.

475. *Journal of Discourses*, 4:43, 52.

476. John 5:1–4.

477. *Wilford Woodruff's Journal*, 4:458–59.

478. Ibid., 4:460. October 2, 1856.

479. Ibid., 4:461. The font had to be filled with buckets from City Creek which ran by the Temple Block. Ibid., 4:524, December 30, 1856.

480. *Journal of Discourses*, 4:97, October 6, 1856.

481. *Wilford Woodruff's Journal*, 4:463, October 5, 1856.

482. In spite of the fact that the dedication of the font in 1856 included the words, "We now dedicate this font to baptize the living and the living for the dead," according to Wilford's journal the only baptisms performed in the first eight years were for the living.

483. *Wilford Woodruff's Journal*, 5:42, March 23, 1857.

484. "Foreign Correspondence," *Millennial Star* 19:35 (August 29, 1857), 557. http://contentdm.lib.byu.edu/cdm/compoundobject/collection/MStar/id/2993/rec/19.

485. *Wilford Woodruff's Journal*, 6:173. In his annual summary for 1864, Wilford described the dedication of the new font as specifically for proxy baptisms. Ibid., 7:101.

486. Ibid., 6:240, August 19, 1865.

487. Between 1855 and 1884 54,170 persons received their washings and anointings and endowments in the Endowment House. Between 1855 and 1889, there were 68,767 sealings: 31,052 living couples were sealed and 37,715 couples were sealed by proxy. See Tingen, "The Endowment House, 1855–1889."

488. During the Sixth Session from 1856 to 1857, when the Territorial Legislature of Utah was rebaptized, the Territorial Council consisted of Heber C. Kimball, Daniel H. Wells, Albert Carrington, Franklin D. Richards, Wilford Woodruff, Leonard E. Harrington, Benjamin F. Johnson, Isaac Morley, William Fenshaw, William H. Dame, Lorin Farr, Lorenzo Snow and John Stoker. Council officers were Leo Hawkins, John T. Caine, George D. Grant, Samuel L. Sprague, Richard Harrison, and Cyrus H. Wheelock. Members of the House of Representatives included Hosea Stout, Hiram B. Clawson, Albert P. Rockwood, Samuel W. Richards, Daniel Spencer, William W. Phelps, James W. Cummings, Jesse C. Little, Alexander McRae, Joseph A. Young, Thomas Grover, John D. Parker, Chauncey W. West, Jonathan C. Wright, James C. Snow, Aaron Johnson, David Evans, Jacob G. Bigler, George Peacock, N. W. Bartholomew, Isaac C. Haight, James Lewis,

Isaac Bullock, Peter Maughan and Enoch Reese. The officers of the House were James Ferguson, James H. Martineau, William H. Kimball, Brigham Young Jr., William Derr, and Jesse Haven.

489. *Wilford Woodruff's Journal,* 4:524. Of the Territorial Legislators who were rebaptized, five were concurrently in the Quorum of Twelve: Brigham Young, Heber C. Kimball, Wilford Woodruff, Lorenzo Snow, and Franklin D. Richards; three were future members of the Twelve: Daniel H. Wells, Brigham Young Jr., and Albert Carrington.

490. Ibid., 4:502, December 7, 1856.

491. Ibid., 4:504, December 8, 1856.

492. *Journal of Discourses,* 13:323, September 5, 1869.

493. *Wilford Woodruff's Journal,* 4:147, December 21, 1856.

494. The list of twenty-seven questions expanded from thirteen questions asked by Brigham Young at a priesthood meeting on November 3, 1856. See Gustave O. Larson, "The Mormon Reformation," *Utah Historical Quarterly,* 26, no. 1 (January 1958): 45.

495. Wilford Woodruff, Letter to George A. Smith, February 2, 1857, *Wilford Woodruff Journals and Papers 1828–1898,* MS 1352, Church History Library, Salt Lake City.

496. See Richard E. Bennett, "Wilford Woodruff and the Rise of Temple Consciousness among the Latter-day Saints, 1877–84," in *Banner of the Gospel: Wilford Woodruff,* edited by Alexander L. Baugh and Susan Easton Black (Provo: Religious Studies Center, Brigham Young University, 2010). The phrase "temple consciousness" was first used by Professor N. L. Nelson in his article "Temple Consciousness for the Dead" published in the *Improvement Era,* March 1940.

497. *Journal of Discourses,* 16:269, October 8, 1873.

498. Ibid., 15:77, April 8, 1872; 9:325–26, April 8, 1862; 17:270–71, May 8, 1874; 18:127, October 8, 1875; 21:302, August 1, 1880.

499. The standing army of the United States after the war with Mexico was only 10,317, so the force sent to Utah was substantial. See John Whiteclay Chambers II, ed., *The Oxford Companion to American Military History,* (Oxford: Oxford University Press, 1999), 50.

500. *Wilford Woodruff's Journal,* 5:69, July 24, 1857.

501. Ibid., 2:42, 2:253–54, 2:272; 3:334, 3:407–9, 3:464; 4:176; 5:140–41; 6:6; 7:261, 7:460–61. See also *Journal of Discourses,* 12:275–76; 22:341–42, 22:346; 24:237, 24:243; 25:11, 25:38–9.

502. *Journal of Discourses,* 7:104–5, January 10, 1858.

503. Ibid., 5:270, September 27, 1857.

504. This legislation was designed "to punish and prevent the practice of polygamy in the Territories of the United States" and under this act, bigamy was punishable by a $500 fine and imprisonment up to five years. In addition, it established a limit of $50,000 of real property that a religious organization in a territory of the United States could hold; any amount exceeding that limit was to be forfeited and escheated to the United States government.

505. The Poland Act redefined the jurisdiction of Utah courts by giving the United States district courts exclusive jurisdiction over all civil and criminal cases in

the Territory of Utah. The Poland Act also eliminated the territorial marshal and attorney and transferred their duties to a federal marshal and a United States Attorney. The Act altered the rules which applied to juries, so anyone practicing polygamy could not serve as a juror.

506. Ibid., 6:378, December 2, 1867.

507. *Wilford Woodruff's Journal,* 6:307–9, December 26, 1866.

508. Ibid., 6:307, 6:317, 6:324–27, 6:332–33, 6:366–67, 6:379, December 30, 1866–December 10, 1867. The apostles were divided into three teams to administer the second anointings. One group met in the Historian's Office, one in Brigham Young's Office, and one in the Endowment House. Ibid., 6:317.

509. Ibid., 6:384, December 31, 1867.

510. *Journal of Discourses,* 12:13–14, May 19, 1867.

511. In May 1831 Joseph Smith received a revelation regarding organizing the church according to God's laws, including the law of consecration, that all would receive their portions according to their individual circumstances, wants and needs. Doctrine and Covenants 51:2–3. In March 1832 Joseph Smith was told to establish a system for the welfare of the poor, as "a permanent and everlasting establishment and order unto my church . . . for if ye are not equal in earthly things, ye cannot be equal in heavenly things," Doctrine and Covenants 78:4, 6. The storehouse for the poor was to be kept "by the consecrations of the church," Doctrine and Covenants 83:6. In a revelation given in June 1834 the Lord explained that the law of consecration is a "law of the celestial kingdom; And Zion cannot be built up unless it is by the principles of the law of the celestial kingdom; otherwise I cannot receive her unto myself," Doctrine and Covenants 105:4–5. See infra endnote 36 regarding Wilford's consecration of all his earthly belongings to the Church when he arrived in Kirtland in 1834. See also Doctrine and Covenants 42:30–42; 51:1–15; 58:34–36; 78:1–22; and 105:1–9, 27–30.

512. *Journal of Discourses,* 17:73, May 8, 1874.

513. An example of the rules from the United Order established in St. George: "We will not take the name of Deity in vain, nor speak lightly of his character, or of sacred things. We will pray with our families morning and evening and also attend to secret prayer. We will observe and keep the Word of Wisdom, according to the spirit and the meaning thereof. We will treat our families with due kindness and affection, and set before them an example worthy of imitation. In our families and intercourse with all persons, we will refrain from being contentious or quarrelsome, and we will cease to speak evil of each other, and will cultivate a spirit of charity towards all. We consider it our duty to keep from acting selfishly or from covetous motives, and will seek the interest of each other and the salvation of all mankind. We will observe the Sabbath day to keep it holy, in accordance with the revelations. . . . In our apparel and deportment we will not pattern after nor encourage foolish and extravagant fashions. . . . We will be simple in our dress and manner of living, using proper economy and prudence in the management of all entrusted to our care. . . . We will honestly and diligently labor and devote ourselves and all we have to the 'order' and to the building of the kingdom of God." See B. H. Roberts, *A Comprehensive History of the Church of Jesus Christ of Latter-day Saints,* 6 vols. (Salt Lake City, Deseret News Press, 1930), 4:485–86.

514. *Journal of Levi Mathers Savage*, (Provo: Brigham Young University Press, 1955), 15.

515. *Wilford Woodruff's Journal*, 7: 233, July 13, 1874.

516. Ibid., 7:234.

517. Ibid.

518. Ibid., 7:239.

519. Isaiah 2:2.

CHAPTER 9

520. *Journal of Discourses*, 26 vols. (Liverpool and London: F. D. and S. W. Richards, 1854–86), 8:203. October 29, 1876.

521. *Wilford Woodruff's Journal, 1833–1898, Typescript*, edited by Scott G. Kenney, 9 vols. (Midvale, Utah: Signature Books, 1983–1984), 7:33, October 6, 1871. Spelling is modernized, and punctuation, capitalization, and paragraphing are sometimes altered for clarity.

522. *Journal of Discourses*, 17:250, October 9, 1874.

523. Charles L. Walker, Andrew Karl Larson, and Katharine Miles Larson, *Diary of Charles Lowell Walker*, 2 vols. (Logan: Utah State University Press, 1980), 1:413–14.

524. Account of Joseph Smith's discourse given June 11, 1843, in *Wilford Woodruff's Journal*, 2:240, and quoted in *History of the Church*, 5:423.

525. *Journal of Discourses*, 18:113–14, September 12, 1875.

526. Ibid., 18:114, September 12, 1875. Matthew 16:19. See also *Wilford Woodruff's Journal*, 8:154: "And my reflections were these that while the Lord holds Moroni responsible for delivering the record of the Book of Mormon to Joseph Smith, and John the Baptist for delivering the Aaronic Priesthood and Peter James and John in delivering the Melchizedek Priesthood and Apostleship to Joseph Smith, and Elijah and Moses for delivering the keys which they held, So will the God of Heaven hold all men from Joseph Smith to the last Deacon responsible for the manner and use they make of the Holy Priesthood and keys that are bestowed upon them."

527. *Journal of Discourses*, 13:165, December 12, 1869.

528. *Wilford Woodruff's Journal*, 1:163.

529. *Journal of Discourses*, 12:276–77, July 19, 1868.

530. Ibid., 22:210, January 9, 1881.

531. Ibid., 15:138, August 24, 1872.

532. Ibid., 18:191, April 6, 1876.

533. See, for example, *Wilford Woodruff's Journal*, 7:180, 221, 227, 244, 262, 263, 276, 277, 328.

534. Wilford Woodruff, "Epistle," *The Contributor* (April 1887): 235; *Wilford Woodruff's Journal*, 6:538, April 14, 1870; 7:292, November 16, 18, 1876; 7:341, March 24, 1877; and 7:607, December 2, 1880.

535. *Wilford Woodruff's Journal*, 7:176, 7:180, April 7 and May 3, 1874.

536. Ibid., 7:220–22, March 13–16, 18, 23, 1875.

537. Ibid., 7:244.

538. Alfred Andrews, *Genealogical History of Deacon Stephen Hart and His Descendants* (New Britain: Austin Hart, 1875). *Wilford Woodruff's Journal*, 7:265–68, January 28, February 9, 14–18, March 22, 1876.

539. Ibid., 7:276–77, June 20, 22, 1876.

540. Ibid., 6:390, January 24, 1868. See also Joseph Smith and B. H. Roberts, *History of the Church of Jesus Christ of Latter-day Saints* (Salt Lake City: Deseret Book Co., 1970), 6:183–84, January 21, 1844.

541. "Discourse by President Wilford Woodruff," *Latter-day Saints' Millennial Star* 58:20 (May 14, 1896), 309. http://contentdm.lib.byu.edu/cdm/compound object/collection/MStar/id/36073/rec/58.

542. Ibid.

543. *Wilford Woodruff's Journal*, 7:287. However, after Brigham Young's death, John Taylor reopened the Endowment House on November 29, 1877. See Ibid., 7:384. Initially if was for use by those who could not travel to St. George because of age or health, and President Taylor allowed marriages to be performed there for time but not sealed for eternity. The use of the Endowment House continued even after the Logan and Manti Temples were completed in 1884 and 1888 respectively. In October 1889 Wilford Woodruff ordered the building razed when an allegedly unauthorized sealing was performed there. (See Official Declaration – 1 in the Doctrine and Covenants.) It was demolished in November 1889. "The Endowment House Going," *Salt Lake Daily Tribune*, (November 17, 1889), 4.

544. *Wilford Woodruff's Journal*, 7:288.

545. Ibid., 2:197, December 31, 1842.

546. Ibid., 7:291, November 9, 1876.

547. Ibid., 1:106, November 25, 1836. See infra page 39.

548. Ibid., 7:291, November 9, 1876.

549. For a history of the construction of the St. George Temple, see Blaine Yorgason, Richard A. Schmutz, and Douglas D. Alder, *All That Was Promised: The St. George Temple and the Unfolding of the Restoration* (Salt Lake City: Deseret Book, 2012).

550. *Wilford Woodruff's Journal*, 7:292, November 13, 1876; 7:297, December 25, 1876; and 7:305, January 1, 1877.

551. Ibid., 7:292, November 13, 1876.

552. Ibid., 7:297, December 25, 1876.

553. Ibid., 7:297, December 27, 28, 29, 30, 1876.

554. Ibid., 7:303, January 1, 1877.

555. Ibid.

556. Ibid.

557. Ibid., 7:304, January 1, 1877.

558. Ibid., 7:309.

559. Ibid., 7:313.

560. Ibid., 7:314–15.

561. Ibid., 7:317.

562. Ibid., 7:318.

563. Ibid., 7:319.

564. Ibid., 7:321, January 9, 1877.

565. Ibid. See also Walker et al, *Diary of Charles Lowell Walker*, 1:445, January 9, 1877.

566. *Wilford Woodruff's Journal*, 4:6, January 19, 1851.

567. Ibid., 3:259, August 15, 1847.

568. *Journal of Discourses*, 10:309, June 11, 1864. This idea was also suggested during the presidencies of John Taylor and Wilford Woodruff. See, for example, Merle H. Graffan, ed., *Salt Lake City School of the Prophets Minute Book*, (Palm Desert: ULC Press), October 12, 1883; and George Q. Cannon's January 14, 1894, address "Blessings Not Appreciated," *Deseret Weekly*, March 10, 1894, 349. http://content dm.lib.byu.edu/cdm/compoundobject/collection/desnews7/id/6755/rec/10.

569. See also *Wilford Woodruff's Journal*, 4:391, January 13, 1856. "I say to you don't hurry in the ordinances. Don't do what you ought not. It is not time to hurry. We should not undertake to do now what we ought to do 50 years hence. . . . You will be just as busy as you can be to do the things which are to be done to day."

570. Ibid., 7:321, January 11, 1877. I have found no mention of proxy ordinations before this time. However Joseph Smith taught of the need to ordain men by proxy along with baptizing, confirming, washing, anointing, ordaining, endowing, and sealing them by proxy. Ibid., 2:341, January 21, 1844. Note: Brigham Young used the example of proxy ordination (to illustrate why women should only be baptized by proxy for women and men for men) in his April 6, 1845, discourse, but his reference appears to be hypothetical indicating proxy ordinations in the future rather than proxy ordinations being administered in Nauvoo. See "Speech Delivered by Brigham Young . . . April 6th, 1845," *Times and Seasons,* (July 1, 1845), 953–57. http://contentdm.lib.byu.edu/cdm/ref/collection/NCMP1820-1846/id/9684.

571. *History of the Church*, 6:50, October 9, 1843.

572. For a detailed analysis on the power of temple rites as perceived by Kathleen Flake, see her article "'Not to be Riten,' The Mormon Temple Rite as Oral Canon," *Journal of Ritual Studies*, 9, no. 2 (Summer 1995).

573. *Wilford Woodruff's Journal*, 7:321, January 11–12, 1877.

574. Ibid., 7:322.

575. Ogden Kraut, comp., *L. John Nuttall Diary Excerpts* (Salt Lake City: Pioneer Press, Salt Lake City, 1994), 24, April 2, 1877.

576. *Wilford Woodruff's Journal,*7:322, 326, January 14 and February 10, 1877.

577. Brigham Young, *Letters of Brigham Young to His Sons*, edited by Dean C. Jessee (Salt Lake City: Deseret Book Company, 1974), 205. See original letter from Brigham Young to Willard Young dated May 23, 1877, in *Brigham Young Office Files Transcriptions*, MS 2736, Letterbook Volume 14, 204–6, Church History Library, Salt Lake City.

578. Nauvoo Relief Society Minute Book, April 28, 1842, 33, The Joseph Smith Papers. Accessed January 19, 2014, http://josephsmithpapers.org/paper Summary/nauvoo-relief-society-minute-book?p=33.

579. Brigham Young, *Letters*, 205.

580. See William G. Hartley, "The Priesthood Reorganization of 1877: Brigham Young's Final Achievement", *BYU Studies* 20, no.1 (Fall 1979): 3–36.

581. Moroni 6:4. See also James R. Clark, comp., "Circular of the First Presidency, July 11, 1877," *Messages of the First Presidency*, 6 vols. (Salt Lake City: Bookcraft, 1965–75), 2:283.

582. For more detail on this period in Church history see Hartley, "The Priesthood Reorganization of 1877," 3–36.

583. *David H. Cannon diaries, 1894–1895*, December 31, 1894, MS 8540, Church History Library, Salt Lake City.

584. Ogden Kraut, comp., *L. John Nuttall Diary Excerpts* (Salt Lake City: Pioneer Press, Salt Lake City, 1994), 24, April 3, 1877.

585. Minutes, Special Bishop's Meeting, November 6, 1885, in Devery S. Anderson, ed., *The Development of LDS Temple Worship* (Salt Lake City: Signature Books, 2011), 54.

586. Ibid. However, compliance with the Word of Wisdom as a prerequisite for temple worthiness was not a strict rule. The elderly who had used tobacco or liquor for many years, presumably before knowing about the revelation prohibiting it, were given more leeway than young members of the Church. In 1889, Wilford cautioned Church authorities to be fair when using their discretion to make exceptions. See Letter from First Presidency (Wilford Woodruff, George Q. Cannon, and Joseph F. Smith) to O. G. Larsen and Counselors, November 25, 1889. Anderson, ed., *Development of LDS Temple Worship*, 83.

CHAPTER 10

587. *Wilford Woodruff's Journal, 1833–1898, Typescript*, edited by Scott G. Kenney, 9 vols. (Midvale, Utah: Signature Books, 1983–1984), 7:395–405, January 23–March 20, 1878. Spelling is modernized, and punctuation, capitalization, and paragraphing are sometimes altered for clarity.

588. When the temple was closed due to the heat, Wilford left St. George July 10 to meet with the Saints throughout Southern Utah. Among other things, he helped organize stakes in Fillmore and Beaver. He returned to St. George on August 14 and began officiating in the temple the following day. Ibid., 7:366.

589. Lorenzo Snow served as President of the Salt Lake Temple from 1893 to 1898. Like Wilford Woodruff's room in the St. George Temple, Lorenzo Snow had a personal room in the Salt Lake Temple where he stayed overnight on occasion.

590. *Wilford Woodruff's Journal*, 7:322, January 14, 1877. Alonzo Raleigh and George Q. Cannon also assisted in writing the ceremonies. See Wilford Woodruff, signed statement, March 26, 1883, entitled "History of the St. George Temple. Its Cost and Dedication and the Labor Therein," *David H. Cannon Collection, 1883–1894*, MS 5035, Church History Library, Salt Lake City. Some historians have referred to a discourse by Joseph Smith to claim that the endowment could or should not be written down. However, in his discourse on October 9, 1843, honoring the recently deceased James Adams, Joseph Smith said that the instruction in the endowment (which James Adams had received) was through spiritual, not written communication, just as the Saints Paul refers to in Hebrews 12:18–29 learned through spiritual not written communication. Joseph Smith "assured the Saints that truth in reference to these matters, can, and may be known, through the

revelations of God in the way of his ordinances, and in answer to prayer. The Hebrew church 'came unto the spirits of just men made perfect, and unto an innumerable company of angels, unto God the Father of all, and to Jesus Christ the Mediator of the new Covenant;' but what they learned, has not been, and could not have been written." "Minutes of a Special Conference," *Times and Seasons,* September 15, 1843, 331. http://contentdm.lib.byu.edu/cdm/ref/collection/NCMP1820-1846/id/8618. (Note: the discrepancy in discourse vs. publication dates is due to the delay in publication of this issue of the *Times and Seasons.*)

591. Kraut, *Nuttall Diary,* 14, February 7, 1877.

592. In 1844 Joseph Smith "was led, before his death, to call the Twelve together from time to time and to instruct them in all things pertaining to the kingdom, ordinances and government of God. He often observed that he was laying the foundation, but it would remain for the Twelve to complete the building. Said he, 'I know not why; but for some reason I am constrained to hasten my preparations, and to confer upon the Twelve all the ordinances, keys, covenants, endowments, and sealing ordinances of the priesthood, and so set before them a pattern in all things pertaining to the sanctuary and the endowment therein. . . . He conferred on Elder Young, the President of the Twelve, the keys of the sealing power. This last key of the priesthood is the most sacred of all, and pertains exclusively to the first presidency of the church, without whose sanction, and approval or authority, no sealing blessing shall be administered pertaining to things of the resurrection and the life to come." "[Parley P. Pratt's] Proclamation to the Church of Jesus Christ of Latter-day Saints," *Latter-day Saints' Millennial Star* (Liverpool, England: April 1842 – March 3, 1932), 5:10 (March 1845), 151. http://contentdm.lib.byu.edu/cdm/compoundobject/collection/MStar/id/390/rec/5. See also Wilford Woodruff's discourse, "The Keys of the Kingdom," Ibid., 51:35 (September 2, 1889), 545–49. http://contentdm.lib.byu.edu/cdm/compound object/collection/MStar/id/18767/rec/51.

593. Ibid., 5:10 (March 1845), 151. http://contentdm.lib.byu.edu/cdm/compoundobject/collection/MStar/id/390/rec/5.

594. George A. Smith told Robert Gardner, "You cannot realize . . . how anxious [President Young] is to get this temple completed. He feels he is getting old, and is liable to drop off anytime, and he has keys he wants to give in the Temple. They can be given only in a temple." Karl S. Snow, "Robert Gardner: Utah Pioneer 1847," (February 25, 1971), 53, MS 5175, International Society of the Daughters of Utah Pioneers Museum, Salt Lake City. Erastus Snow said: "It is a great joy and comfort to know that [Brigham Young] had the privilege of living to complete one Temple and to see it dedicated, and that he superintended the setting in order of the priesthood and the ordinances for the redemption of the dead . . . something he greatly desired to see done before he should pass away." See *Death of President Brigham Young. Brief Sketch of His Life and Labors. Funeral Ceremonies with Full Report of the Addresses* (Salt Lake City: Deseret News Steam Printing Establishment, 1877), 20. http://openlibrary.org. See also B. H. Roberts, *A Comprehensive History of the Church of Jesus Christ of Latter-day Saints,* 6 vols. (Salt Lake City, Deseret News Press, 1930), 5:516–17n2. Initially, however, Brigham Young had not pushed for the completion of the Salt Lake Temple because the temple in Jackson County, Missouri, was to be

the first temple completed and he expected to return there soon. On August 23, 1862, Wilford recorded a conversation with Brigham Young: "I do not want to quite finish this temple for there will not be any temple finished until the one is finished in Jackson County, Missouri, pointed out by Joseph Smith. Keep this a secret to yourselves lest some may be discouraged." *Wilford Woodruff's Journal*, 6:71. Brigham also stated that he expected the Saints would be back in Missouri before 1870.

595. *Wilford Woodruff's Journal*, 7:322–40, January 15–February 12, 1877. See also Kraut, *Nuttall Diary*, 16–21, February 10–13, 19, 21, 24, 27. March 5, 16–18, 1877.

596. Kraut, *Nuttall Diary*, 13, February 1, 1877. "President Young was present and gave some instructions [at the veil] not previously given which I wrote for safe keeping and reference hereafter." See also Kraut, *Nuttall Diary*, June 3, 1892, and *Wilford Woodruff's Journal*, 7:325. Brigham Young's lecture at the veil included his teaching that Adam was the father of Jesus Christ. After Brigham's death, inclusion of the Adam-God teaching in the lecture at the veil was discontinued at some point. Although I have found no document giving an exact date, my research indicates it was sometime between 1894 and 1904. According to Charles L. Walker, Wilford Woodruff and the First Presidency attended the High Council meeting in St. George held to discuss Edward Bunker Sr.'s concerns regarding the practice of adoption, controversies involving Adam, resurrection, and other subjects. Wilford Woodruff's counsel was, "[I]t was not wisdom for the Elders to contend about such matters and things they did not understand." George Q. Cannon followed and said, "[I]t was not necessary that we should or endorse the doctrine that some men taught that Adam was the Father of Jesus Christ." Andrew Karl Larson, and Katharine Miles Larson, *Diary of Charles Lowell Walker*, 2 vols. (Logan: Utah State University Press, 1980)2:740–41, (June 11, 1892). The Adam-God teaching was controversial when it was introduced by Brigham Young in 1852 (see for example, *Wilford Woodruff's Journal*, 4:129, and *Journal of Discourses*, 1:50–51), and it remains controversial. It is not addressed in this book because Wilford Woodruff did not address it as part of the temple ordinances. References to the teachings regarding Adam and God in *Wilford Woodruff's Journal* are: 1:468, 2:383–385; 4:129–130, 4:250, 4:288–290, 4:316–317; 5:493; 6:343, 6:381, 6:389–390, 6:508, 6:576. See also his April 7, 1895, discourse in General Conference: "Cease troubling yourselves about who God is, who Adam is, who Christ is, who Jehovah is. For heaven's sake, let these things alone . . . God is God. Christ is Christ. The Holy Ghost is the Holy Ghost. . . . I say this because we are troubled every little while with inquiries from Elders anxious to know who God is, who Christ is, and who Adam is. . . . The Lord . . . the Son of God is the same. He is the Savior of the world. He is our advocate with the Father. . . . Adam is the first man. He was placed in the Garden of Eden and is our great progenitor. God the Father, God the Son, and God the Holy Ghost are the same yesterday, to-day and forever. That should be sufficient for us to know." "Discourse by President Wilford Woodruff," *Millennial Star* 57:23, (June 6, 1895), 355–356. http://contentdm.lib.byu.edu/cdm/compoundobject/

collection/MStar/id/33934/rec/57. See also Abraham H. Cannon, *Candid Insights of a Mormon Apostle: The Diaries of Abraham H. Cannon 1889–1895*, edited by Edward Leo Lyman (Salt Lake City: Signature Books, 2010), 636. April 7, 1895.

597. *Journal of Discourses*, 26 vols. (Liverpool and London: F. D. and S. W. Richards, 1854–86), 17:39, April 7, 1873.

598. On August 24, 1877, L. John Nuttall recorded contents of letter received from Brigham Young in answer to L. John Nuttall's letter dated March 18. Kraut, *Nuttall Diary*, 35–37.

599. Doctrine and Covenants 68:24.

600. *Wilford Woodruff's Journal*, 6:232–33.

601. Kraut, *Nuttall Diary*, 36, August 24, 1877.

602. Anderson, ed., *Development of LDS Temple Worship*, 68. Original Wilford Woodruff, Letter to Marriner Wood Merrill, September 9, 1887, MS 3923, Church History Library, Salt Lake City.

603. *Wilford Woodruff's Journal*, 4:391, January 13, 1856.

604. Ibid., 1:265, July 1, 1838.

605. 3 Nephi 9:20, and Doctrine and Covenants 59:8.

606. Kraut, *Nuttall Diary*, 18, March 1, 1877. See also Kraut, *Nuttall Diary*, 24. On April 2, 1877, L. John Nuttall sent a statement to Brigham Young detailing the ordinances that had been completed between January 9 and March 31, 1877. During that time, 24 days were devoted to baptisms and 8,733 were completed; 29 days were devoted to endowments and 581 were administered to the living and 3,208 by proxy; 169 ordinations for the living and 1,193 by proxy; 195 sealings for the living and 961 by proxy; 127 second anointings.

607. *Journal of Discourses*, 23:131, May 14, 1882.

608. Wilford Woodruff, "Discourse Delivered by President Wilford Woodruff at the General Conference, in the Tabernacle, Salt Lake City, Monday Morning, April 6, 1891," *Deseret Weekly*, April 25, 1891, 554. http://lib.byu.edu/digital/deseret_news/.

609. *Wilford Woodruff's Journal*, 7:340, March 21, 1877; and Wilford Woodruff, "History of the St. George Temple: Its Cost and Dedication and the Labor Thereon," March 26, 1883, in David Henry Cannon Collection, 1883–1924, Church History Library, Salt Lake City.

610. *Wilford Woodruff's Journal*, 7:359, July 5, 1877.

611. On January 31, 1877, Brigham Young appointed the following to officiate in the St. George Temple: Wilford Woodruff to preside, and as workers: John O. Angus, Henry W. Bigler, James G. Bleak, David H. Cannon, Jesse W. Crosby, Henry Eyring, William Fawcett, John Lytle, Alexander F. MacDonald, John D. T. McAllister, John M. Moody, L. John Nuttall, Alonzo H. Raleigh, John L. Smith, William H. Thompson, and Anson P. Winsor. Brigham also asked his wife Lucy Bigelow Young to preside over the sisters, and called as workers Sarah Ann Pulsipher Alger, Elizabeth Price Bentley, Frances C. Brown, Eliza S. Calkin, Nanette S. B. Calkin, Sarah A. Church, Hannah E. B. Crosby, Eudora L. Young Dunford, Susan Amelia ("Susa") Young Dunford, Annie L. I. Ivins, Hannah G. Perkins, Minerva W. Snow, and Annie T. Wells. See *Annals of the Southern Utah Mission 1877*, 45–46, MS 318, Church History Library, Salt Lake City.

612. *Wilford Woodruff's Journal,* 7:344, April 8, 1877.

613. The shirts were to "reach down to the knees or a little below." "Letter of Special Instructions to Bishops dated January 13, 1877, from Brigham Young, Wilford Woodruff, Erastus Snow, John W. Young, and Brigham Young Jr.," *Annals of the Southern Utah Mission 1877,* 34–35, Church History Library, Salt Lake City.

614. *Wilford Woodruff's Journal,* 7:325, February 1, 1877. Brigham Young subsequently directed that white leather (deerskin) suits be sewn for the men officiating in the temple.

615. Speaking at the Church Conference held in conjunction with the dedication of the St. George Temple, John Taylor called this time "the commencement of an epoch which reaches back to eternity and forward to eternity." *Annals of the Southern Mission,* April 4, 1877, 62, Church History Library, Salt Lake City. http:// eadview.lds.org/findingaid/viewer?pid=IE436352&pds_handle=. He understood that these changes would give the Saints a new understanding of their role as "saviors on Mount Zion" and their unique position in the world. See also *Journal of Discourses,* 20:177, April 8, 1879.

616. *Journal of Discourses,* 17:39, April 7, 1873.

617. Ibid., 13:327, September 5, 1869.

618. *Wilford Woodruff's Journal,* 7:293, November 20–24, 1876.

619. Ibid., 6:558, June 22, 1870.

620. Wilford Woodruff, "Discourse Delivered by President Wilford Woodruff at the General Conference, in the Tabernacle, Salt Lake City, Monday Morning, April 6, 1891," in *Deseret Weekly,* April 25, 1891, 554. http://lib.byu.edu/digital/ deseret_news/.

621. *Journal of Discourses,* 22:34, June 26, 1881. Ibid., 19:228, September 16, 1877.

622. Kraut, *Nuttall Diary,* 24, April 2, 1877.

623. *Journal of Discourses,* 15:11, April 6, 1872.

624. *Wilford Woodruff's Journal,* 7:329, February 23, 1877.

625. "Discourse by President Wilford Woodruff," *Millennial Star* 56:22 (May 28, 1894), 339–41. http://contentdm.lib.byu.edu/cdm/compoundobject/ collection/MStar/id/20113/rec/56.

626. *Wilford Woodruff's Journal,* 7:332–33, March 1, 1877.

627. Ibid., 7:329–36, March 10, 1877.

628. Ibid., 7:330, March 1, 1877.

629. Ibid., 7:338, March 10, 1877.

630. *Martha C. Cox Autobiography,* MS 1661, 149–50, Church History Library, Salt Lake City.

631. *Journal of Discourses,* 21:192, July 3, 1880.

632. It is important to note the difference between Wilford, as the designated representative or "heir" of his family within the Church asking others to assist him in completing proxy ordinances for his relatives, and someone randomly performing work for individuals they have no relation to. See infra pages 219–21 for discussion on "heirship."

633. Others pictured seated on the floor are Julina and Edna Lambson Smith (sisters and plural wives of Joseph F. Smith), and Christina Willardson. Standing are

Esther Parkinson, Frances Cann Brown, Adeline Hatch Barber, and Ellen Barton Ray Matheny. The picture and life sketches of the women were featured in *The Young Women's Journal*, 4 (April 1893): 288–306.

634. Susa Young Gates, *Lucy Bigelow Young*, Typescript, 87, Utah State Historical Society Archives, Salt Lake City.

635. Emmeline B. Wells, "Lucy Bigelow Young," *Young Women's Journal* 3 (January 1892): 146.

636. Susa Young Gates, *Lucy Bigelow Young*, 89.

637. *Wilford Woodruff's Journal*, 7:341–45, March 27 to April 14, 1877.

638. Ibid., 7:343, April 6, 1877.

639. Ibid., 7:342, March 30, 1877.

640. Ibid., 7:340–41. See also *Henry Eyring's Journal*, February 24, 1877: "[M]yself and wives received our second anointing under the hands of Elder Wilford Woodruff, to whom we were subsequently adopted as son and daughter." "Subsequently" in this case apparently meant on a different day. http://www.bunker.org/henryeyring.html. Original in Henry Eyring Journals 1877–1896, MS0008, Special Collections, J. Willard Marriott Library, University of Utah, Salt Lake City.

641. *Wilford Woodruff's Journal*, 7:344, April 11, 1877. Samuel and Josiah Hardy were friends of Wilford Woodruff and cousins of Leonard W. Hardy.

642. Ibid., 7:345.

643. Ibid., 7:347, April 25, 1877; and 7:350, May 18, 1877.

644. Ibid., 7:359, July 5, 1877.

645. Ibid., 7:354–55, June 16, 1877. On page 499 of his biography of Wilford Woodruff, *Wilford Woodruff: History of His Life and Labors As Recorded in His Daily Journals*, Matthias F. Cowley adds the phrase "to labor among those for whom we are officiating in the Temple of the Lord" at the end of this sentence. The phrase is not in Wilford Woodruff's Journal although it was Wilford's belief that those in the spirit world were preaching the gospel to others and aiding those on earth in their efforts to redeem the dead. http://books.google.com/books/about/Wilford_Woodruff.html?id=UsoEAAAAYAAJ.

646. See for example, *Wilford Woodruff's Journal*, 7:262, January 10, 1876; 7:604, November 17, 1880; 8:222, January 8, 1884; 9:229, December 9, 1892.

647. Letter, Phebe Woodruff to Wilford Woodruff, October 6, 1840, MS 19509, Church History Library, Salt Lake City.

CHAPTER 11

648. *Wilford Woodruff's Journal, 1833–1898, Typescript*, edited by Scott G. Kenney, 9 vols. (Midvale, Utah: Signature Books, 1983–1984), 7:367–68, 389. Spelling is modernized, and punctuation, capitalization, and paragraphing are sometimes altered for clarity.

649. *Journal of Discourses*, 26 vols. (Liverpool and London: F. D. and S. W. Richards, 1854–86), 18:304, January 1, 1877, remarks delivered at the dedication of the St. George Temple.

650. Ibid., 19:230, September 16, 1877.

651. Ibid., 19:229–30.

652. Wilford Woodruff, *Conference Report*, April 1898, 89–90. See Joseph Smith's testimony regarding these men in Doctrine and Covenants 101:80.

653. *Journal of Discourses*, 22:332, October 8, 1881.

654. Ibid., 22:331–32.

655. He mentions this experience several more times in his journal. See *Wilford Woodruff's Journal*, 7:389, December 31, 1877; and 8:156, March 1, 1883.

656. Ibid., 5:142, December 21, 1857; and 6:5, January 6, 1862.

657. Only one of the Signers of the Declaration of Independence, Charles Carroll, was still living when the Church was officially organized in 1830, and he died in 1832 at the age of 93.

658. Wilford read whenever he had a chance. He records information in his journal on 148 books that he read, and simply notes on other days, "I spent my time reading." He was particularly interested in United States and world history. He specifically mentions reading the biographies of explorers like Daniel Boone, David Livingstone and John L. Stephens, American statesmen Abraham Lincoln and Benjamin Franklin, as well as the History of Russia and the account of the French Revolution.

659. On May 6, 1843, Joseph Smith said, ". . . when we have petitioned those in power for assistance, they have always told us they had no power to help us. Damn such traitors! When they give me the power to protect the innocent, I will never say I can do nothing: I will exercise that power, so help me God." See Joseph Smith and B. H. Roberts, *History of the Church of Jesus Christ of Latter-day Saints* (Salt Lake City: Deseret Book Co., 1970), 5:384. This comment alludes to the response Joseph received from President Martin Van Buren on November 29, 1839, when Joseph met with him to personally deliver the Saints' petitions for redress of grievances for the losses they suffered in Missouri in 1838 and 1839. Documents, Petition to United States Congress, November 29, 1839, The Joseph Smith Papers. President Van Buren's response to Joseph Smith was, "What can I do? I can do nothing for you. If I do anything, I shall come in contact with the whole state of Missouri." See *History of the Church*, 4:40, 80. In 1857 President James Buchanan accused Governor Brigham Young of treason and declared Utah Territory in rebellion. Buchanan sent a regiment of the United States Army to Utah to accompany a newly appointed governor and, the Saints believed, to destroy the Church and its members. See *Wilford Woodruff's Journal*, 5:90, 162-65.

660. The presidents of the United States and their wives that were included were George Washington and Martha Dandridge Custis; John Adams and Abigail Smith; Thomas Jefferson and Martha Wayles; James Madison and Dorothy ("Dolley") Payne; and Andrew Jackson and Rachel Donelson. (Wives of five of the other presidents were still alive.)

661. The information on the Signers of the Declaration of Independence would have been readily available, particularly given the fact that the Centennial of the Declaration had been celebrated the year before his vision. Although Wilford Woodruff did not include the source or sources he used to compile the list of other eminent men and the eminent women, based on the information he does include, his main source was Evert Duyckinck's two volume work published in 1873:

"Portrait Gallery of Eminent Men and Women of Europe and America: Embracing History, Statesmanship, Naval and Military Life, Philosophy, The Drama, Science, Literature and Art. With Biographies." Duyckinck includes information on all the other eminent men, except Count Demetrius Parepa, and sixty-six of the sixty-eight eminent women. The two women his work does not include are Euphroynse Parepa-Rosa and her mother Elizabeth Sequinn. Perhaps Lucy Bigelow Young was impressed by the incredible talent of Euphroynse when she attended Parepa-Rosa's concert in the Salt Lake Theater on November 14, 1868, and added her name as well as the names of her parents to the list she helped Wilford Woodruff prepare. One mistake in the list of eminent women is the substitution of Princess Charlotte for Margarita Maza as the wife of Benito Juárez. Margarita was not mentioned in Duyckinck's work, and Charlotte was actually the wife of Maximilian I of Austria, appointed Emperor of Mexico by Napoleon III and defeated by Benito Juárez.

662. "Biography of Charlotte Corday," by T.Y. Stanford and Joseph Stanford was later published in the Church periodical, *"The Contributor,"* 13 (1892): 30.

663. Although only 75 of the 100 eminent men Wilford Woodruff lists in his journal appear on the Baptismal Records in the St. George Temple, all 100 men are listed in the St. George Temple Endowment Records with the baptismal date of August 21, 1877. In addition to the 100 men for whom Wilford acted as proxy, he baptized John D. T. McAllister for another 21 eminent men on the same day. By combining the list in Wilford's journal and the recorded information in the temple records, the total number of individuals included in his group of eminent men and women is 189: 121 men and 68 women. The lists created by Brian H. Stuy in his article "Wilford Woodruff's Vision of the Signers of the Declaration of Independence," *Journal of Mormon History*, 26 no. 1 (Spring 2000), 83–90, and Vicki Jo Anderson in her book, *The Other Eminent Men of Wilford Woodruff*, (Cottonwood: Zichron Historical Research Institute, 1994), 411–18, differ from each other and from my research. Brian Stuy includes Mrs. Elijah Gibbs and Maria Fackrell for whom Lucy Bigelow Young was baptized the same day as the eminent women. However, Mrs. Elijah Gibbs (Lydia Knapp) was the wife of Lucy Bigelow Young's great-uncle (Lucy Bigelow's mother was Mary Gibbs), and Maria Fackrell was a member of the Church (as noted next to her name in the endowment record). Presumably Maria Fackrell's baptism on August 21, 1877 was to facilitate her subsequent endowment and sealing to John D. T. McAllister, Wilford Woodruff's counselor in the St. George Temple (with his wife Ann McAllister acting as proxy) on August 23, 1877. See *St. George Sealing Records*, January–October 1877, Microfilm No. 170595, Family History Library, Salt Lake City (hereafter FHL). Other eminent men and women baptized on August 21, 1877, but not included on Wilford Woodruff's list, are Edmund Burke, his wife Jane Nugent, and President Andrew Jackson's parents, Andrew and Elizabeth Hutchinson Jackson.

664. Benjamin Franklin, for example, was baptized by proxy in Nauvoo in 1841 (see *Nauvoo Baptismal Record Index*, Microfilm No. 820155, FHL), in the Endowment House font in 1871 (see *Endowment House Baptism for the Dead*, Microfilm No. 183384, FHL) and again in 1876 (see Ibid., Microfilm No. 183388).

665. Wilford apparently did not include William Floyd's name on the list to be baptized because he was aware that Addison Everett had been baptized for "Wil-

liam Floid" (sic) on March 13, 1877 (See *St. George Temple Baptisms for the Dead*, Microfilm No. 170841, Vol. B, 36–37, FHL). William Floyd's endowments were completed along with the other Signers of the Declaration of Independence on August 22, and Addison Everett again acted as proxy for William Floyd in receiving the endowment. Wilford must also have been aware that Levi Ward Hancock, John Hancock's third cousin, was baptized for John on May 29, 1877, and endowed for John on May 30, 1877. (See *St. George Temple Baptisms for the Dead*, Microfilm No. 170843, Vol. D, FHL; and *St. George Temple Endowments*, Microfilm No. 170542, 16–17, FHL).

666. *Wilford Woodruff's Journal*, 7:389, December 31, 1877.

667. *Journal of Discourses*, 19:229–30.

668. Doctrine and Covenants 137:7–8.

669. *Wilford Woodruff's Journal*, 7:369. August 22–23, 1877.

670. Ibid., August 22–24, 1877 and *St. George Temple Endowments*, Microfilm No. 170542, 224-27, FHL. On March 19, 1894, Wilford recorded the following: "I had a dream in the night. I met with Benjamin Franklin. I thought he was on the earth. I spent several hours with him and we talked over our endowments. He wanted some more work done for him than had been done, which I promised him he should have. I thought then he died and, while waiting for burial, I awoke. I thought very strange of my dream. I made up my mind to get second anointing for Benjamin Franklin and George Washington." *Wilford Woodruff's Journal*, 9:293.

671. Martha Dandridge Custis Washington was baptized by proxy on August 21, 1877, endowed on August 22 (*St. George Temple Endowment Record*, Microfilm No. 170542, Book B, 288, FHL), and sealed (*St. George Temple sealings Jan 1877–Oct 1877*, Microfilm No. 179595, 288, FHL) the same day. Lucy Bigelow Young served as proxy for all three ordinances. Daniel Parke Custis was baptized by proxy on August 21, 1877, and endowed the following day with Henry W. Bigler as proxy (*St. George Temple Endowment Record*, Microfilm No. 170542, Book B, 226, FHL). George Washington was vicariously baptized on August 21, endowed on August 22 (*St. George Temple Endowment Record*, Microfilm No. 170542, Book B, 226, FHL) and sealed the same day with John D. T. McAllister acting as proxy. George Washington was also baptized in 1841 by Don Carlos Smith and Stephen Jones (see *Nauvoo Baptismal Record Index*, Microfilm No. 820155, FHL) and in 1876 by John Bernhisel (see *Endowment House Baptisms for the Dead*, Microfilm No. 183388, FHL).

672. *St. George Temple Sealing record November 1877–December 1878*, Microfilm No. 170595, 292, FHL. Lucy Bigelow Young was baptized on August 21 for Mary Ball Washington and Ann McAllister served as proxy in Mary's endowment (*St. George Temple Endowment Record*, Microfilm No. 170542, Book B, 288, FHL) and sealing on August 22. John D. T. McAllister was baptized for Lawrence Washington on August 21, 1877. Charles A Terry served as proxy for Lawrence Washington in his endowment and sealing (*St. George Temple Endowment record*, Microfilm No. 170542, Book B, 226, FHL).

673. *Journal of Discourses*, 19:229, September 16, 1877.

674. Ibid., 19:229–30.

675. Kraut, *Nuttall Diary*, 24, April 3, 1877.

676. Doctrine and Covenants 128:15.

677. "Remarks Made at the Salt Lake Stake Conference Sunday, December 12th, 1897 by President Wilford Woodruff," *Deseret Evening News*, December 18, 1897, 9.

678. Ibid.

679. Ibid.

680. *Journal of Discourses*, 23:330–31, December 10, 1882. See also Ibid., 21:302, August 1, 1880.

681. Ibid., 19:135–36,October 13, 1877.

682. Ibid., 22:210, January 9, 1881.

683. For additional information on Wilford Woodruff's time in St. George see Thomas G. Alexander, "*An Apostle in Exile: Wilford Woodruff and the St. George Connection*," paper presented at the Juanita Brooks Lecture Series, St. George, Utah, 1994, Dixie State College, St. George, Utah. http://library.dixie.edu/special_collections/Juanita%20Brooks%20lectures/1994%20-20An%20Apostle%20in%20Exile.html.

684. Ibid., 19:155, 157, November 14, 1877.

CHAPTER 12

685. George Reynolds, a secretary in the office of the President of the Church, agreed to serve as a test case and was convicted for bigamy under the 1862 Morrill Act. See infra endnote 724 for the Court's reasoning for upholding his conviction.

686. See *Miles v. United States*, 103 U.S. 304 (1880); *In re Snow*, 120 U.S. 274 (1887); and *Ex Parte Nielsen*, 131 U.S. 176 (1889). For example, the Supreme Court overturned John Miles' bigamy conviction because his wives were compelled to testify, in violation of the spousal privilege. (Under the spousal privilege, a rule of evidence, one spouse cannot be forced to testify against the other.)

687. *Wilford Woodruff's Journal, 1833–1898, Typescript*, edited by Scott G. Kenney, 9 vols. (Midvale, Utah: Signature Books, 1983–1984), 8:90, March 14, 1882.

688. John Taylor instructed the temple presidents to ensure those whose civil marriage ceremonies were later sealed in the temple properly filed their marriage/sealing certificates with the probate court to satisfy the requirements of the Edmunds Act. However, proxy sealings did not have to be recorded. See John Taylor and George Q. Cannon, Letter to Marriner W. Merrill, President of the Logan Temple, April 7, 1887, Devery S. Anderson, ed., *The Development of LDS Temple Worship* (Salt Lake City: Signature Books, 2011), 63.

689. The Supreme Court upheld the Utah Territorial Court's ruling that a man, in this case Angus Cannon, was guilty of unlawful cohabitation, not because he was intimate with his wives, but because he ate dinner with them and continued to support and provide for them, *Cannon v. United States* (December 15, 1885).

690. See "Remarks by George Q. Cannon . . . Oct 6th, 1890," *Deseret Weekly*, October 18, 1890, 550. http://contentdm.lib.byu.edu/cdm/compoundobject/collection/desnews4/id/15816/rec/84; and B. H. Roberts, *A Comprehensive History of the Church of Jesus Christ of Latter-day Saints*, 6 vols. (Salt Lake City, Deseret News Press, 1930), 6:210–11.

691. Prisoners pictured (from left to right): Francis A. Brown (sentenced July 11, 1885, for unlawful cohabitation to six months and a $300 fine); Freddy Self (?); Moroni Brown (served six months, May 15, 1885, to January 13, 1886, and paid a $300 fine for unlawful cohabitation); Amos Milton Musser (sentenced to six months and a $300 fine for unlawful cohabitation; served May 9, 1885, to October 12, 1885; assistant Church Historian; his son Joseph W. Musser became a leader of the Short Creek Fundamentalist group); George H. Kellogg (served February 14 to December 23, 1885, for stealing a horse and buggy; worked in the prison kitchen); Parley P. Pratt Jr. (son of Parley P. Pratt and his first wife Thankful Halsey; sentenced to six months for unlawful cohabitation; served May 2 to October 15, 1885, with extra days for violating prison rule by delivering a letter); Rudger J. Clawson (missionary companion of martyr Joseph Standing; sentenced on November 3, 1884, to 3½ years and an $800 fine on two counts; served November 1884 to December 1887; later served in Quorum of the Twelve Apostles from 1898 to 1943); and Job Pingree (sentenced July 13, 1885, to five months and a $300 fine for unlawful cohabitation; released November 17, 1885).

692. *Wilford Woodruff's Journal*, 8:421, 426.

693. For example, the Gardo House was used by Church leaders for offices and meetings. After paying $28,000 ($450 a month) "on our own property since the government had taken possession of it," Church leaders moved out on November 30, 1891, because, wrote Wilford, "we thought it was time to stop." Ibid., 9:174.

694. The Valley House was the name given to the home Wilford Woodruff built in 1851 on the southwest corner of South Temple and West Temple streets in Salt Lake City. It was constructed of "adobe and plaster with heavy timbers and beams held together by buckskin thongs and wooden spikes." He later expanded it to accommodate his families, and after he relocated his families, it was remodeled in 1879 for use as a forty-room hotel that could serve sixty guests. The Valley House gained a national reputation and stood until it was demolished in 1915 to make way for the rail depot. Abravanel Hall now occupies the site.

695. Mary Ann Jackson arrived in Salt Lake City on September 25, 1847, in the care of Wilford's father, Aphek Woodruff. Wilford had been sent east from Winter Quarters to gather more Saints, and did not return to Salt Lake City until October 1850. The situation was apparently too hard for Mary Ann as she divorced Wilford on May 11, 1848. Wilford continued to provide a home for her to live in and supported their son James. In 1857, Mary Ann asked Wilford if he would remarry her, but he declined based on their past experience. She married David James Ross, a widower with three children, in December 1857. After David abandoned her and their two children in the 1860s, Wilford brought James into his household in 1863 to raise him. According to two cryptic notes in his journal, Wilford and Mary Ann may have been resealed in 1878. See *Wilford Woodruff's Journal*, 7:441, December 2 and 4, 1878.

696. Wilford helped support Mary Ann Jackson until her death on October 25, 1894, and she was buried in the Woodruff family plot in Salt Lake City.

697. *Wilford Woodruff's Journal*, 7:338, 339, 340. Mike Quinn believes that Wilford and Eudora's child was born and died on April 1, 1878. See D. Michael Quinn, "LDS Church Authority and New Plural Marriages, 1890–1904," *Dialogue: A Journal*

of Mormon Thought 18, no. 1 (Spring 1985): 64. Wilford's journal entry states, "I got a telegram saying that [–] had a son born at 3 o'clock and died at 12 o'clock." See *Wilford Woodruff's Journal*, 7:407, April 1, 1878.

698. *Journal of Discourses*, 26 vols. (Liverpool and London: F. D. and S. W. Richards, 1854–86), 24:55–56, January 27, 1883.

699. Ibid., 22:234, June 26, 1881.

700. Ibid., 23:329, December 10, 1882.

701. Ibid., 19:229, September 16, 1877.

702. Ibid.

703. Ibid., 19:230, September 16, 1877.

704. *Wilford Woodruff's Journal*, 7:374.

705. "The Logan Temple: Laying the Cornerstones," *Deseret Weekly*, September 26, 1877, 1. http://lib.byu.edu/digital/deseret_news/.

706. *Wilford Woodruff's Journal*, 7:377.

707. Ibid., 7:383.

708. Ibid., 8:139, December 18, 1882. "We visited the Temple. It was Beautiful. The outside was painted with something like the Cream Color. It took 15,000 pounds of white lead to paint it and the material cost $2,000. The font was in its place."

709. John Taylor, Letter to Stake Presidents, November 15, 1877, Anderson, ed., *Development of LDS Temple Worship*, 42–43.

710. *Wilford Woodruff's Journal*, 7:384, November 29, 1877.

711. Wilford Woodruff ordered the razing of the Endowment House, in October 1889, after an allegedly unauthorized sealing was performed there. (See Official Declaration – 1 in the Doctrine and Covenants. See also Abraham H. Cannon, *Candid Insights of a Mormon Apostle: The Diaries of Abraham H. Cannon 1889–1895*, edited by Edward Leo Lyman (Salt Lake City: Signature Books, 2010), 15, October 18, 1889. On November 17, the Salt Lake Tribune reported that the building was "being demolished" and by the end of November the Endowment House was completely gone. "The Endowment House Going," *The Salt Lake Daily Tribune*, November 17, 1889, 4.

712. *Journal of Discourses*, 19:298, April 6, 1878.

713. *Wilford Woodruff's Journal*, 7:396–405, January 22 to March 20, 1878.

714. Ibid., 7:396, January 23, 1878.

715. Ibid., 7:397, February 5, 1878.

716. *St. George Temple Endowment Record*, Microfilm No. 170542, Book B, FHL, Salt Lake City.

717. *Wilford Woodruff's Journal*, 7:401, March 1, 1878.

718. Ibid., 7:404, March 15, 1878.

719. From "Totals of Ordinance work in St. George Temple" sent to President J. D. T. McAllister by Moses Farnsworth 1877–1883. Manuscript MSS SC 2670, Harold B. Lee Library Special Collections, Brigham Young University, Provo, Utah.

720. *Journal of Discourses*, 19:296, April 6, 1878.

721. Ibid., 19:362–63, June 30, 1878.

722. Ibid., 19:296, April 6, 1878.

723. Comparing polygamy to "one feather in a bird, one ordinance in the Church and Kingdom," Wilford said, "Do away with that, then we must do away with prophets and Apostles, with revelation and the gifts and graces of the Gospel, and finally give up our religion altogether." He concluded, "We just can't do that." See *Journal of Discourses*, 13:166, December 12, 1869.

724. *Reynolds v. United States*, 98 U.S. 145 (1879). Congress did not have power over religious belief or opinion, "but was left free to reach actions which were in violation of social duties or subversive of good order," Ibid., 165. Comparing polygamy to human sacrifice the Court continued, "So here, as a law of the organization of society under the exclusive dominion of the United States, it is provided that plural marriages shall not be allowed. Can a man excuse his practices to the contrary because of his religious belief? To permit this would be to make the professed doctrines of religious belief superior to the law of the land, and in effect to permit every citizen to become a law unto himself," Ibid., 166–67.

725. *Wilford Woodruff's Journal*, 7:444, January 2, 1879.

726. Ibid., 7:448, 450, January 8 and 21, 1879.

727. Ibid., 7:453, February 5, 1879.

728. Ibid., 7:454, February 7, 1879.

729. Ibid., 7:457. He later wrote in his journal that his testimony was indeed published in newspapers: Ibid., 7:481, April 26, 1879; and Ibid., 7:528–29, November 10, 1879.

730. Ibid., 7:460, February 26, 1879.

731. Ibid., 7:448, February 22, 1879.

732. Ibid., 7:466, February 28, 1879.

733. Ibid., 7:468, March 1, 1879.

734. Ibid. Wilford Woodruff concluded that he had had 267 women sealed to him by proxy in the Endowment House and the St. George Temple.

735. Ibid., 7:471, March 4, 1879.

736. Ibid., 7:444. A total of 269 of Wilford's ancestors were sealed by proxy in 1878, and 180 between January and March 1879.

737. Ibid., 7:472, March 6, 1879.

738. Ibid., 7:477, March 29, 1879.

739. For example see Ibid., 7:496, July 16, 1879; and 7:512–13, September 6, 1879.

740. Ibid., 7:537, December 25, 1879.

741. Ibid., 7:544–45, January 17, 1880. President Ulysses S. Grant was elected in 1868. Tension between the federal government and Utah Territory began rising again in 1870 and escalated in 1871. Martial law was threatened on July 4 to prevent the local Mormon militias from joining in the parade, and although the territorial troops were called in, fighting was avoided. President Grant, however, believed Utah was in a state of rebellion and determined the best course was to arrest those who were practicing polygamy. In October 1871, hundreds were arrested by U.S. marshals and imprisoned under the Morrill Act. President Grant visited Salt Lake City in October 1875. In his annual address to Congress on December 7, 1875, he said, "In nearly every annual message that I have had the honor of transmitting to Congress I have called attention to the anomalous, not to say scandalous, condition

of affairs existing in the Territory of Utah, and have asked for definite legislation to correct it. That polygamy should exist in a free, enlightened, and Christian country, without the power to punish so flagrant a crime against decency and morality, seems preposterous. True, there is no law to sustain this unnatural vice; but what is needed is a law to punish it as a crime, and at the same time to fix the status of the innocent children, the offspring of this system, and of the possibly innocent plural wives. But as an institution polygamy should be banished from the land." See Ulysses S. Grant: "Seventh Annual Message," December 7, 1875, *The American Presidency Project*, Gerhard Peters and John T. Woolley. http://www.presidency.ucsb.edu/ws/?pid=29516.

742. *Wilford Woodruff's Journal*, 7:546–47, 7:615–25.
743. *Journal of Discourses*, 22:148, April 3, 1881.
744. Ibid., 22:147, April 3, 1881.
745. *Wilford Woodruff's Journal*, 7:560, February 29, 1880.
746. Ibid., 8:17, March 5, 1881.
747. *Journal of Discourses*, 21: 301–2, August 1, 1880.
748. Ibid., 21:127, June 6, 1880.
749. Ibid., 21:301, August 1, 1880.
750. Ibid., 21:302, August 1, 1880.
751. Ibid., 21:189, July 3, 1880.
752. Ibid., 21:192.

CHAPTER 13

753. *Wilford Woodruff's Journal, 1833–1898, Typescript*, edited by Scott G. Kenney, 9 vols. (Midvale, Utah: Signature Books, 1983–1984), 7:595.
754. Ibid., 7:595–6. On April 10, 1875, the seniority of the Quorum of the Twelve had been adjusted according to ordination date, rather than age or length of time in the Quorum, placing John Taylor ahead of Wilford Woodruff, and both men ahead of Orson Pratt and Orson Hyde. Ibid., 7:224.
755. *Journal of Discourses*, 26 vols. (Liverpool and London: F. D. and S. W. Richards, 1854–86), 21:317, October 10, 1880.
756. Ibid., 22:234, June 26, 1881.
757. *Wilford Woodruff's Journal*, 8:15, February 25, 1881.
758. Ibid., 8:15–16, March 1, 1881.
759. Ibid., 8:18, March 11–12, 1881.
760. Ibid., 8:28, April 30, 1881.
761. Letter, Phebe Woodruff to Wilford Woodruff, October 6, 1840, MS 19509, Church History Library, Salt Lake City.
762. *Journal of Discourses*, 16:188, September 4, 1873.
763. See explanation in endnote 765 below regarding correspondence between Wilford Woodruff and Logan Temple President Marriner W. Merrill.
764. *Journal of Discourses*, 16:188, September 4, 1873.
765. Wilford Woodruff, Letter to Marriner W. Merrill, September 5, 1887, in Devery S. Anderson, ed., *The Development of LDS Temple Worship* (Salt Lake City: Signature Books, 2011), 67–68, written in response to a request from James H.

Martineau for permission to do proxy work for some early Christian martyrs. [See James H. Martineau, Donald G. Godfrey, and Rebecca S. Martineau-McCarty, *An Uncommon Common Pioneer: The Journals of James Henry Martineau, 1828–1918* (Provo: Religious Studies Center, Brigham Young University, 2008), 614–15.] Wilford gave permission for James H. Martineau to perform the work because they were his ancestors, but sent a copy of the letter to Logan Temple President Marriner W. Merrill with additional instructions. Original Wilford Woodruff, Letter to Marriner W. Merrill, September 5, 1887, MS 2084, Church History Library, Salt Lake City.

766. Reprint of June 23, 1893 letter from Lorenzo Snow, President of the Salt Lake Temple, *Church News*, December 5, 1964. See Anderson, ed., *Development of LDS Temple Worship*, 93.

767. See Section 5.4. Temple and Family History Work, *Handbook 2: Administering the Church* (Salt Lake City: The Church of Jesus Christ of Latter-day Saints, 2010).

768. "Remarks by President Wilford Woodruff, at the Sanpete Stake Conference, held at Manti, Utah, Sunday and Monday, May 19 and 20, 1889," *Deseret Weekly*, June 22, 1889, 824. http://lib.byu.edu/digital/deseret_news/.

769. Instruction by John D. T. McAllister in regard to temple clothing in Temple Minute Book, St. George, December 1, 1877. See Anderson, ed., *Development of LDS Temple Worship*, 69.

770. *Journal of Discourses*, 23:328–29, December 10, 1882.

771. Ibid., 23:331.

772. "General Conference," *Latter-day Saints' Millennial Star* (Liverpool, England: April 1842 – March 3, 1932), 49:47 (November 21, 1887), 742–43, referencing Obadiah 1:21. http://contentdm.lib.byu.edu/cdm/compoundobject/collection/MStar/id/32536/rec/49.

773. *Journal of Discourses*, 24:55–56, January 27, 1883.

774. *Wilford Woodruff's Journal*, 8:91, March 14, 1882.

775. Quoted in Mari Grana, "Pioneer, Polygamist, Politician: The Life of Dr. Martha Hughes Cannon" (TwoDot, 2009), 37.

776. *Wilford Woodruff's Journal*, 8:92, March 24, 1882.

777. *Journal of Discourses*, 23:132–33, May 14, 1882.

778. Ibid.

779. George Q. Cannon, *A Review of the Decision of the Supreme Court of the United States, in the Case of Geo[rge]. Reynolds vs. the United State*, (Salt Lake City: Deseret News Printing and Publishing Establishment, 1879), 52. http://books.google.com/books/about/A_Review_of_the_Decision_of_the_Supreme.html?id=xoYuAAAAYAAJ.

780. *"Edmunds Act, Report of Commission"* (Salt Lake City: Tribune Printing and Publishing Company, 1883), 12. https://archive.org/details/edmundsactreport00unitrich.

781. *Wilford Woodruff's Journal*, 8:250, May 17, 1884.

782. Ibid., 6:126, August 22, 1863.

783. Ibid., 8:246–48, May 8, 1884.

784. Ibid., 8:250, May 17, 1884.

785. Ibid., 8:298–99, January 11–17, 1885.

786. Ibid., 8:299–341.
787. Ibid., 8:341, November 1, 1885.
788. Ibid., 8:342, November 9, 1885.
789. Ibid., 8:343 and 9:426.
790. Ibid., 8:344–45, November 13–23, 1885.
791. Ibid., 8:416.
792. Ibid., 8:400, August 7, 1886.
793. Heber J. Grant, *diary*, September 29, 1887, Heber J. Grant Collection, 1852–1945, MS 1233, Church History Library, Salt Lake City.
794. *Journal of Discourses,* 21:190, July 3, 1880.
795. *Wilford Woodruff's Journal,* 8:423.
796. Ibid., 8:449, July 29, 1887.
797. Ibid., 8:447, July 25, 1887.
798. Ibid., 8:468, 470.

CHAPTER 14

799. "General Conference," *Latter-day Saints' Millennial Star* (Liverpool, England: April 1842 – March 3, 1932), 52:47 (November 24, 1890), 739. http://content dm.lib.byu.edu/cdm/compoundobject/collection/MStar/id/33305/rec/52. "Box Elder Stake Conference," *Deseret Weekly*, November 7, 1891, 627. http://content dm.lib.byu.edu/cdm/compoundobject/collection/desnews9/id/26044/rec/91. "Remarks Made by President Wilford Woodruff at Cache Stake Conference . . . November 1, 1891," Ibid., November 14, 1891, 659. http://contentdm.lib.byu.edu/cdm/compoundobject/collection/desnews4/id/22707/rec/5.
800. The majority of members of the Church attending general conference sustained the Manifesto. See *Wilford Woodruff's Journal, 1833–1898, Typescript,* edited Scott G. Kenney, 9 vols. (Midvale, Utah: Signature Books, 1983–1984), 9:117, October 6, 1890.
801. "The exact percentage of Latter-day Saints who participated in the practice [of plural marriage] is not known, but studies suggest a maximum of from 20 to 25 [percent] of LDS adults were members of polygamous households." Ronald K. Esplin and Daniel Bachman, "Plural Marriage," *Encyclopedia of Mormonism,* ed. Daniel H. Ludlow, 4 vols. (New York: Macmillan, 1992), 3:1095. According to George D. Smith, before Joseph Smith was killed in June 1844 there were thirty men who had married additional wives. By the time the Saints left Nauvoo in February 1846, 153 men had been sealed to a total of 587 wives. (Church membership at that time was approximately 30,000, which would mean 2.6% were part of polygamous relationships.) George D. Smith estimates that by 1890, when the Manifesto was issued, approximately 2,450 husbands were plurally married to 6,200 wives. (Church membership at that time was approximately 188,000, so that means approximately 4.6% were in polygamous relationships.) See "Nauvoo Roots of Mormon Polygamy, 1841–46: A Preliminary Demographic Report," *Dialogue: A Journal of Mormon Thought,* 27, no. 1 (Spring 1994), 1–72. These figures are consistent with the assessments made at the time. See "Comments of Nobel and Miller on the Manifesto," *Deseret Weekly*, October 18, 1890, 540. http://contentdm.lib.byu.edu/cdm/

compoundobject/collection/desnews4/id/15816/rec/84.

802. B. H. Roberts, *A Comprehensive History of the Church of Jesus Christ of Latter-day Saints,* 6 vols. (Salt Lake City, Deseret News Press, 1930), 5: 527.

803. Jedediah Rogers, ed., *In the President's Office: The Diaries of L. John Nuttall 1879–1892* (Salt Lake City: Signature Books, 2007), 298, December 19, 1888.

804. Heber J. Grant, *diary,* December 20, 1888. Heber J. Grant Collection, 1852–1945, MS 1233, Church History Library, Salt Lake City. See also George Q. Cannon's discourse, "Box Elder Stake Conference," *Deseret Weekly,* November 7, 1891, 627. http://lib.byu.edu/digital/deseret_news/.

805. "Remarks Made by President Wilford Woodruff at Cache Stake Conference . . . November 1, 1891," *Deseret Weekly,* November 14, 1891, 659. http://lib.byu.edu/digital/deseret_news/.

806. "Box Elder Stake Conference," Ibid., November 7, 1891, 627.

807. "Remarks by President Wilford Woodruff . . . July 29, 1889," *Millennial Star* 51:30 (September 23, 1889), 595. http://contentdm.lib.byu.edu/cdm/compoundobject/collection/MStar/id/18767/rec/51.

808. *Journal of Discourses,* 26 vols. (Liverpool and London: F. D. and S. W. Richards, 1854–86), 22:147, April 3, 1881.

809. Ibid.

810. Ibid.

811. The following is a brief chronology of the government actions leading up to the Manifesto: January 18, 1888, Utah Territorial Supreme Court denies an appeal to the U.S. Supreme Court in the case of appointing a receiver for the Church property. July 6, 1888, Church farm in Salt Lake County is turned over to Receiver Frank Dyer. July 9, 1888, Dyer petitions the Supreme Court of Utah to have over $157,000 worth of Church property delivered to him. July 10, 1888, Majority of Church property is turned over to Dyer on compromise regarding temples, pending appeal to the U.S. Supreme Court. September 17, 1888, Dyer threatens to break agreement not to confiscate the temples. October 9, 1888, the Utah Supreme Court approves the agreement reached in July to end the lawsuit and the Temple Block is returned to the Church. January 19, 1889, U.S. Supreme Court arguments heard in *Mormon Church v. United States* 136 U.S. 1. February 18, 1889, Receiver Dyer is examined in court, and nothing is found against his actions regarding the Church property. July 12, 1889, Charles S. Varian appointed as United States Attorney for Utah. September 27, 1889, Utah Commission report says Utah needs harsher measures. November 30, 1889, Third District Court Judge Anderson rules that Mormons immigrating to United States cannot be admitted as citizens. February 3, 1890, U.S. Supreme Court affirms the constitutionality of the Idaho test oath in the case of *Davis v. Beason.* March 1890, Utah Supreme Court terminated the lease of the Church offices. April 11, 1890, Cullom-Struble Bill introduced in Congress to disenfranchise all Utah Mormons through test oath similar to Idaho test oath. July 10, 1890, Receiver Dyer resigns. July 16, 1890, Utah Supreme Court appoints Henry W. Lawrence as Receiver. Special Commission appointed in August 1890 to review Utah Supreme Court's approval of 1888 agreement exempting temples from seizure by the government and Dyer's subsequent actions. Court hearings scheduled for September 1890.

812. *Wilford Woodruff's Journal*, 8:499–500, May 17–21, 1888.

813. Ibid., 8:498, May 15, 1888.

814. Ibid., 8:499, May 17, 1888.

815. Ibid.

816. Ibid. See also Heber J. Grant, *diary*, August 3, 1887, Heber J. Grant Collection, 1852–1945, MS 1233, Church History Library, Salt Lake City. "This morning at 10 o'clock attended a meeting at the President's office. . . . [Wilford Woodruff] had felt strong desires that our temples might be preserved from our enemies and had pray[ed] earnestly to God that they might not be defiled and his hopes and faith were that they would be protected."

817. *Wilford Woodruff's Journal*, 8:502, May 30, 1888; 8:504, June 13, 1888; and 8:506, June 28, 1888. See also Rogers, *In the President's Office*, 258, July 19, 1888.

818. *Wilford Woodruff's Journal*, 8:520, October 8, 1888.

819. Ibid., 8:507, July 2, 1888. "We closed our U.S. suit with Peters and Dyer. . . . It has been a hard piece of work to form this settlement with Peters and Dyer," Ibid., 8:508, July 9, 1888. "I had an interview . . . concerning our settlement with Dyer and Peters and we find that they are determined to try to break the Settlement." Ibid., 8:517, September 17, 1888.

820. Ibid., 8:489–91, March 20–26, 1888.

821. Rogers, *In the President's Office*, 320, February 27, 1889. This difficult transition was the reason Wilford instructed the Quorum of the Twelve Apostles to immediately reorganize the First Presidency upon his death, rather than allow the multi-year apostolic interregna that had followed the deaths of Joseph Smith, Brigham Young, and John Taylor.

822. *Wilford Woodruff's Journal*, 9:15, April 3–5, 1889.

823. Ibid., 9:16, April 7, 1889.

824. Wilford Woodruff, *Leaves from My Journal* (Salt Lake City: Juvenile Instructor Office, 1882), 3. See also *Journal of Discourses*, 4:99, October 6, 1856. With the death of Erastus Snow on May 27, 1888, Wilford was the only living Apostle within the Church called by Joseph Smith. See *Wilford Woodruff's Journal*, 8:501.

825. *Wilford Woodruff's Journal*, 9:16, April 7, 1889.

826. Ibid., 9:235, January 5, 1893.

827. Ibid., 9:284, January 9, 1894.

828. Ibid., 9:224, October 28, 1893; 9:275, December 13, 1893; and 9:276, December 19, 1893.

CHAPTER 15

829. James R. Clark, *Messages of the First Presidency of The Church of Jesus Christ of Latter-day Saints 1833-1964*. 6 vols. (Salt Lake City: Bookcraft, Inc., 1966), 3:183–87. Published in *Deseret Weekly*, December 21, 1889, 809–10. http://contentdm.lib. byu.edu/cdm/compoundobject/collection/desnews7/id/2316/rec/5. See also Abraham H. Cannon, *Candid Insights of a Mormon Apostle: The Diaries of Abraham H. Cannon 1889–1895*, edited by Edward Leo Lyman (Salt Lake City: Signature Books, 2010), 36.

830. *Journal of Discourses,* 26 vols. (Liverpool and London: F. D. and S. W. Richards, 1854–86), 25:210–11, June 29, 1884.

831. Ibid.

832. *Wilford Woodruff's Journal, 1833–1898, Typescript,* edited by Scott G. Kenney, 9 vols. (Midvale, Utah: Signature Books, 1983–1984), 9:94, May 19, 1890. Late Corporation of the Church of Jesus Christ of Latter-day Saints v. United States (136 US 1, 1890). (US Reports 136:1–68 *The late corporation of the Church of Jesus Christ of Latter-day Saints vs. U.S.,* Numbers 1030, 1054).

833. "The Church Cases," *Deseret Weekly,* September 13, 1890, 380–83. http://contentdm.lib.byu.edu/cdm/compoundobject/collection/desnews9/id/185 76/rec/74; "The Church Cases," Ibid., September 20, 1890, 433–35. http:// contentdm.lib.byu.edu/cdm/compoundobject/collection/desnews4/id/15346/ rec/77; "The Church Cases," Ibid., September 27, 1890, 455–58. http://content dm.lib.byu.edu/cdm/compoundobject/collection/desnews4/id/15450/rec/79.

834. Section 13 of the Edmunds-Tucker Act, 24 Stat. 635, c. 397, included the following provision: "That it shall be the duty of the attorney general of the United States to institute and prosecute proceedings to forfeit and escheat to the United States the property of [the Church] . . . provided, that no building, or the grounds appurtenant thereto, which is held and occupied exclusively for purposes of the worship of God, or parsonage connected therewith, or burial-ground, shall be forfeited."

835. *Wilford Woodruff's Journal,* 2:297, September 10, 1843.

836. *Diary Excerpts of Brigham Young Jr.,* 1874–1899. New Mormon Studies [CD ROM]. (Salt Lake City: Signature Books, 1997), September 24, 1890. "I can see the necessity of the Presidency and Twelve coming to the front to assure the nation we mean what we say. Pres[iden]t Woodruff said before I left, 'we must do something to save our Temples.' Someone may ask Can't God save them? I answer yes, and you might even now be redeemed had the people obeyed the counsel our leaders were inspired to give them in the past. I will do whatever my leaders counsel, but the base thought of taking clemency from U.S.A. that has destroyed the prophets and has thrust us out to perish, pains me more than I can tell."

837. "Remarks Made by President George Q. Cannon, at Cache Stake Conference . . . November 1st, 1891," *Deseret Weekly,* November 21, 1891, 691. http:// contentdm.lib.byu.edu/cdm/compoundobject/collection/desnews4/id/22707/ rec/5.

838. Ibid.

839. *Wilford Woodruff's Journal,* 9:168–70, October 25, 1891. "Remarks Made by President Wilford Woodruff at Cache Stake Conference . . . November 1, 1891," *Deseret Weekly,* November 14, 1891, 659. http://contentdm.lib.byu.edu/cdm/ compoundobject/collection/desnews4/id/22707/rec/5.

840. *Wilford Woodruff's Journal,* 9:112–13, September 25, 1890. In the December 19, 1891, petition to President Benjamin Harrison requesting amnesty, the First Presidency and Quorum of Twelve stated, "According to our faith the head of the Church receives from time to time, revelations for the religious guidance of his people. In September, 1890, the present head of the Church, in anguish and prayer, cried to God for help for his flock, and received the permission to advise the

members of the Church of Jesus Christ of Latter-day Saints that the law command-
ing polygamy was henceforth suspended," *Messages of the First Presidency*, 3:230.
Benjamin Harrison: "Proclamation 346 – Granting Amnesty and Pardon for the
Offense of Engaging in Polygamous or Plural Marriage to Members of the Church
of Latter-Day Saints," January 4, 1893, Gerhard Peters and John T. Woolley, *The
American Presidency Project.* http://www.presidency.ucsb.edu/ws/?pid=71164. The
Manifesto was incorporated into the Doctrine and Covenants in 1908.

841. Marriner Wood Merrill, *Utah Pioneer and Apostle Marriner Wood Merrill and
His Family.* Edited by Melvin Clarence Merrill. (Salt Lake City: Deseret News, 1937),
September 24, 1890, 127.

842. "Remarks Made by President Wilford Woodruff at Cache Stake Conference . . . November 1, 1891," *Deseret Weekly*, November 14, 1891, 659. http://
contentdm.lib.byu.edu/cdm/compoundobject/collection/desnews4/id/22707/
rec/5.

843. "We received a telegram from President Woodruff containing a declaration ^or manifesto^ from him in regard to recent report of the Utah Commission
on the subject of Polygamous Marriages & of the preaching of that doctrine by the
Church Authorities, in which he denies their statements and declares himself as
willing to obey the laws of the nation on that subject & to advise the members of
the church to do likewise, &c. Bro [John T]. Caine made arrangements to have the
declaration ^or manifesto^ published in the Evening "Star ^& Critic"^ and to have
it printed in a circular letter or pamphlet for distribution to the President, Cabinet,
Senate & House of Reps & other leading men." See Jedediah Rogers, ed., *In the
President's Office: The Diaries of L. John Nuttall 1879–1892* (Salt Lake City: Signature
Books, 2007), 417–18, September 25, 1890. Note: ^^ marks in the quote above
indicate what John Nuttall wrote above the lines of text in his journal.

844. *Wilford Woodruff's Journal*, 9:117, October 6, 1890.

845. "Remarks by President George Q. Cannon and President Wilford
Woodruff ... immediately following the adoption by the General Assembly of the
Manifesto . . . ." *Deseret Weekly*, October 18, 1890, 551. http://contentdm.lib.byu.
edu/cdm/compoundobject/collection/desnews4/id/15816/rec/84.

846. "General Conference," *Latter-day Saints' Millennial Star* 52:46, (November
17, 1890), 723–25. http://contentdm.lib.byu.edu/cdm/compoundobject/
collection/MStar/id/33305/rec/52. See also "General Conference," *Millennial Star*
52:47 (November 24, 1890), 737–38; and "Discourse by President Wilford Woodruff," *Millennial Star* 56:22 (May 28, 1894), 337. "There has never been a time when
a doctrine has been presented to us by the servants of God that has appeared new
or mysterious, but what the Spirit of God has been ready to bear testimony to the
truth of the same."

847. "General Conference," *Millennial Star* 52:47 (November 24, 1890), 739.
http://contentdm.lib.byu.edu/cdm/compoundobject/collection/MStar/id/33305/
rec/52.

848. *Wilford Woodruff's Journal*, 9:67–69, November 24, 1889.

849. See Rogers, *In the President's Office*, 393–94, September 24, 1889.

850. *Wilford Woodruff's Journal*, 8:133, November 22, 1882.

851. Cannon, *Candid Insights*, 135, September 26, 1890. "In his declaration . . . there is no renunciation of principle nor abandonment of families recommended, as some fault-finders try to make it appear."

852. See, for example, Rogers, *In the President's Office*, 309, January 23, 1889. "A letter was written to Pres[iden]t M[arriner] W[ood] Merrill of Logan Temple to discontinue Plural Marriages for the present and until further advised unless for special occasions, for prudential reasons."

853. Doctrine and Covenants, Official Declaration-1.

854. Ibid., Excerpts from Three Addresses by President Wilford Woodruff Regarding the Manifesto.

855. *Wilford Woodruff's Journal*, 8:520, October 5, 1888; 7:457–67, February 21, 1879; and 9:58–59, December 20, 1888.

856. "Remarks Made by President Wilford Woodruff at Cache Stake Conference . . . November 1, 1891," *Deseret Weekly*, November 14, 1891, 660. http://lib.byu.edu/digital/deseret_news/.

857. Cannon, *Candid Insights*, 38–39, December 20, 1889.

858. *Wilford Woodruff's Journal*, 9:69, November 24, 1889.

859. *Messages of the First Presidency*, "First Presidency, October 6, 1885," 3:26–27, 3:32–33.

860. Quoting "testimony of the witnesses on the defendant's side," made Wednesday, October 28, 1891, before Judge Loofbourrow in "Arguments in the Church Cases," *Deseret News Weekly*, October 31, 1891, 611. http://lib.byu.edu/digital/deseret_news/.

861. Ibid. Quoting Charles S. Varian, US Attorney for the Territory of Utah.

862. "Remarks Made by President Wilford Woodruff at Cache Stake Conference . . . November 1, 1891," *Deseret Weekly*, November 14, 1891, 659–60. http://lib.byu.edu/digital/deseret_news/.

863. Jacob 2:27–30. See also *Wilford Woodruff's Journal*, 7:459, February 22, 1879.

864. Cannon, *Candid Insights*, 135, September 26, 1890.

865. See, for example, Ibid., 147, 261.

866. Joseph Smith was told, "If thou livest until thou art eighty-five years old, thou shalt see the face of the Son of Man" (See Doctrine and Covenants 130:14–17; April 6, 1843); and as a result, some Saints believed the Second Coming of Christ would take place in 1890 or 1891 because Joseph Smith was born December 23, 1805. However, Joseph believed the revelation simply meant Christ would not come before that time. In an 1844 discourse, Joseph Smith prophesied that Christ would not come before 1884. See *Wilford Woodruff's Journal*, 2:365, March 10, 1844.

867. *Journal of Discourses*, 18:116.

868. Ibid., 23:132–33, May 14, 1882. See also "The Manifesto and the End of Plural Marriage," October 27, 2014, https://www.lds.org/topics/the-manifesto-and-the-end-of-plural-marriage?lang=eng.

869. "Box Elder Stake Conference," *Deseret Weekly*, November 7, 1891, 627. (Discourse delivered October 25, 1891.) http://contentdm.lib.byu.edu/cdm/compoundobject/collection/desnews9/id/26044/rec/91.

870. *Wilford Woodruff's Journal*, 9:235, January 5, 1893.

871. Ibid., 3:175, May 13, 1847.

872. Ibid., 9:187, March 2, 1892.

873. Ibid., 9:193, April 6, 1892.

874. Ibid.

875. Ibid., 9:194.

876. Ibid., 9:246, April 6, 1893.

877. "Annual Conference," *Deseret Weekly*, April 15, 1893, 514. http://content dm.lib.byu.edu/cdm/compoundobject/collection/desnews4/id/31956/rec/17. See also James E. Talmage, *The House of the Lord* (Salt Lake City: Deseret Book Co., 1968), 134–43.

878. Andrew Jenson, *Diaries*, April 7, 1893, Church History Library, Salt Lake City.

879. Doctrine and Covenants, Official Declaration-1, Excerpts from Three Addresses by President Wilford Woodruff Regarding the Manifesto.

880. Ibid. From a discourse at the sixth session of the dedication of the Salt Lake Temple, April 1893. Typescript of Dedicatory Services, Church History Library, Salt Lake City.

881. *Wilford Woodruff's Journal*, 9:259–64, August 29, 1893.

882. *Report of the commissioners from Connecticut of the Columbian Exhibition of 1893 at Chicago* by Morris Woodruff Seymour (Connecticut: Board of World's Fair Managers, Connecticut at the World's Fair, 1893), 188. https://archive.org/stream/connecticutatwor00conn#page/188/mode/2up/search/wilford.

883. *Wilford Woodruff's Journal*, 9:279, December 31, 1893.

884. Ibid.

885. Ibid., 9:311.

886. Ibid., 9:342–51.

887. Ibid., 9:385, January 4, 1896.

888. Ibid., January 6, 1896.

889. Ibid., 9:386.

890. Ibid., 9:267, October 17, 1893. The Logan Temple was dedicated in 1884, the Manti Temple in 1888, and the Salt Lake Temple in 1893.

891. First Presidency (Wilford Woodruff, George Q. Cannon, and Joseph F. Smith), Letter to Lorenzo Snow, President of the Salt Lake Temple, August 31, 1894. Devery S. Anderson, ed., *The Development of LDS Temple Worship* (Salt Lake City: Signature Books, 2011), 99–100. Original in *Wilford Woodruff Correspondence, 1887–1898*, MS 2081, Church History Library, Salt Lake City.

892. *Wilford Woodruff's Journal*, 9:298.

893. See Alma 5:21, 27; Doctrine and Covenants 82:14; Revelation 3:4–5.

894. Carlos E. Asay, "The Temple Garment: 'An Outward Expression of an Inward Commitment'," *The Ensign of The Church of Jesus Christ of Latter-day Saints* (August 1997): 19; Joseph F. Smith, *Improvement Era* (August 1906); 813. In 1923, Church leaders authorized changes in the one-piece pattern including the use of buttons instead of strings, sleeves above the elbow rather than down to the wrist, and legs that ended a few inches below the knee rather than extending down to the ankle. See First Presidency (Heber J. Grant, Charles W. Penrose, and Anthony W. Ivins) Letter to Stake and Temple Presidents, June 14, 1923. Anderson, ed.,

Development of LDS Temple Worship, 201. The two-piece garment was authorized in 1979.

895. William Clayton and George D. Smith, *An Intimate Chronicle: The Journals of William Clayton*, (Salt Lake City: Signature Books in Association with Smith Research Associates, 1995), 212, December 14, 1845.

896. Clayton, *An Intimate Chronicle*, 227–28, December 21, 1845.

897. Ibid.

898. Cannon, *Candid Insights*, 443, December 7, 1893.

899. Boyd K. Packer, *The Holy Temple*, (Salt Lake City: Bookcraft, 1980), 75–79.

900. First Presidency (Wilford Woodruff, George Q. Cannon, and Joseph F. Smith), Letter to Lorenzo Snow, President of the Salt Lake Temple, August 31, 1894. See Anderson, ed., *Development of LDS Temple Worship*, 99.

901. Evelyn T. Marshall, "Garments," in *Encyclopedia of Mormonism*, ed. Daniel H. Ludlow, 4 vols. (New York: Macmillan, 1992), 2:534.

902. *Messages of the First Presidency*, "Circular Letter from Wilford Woodruff, George Q. Cannon, and Joseph F. Smith, November 6, 1891," 3:228.

903. *Wilford Woodruff's Journal*, 9:73, 1889 Summary on December 31, 1889; 9:129, Synopsis of Labors December 31, 1890; and 9:177, 1891 Synopsis of *Journal* on December 31, 1891. Examples of per day numbers in Ibid., 9:95, May 29, 1890; and 9:119, October 16, 1890.

904. *Messages of the First Presidency*, "Circular Letter from Wilford Woodruff, George Q. Cannon, and Joseph F. Smith, November 6, 1891," 3:228.

905. Cannon, *Candid Insights*, 6, October 7, 1889.

906. Wilford Woodruff, Letter to Samuel A. Wooley, May 22, 1888. Anderson, ed., *Development of LDS Temple Worship*, 74.

907. Wilford Woodruff, Letter to Daniel H. Wells, September 18, 1888. Ibid., 76.

908. Doctrine and Covenants 2:2. See also Joseph Smith and B. H. Roberts, *History of the Church of Jesus Christ of Latter-day Saints* (Salt Lake City: Deseret Book Co., 1970), 6:251–54.

CHAPTER 16

909. *Journal of Discourses*, 26 vols. (Liverpool and London: F. D. and S. W. Richards, 1854–86), 2:196, February 25, 1855.

910. Ibid.

911. "General Conference," *Latter-day Saints' Millennial Star* (Liverpool, England: April 1842 – March 3, 1932), 53:26 (June 29, 1891), 403. http://contentdm.lib.byu.edu/cdm/compoundobject/collection/MStar/id/31248/rec/53.

912. "Speech Delivered by President B. Young . . . April 6th, 1845," *Times and Seasons,* July 1, 1845, 955. http://contentdm.lib.byu.edu/cdm/ref/collection/NCMP1820-1846/id/9684. "Joseph in his life time did not receive every thing (sic) connected with the doctrine of redemption, but he has left the key with those who understand how to obtain and teach to this great people all that is necessary for their salvation and exaltation in the celestial kingdom of our God."

913. *Journal of Discourses*, 5:84, April 9, 1857.

914. See examples in *Wilford Woodruff's Journal, 1833–1898, Typescript*, edited by Scott G. Kenney, 9 vols. (Midvale, Utah: Signature Books, 1983–1984), 6:39. See also Ibid., 5:553.

915. Ibid., 9:370.

916. Abraham H. Cannon, *Candid Insights of a Mormon Apostle: The Diaries of Abraham H. Cannon 1889–1895,* edited by Edward Leo Lyman (Salt Lake City: Signature Books, 2010.), 302–3, February 11, 1892. "We had some talk as to the correct form to be used by the person who administers the ordinance of baptism, and President Woodruff expressed himself in favor of adhering to the words used in the revelations of the Lord as contained in [Doctrine and Covenants 20:73], except in the case of baptism for the health, when the object of the ordinance might be mentioned [i.e. the phrase "for the restoration of health"]." See also Ibid., 441–42, 495–96.

917. *Wilford Woodruff's Journal,* 9:243, March 14, 1893.

918. Ibid., 9:243–44, March 14 and 18, 1893. See also *Messages of the First Presidency,* "Letter to Stake Presidencies, May 9, 1893," 3:245–46.

919. *Cannon, Candid Insights,* 441–42, November 29, 1893. "It was also decided that only the form given for baptism in the Doctrine and Covenants shall be used in the administration of this ordinance, except in the performance of baptism for the dead in the temples, where for adults they use the words, 'Being commissioned of Jesus Christ I baptize you ---- for and in behalf of ----, who is dead for the remission of your sins,' etc. It was decided that his matter of temple work shall be considered later." See also Ibid. 495–596; Jean Bickmore White, ed., *Church, State, and Politics: The Diaries of John Henry Smith,* (Salt Lake City: Signature Books, 1990), 302; and Charles L. Walker, Andrew Karl Larson, and Katharine Miles Larson, *Diary of Charles Lowell Walker,* 2 vols. (Logan: Utah State University Press, 1980), 2:302.

920. See George Q. Cannon's discourse as recorded by Charles O. Card in Donald G. Godfrey and Brigham Y. Card, eds., *The Diaries of Charles Ora Card: The Canadian Years 1886–1903* (Salt Lake City: University of Utah Press, 1993), 286; Thomas G. Alexander, *Mormons in Transition: A History of the Latter-Day Saints, 1890–1930,* (Urbana and Chicago: University of Illinois Press, 1996), 290–91; and Marriner W. Merrill, "Cache Stake Conference, Logan, Utah, July 12, 1897," *Deseret Weekly,* July 17, 1897, 148. "He thought there was a danger of invading the sanctity of these ordinances [administration to the sick and baptism] by making too common a use of them. . . . Christ was baptized but once and he is an example to all. If any who are baptized by proper authority have sinned they should repent and seek forgiveness and that is all that is necessary." http://lib.byu.edu/digital/deseret_news/.

921. Anecdotal evidence of the waning of rebaptism is the fact that, following the Church-wide reorganization in 1877 and the death of President Brigham Young, rebaptism is only mentioned five times in Wilford's journals. See *Wilford Woodruff's Journal,* 7:598, October 21, 1880; 8:211, December 12, 1883; and 8:289, December 9, 1884. However, the distinction between baptism for a remission of sin and baptism for the renewal of covenants is evidenced by a letter George Reynolds wrote on behalf of the First Presidency to Arthur Eroppe. In 1888 he told Arthur

that the "universal rule"—that all emigrants should be rebaptized and reconfirmed when they reached Zion—was still in force: "This requirement has been observed by the President of the Church, and all its officers and members, and would be required of you on your arrival." See George Reynolds, on behalf of the First Presidency, Letter to Arthur Eroppe, March 9, 1888, typescript, Scott Kenney Research Collection, First Presidency, Correspondence (1887–1896), Special Collections, J. Willard Marriott Library, University of Utah, Salt Lake City.

922. The First Presidency under Heber J. Grant sent instructions to all temple presidents calling attention to the custom prevailing "to some extent in our temples" of baptizing for health, stating it was detrimental to temple work. The letter also indicated that the practice of Church members going to the temples to be administered to was also a departure from revealed instruction and should be stopped. See *Messages of the First Presidency,* 5:224. (Letters dated December 15, 1922 and January 18, 1923.)

923. *Wilford Woodruff's Journal,* 9:370.

924. "President Lorenzo Snow called attention to the form of baptism used in the temples on behalf of the dead, in which the words 'for the remission of your sins' were interpolated, being different from the form of baptism for the living. President Joseph F. Smith said he had noticed in baptizing a person for health the words were used 'for the renewal of your covenants, the remission of your sins and the restoration of your health'. It was the unanimous sense of the Council that these forms should be corrected by letter of instructions to the Temple Presidents." Minutes of May 7, 1896, meeting of the First Presidency and Apostles, *Church Historian's Office Journal History of the Church 1896–2001,* CR 100 137, vol. 323, image 59. http://eadview.lds.org/findingaid/viewer?pid=IE502434&pds_handle=.

925. George Q. Cannon, October 6, 1897, *Conference Report,* October 1897, 68. See also Joseph Fielding Smith, *Doctrines of Salvation,* compiled by Bruce R. McConkie, 3 vols. (Salt Lake City: Bookcraft, 1960), 2:335.

926. In the Manti Temple, the number of baptisms for renewal of covenants decreased from 835 in 1888, the year it was dedicated, to zero in 1897; the only year baptisms for renewal of covenants were performed in the Salt Lake Temple was 1893, the year it was dedicated, and there were thirty-four. Rebaptisms for remission of sins were still performed in the St. George Temple until 1900: twenty-six in 1898, seven in 1899 and three in 1900; rebaptisms continued in the Logan Temple until 1907. Rebaptism was specifically allowed for individuals subject to Church discipline who were not excommunicated.

927. "Minutes of May 7, 1896, meeting of the First Presidency and Apostles," *Church Historian's Office Journal History of the Church 1896–2001,* CR 100 137, vol. 323, image 59. http://eadview.lds.org/findingaid/viewer?pid=IE502434&pds_handle=.

928. First Presidency (Wilford Woodruff, George Q. Cannon, and Joseph F. Smith), Letter to Temple Presidents, May 20, 1896. See Devery S. Anderson, ed., *The Development of LDS Temple Worship* (Salt Lake City: Signature Books, 2011, 103–104.

929. Ibid.

930. *Messages of the First Presidency,* 5:224–25.

931. Baptisms for healing were ended altogether in 1923 under the direction of President Heber J. Grant. First Presidency, Letter to Temple Presidents, December 15, 1922; and Circular Letter to Stake Presidents, January 18, 1923, *Messages of the First Presidency*, 5:224.

932. *Journal of Discourses*, 8:265, April 22, 1860.

933. "Discourse by President Wilford Woodruff," *Millennial Star*, 56:22 (May 28, 1894), 338. http://contentdm.lib.byu.edu/cdm/compoundobject/collection/MStar/id/20113/rec/56. See Malachi 4:5–6. See also *Journal of Discourses*, 9:325 for statement by Wilford Woodruff on spiritual confirmation of doctrinal changes.

934. "Discourse by President Wilford Woodruff," *Millennial Star* 56:22 (May 28, 1894), 337. http://contentdm.lib.byu.edu/cdm/compoundobject/collection/MStar/id/20113/rec/56. See also *Wilford Woodruff's Journal*, 3:134.

935. *Journal of Discourses*, 5:85, April 9, 1857.

936. George Q. Cannon, "President Woodruff's Birthday," *Deseret Weekly*, March 6, 1897, 371. http://lib.byu.edu/digital/deseret_news/.

937. See discourses delivered prior to his death in Joseph Smith and B. H. Roberts, *History of the Church of Jesus Christ of Latter-day Saints* (Salt Lake City: Deseret Book Co., 1970), 5:530–31, August 13, 1843, and 5:554–55, August 27, 1843.

938. *Wilford Woodruff's Journal*, 6:507–508, December 11, 1869. See also "Minutes of the Thirty-fifth Semi-annual Conference . . . October 6, 7, 8, and 9, 1865," *Millennial Star* 27:49 (December 9, 1865), 771; "Discourse by Brigham Young . . . January 24, 1869," *Millennial Star* 31:13, 203–204, March 27, 1869; and *Journal of Discourses*, 10:254; 12:161–67; 16:185–89.

939. *Wilford Woodruff's Journal*, 4:390, January 13, 1856.

940. Ibid.

941. Ibid.

942. *Journal of Discourses*, 9:269, April 6, 1862.

943. Ibid.

944. Ibid., 11:326, February 10, 1867.

945. See Daniel H. Wells, "Minutes of a Meeting at Ogden," *Millennial Star* 34:27 (July 2, 1872), 417. http://contentdm.lib.byu.edu/cdm/compoundobject/collection/MStar/id/25727/rec/34; and Brigham Young, *Journal of Discourses*, 16:185–89, September 4, 1875.

946. See, for example, *Wilford Woodruff's Journal*, 8:154, February 18, 1883.

947. *Journal of Discourses*, 21:284, July 4, 1880.

948. *Wilford Woodruff's Journal*, 7:340, March 22, 1877.

949. Ibid., 9:408.

950. Ibid., 4:133, April 11, 1852.

951. Jedediah Rogers, ed., *In the President's Office: The Diaries of L. John Nuttall 1879–1892* (Salt Lake City: Signature Books, 2007), 152–53, June 16, 1884. "[A]fter due consideration of the whole case the First Presidency decided that Sister Ellen Clifford be permitted to make her choice as to whether she will be sealed to her first husband Thomas Andrews (dead) or to her second husband John E. Hansen (now living) and in case she chooses to be sealed to Brother Hansen, that Brother Hansen . . . and Sister Hansen have some woman sealed to Brother Andrews and also have the children and Brother Andrews adopted into their family."

952. *Wilford Woodruff's Journal*, 6:232, July 13, 1865.

953. Ibid., 8:64. Sarah Emma was born July 14, 1838, and died July 17, 1840.

954. James B. Allen, "Line Upon Line," *The Ensign of The Church of Jesus Christ of Latter-day Saints* (July 1979): 37.

955. *Wilford Woodruff's Journal*, 6:349, June 15, 1867. See also Ibid., 6:553, 6:561.

956. Gordon Irving, "The Law of Adoption: One Phase of the Development of the Mormon Concept of Salvation," 1830–1900, *BYU Studies* 14, no. 3 (1974), 302.

957. Ogden Kraut, comp., *L. John Nuttall Diary Excerpts* (Salt Lake City: Pioneer Press, Salt Lake City, 1994), 105.

958. Ibid.

959. Ibid.

960. Ibid.

961. *Wilford Woodruff's Journal*, 9:203.

962. Ibid., 5:3–4, January 3, 1857.

963. Ibid., 9:204, June 13–15, 1892. See also Ibid., 6:553.

964. Ibid., 9:203, June 11, 1892. Walker et al, *Diary of Charles Lowell Walker*, 2:740–41, June 11, 1892.

965. *Wilford Woodruff's Journal*, 3:130–131, February 16, 1847.

966. "The Law of Adoption," *Deseret Weekly*, April 21, 1894, 541–44. http://contentdm.lib.byu.edu/cdm/compoundobject/collection/desnews7/id/7443/rec/16.

967. "Discourse by President Wilford Woodruff," *Millennial Star* 56:22 (May 28, 1894), 337. http://contentdm.lib.byu.edu/cdm/compoundobject/collection/MStar/id/20113/rec/56. See also "Speech Delivered by President B. Young . . . April 6th, 1845," *Times and Seasons*, July 1, 1845, 954–955. http://contentdm.lib.byu.edu/cdm/ref/collection/NCMP1820-1846/id/9684.

968. "Discourse by President Wilford Woodruff," *Millennial Star*, 56:22 (May 28, 1894), 337. http://contentdm.lib.byu.edu/cdm/compoundobject/collection/MStar/id/20113/rec/56.

969. Ibid.

970. Ibid., 337–38.

971. Wilford himself had given this answer when asked by Eliza I. Jones in 1888. "We do not consider it safe for a woman in the Church to be sealed to a man who died before receiving the gospel." Wilford Woodruff, Letter to Eliza I. Jones, February 24, 1888. Anderson, ed., *Development of LDS Temple Worship*, 71.

972. "Discourse by President Wilford Woodruff," *Millennial Star*, 56:22 (May 28, 1894), 339. http://contentdm.lib.byu.edu/cdm/compoundobject/collection/MStar/id/20113/rec/56.

973. Ibid.

974. Doctrine and Covenants 128:9–10.

975. "Discourse by President Wilford Woodruff," *Millennial Star*, 56:22 (May 28, 1894), 337. http://contentdm.lib.byu.edu/cdm/compoundobject/collection/MStar/id/20113/rec/56. "There has never been a time when a doctrine has been presented to us by the servants of God that has appeared new or mysterious, but

what the Spirit of God has been ready to bear testimony to the truth of the same." *Journal of Discourses,* 9:325, April 8, 1862.

976. *Journal of Discourses,* 18:190–91, April 6, 1876.

977. "Discourse Delivered by President Wilford Woodruff at the General Conference . . . April 6, 1891," *Deseret Weekly,* April 25, 1891, 554. http://lib.byu. edu/digital/deseret_news/. See also "General Conference," *Millennial Star* 53:26 (June 29, 1891), 406. http://contentdm.lib.byu.edu/cdm/compoundobject/ collection/MStar/id/31248/rec/53.

978. "The Law of Adoption," *Deseret Weekly,* April 21, 1894, 541–43. http://contentdm.lib.byu.edu/cdm/compoundobject/collection/desnews7/id/744 3/rec/16.

979. "Discourse by President Wilford Woodruff," *Millennial Star* 56:22 (May 28, 1894), 339–41. http://contentdm.lib.byu.edu/cdm/compoundobject/ collection/MStar/id/20113/rec/56.

980. "Discourse by President Wilford Woodruff," *Millennial Star* 56:21 (May 21, 1894), 325. http://contentdm.lib.byu.edu/cdm/compoundobject/collection/ MStar/id/20113/rec/56.

981. "Discourse by President George Q. Cannon," Ibid., 56:23 (June 4, 1894), 355, 358. http://contentdm.lib.byu.edu/cdm/compoundobject/collection/MStar/ id/20113/rec/56.

982. *Wilford Woodruff's Journal,* 9:461, April 17, 1897.

983. See Cannon, *Candid Insights,* 520, June 14, 1894. Wilford Woodruff did authorize the cancellation of some of the first adoptions performed to Church leaders in the Nauvoo Temple. See, for example, Devery S. Anderson and Gary James Bergera, eds, *The Nauvoo Endowment Companies, 1845–1846,* (Salt Lake City: Signature Books, 2005), 497, 583.

984. "Temple Policies and the New Family Search Website," accessed January 2, 2014, https://help.familysearch.org/publishing/620/110136_f.SAL_Member. html.

985. Doctrine and Covenants 138:34.

986. 2 Nephi 28:30.

987. "Discourse by President Wilford Woodruff," *Millennial Star* 56:21 (May 21, 1894), 325. http://contentdm.lib.byu.edu/cdm/compoundobject/collection/ MStar/id/20113/rec/56.

988. Ibid.

989. *Pearl of Great Price,* Articles of Faith 1:9

990. *Journal of Discourses,* 21:194, July 3, 1880.

991. Ibid., 18:190–91. April 6, 1876.

992. N. B. Lundwall, *Temples of the Most High* (Salt Lake City: Press of Zion's Printing & Publishing Co., 1943), 122.

993. Joseph Christenson's statement in *Utah Genealogical and Historical Magazine,* 28 (1937):149.

994. Franklin D. Richards' personal library of genealogical reference publications became the basis for the first genealogical library in 1884 that was housed in the Church Historian's Office. Each temple also had a genealogical library. See James B. Allen, Jessie L. Embry, and Kahlile B. Mehr. *Hearts Turned to the Fathers: A*

History of the Genealogical Society of Utah, Provo, Utah: BYU Studies Monograph Series, 1995.

CHAPTER 17

995. "Discourse by President Wilford Woodruff," *Latter-day Saints' Millennial Star* (Liverpool, England: April 1842 – March 3, 1932), 58:20 (May 14, 1896), 309. http://contentdm.lib.byu.edu/cdm/compoundobject/collection/MStar/id/36073/rec/58.

996. *Journal of Discourses*, 26 vols. (Liverpool and London: F. D. and S. W. Richards, 1854–86), 18:192, April 6, 1876.

997. "Discourse by President Wilford Woodruff," *Millennial Star* 58:47 (November 19, 1896), 742. http://contentdm.lib.byu.edu/cdm/compoundobject/collection/MStar/id/36073/rec/58.

998. "Remarks made at the Salt Lake Stake Conference Sunday, December 12, 1897, by President Wilford Woodruff," *Deseret Evening News*, December 18, 1897, 9. http://lib.byu.edu/digital/deseret_news/.

999. "Talks to the Sisters," *Deseret Weekly*, February 24, 1894, 288. http://contentdm.lib.byu.edu/cdm/compoundobject/collection/desnews7/id/6522/rec/8. See also "The Law of Adoption," Ibid., April 21, 1894, 541-544. http://contentdm.lib.byu.edu/cdm/compoundobject/collection/desnews7/id/7443/rec/16.

1000. "Discourse by President Wilford Woodruff," *Millennial Star* 58:20 (May 14, 1896), 309. http://contentdm.lib.byu.edu/cdm/compoundobject/collection/MStar/id/36073/rec/58.

1001. Ibid.

1002. *Journal of Discourses*, 18:188, April 6, 1876.

1003. Ibid., 18:188–89.

1004. Ibid., 22:147, April 3, 1881.

1005. Ibid., 18:190, April 6, 1876.

1006. "Discourse by President Wilford Woodruff," *Millennial Star* 56:22 (May 28, 1894), 341. http://contentdm.lib.byu.edu/cdm/compoundobject/collection/MStar/id/20113/rec/56.

1007. *Journal of Discourses*, 10:218–19, June 2, 1863.

1008. Ibid., 18:191, April 6, 1876.

1009. Ibid., 18:190.

1010. "Discourse delivered by President Wilford Woodruff . . . on August 3, 1890," *Deseret Weekly*, August 30, 1890, 308. http://contentdm.lib.byu.edu/cdm/compoundobject/collection/desnews9/id/18576/rec/74.

1011. Ibid.

1012. "As a people we aim at celestial glory; we aim at the establishment of the Kingdom of God." See *Journal of Discourses*, 21:192, July 3, 1880.

1013. Ibid., 13:167, December 12, 1869.

1014. First mission to the Southern United States from January 13, 1835 to November 25, 1836 (22.5 months); second mission to Connecticut and the Fox Islands, Maine, from May 31, 1837 to December 19, 1838 (18.5 months); third mission to the British Isles from August 8, 1839 to October 6, 1841 (26 months); fourth mission to the eastern United States from July 7 to November 4, 1843 (4 months); fifth mission to the eastern United States from May 9 to August 6, 1844 (3 months); sixth mission to the British Isles from August 12, 1844 to April 13, 1846 (20 months); seventh mission to the eastern United States from June 21, 1848 to October 14, 1850 (28 months). Total: 10 years and 2 months.

1015. Doctrine and Covenants 128:18.

1016. *Pearl of Great Price,* Moses 1:39.

1017. Joseph Fielding Smith, *Doctrines of Salvation,* compiled by Bruce R. McConkie, 3 vols. (Salt Lake City: Bookcraft, 1960), 2:122.

1018. *Journal of Discourses,* 19:228, September 16, 1877.

1019. "Discourse by President Wilford Woodruff," *Millennial Star* 58:20 (May 14, 1896), 307. http://contentdm.lib.byu.edu/cdm/compoundobject/collection/MStar/id/36073/rec/58.

1020. Transcript of Wilford Woodruff's Testimony, March 19, 1897, AV1, Church History Library, Salt Lake City. Spelling and punctuation modernized.

1021. "Remarks Made at the Salt Lake Stake Conference . . . December 12, 1897, by President Wilford Woodruff," *Deseret Evening News,* December 18, 1897, 9. http://udn.lib.utah.edu/cdm/compoundobject/collection/den1895/id/138051/rec/289.

1022. *Conference Report,* April 1898, 89–90.

1023. Ibid.

1024. *Journal of Discourses,* 8:269, August 26, 1860.

1025. Ibid.

1026. Ibid., 13:327. September 5, 1869.

1027. *Wilford Woodruff's Journal,* 9:556, July 24, 1898.

1028. Ibid., 9:561, September 2, 1898. Wilford was preceded in death by fourteen of his thirty-four children. Lucy Woodruff Smith, "President Wilford Woodruff," *Young Woman's Journal,* 9, no. 10 (October 1898), 437.

1029. Romans 14:9.

1030. 1 Peter 3:18–20; Doctrine and Covenants 138:30.

1031. 1 Peter 4:6.

1032. 1 Corinthians 15:22.

1033. *Conference Report,* October 1897, 47.

1034. Ibid. See "Discourse by President Wilford Woodruff," *Millennial Star* 56:22 (May 28, 1894), 341. http://contentdm.lib.byu.edu/cdm/compoundobject/collection/MStar/id/20113/rec/56.

1035. *Journal of Discourses,* 18:112, September 12, 1875.

1036. "Remarks made by President Wilford Woodruff at the St. George Stake Conference . . . June 12th and 13th, 1892," *Deseret Weekly,* August 6, 1892, 193. http://lib.byu.edu/digital/deseret_news/. See also *Journal of Discourses,* 21:301–2, August 1, 1880.

1037. *Journal of Discourses,* 18:189, April 6, 1876.

APPENDICES

Abbreviations:

D & C	*The Doctrine and Covenants*
EJ	*Elders' Journal of the Church*
HC	*History of the Church of Jesus Christ of Latter-day Saints*
JS—H	Joseph Smith—History in the *Pearl of Great Price*
MHC	*Manuscript History of the Church* at josephsmithpapers.org
WWJ	*Wilford Woodruff's Journal* Typescript

Appendix 1: Temple Ordinance Chronology

Location	Initial washings & anointings	Proxy baptisms	Endowments for the living	Proxy endowments	Rebaptisms	Baptisms for health/healing
Kirtland, Ohio	Mar 30, 1836– Apr 7, 1837	N/A	N/A	N/A	N/A	N/A
Nauvoo, Illinois	N/A	Sep 12, 1840– Aug 26, 1844	May 4, 1842--1845	N/A	1841–1842	1841–1845
Nauvoo Temple	N/A	Nov 21, 1841– Jan 9, 1845	Dec 10, 1845– Feb 7, 1846	N/A	1841–1845	1841–1845
During Exodus	N/A	Apr 4, 1848	N/A	N/A	Aug 8, 1846 Apr 4, 1847	Aug 8, 15, 1846 Jul 20, 1847 Jul 10, 1850
Salt Lake City	N/A	Aug 21, 1855	Oct 21, 1849–1851	N/A	Aug 6, 1847–?	1847–1923
Prophet's Office	N/A	N/A	N/A	N/A	N/A	N/A
Council House	N/A	N/A	Feb 21, 1851–55	N/A	N/A	N/A
Salt Lake Endowment House	N/A	Oct 23, 1857 Aug 19, 1865 Jul 25, 1867– Oct 26, 1876	May 5, 1855– Oct 26, 1876 Dec 29, 1877–1884	N/A	Oct 2, 1856– 1876	1856–1876
St. George Temple	N/A	Jan 9, 1877–	Jan 11, 1877–	Jan 11, 1877–	1877–1900	1877–1923
Logan Temple	N/A	May 21, 1884–	May 21, 1884–	May 21, 1884–	1884–1907	1884–1923
Manti Temple	N/A	May 29, 1888–	May 30, 1888–	May 30, 1888–	1888–1897	1888–1923
Salt Lake Temple	N/A	May 23, 1893–	May 24, 1893–	May 24, 1893–	1893	Apr 23, 1893–1923

Location	Sealing of spouses	Proxy sealing of spouses	Proxy priesthood ordinations	Sealing children to parents (living/proxy)	Priesthood adoptions (living/proxy)	Second anointings	Proxy second anointings
Kirtland, Ohio	1830s FA–JS?	N/A	N/A	N/A	N/A	N/A	N/A
Nauvoo, Illinois	Apr 5, 1841 (LB–JS?)– May 17, 1843	1842–1845	N/A	N/A	N/A	Sept 28, 1843–1844?	Nov 12, 1843–1844?
Nauvoo Temple	Jan 7– Feb 7, 1846	Jan 7–Feb 7, 1846	N/A	Jan 11–Feb 6, 1846	Jan 25–Feb 6, 1846	Jan 8–Feb 7, 1846	Jan 12–Feb 7, 1846
During Exodus	Nov 8, 1846–?	N/A	N/A	N/A	N/A	N/A	N/A
Historian's Office	Oct 13, 1849–?	N/A	N/A	N/A	N/A	Jan 7, 1867– Feb 28, 1869	Jan 24, 1867– Feb 28, 1869
Prophet's Office	1850s	?	N/A	N/A	N/A	Jan 7, 1867– 1868	?
Council House	1851–1855	?	N/A	N/A	N/A	Jan 14, 1867–1868	?
Salt Lake Endowment House	1855–1876 1877–1889	1855–1889?	N/A	N/A	N/A	Dec 31, 1866–1889	?
St. George Temple	Jan 11, 1877–	Jan 11, 1877–	Jan 11, 1877–	Mar 22, 1877–	Mar 2, 1877–?	Jan 16, 1877–	Feb 7, 1877–
Logan Temple	May 21, 1884–	May 1884–	May 1884–	May 21, 1884–	May 1884–?	May 1884–	1884–
Manti Temple	May 30, 1888–	1888–	1888–	Jun 6, 1888–	May 1888–1897	1888–	1888–
Salt Lake Temple	Apr 23, 1893–	1893–	1893–	Apr 8, 1893–	Apr 1893–?	Jun 7, 1893–	1893–

Appendix 2: Wilford Woodruff's Children

	Name	Birth Date	Place of birth	Death Date	Place of death	Mother
1	Sarah Emma	July 14, 1838	Scarborough, ME	July 17, 1840	Nauvoo, IL,	Phebe W. Carter
2	Wilford	March 22, 1840	Montrose, IA	May 6, 1921	Salt Lake City, UT	Phebe W. Carter
3	Phebe Amelia	March 4, 1842	Nauvoo, IL	Feb 15, 1919	Salt Lake City, UT	Phebe W. Carter
4	Susan Cornelia	July 25, 1843	Nauvoo, IL	Oct 6, 1897	Sioux City, IA	Phebe W. Carter
5	Joseph	July 18, 1845	Liverpool, England	Nov 12, 1846	Winter Quarters, NE	Phebe W. Carter
6	Ezra	Dec 8, 1846	Winter Quarters, NE	Dec 10, 1846	Winter Quarters, NE	Phebe W. Carter
7	James Jackson	May 25, 1847	Winter Quarters, NE	Dec 8, 1927	Salt Lake City, UT	Mary Ann Jackson
8	Shuah Carter	Oct 28, 1847	Council Bluffs, IA	July 22, 1848	Lost Grove, IL	Phebe W. Carter
9	Beulah Augusta	July 19, 1851	Salt Lake City, UT	Jan 13, 1905	Salt Lake City, UT	Phebe W. Carter
10	Aphek	Jan 25, 1853	Salt Lake City, UT	Jan 25, 1853	Salt Lake City, UT	Phebe W. Carter
11	David Patten	April 4, 1854	Salt Lake City, UT	Jan 20, 1937	Long Beach, CA	Sarah Brown
12	Brigham Young	Jan 18, 1857	Salt Lake City, UT	June 16, 1877	Smithfield, UT	Sarah Brown
13	Hyrum Smith	Oct 4, 1857	Salt Lake City, UT	Nov 24, 1858	Salt Lake City, UT	Emma Smith
14	Phebe Arabell	May 30, 1859	Salt Lake City, UT	Sept 7, 1939	Clearfield, UT	Sarah Brown
15	Emma Manella	July 4, 1860	Salt Lake City, UT	Nov 30, 1905	Vernal, UT	Emma Smith
16	Marion	June 1, 1861	Salt Lake City, UT	Feb 5, 1946	Tremonton, UT	Sarah Delight Stocking

17	Sylvia Melvina	Jan 14, 1862	Salt Lake City, UT	Aug 7, 1940	American Falls, ID	Sarah Brown
18	Asahel Hart	Feb 3, 1863	Salt Lake City, UT	July 2, 1939	Salt Lake City, UT	Emma Smith
19	Emeline	July 25, 1863	Salt Lake City, UT	May 25, 1915	Salt Lake City, UT	Sarah Delight Stocking
20	Newton	Nov 3, 1863	Salt Lake City, UT	Jan 21, 1960	Salt Lake City, UT	Sarah Brown
21	Ensign	Dec 23, 1865	Salt Lake City, UT	May 1, 1955	Murray, UT	Sarah Delight Stocking
22	Ann Thompson	April 10, 1867	Salt Lake City, UT	April 11, 1867	Salt Lake City, UT	Emma Smith
23	Mary	Oct 26, 1867	Salt Lake City, UT	Feb 15, 1903	Provo, UT	Sarah Brown
24	Clara Martisha	July 23, 1868	Salt Lake City, UT	Dec 29, 1927	Salt Lake City, UT	Emma Smith
25	Jeremiah	Aug 29, 1868	Fort Herriman, UT	Dec 16, 1869	Salt Lake City, UT	Sarah Delight Stocking
26	Charles Henry	Dec 5, 1870	Salt Lake City, UT	Feb 2, 1871	Salt Lake City, UT	Sarah Brown
27	Rosannah	April 17, 1871	Salt Lake City, UT	Oct 22, 1872	Salt Lake City, UT	Sarah Delight Stocking
28	Abraham Owen	Nov 23, 1872	Salt Lake City, UT	June 21, 1904	El Paso, TX	Emma Smith
29	Edward Randolph	Feb 2, 1873	Randolph, UT	Feb 8, 1873	Randolph, UT	Sarah Brown
30	John Jay	Aug 14, 1873	Salt Lake City, UT	Nov 1, 1964	Boise, ID	Sarah Delight Stocking
31	Winnifred Blanche	April 9, 1876	Salt Lake City, UT	April 28, 1954	Salt Lake City, UT	Emma Smith
32	Son	April 1, 1878?	Salt Lake City, UT?	April 1, 1878	Salt Lake City, UT?	Eudora Lovina Young?
33	Julia Delight Stocking	June 28, 1878	Salt Lake City, UT	Jan 8, 1954	Granger, UT	Sarah Delight Stocking
34	Mary Alice	Jan 2, 1879	Salt Lake City, UT	Jan 14, 1916	Salt Lake City, UT	Emma Smith

Appendix 3: Wilford Woodruff's Wives

	Parents	Relationship	Marriage/sealing	Divorce	Prior marriage	Subsequent marriage
Phebe Whittemore Carter Mar 8, 1807-Nov 10, 1885	Ezra Carter Sarah Fabyan	Wilford met Phebe in Kirtland, Ohio	Married April 13, 1837 in Kirtland, OH/Sealed Nov 11, 1843 in Nauvoo, Il.	N/A	N/A	N/A
Mary Ann Jackson Feb 18, 1818-Oct 25, 1894	William Jackson Elizabeth Lloyd	Woodruffs met Mary Ann on their mission in England	Aug 2, 1846 in Cutler's Park, Nebraska then Resealed Dec 1878?	May 11, 1848	N/A	David J. Ross Dec 13, 1857
Sarah Elinor Brown Aug 22, 1827-Dec 25, 1915	Charles Brown Mary Arey	Wilford met the Browns on his mission in Maine	Aug 2, 1846 in Cutler's Park, Nebraska	Aug 29, 1846	N/A	Lisbon Lamb Feb 15, 1849
Mary Caroline Barton Jan 12, 1829-Aug 10, 1910	William Allen Barton Mary Ann Swain	None known	Aug 2, 1846 in Cutler's Park, Nebraska	Aug 29, 1846	N/A	Erastus Curtis Feb 4, 1848
Mary Meek Giles Sept 6, 1802-Oct 3, 1852	Samuel Giles Elizabeth Reith	Woodruffs met Mary on their mission in Massachusetts?	Mar 26, 1852 in Woodruff's home in Salt Lake City, Utah	N/A	Nathan Webster	N/A
Sarah Brown Jan 1, 1834-May 9, 1909	Harry Brown Rhoda North	Wilford met Harry Brown in New York in 1834	Mar 13, 1853 in Endowment House in Salt Lake City, Utah	N/A	N/A	N/A
Emma Smith Mar 1, 1838-Mar 4,1912	Samuel Smith Martisha Smoot	Wilford met the Smiths on his mission in Kentucky	Mar 13, 1853 in Endowment House in Salt Lake City, Utah	N/A	N/A	N/A
Sarah Delight Stocking July 26, 1838-May 28, 1906	John Jay Stocking Catherine E. Ensign	Woodruffs knew the Stockings in Nauvoo	July 31, 1857 in Endowment House in Salt Lake City, Utah	N/A	N/A	N/A
Eudora Lovina Young May 12, 1852-Oct 21, 1921	Brigham Young Lucy Bigelow	Wilford met Eudora in St. George, Utah	Mar 10, 1877 in St. George Utah Temple	Nov 25, 1878	Moreland Dunford	Albert Hagen 1878 or 1879

Appendix 4: Timeline of Wilford Woodruff's Life

March 1, 1807	Wilford is born in Farmington Township (Avon), CT, to Beulah Thompson and Aphek Woodruff. WWJ 1:5
June 7, 1807	Wilford is baptized in the Northington Connecticut (Congregational) Church by Reverend Rufus Hawley.
June 11, 1808	Wilford's mother, Beulah Thompson Woodruff, dies at age 26 of spotted fever. WWJ 1:160, 215
1801–1809	Thomas Jefferson is third President of 16 United States.
March 4, 1809	James Madison is inaugurated as fourth President of 17 United States.
Nov 9, 1810	Wilford's father Aphek marries Azubah Hart; only two of their six children live to adulthood. WWJ 1:161, 215
March 4, 1817	James Monroe inaugurated as fifth President of 17 United States.
Spring 1820	Joseph Smith's First Vision. Joseph Smith—History 1:14–20
May 1, 1821	Wilford completes general education at age 14; lives with George Cowles for two years to learn miller's trade.
1821–1826	Wilford works summers, continues schooling at Farmington Academy during the winters. WWJ 1:260
Sept 21, 1823	Joseph Smith's second vision: instruction about the Book of Mormon and mission of Elijah. JS—H 1:30–54
March 4, 1825	John Quincy Adams is inaugurated as sixth President of 24 United States.
1827	Wilford begins managing mill for his Aunt Helen Wheeler.
Sept 22, 1827	Joseph Smith receives records to begin translation of the Book of Mormon. JS—H 1:59
March 4, 1829	Andrew Jackson is inaugurated as seventh President of 24 United States.
May–June 1829	Aaronic and Melchizedek priesthoods are restored. JS—H 1:68–72; Doctrine and Covenants 27:7–8, 12
June 1829	Joseph Smith finishes translating the Book of Mormon.
March 26, 1830	First copies of the Book of Mormon are available in Palmyra, New York.
April 6, 1830	Joseph Smith officially organizes the Church in Fayette Township, New York.
Spring 1830	Wilford is age 23 when Robert Mason prophesies of the restoration of the gospel and Wilford's place in it.
1830	Church membership reaches 200; the population of the 24 United States is 12,866,000.
May 1830	Wilford hired by Collins Ax Company to run their mill; works in Collinsville (South Canton), CT
Dec 1830	Joseph Smith is instructed to move the Church to Kirtland to receive endowment. D & C 37; 38:32
1831	Wilford works in Cowles mill in Farmington, Connecticut.
May 5, 1831	Wilford is baptized by immersion by George Phippen, a Baptist minister; does not join Baptist Church.
Feb 16, 1832	Joseph Smith receives revelation regarding the three degrees of glory. Doctrine and Covenants 76

March 8, 1832	First Presidency of the High Priesthood organized with Joseph Smith, Jesse Gause, and Sidney Rigdon
Spring 1832	Wilford reads newspaper article about the Mormons; intrigued by similarities to New Testament church.
Spring 1832	Wilford feels inspired to go to Rhode Island, but does not follow prompting.
May 1832	Wilford and his brothers purchase a farm, sawmill, and orchard in Richland, Oswego Co, NY. WWJ 1:215
Dec 1832	Joseph Smith commanded to build a temple in order to receive priesthood keys. D & C 88:119–120
June 5, 1833	Construction of the Kirtland Temple begins.
July 23, 1833	Cornerstones laid for the Kirtland Temple.
Dec 29, 1833	Wilford hears the restored gospel for the first time from Zerah Pulsipher and Elijah Cheney. WWJ 1:5–6
Dec 31, 1833	Wilford is baptized and confirmed by Zerah Pulsipher; Wilford's brother Azmon also baptized. WWJ 1:6
Jan 2, 1834	Richland Branch of Church organized; Azmon ordained a priest, Wilford ordained a teacher. by Zerah Pulsipher.
Jan 1834	Wilford begins preaching with Harry Brown (father of future wife Sarah) and James Blakesly. WWJ 1:6, 215.
April 1, 1834	Wilford is directed by Parley P. Pratt and Harry Brown to join Zion's Camp. WWJ 1:7
April 11, 1834	Wilford leaves New York to join Saints in Kirtland, Ohio. WWJ 1:7
April 25, 1834	Wilford arrives in Kirtland, Ohio, where he meets Joseph Smith and stays at his house for the week. WWJ 1:8
May–June 1834	Wilford travels with Zion's Camp to Missouri to help protect and defend persecuted Saints there. WWJ 1:9–12
July–Dec 1834	Wilford works in Clay County, Missouri, making brick to build the home of Michael Arthur. WWJ 1:14
Nov 5, 1834	Wilford ordained a priest by Simeon Carter at Adam-ondi-Ahman in Clay County, Missouri. WWJ 1:14, 215
Nov 13, 1834	Wilford licensed by Edward Partridge as a representative of the Church in order to serve a mission. WWJ 1:15
Dec 31, 1834	Wilford consecrates himself and all his earthly possessions to the Church. WWJ 1:16
Jan 13, 1835	Wilford leaves for his first mission in Arkansas, Kentucky, and Tennessee with Harry Brown. WWJ 1:17
Feb 14, 1835	The first Quorum of the Twelve Apostles is organized in Kirtland, Ohio. Doctrine and Covenants 107:23–24
June 28, 1835	Wilford ordained an Elder by Warren Parrish at Eagle Creek, Tennessee. WWJ 1:33, 215
Jan 21, 1836	First washings and anointings administered; vision of celestial kingdom in Kirtland Temple. D & C 137
March 27, 1836	Kirtland Temple is dedicated. Doctrine and Covenants 109
April 3, 1836	Jesus Christ appears in Kirtland Temple; Moses, Elias, Elijah confer priesthood keys. D & C 110; WWJ 1:67
April 19, 1836	Wilford called to be a member of the Second Quorum of the Seventy at age 29. WWJ 1:63
April 22, 1836	Wilford stays in Samuel Smith's home (father of future wife Emma Smith). WWJ 1:67
May 31, 1836	Wilford ordained a Seventy in Second Quorum of Seventy by David Patten and Warren Parrish. WWJ 1:74

Oct 25, 1836   Wilford leaves Kentucky to return to Ohio. WWJ 1:102

Nov 7, 1836   Wilford votes in national elections for Martin Van Buren (Pres.) and Richard Johnson (VP). WWJ 1:104

Nov 25, 1836   Wilford returns to Kirtland from mission to Southern states and tours Kirtland Temple. WWJ 1:106

December 1836   Wilford studies Latin and Greek in the Kirtland School (held in the attic of the temple). WWJ 1:111–141

Jan–Apr 1837   Wilford attends School of the Prophets. WWJ 1:118–126

Jan 3, 1837   Wilford called to be a member of the First Quorum of the Seventy. WWJ 1:118, 216

Jan 28, 1837   Wilford introduced to Phebe Whittemore Carter, a recent convert from Maine. WWJ 1:139

March 4, 1837   Martin Van Buren inaugurated as the eighth President of 26 United States.

March 23, 1837   Wilford spends his first day in the Kirtland Temple. WWJ 1:126–127

April 4–6, 1837   Wilford attends Solemn Assembly and receives washings and anointings in Kirtland Temple. WWJ 1:128–137

April 13, 1837   Wilford and Phebe married by Frederick G. Williams in Joseph Smith's home in Kirtland. WWJ 1:140–45

April 15, 1837   Wilford receives his patriarchal blessing from Joseph Smith Sr. WWJ 1:142–43

April–May 1837   Wilford and Phebe live with Warren and Martha Parrish; Wilford works for Heber C. Kimball. WWJ 1:146–7

May 1837   Woodruffs live with Jonathan and Olive Hale; Wilford records patriarchal blessings for Joseph Smith Sr.

June–Aug 1837   Phebe stays with Olive; Wilford leaves on mission to Canada/Maine with Jonathan Hale. WWJ 1:149

June 12, 1837   Wilford visits childhood home in Farmington, Connecticut and stays with his family. WWJ 1:258–270

July 6–20, 1837   Wilford meets with relatives in Connecticut. WWJ 1:159–165

July 12, 1837   Wilford baptizes his Uncle Ozem, Aunt Hannah, and cousin John Woodruff. WWJ 1:163

Aug 8, 1837   Wilford meets Phebe's family for the first time while visiting Scarborough, Maine. WWJ 1:167–169

Aug 19, 1837   Wilford arrives in the Fox Islands, Maine. WWJ 1:169

Dec 29, 1837   Wilford stays with Charles Brown (father of future wife Sarah E. Brown) WWJ 1:193

Jan 12, 1838   Joseph Smith moves Church to Far West, Missouri, to escape persecution in Ohio.

Apr 19, 1838   Wilford stays with Charles Brown (father of future wife Sarah E. Brown) WWJ 1:241

May 14, 1838   Wilford reads Parley P. Pratt's explanation of adoption by baptism into kingdom of God. WWJ 1:249

July 1838   Joseph Smith explains the need for all living and dead to receive ordinances. EJ 1:43

July 1, 1838   Wilford baptizes father Aphek, stepmother Azubah, half-sister Eunice in Farmington, CT. WWJ 1:264.

July 8, 1838   Wilford called to the Quorum of the Twelve Apostles. Doctrine and Covenants 118

July 14, 1838   Wilford present for birth of his first child, Sarah Emma, in Scarborough, Maine. WWJ 1:271–272

Aug 7, 1838   Wilford returns to his mission in the Fox Islands. WWJ 1:275

Aug 9, 1838	Wilford receives news of calling as an Apostle; call to go on mission to England with apostles. WWJ 1:276–277
Oct 4, 1838	Woodruffs begin trek from Maine to Missouri with group of converts to gather with the Saints. WWJ 1:294
Oct 27, 1838	Governor Boggs issues order expelling Saints from Missouri under threat of extermination. (WWJ 1:321)
Oct 30, 1838	Haun's Mill massacre in Caldwell County, Missouri, and surrender of Church leaders in Far West demanded.
Nov 1, 1838	Joseph and Hyrum Smith and other Church leaders surrender; General Samuel Lucas orders their execution.
November 1838	Court hearings to determine Church leaders' fate; Joseph, Hyrum and others are incarcerated in Liberty Jail.
Dec–Apr 1839	While Church leaders remain in Liberty Jail, the Saints are forced from Missouri and relocate in Illinois.
Nov–Dec 1839	Phebe deathly ill with brain fever; after her spirit leaves her body Wilford restores her to life. WWJ 1:303–306
Dec 11, 1839	Wilford's half-brother Asahel dies in Indiana at the age of 24 (last living of 5 half-brothers). WWJ 1:307–311
Dec '38–Mar 1839	Woodruffs winter in Rochester, IL with Brown family; Charles and Rebecca Brown die. WWJ 1:312–319, 351
March 16, 1839	Wilford, Phebe, and Sarah Emma finally arrive in Quincy, Illinois. WWJ 1:322
April 16, 1839	Church leaders escape Liberty Jail with help of guards; Saints move to Commerce, ILs and establish Nauvoo.
April 26, 1839	At age 32 Wilford is ordained an Apostle at the temple site in Far West, Missouri. WWJ 1:325–27
May 4, 1839	Wilford records his call to serve his third mission. WWJ 1:336
May 18, 1839	Woodruffs move to Montrose, IA, live in abandoned barracks with Brigham Young's family. WWJ 1:332
June 11, 1839	Joseph Smith begins dictating history to scribe James Mulholland; used in *Manuscript History of the Church*.
Aug 8, 1839	Wilford leaves on two year mission to England with John Taylor. WWJ 1:349
November 1839	*Times and Seasons* published in Nauvoo, Illinois through 1846.
Nov 3, 1839	Church historian James Mulholland dies; completed *Manuscript History of the Church* up to Sept 30, 1830.
Nov 29, 1839	Joseph Smith travels to Washington, D.C. to deliver Missouri redress petition to President Van Buren.
1840	Church membership is 16,800; population of the 26 United States is 17,100,000.
Jan 11, 1840	Wilford arrives in Liverpool, England; helps convert 1,800 people; serves until May 1841. WWJ 1:402–2:102
Feb 10, 1840	Wilford celebrates Queen Victoria's marriage to Prince Albert by preaching the gospel. WWJ 1:417
March 5, 1840	Wilford arrives at John Benbow's home; over 600 people baptized in 35 days. WWJ 1:424–439
March 22, 1840	Phebe's second child Wilford Jr. is born in Montrose, Iowa in Wilford's absence. WWJ 1:426
May 1840	*The Latter-Day Saints' Millennial Star* first published in Manchester, England by Parley P. Pratt.
July 17, 1840	Phebe's first child Sarah Emma dies at age two in Montrose, IA. WWJ 1:537, 541–542
Aug 14, 1840	Joseph Smith's first explanation of doctrine on baptism for the dead by living relatives. HC 4:179, 231

392

Aug 15, 1840	First baptisms for the dead performed in the Mississippi River.
September 1840	Joseph Smith announces the need to build a temple in Nauvoo.
Jan 19, 1841	Revelation to Joseph Smith on building Nauvoo Temple; place for baptisms and endowment. D &C 124:28–42
March 4, 1841	William Henry Harrison inaugurated as ninth President of 26 United States.
April 6, 1841	John Tyler inaugurated as tenth President of 26 United States after death of President Harrison.
April 6, 1841	Cornerstones are laid for the Nauvoo Temple.
April 20, 1841	Wilford leaves England for America with other members of Quorum of the Twelve. WWJ 2:92
May 20, 1841	Wilford arrives in New York. WWJ 2:102
June 2, 1841	Reunited with Phebe after 2 years; meets his 15-month-old son Wilford Jr. WWJ 2:105
Jul–Aug 1841	Wilford spends time with family, officiates in marriage of sister Eunice to Dwight Webster on August 4. WWJ 2:114
Aug 27, 1841	Church historian Robert B. Thompson dies; he completed *Manuscript History of the Church* Sept to Nov 1830.
1841–1842	W. W. Phelps writes *Manuscript History of the Church* Vol. A–1 for Nov 1830 to Nov 1, 1831.
Oct 3, 1841	Joseph Smith directs Saints to stop proxy baptisms in Mississippi River, wait for completion of temple font.
Oct 6, 1841	Woodruffs arrive in Nauvoo. WWJ 2:131
Oct 19, 1841	Wilford and Phebe move into their own home for the first time in their married life. WWJ 2:134
Oct 30, 1841	Wilford is appointed to Nauvoo City Council. WWJ 2:135
Nov 8, 1841	Wooden font completed in the unfinished basement of Nauvoo Temple.
Nov 21, 1841	Wilford witnesses first baptisms for the dead in the Nauvoo Temple. HC 4:426, 454. WWJ 2:138–139
Dec 27, 1841	Wilford sees Urim and Thummim. WWJ 2:144
January 1842	Wilford helps haul stone for the Nauvoo House and Nauvoo Temple. WWJ 2:149
Feb 3, 1842	Wilford appointed manager of the Church's official newspaper *Times and Seasons*. WWJ 2:153
Feb 19, 1842	Wilford sets type for printing/publishing the *Book of Abraham* in *Times and Seasons* WWJ 2:155–156
March 4, 1842	Phebe's third child Phebe Amelia is born in Nauvoo, Illinois. WWJ 2:157
March 15, 1842	Serial publication of *Manuscript History of the Church* in *Times and Seasons* as "History of Joseph Smith."
March 27, 1842	Nauvoo Reformation included rebaptisms; Wilford rebaptized for the first time. WWJ 2:165
April 21, 1842	Wilford baptized for mother Beulah; half-brothers Philo and Asahel; Phebe for grandparents. WWJ 2:171, 177
May 3, 1842	Joseph receives revelation regarding the meaning of endowment; prepares place to administer endowment.
May 4, 1842	Joseph administers first endowment ordinances in room above the Red Brick Store in Nauvoo. HC 5:1–3
May 7, 1842	Wilford baptized by proxy for great-grandparents Josiah and Sarah Woodford Woodruff. WWJ 2:175

May 15, 1842	Wilford baptized by proxy for more great-grandparents. WWJ 2:176
May 29, 1842	Wilford and Phebe baptized for six family members. WWJ 2:177
Aug–Sept, 1842	Wilford is confined to his bed with illness for 40 days. WWJ 2:184-188
June 1842	*Millennial Star* begins serial publication of *Manuscript History of the Church* in England.
Sept 6, 1842	Joseph Smith's letter states baptism for the dead is welding link between fathers and children. D & C 128
Oct 30, 1842	3,000 gather in unfinished temple for the first official meeting (the walls were only 4 feet high). WWJ 2:191
Dec 21, 1842	Willard Richards starts writing *Manuscript History of the Church* Nov 1, 1831–Aug 30, 1834.
May 1843	Wilford assists in publication of the *Nauvoo Neighbor* (published until Saints leave Nauvoo in 1846).
May 16–17, 1843	Revelation received by Joseph Smith explaining the necessity of eternal marriage for exaltation. D & C 131
July–Nov 1843	Wilford serves fourth mission in eastern states (with other apostles) to raise funds for temple. WWJ 2:259–325
July 12, 1843	Revelation regarding new and everlasting covenant of marriage for eternity dictated. D & C 132:15–20
July 25, 1843	Phebe's fourth child Susan Cornelia born in Nauvoo, Illinois, in Wilford's absence. WWJ 2:264
Aug 5, 1843	Wilford arrives in Philadelphia. WWJ 2:270
Oct 1, 1843	Willard Richards starts Volume B–1 of the *Manuscript History of the Church* commencing with Sept 1, 1834.
Nov 4, 1843	Wilford returns to Nauvoo from mission to England. (Age 36.) WWJ 2:325
Nov 11, 1843	Wilford's marriage to Phebe sealed for eternity by Hyrum Smith. WWJ 2:326–327
Dec 2, 1843	Wilford receives washings, anointings, and endowment. WWJ 2:329
Dec 23, 1843	Phebe receives washings, anointings, and endowment. WWJ 2:332
Jan 28, 1844	Wilford and Phebe receive second anointings. WWJ 2:344
March 2, 1844	Willard Richards completes *Manuscript History of the Church* Vol. B–1 covering Sept 1, 1834–Aug 5, 1838.
1844	Publication of "The History of Joseph Smith" in the *Times and Seasons* covering period up to Jan 7, 1832.
March 26, 1844	Wilford attends meeting when Joseph Smith confers priesthood keys on Quorum of the Twelve. WWJ 2:371
April 7, 1844	Wilford records Joseph Smith's discourse on important doctrines at funeral of King Follett. WWJ 2:378–88
May 4, 1844	Wilford completes brick home in Nauvoo; over the next 2 years lives in it for less than 6 weeks. WWJ 2:393
May–Aug, 1844	Wilford serves fifth mission in the eastern states; holds conferences, campaigns for Joseph Smith. WWJ 2:394
June 26, 1844	Wilford arrives in Boston to attend convention; nominate Joseph Smith for President of the U. S. WWJ 2:413
June 27, 1844	Joseph and Hyrum Smith murdered while in Carthage Jail. WWJ 2:413–414
July 1, 1844	Wilford attends Jeffersonian Democracy Convention in Boston to nominate Joseph Smith. WWJ 2:415

July 7, 1844	Work on the Nauvoo Temple resumes.
July 9, 1844	Wilford learns of Joseph and Hyrum's death through newspaper article in *Boston Times*. WWJ 2:419–20, 423
Aug 6, 1844	Wilford returns to Nauvoo with other members of the Quorum of the Twelve. WWJ 2:433–34
Aug 8, 1844	Meeting where majority of Saints sustain Quorum of Twelve as governing body of the Church. WWJ 2:434–40
Aug 12, 1844	Wilford accepts call to preside over the European Mission for one year. WWJ 2:441
Aug 26, 1844	Wilford and Phebe baptized in Mississippi River for deceased relatives. WWJ 2:455–456
Aug 28, 1844	Wilford and Phebe and their children leave Nauvoo for England; Wilford's sixth mission. WWJ 2:459
Dec 6, 1844	Woodruffs board ship to sail from New York City to Liverpool. WWJ 2:488
Dec 11, 1844	Willard Richards, under the direction of Brigham Young, resumes work on *Manuscript History of the Church*.
Jan 3, 1845	Woodruffs arrive in Liverpool. WWJ 2:498–3:8
March 4, 1845	James K. Polk inaugurated as eleventh President of 27 United States.
June 15, 1845	Willard Richards and Thomas Bullock resume work on *Manuscript History of the Church* begin at Aug 5, 1838.
June 25, 1845	First stone laid for the new baptismal font in the Nauvoo Temple.
July 18, 1845	Phebe's fifth child, Joseph, is born in Liverpool, England. WWJ 2:581
Oct 5, 1845	Church Conference is held in the Nauvoo Temple; pulpits are complete and windows installed.
Dec 10, 1845	First endowments for the living performed in the Nauvoo Temple. HC 7:543
Jan 8, 1846	First priesthood adoptions performed in the Nauvoo Temple.
Jan 11, 1846	First sealings of children to parents performed in the Nauvoo Temple.
Jan 16, 1846	Phebe and 40 other Saints (incl. Wilford's future wife Mary Ann Jackson) leave England. WWJ 3:5
Jan 20, 1846	Willard Richards and Thomas Bullock stop work on *Manuscript History of the Church* (until July 1, 1854).
Jan 22, 1846	Wilford leaves England for New York; experiences terrible Atlantic storm. WWJ 3:8–25
Feb 4, 1846	First Saints leave Nauvoo for Iowa.
1846	Population of Nauvoo 14,000–15,000; population of Illinois 500,000–600,000.
Feb 7, 1846	On final day of work in temple, 600 received ordinances; total of 5,615 received endowments in Nauvoo.
Feb 15, 1846	*Times and Seasons* stops serial publication of the *Manuscript History of the Church*; final entry re: Aug 11, 1834.
Feb–Mar 1846	Main exodus of Saints from Nauvoo. Brigham Young's family leaves Feb 15. Temperature -12° F on Feb 24.
March 17, 1846	Wilford retrieves daughter from sister-in-law's where she lived during his mission to England. WWJ 3:28
March 20, 1846	Wilford returns to Farmington, CT; parents and cousin Betsey Cossett accompany him to Nauvoo. WWJ 3:33
April 13, 1846	Wilford arrives in Nauvoo with daughter, cousin, and parents; Phebe arrived a few days before. WWJ 3:38

April 15, 1846	Woodruffs tour Nauvoo Temple with others. WWJ 3:39
April 30, 1846	Private dedication of Nauvoo Temple. WWJ 3:41
May 1–3, 1846	Public dedication of Nauvoo Temple; Wilford attends with parents, Phebe, Mary Ann Jackson. WWJ 3:42–47
May 13, 1846	United States Congress declares war on Mexico.
May 22, 1846	Woodruffs leave Nauvoo to join Saints in Iowa. WWJ 3:49
June 26, 1846	Wilford at Mt. Pisgah when Captain Allen arrives to recruit Mormon Battalion. WWJ 3:54–56
July 9, 1846	Woodruffs reach Council Bluffs. WWJ 3:58
July 16–17, 1846	Mormon Battalion recruited by United States Army. WWJ 3:59–61
July 25, 1846	Woodruffs cross Missouri River to Cutler's Park, Nebraska. WWJ 3:63
Aug 2, 1846	Wilford sealed to Mary Ann Jackson, Sarah Elinor Brown, Mary Caroline Barton. WWJ 3:64–65; MHC 16:127
Aug 8, 1846	Wilford rebaptized 2nd time; rebaptizes Phebe, S. Brown, M. Barton, M. Jackson, Rosetta King. WWJ 3:66
Aug 29, 1846	Wilford expels Sarah E. Brown and Mary C. Barton from his family. WWJ 3:71; MHC 15:210.
August 1846	Wilford moves his family to Winter Quarters and begins building a cabin to house them for the winter.
Oct 15, 1846	Wilford severely injured by falling tree: breaks breastbone, three ribs, suffers internal injuries. WWJ 3:93–94
Nov 12, 1846	Phebe's fifth child Joseph dies at age 16 months in Winter Quarters, Nebraska. WWJ 3:95
Dec 8–10, 1846	Phebe's sixth child Ezra born in Winter Quarters, Nebraska, and dies 2 days later. WWJ 3:97
Dec 13, 1846	483 Saints at Winter Quarters: 334 sick, 53 wives of Mormon Battalion soldiers, 75 widows. WWJ 3:103
Jan 19, 1847	Wilford organizes "adopted" family (40 heads of households) under covenant to abide rules. WWJ 3:119
April 14, 1846	Wilford leaves for the Salt Lake Valley with the first company of pioneers. WWJ 3:146
May 25, 1847	James Jackson Woodruff born (only child of Mary Ann Jackson and Wilford).
1847	Church membership is 34,694.
June 14, 1847	Mary Ann Jackson and her 19-day-old son James start journey to Salt Lake with Wilford's father Aphek.
July 22, 1847	Advance company arrives in Salt Lake Valley (still Mexican territory at the time); sets up camp. WWJ 3:234
July 24, 1847	Wilford arrives in Salt Lake Valley with Brigham Young and plants potatoes. WWJ 3:233–234
July 26, 1847	Wilford first to climb Ensign Peak. WWJ 3:236
July 26, 1847	Location for Salt Lake Temple Block designated (originally 40 acres). WWJ 3:236, 239
July 31, 1847	First bowery built on Temple Block by Mormon Battalion. WWJ 3:244–245
Aug 6, 1847	Wilford, Brigham Young, and other apostles are rebaptized (Wilford's third rebaptism). WWJ 3:248–249

Aug 26, 1847	After planting crops and building cabins, Wilford leaves Salt Lake to return to Winter Quarters. WWJ 3:263
Sept 3–5, 1847	Wilford's group meets companies heading west incl. father Aphek, wife Mary Ann, son James. WWJ 3:264–267
Oct 28, 1847	Phebe's seventh child Shuah Carter born in Council Bluffs, Iowa, in Wilford's absence. WWJ 3:287–288
Oct 31, 1847	Wilford arrives in Council Bluffs/Kanesville, Iowa. WWJ 3:288
Dec 5, 1847	First Presidency reorganized with Brigham Young as President of the Church. WWJ 3:294–295
December 1847	Log tabernacle built in Council Bluffs. WWJ 3:299
Dec 27, 1847	Brigham Young sustained as President of the Church by the Saints. WWJ 3:300–301
Feb 2, 1848	Treaty signed ending Mexican–American War. Mexico cedes to US: present day CA, NV, NM, WY, AZ, CO
March 18, 1848	Wilford baptizes 8-year-old son Wilford Jr. WWJ 3:333
May 11, 1848	Mary Ann Jackson divorces Wilford.
June 21, 1848	Wilford leaves Iowa with family to preside over Church in Eastern United States and Canada. WWJ 3:353
July 22, 1848	Phebe's seventh child Shuah Carter dies in LaMoille, Illinois at age 9 months. WWJ 3:359
Aug 12, 1848	Woodruffs arrive in Boston, Massachusetts. WWJ 3:361–544
March 5, 1849	Zachary Taylor inaugurated as twelfth President of 30 United States.
March 8, 1849	Constitutional convention held to form the State of Deseret: UT, NV, AZ, parts of CA, WY, CO, NM, OR, ID.
March 22, 1849	Wilford baptizes father-in-law Ezra Carter. WWJ 3:433–434
Spring 1849	Second bowery built on Temple Block in Salt Lake City.
1850	Church membership 61,000; population of Utah Territory 11,380; population of United States 23,192,000.
April 9, 1850	Woodruffs leave Boston with a group of 209 converts to join the Saints in Utah. WWJ 3:544
May 16, 1850	Woodruffs return to Council Bluffs, Iowa. WWJ 3:552
June 15, 1850	Woodruffs leave for Salt Lake Valley from Kanesville, Iowa. WWJ 3:557
July 10, 1850	Millard Fillmore inaugurated as thirteenth President of 30 United States.
Sept 9, 1850	Under Compromise of 1850, Congress created the Utah Territory; Brigham Young appointed as Governor.
Oct 14, 1850	Woodruffs arrive in Salt Lake Valley and live in cabins Wilford built in 1847. WWJ 3:577
Dec 5, 1850	Wilford appointed to the Council (Legislature) of the State of Deseret (serves a total of 21 terms). WWJ 3:582
1851	Wilford moves his cabins from Old Fort to construct home on South Temple and West Temple
1851–1854	Marriage sealings and endowments administered in the Utah Territorial Council House in Salt Lake City.
Jan 6, 1851	Wilford begins serving as member of Utah Territorial Legislature. WWJ 4:4
March 20, 1851	Wilford's stepmother Azubah Hart dies in Burlington, Vermont. WWJ 4:64

Spring 1851	Plans announced for construction of adobe Tabernacle on Temple Block.
July 19, 1851	Phebe's eighth child Beulah Augusta born in Salt Lake City. WWJ 4:48
Aug 2, 1851	Groundbreaking for adobe Tabernacle on Temple Square.
Nov 15, 1851	Publication of the *Manuscript History of the Church* begins in the *Deseret News*.
Jan–Mar 1852	Wilford serves second term as member of Territorial Legislature. WWJ 4:89–102
March 28, 1852	Wilford sealed to plural wife Mary Meek Giles Webster by Brigham Young in Woodruff's home. WWJ 4:103
1852	First Thursday of the month designated for fasting and prayer (later changed to first Sunday by Wilford).
April 6, 1852	General Conference held in new adobe Tabernacle on Temple Block. WWJ 4:104–105
April 7, 1852	Brigham Young sustained as Governor of the State of Deseret. WWJ 4:112
July 7, 1852	Endowments resumed in Council House by Heber C. Kimball at the direction of Brigham Young. MHC 22:62
July 25, 1852	Wilford rebaptizes plural wife Mary Webster and baptizes 8-year-old daughter Susan. WWJ 4:141
Aug 3, 1852	Workers began laying foundation stones for the wall around the Temple Block. MHC 22:67.
Aug 8, 1852	Revelation on patriarchal marriage first made public by Brigham Young. WWJ 4:142
Oct 3, 1852	Wilford's plural wife Mary Meek Giles Webster dies. WWJ 4:149
Dec 21, 1852	Wilford appointed clerk and historian of the Quorum of the Twelve Apostles at age 45. WWJ 4:161–162
Jan 2–14, 1853	Wilford serves third term as member of Utah Territorial Legislature. WWJ 4:179
Jan 25, 1853	Phebe's ninth child Aphek born in Salt Lake City and only lives two hours. WWJ 4:183
Feb 14, 1853	Wilford attends groundbreaking ceremony and dedication of Salt Lake Temple site. WWJ 4:195–199
Feb–Apr 1853	Wilford assigned to supervise construction of temple foundation; started digging Feb 23. WWJ 4:207–213
March 4, 1853	Franklin Pierce inaugurated as fourteenth President of 31 United States.
March 13, 1853	Wilford sealed to Emma Smith and Sarah Brown in Council House; resealed to Phebe. WWJ 4:211
April 6, 1853	Cornerstones of Salt Lake Temple were laid. WWJ 4:213–214
June 15, 1853	Eunice, Wilford's only sister, dies in Burlington, Vermont. WWJ 4:219
July 1, 1853	Thomas Bullock and Willard Richards resume work on the *Manuscript History of the Church*.
Dec 1, 1853	*Manuscript History of the Church* completed to March 1, 1843: Vol. D–1 is Aug 1, 1842 to July 1, 1843.
Dec 13, 1853	Sealing to Mary Ann Jackson cancelled?
Jan 4–20, 1854	Wilford serves fourth term in Utah Territorial Legislature. WWJ 4:240–241
April 4, 1854	Sarah Brown's first child David Patten Woodruff is born in Salt Lake City. WWJ 4:258

April 7, 1854	George A. Smith appointed Church Historian; *Manuscript History of the Church* Jul 1, 1843–Apr 30, 1844.
Summer 1854	Third bowery built on Temple Square, north of adobe Tabernacle.
Dec 11, 1854	Wilford serves in Territorial Legislature December 11 to January 19, 1855. WWJ 4:294–301
Feb 3, 1855	Wilford elected president of the Universal Scientific Society established in the Territory. WWJ 4:302
May 5, 1855	Wilford attends dedication of Endowment House in Salt Lake City. WWJ 4:316
May 5, 1855	First endowments for the living administered in the Endowment House. WWJ 4:316
1855–1857	Church Reformation takes place in Utah.
May 9–27, 1855	Wilford tours southern Utah settlements with Brigham and apostles. WWJ 4:318–327
Sept 13, 1855	Wilford helps establish the Deseret Horticultural Society. WWJ 4:336
Dec '55–Jan '56	Wilford serves fifth term in Territorial Legislature. WWJ 4:361–395
March 17, 1856	Second Constitutional Convention held and petition for State of Deseret delivered to Washington, D.C.
March 17, 1856	Wilford rebaptizes family members over the age of 8 (3 wives, 3 children, and "Lamanite" boy Moroni). WWJ 4:407
April 7, 1856	Wilford appointed Assistant Church Historian (serves in Historian's Office from 1856 to 1883). WWJ 4:409
April 28, 1856	Wilford poisoned while skinning livestock; life saved through priesthood blessings. WWJ 4:414–419
September 1856	Church-wide reformation includes rebaptizing, restructuring and recommitment to principles and covenants.
Oct 2, 1856	Wilford helps dedicate Endowment House baptismal font. WWJ 4:458–462
Oct 2, 1856	First baptisms performed in font; Quorum of the Twelve rebaptized (4th rebaptism for Wilford). WWJ 4:461–2
Dec 30, 1856	Members of Utah Territorial Legislature rebaptized (Wilford for the fifth time). WWJ 4:524
Dec '56–Jan '57	Wilford serves sixth term in Utah Territorial Legislature to January 16, 1857. WWJ 4:518–5:9
1856–1861	Wilford serves on Board of Directors of Deseret Agriculture and Manufacturing Society.
January 1857	Wilford and George A. Smith complete *Manuscript History of the Church* up to Joseph Smith's death in 1844.
Jan 18, 1857	Sarah's second child Brigham Young Woodruff is born in Salt Lake City. WWJ 5:9–10
March 4, 1857	James Buchanan inaugurated as fifteenth President of 31 United States.
1857	Church membership is 55,236.
July 13, 1857	President Buchanan removes Brigham Young as Governor; sends army to escort new Governor Cumming.
July 24, 1857	Saints receive news that 2,500 U.S. Army troops are coming to Utah. WWJ 5:69
July 31, 1857	Wilford sealed to plural wife Sarah Delight Stocking ("Delight") by Brigham Young. WWJ 5:70
Sept 7-11, 1857	Attack on wagon train of emigrants and massacre at Mountain Meadows.
Sept 29, 1857	John D. Lee gives false report of Mountain Meadows massacre to Wilford and Brigham Young. WWJ 5:102–3

Oct 1, 1857	United States Army winters at Camp Scott, Wyoming, 100 miles from Salt Lake City. WWJ 5:104
Oct 4, 1857	Emma's first child Hyrum Smith Woodruff is born in Salt Lake City. WWJ 5:105
Oct 16, 1857	US Army Colonel Alexander's letter threatens Saints with extermination if they oppose Army. WWJ 5:108
Nov 21, 1857	Alfred Cumming charges Brigham Young with treason; declares Utah citizens in rebellion against U.S.
Dec 13, 1857	Wilford serves seventh term in Territorial Legislature. WWJ 5:134–143
Feb 3, 1858	President Buchanan asks for four more regiments to help quell "rebellion." WWJ 5:162
Spring 1858	Third bowery on Temple Block in Salt Lake City dismantled before arrival of Johnston's Army.
April 8, 1858	Wilford moves to Provo; 30,000 Saints prepare to abandon/burn Salt Lake City ahead of army. WWJ 5:178
April 1858	Governor Cumming enters Salt Lake City without army escort under terms negotiated by Thomas Kane.
June 1858	U. S. Army enters abandoned Salt Lake Valley under terms of brokered peace. WWJ 5:210–211
July–Aug 1858	Saints begin returning to their homes in Salt Lake City. WWJ 5:202
Nov 24, 1858	Emma's first child Hyrum Smith Woodruff dies at age 13 months. WWJ 5:244
Dec 13–31, 1858	Wilford serves eighth term in Utah Legislature. WWJ 5:254–263
Jan 30, 1859	Wilford performs marriage of daughter Susan to Robert Scholes (first child to marry). WWJ 5:280
April 4, 1859	Wilford's daughter Phebe Amelia is sealed to Lorenzo Snow as his eighth wife. WWJ 5:323 and see 5:22
May 30, 1859	Sarah's third child Phebe Arabell is born in Salt Lake City. WWJ 5:341
Oct 16–29, 1859	Wilford is dying; gives family final instructions on funeral and disposition of belongings. WWJ 5:390–393
1860	Church membership 61,000; population of Utah Territory 40,273, population of 37 United States 31,443,000.
May 21, 1860	First grandchild born, Robert and Susan's daughter; four generations living in his home. WWJ 5:459
July 4, 1860	Emma's second child Emma Manella is born in Salt Lake City. WWJ 5:471
Feb 4, 1861	Seven southern states secede from Union. WWJ 5:550 (Confederacy included 15 states and territories by 1862)
March 4, 1861	Abraham Lincoln inaugurated as sixteenth President.
April 21, 1861	News arrives in Utah of firing on Fort Sumter and the beginning of the Civil War. WWJ 5:566
May 28, 1861	Wilford's father Aphek Woodruff dies. WWJ 5:579
June 1, 1861	Delight's first child Marion is born in Salt Lake City WWJ 5:580; Wilford learns of father's death WWJ 5:581
December 1861	Governor John Dawson arrives on 7th departs on 31st, vetoes 3rd Constitutional Convention. WWJ 5:604–615
Jan 14, 1862	Sarah's fourth child Sylvia Melvina is born in Salt Lake City. WWJ 6:7
Jan 20, 1862	Wilford helps draft constitution for State of Deseret; Brigham Young elected first governor. WWJ 6:8–13

June 9, 1862	Congress rejects fourth petition for formation of State of Deseret; Brigham Young still serves as Governor.
1862–1870	Legislature of the State of Deseret meets simultaneously with Utah Territorial Legislature. WWJ 6:52–53
June 10, 1862	Salt Lake Temple foundation razed and top stones removed. WWJ 6:53
July 6, 1862	Wilford baptizes son David Patten Woodruff. WWJ 6:65
July 8, 1862	Morrill Anti-Bigamy Law signed by Abraham Lincoln.
July 6, 1862	Wilford moves plural wife Delight to Fort Herriman. WWJ 6:66
July 22, 1862	Wilford serves as Pres. of Deseret Agriculture and Manufacturing Society for 15 years (1862–1877). WWJ 6:67
Aug 23, 1862	Wilford records Brigham Young's plans for a 15,000-seat tabernacle on Temple Square. WWJ 6:71
Jan 1, 1863	Emancipation Proclamation issued by Abraham Lincoln. WWJ 6:89
Feb 3, 1863	Emma's third child Asahel Hart is born in Salt Lake City. WWJ 6:95
April 6, 1863	Plans announced for construction of Great Tabernacle on Temple Block.
April 7, 1863	Wilford Jr. called to serve a mission in England. WWJ 6:108
May 29, 1863	James Jackson Woodruff returns to live with Wilford. WWJ 6:113
July 25, 1863	Delight's second child Emeline is born in Salt Lake City. WWJ 6:122
Nov 3, 1863	Sarah's fifth child Newton is born in Salt Lake City. WWJ 6:135
March 4, 1865	Abraham Lincoln's second inauguration. WWJ 6:215
April 9, 1865	Civil War ends. WWJ 6:220
April 14, 1865	Abraham Lincoln assassinated. WWJ 6:220
April 15, 1865	Andrew Johnson inaugurated as seventeenth President of 36 United States.
Dec 23, 1865	Delight's third child Ensign is born in Salt Lake City. WWJ 6:266
Dec 26, 1866	Brigham Young reintroduces second anointings. WWJ 6:307–309
Feb 12, 1867	Emma receives her second anointing. WWJ 6:326
Feb 14, 1867	Delight receives her second anointing. WWJ 6:326
April 10, 1867	Emma's fourth child Ann Thompson is born in Salt Lake City and dies the next day. WWJ 6:335–336
Oct 6, 1867	First meeting held in Great Tabernacle on Temple Block. WWJ 6:367
Oct 26, 1867	Sarah's sixth child Mary is born in Salt Lake City. WWJ 6:375
Dec 2, 1867	Wilford participates in reestablishment of the School of the Prophets. WWJ 6:378, 381.
July 23, 1868	Emma's fifth child Clara Martisha is born in Salt Lake City. WWJ 6:416
Aug 29, 1868	Delight's fourth child Jeremiah is born in Fort Herriman, Utah.

March 4, 1869	Ulysses S. Grant inaugurated as eighteenth President of 37 United States.
May 10, 1869	Transcontinental Railroad completed, effectively ending isolation of Utah. WWJ 6:472
Dec 16, 1869	Delight's fourth child Jeremiah dies at age 15 months in Salt Lake City. WWJ 6:510
1870	Church membership 90,130; population of Utah Territory 86,336; population of 38 United States 39,820,000.
Feb 1870	Utah women given the right to vote; Liberal (non-Mormon) Party formed opposing People's (Mormon) Party.
Nov 21, 1870	Wilford comforts Emma through her miscarriage. WWJ 6:582
Dec 5, 1870	Sarah's seventh child Charles Henry is born in Salt Lake City. WWJ 1:205
Jan 31, 1871	Brigham Young proposes idea of building a temple in St. George.
Feb 2, 1871	Sarah's seventh child Charles Henry dies at age two months in Salt Lake City. WWJ 7:7
April 17, 1871	Delight's fifth child Rosannah is born in Salt Lake City. (Not in WWJ)
April 18, 1871	Wilford moves wife Sarah Brown and her children to Randolph, Utah. WWJ 7:15
Oct 6, 1871	Priesthood members vote in favor of building temple in St. George. WWJ 7:33
Nov 9, 1871	Groundbreaking ceremony for St. George Temple.
Feb 18, 1872	Fifth Constitutional Convention held to petition for statehood. WWJ 7:60 (Rejected by Congress April 2)
Sept 9–27, 1872	Wilford travels to California to attend California State Fair. WWJ 7:81–89
Oct 22, 1872	Delight's fifth child Rosannah dies at age 18 months in Salt Lake City. WWJ 7:92
Nov 23, 1872	Emma's sixth child Abraham Owen is born in Salt Lake City. WWJ 7:95
Feb 2, 1873	Sarah's eighth child Edward Randolph is born in Randolph, Utah. WWJ 7:121
Feb 8, 1873	Sarah's eighth child Edward Randolph dies in Randolph. WWJ 7:122
Aug 14, 1873	Delight's sixth child John Jay is born in Salt Lake City. (Not in WWJ)
June 23, 1874	Poland Act passed by Congress becomes legal basis for the prosecution of polygamists in the 1870s and 1880s.
April 10, 1875	Seniority of apostles adjusted according to ordination date, placing John Taylor ahead of Wilford. WWJ 7:224
July 17, 1875	Wilford rebaptized (for the sixth time) along with other members of the Quorum of the Twelve. WWJ 7:234
Aug 11, 1875	St. George Temple baptismal font dedicated; used to rebaptize Saints entering the United Order in St. George.
Oct 3, 1875	President Ulysses S. Grant visits Salt Lake City. WWJ 7:247–248
Oct 9, 1875	Great Tabernacle on Temple Block dedicated by President John Taylor. WWJ 7:250
Jan 3, 1876	Wilford moves Delight into her new house in Salt Lake City. WWJ:7:261
April 9, 1876	Emma's seventh child Winnifred Blanche is born in Salt Lake City. WWJ 7:271

Nov 1, 1876	Wilford moves to St. George to assist in readying temple for dedication WWJ 7:289
Nov 7, 1876	National elections. WWJ 7:290
Nov 13, 1876	Wilford, L. John Nuttall and John D. T. McAllister begin writing down the temple ceremony. WWJ 7:292
1877	Church membership reaches 115,065.
Jan 1, 1877	Wilford, Brigham Young Jr., and Erastus Snow dedicate portions of St. George Temple. WWJ 7:303–315
Jan 9, 1877	First baptism for the dead performed in St. George Temple font. WWJ 7:321
Jan 11, 1877	First proxy endowments performed in this dispensation in St. George Temple. WWJ 7:321
Jan 11, 1877	First proxy sealings and sealings and endowments for the living in St. George Temple. WWJ 7:321
Jan 14, 1877	Brigham Young asked Wilford and others to write out the temple ceremonies. WWJ 7:322–340
Jan 16, 1877	Wilford administers second anointing to the first couple in the St. George Temple. WWJ 7:322
Feb 7, 1877	Wilford administers second anointing by proxy for the first time in the St. George Temple. WWJ 7:326
Feb 23, 1877	Wilford receives revelation authorizing proxy ordinances for his family by non-relatives. WWJ 7:329
March 1, 1877	In honor of Wilford's 70th birthday, 154 women serve as proxies in ordinances for his family. WWJ 7:329–336
March 3, 1877	Rutherford B. Hayes inaugurated as nineteenth President of 38 United States.
March 10, 1877	Wilford sealed to Eudora Lovina Young by her father Brigham Young. WWJ 7:338
March 21, 1877	Wilford and others finished writing down the ceremonies and temple procedures. WWJ 7:340
March 22, 1877	Wilford performed first adoptions (two couples to Brigham Young) in St. George Temple. WWJ 7:340–341
March 27, 1877	Phebe, Wilford Jr., Beulah and Phebe Amelia arrive in St. George to work in temple. WWJ 7:341–345
March 30, 1877	First time Wilford ever acted as proxy in endowment: for "Prophet" Robert Mason. WWJ 7:342
April 1, 1877	General Conference held in completed temple, dedication of entire temple. WWJ 7:343
April 8, 1877	At the age of 70, called to preside over the St. George Temple (served until June 26, 1884). WWJ 7:344
April 11, 1877	First time anyone ever adopted to Wilford: Josiah G. Hardy, Samuel B. Hardy and their wives. WWJ 7:344
April 14, 1877	Wilford's family leaves St. George to return to Salt Lake City. WWJ 7:345
April 16, 1877	Wilford resigns as President of the Deseret Agricultural and Manufacturing Society after 15 years. WWJ 7:346
April 25, 1877	Site for Manti Temple dedicated by Brigham Young. WWJ 7:347
May 18, 1877	Site for Logan Temple dedicated by Brigham Young. WWJ 7:350
June 16, 1877	Wilford's son Brigham drowns in Bear River at age 20. WWJ 7:354–355
July 1877	Church-wide priesthood reorganization included rebaptism. WWJ 7:362
Aug 19–21, 1877	Wilford's vision of Signers of Dec. of Independence; proxy baptisms for Eminent Men/Women. WWJ 7:367–68

Aug 22–24, 1877	Majority of endowments completed for Eminent Men and Women; some sealings also completed. WWJ 7:369
Aug 29, 1877	Brigham Young dies. WWJ 7:370
Sept 1, 1877	Wilford accompanies Lucy Bigelow Young to Salt Lake City for funeral. WWJ 7:370–71
Sept 2, 1877	Funeral service for Brigham Young held in Tabernacle. WWJ 7:371
Sept 2, 1877	Wilford dedicates Brigham Young's grave. WWJ 7:372
Sept 4, 1877	Apostles meet and agree that John Taylor will be President of the Quorum of the Twelve. WWJ 7:372
Sept 16, 1877	Wilford publicly shares his vision of the Signers of the Declaration of Independence. WWJ 7:373
Sept 17, 1877	Wilford participates in the cornerstone laying ceremony for the Logan Temple. WWJ 7:374
Oct 6, 1877	Solemn Assembly to sustain Quorum of Twelve as leading body; John Taylor as Quorum pres. WWJ 7:377
Nov 29, 1877	Endowments resume in Endowment House; for those too ill or elderly to travel to St. George. WWJ 7:384
Jan –Mar 1878	Wilford spends two months working in St. George Temple. WWJ 7:395–405
April 1, 1878	Wilford and Eudora's? son is born and dies nine hours later. WWJ 7:407
June 28, 1878	Delight's seventh child Julia Delight Stocking is born in Salt Lake City. WWJ 7:425
Nov 1878	Wilford is divorced from Eudora Young? ("sent bill" on Nov 25; "signed bill" on Nov 28) WWJ 7:439
Dec 2, 1878	Wilford asks Mary Ann Jackson to be resealed to him. (Note written in shorthand in margin of WWJ 7:441)
Jan 1, 1879	Wilford and Phebe move from Valley House into house next door; lease Valley House to be used as a hotel.
Jan 2, 1879	Emma's eighth child, Wilford's thirty-fourth and last child, Mary Alice is born in Salt Lake City. WWJ 7:489
Jan 6, 1879	Supreme Court denies George Reynolds' challenge to Morrill Law; plural marriage a criminal offense.
Feb 7, 1879	Wilford goes into hiding to avoid arrest for polygamy. WWJ 7:454
Mar '79–Apr 1880	Wilford spends a year in Arizona "on the underground" serving a mission among the Indians. WWJ 7:342–567
1880	Church membership 135,000; Utah Territory 143,963; population of 38 United States 50,190,000.
Jan 26, 1880	Wilford receives Wilderness Revelation re: God's defense of the patriarchal law of marriage. WWJ 7:546
April 2, 1880	Wilford returns to Salt Lake City from exile in Arizona. WWJ 7:567
Oct 10, 1880	First Presidency reorganized with John Taylor President; Wilford President of Quorum of 12. WWJ 7:595–6
Oct 10, 1880	*Pearl of Great Price* officially accepted as scripture by the membership of the Church. WWJ 7:596
Jan 16, 1881	Wilford appointed General President of Young Men's Mutual Improvement Association. WWJ 8:5
Feb–Mar 1881	Wilford works for a month in the St. George Temple. WWJ 8:15–22
March 4, 1881	James A. Garfield inaugurated as twentieth President of 38 United States.

March 5, 1881	Apostles wash feet against enemies as directed in Wilderness Revelation. WWJ 8:17
May '81–Apr 1889	Wilford serves eight years as Church Historian (until becoming President of the Church). WWJ 8:51
Sept 20, 1881	Chester A. Arthur inaugurated as 21st President of 38 United States after assassination of James A. Garfield.
Nov–Dec 1881	Wilford works in St. George Temple. WWJ 8:64–70
Jan 8, 1882	Assembly Hall on Temple Block dedicated by Joseph F. Smith. WWJ 8:80
March 14, 1882	Edmunds Act passed: plural marriage a felony, cohabitation a misdemeanor. WWJ 8:90
March 24, 1882	First Presidency counsels men to live with "only one wife under the same roof." WWJ 8:92
April 1882	Sixth Constitutional Convention for Utah held; Congress rejects petition for statehood on Feb 23, 1883.
Oct 5, 1883	Wilford sustained in General Conference as Church Historian and recorder. (not in WWJ)
Oct 12, 1883	John Taylor reinstitutes the School of the Prophets with "washing of the feet." WWJ 8:201
Dec '83–Jan 1884	Wilford works in St. George Temple. WWJ 8:211–221
May 17, 1884	Wilford helps dedicate Logan Temple. WWJ 8:249–252
May 29–Jun 19 1884	Wilford tours Idaho settlements with wife Sarah and Heber J. Grant. WWJ 8:253–260
Jan '85–Oct 1887	Wilford goes into hiding again to avoid arrest; lives in St. George area from Jan 20 to Nov 5, 1885. WWJ 8:299–341
March 4, 1885	Grover Cleveland inaugurated as twenty-second President of 38 United States. WWJ 8:307
Nov 5, 1885	Wilford called back to Salt Lake City for a meeting of Quorum of the Twelve. WWJ 8:342
Nov 9, 1885	Wilford sees Phebe for the last time and gives her a blessing. WWJ 8:342
Nov 10, 1885	Phebe Woodruff dies; Wilford watches funeral from Church office to avoid arrest. WWJ 8:342–343; 9:426
Jan 13, 1887	Congress passes the Edmunds-Tucker Act; Act becomes law on March 3, 1887. WWJ 8:421, 426
April 24, 1887	John D. T. McAllister becomes St. George Temple President. WWJ 8:435
June–July 1887	Seventh Constitutional Convention for Utah held; Congress rejects petition for statehood.
July 25, 1887	John Taylor dies at the age of eighty. WWJ 8:447
July 25, 1887	Wilford, as President of Quorum of the Twelve, becomes the leader of the Church. WWJ 8:448
July 29, 1887	Wilford watches John Taylor's funeral procession from Church office to avoid arrest. WWJ 8:449
July 30, 1887	Frank H. Dyer appointed receiver for the government; Church property confiscated.
Oct 9, 1887	Wilford meets with Saints in Salt Lake Tabernacle for first time in three years. WWJ 8:461
March 1888	Wilford's reorganization of First Presidency fails due to discord re: George Q. Cannon. WWJ 8:489–91
May 17, 1888	Wilford dedicates the Manti Temple in private services. WWJ 8:499–500
May 21, 1888	Lorenzo Snow dedicates Manti Temple in public ceremony after Wilford returns to Salt Lake City. WWJ 8:500

May 27, 1888	When Erastus Snow dies Wilford is only living Apostle who served in the days of Joseph Smith. WWJ 8:501
June 14, 1888	Wilford directs all 32 stakes to establish Stake Academies to educate youth of the Church. WWJ 8:504
July 9, 1888	Church's attorneys obtain commitment from U.S. Solicitor that temples would not be confiscated. WWJ 8:508
Nov 7, 1888	Benjamin Harrison is elected president. WWJ 8:524
Dec 20, 1888	Apostles refuse to sign document rejecting polygamy. WWJ 8:530
March 4, 1889	Benjamin Harrison inaugurated as twenty-third President of 38 United States.
April 5, 1889	First Presidency reorganized: Wilford President, George Q. Cannon, Joseph F. Smith counselors. WWJ 9:15
April 7, 1889	Solemn Assembly held in Tabernacle to sustain new First Presidency. WWJ 9:16
Oct 21–Nov 16 1889	Wilford travels with Emma and Church leaders to Idaho, Oregon, Washington, and Canada. WWJ 9:59–66
Nov 1889	Endowment House closed and demolished. WWJ 9:62–65
Nov 24, 1889	Wilford receives revelation on politics and polygamy; will not trade religion for statehood. WWJ 9:67–69
Nov 30, 1889	Judge Anderson denies immigrating Church members United States' citizenship. WWJ 9:70
Dec 23, 1889	Church-wide fast day on Joseph Smith's birthday asking for deliverance from persecution. WWJ 9:70, 73
1890	Church membership 188,000; Utah Territory 210,779; population of 44 United States. 62,948,000
May 19, 1890	U.S. Supreme Court sustains Edmunds–Tucker Act and Congress's right to escheat Church property. WWJ 9:94
June 1890	Secretary of State James G. Blaine drafts document renouncing polygamy which Church leaders refuse to sign.
August 1890	Frank H. Dyer is removed as receiver and replaced by Henry W. Lawrence.
Aug 3, 1890	Wilford visits Saints throughout Utah, Wyoming, Colorado, New Mexico and Arizona. WWJ 9:103
Sept 24, 1890	Wilford meets with three apostles regarding decision on polygamy. WWJ 9:112
Sept 25, 1890	Wilford issues Manifesto on polygamy as a press release. WWJ 9:112–116
Oct 6, 1890	Majority of members of the Church attending General Conference sustain the Manifesto. WWJ 9:117
May 9, 1891	Wilford meets President Benjamin Harrison when he visits Salt Lake City. WWJ 9:147
May 29, 1891	People's Party is disbanded; Saints advised to join Democrat/Republican parties. WWJ 9:154
Oct 19, 1891	Wilford testifies in court regarding practice of polygamy. WWJ 9:165–166
Oct 25, 1891	Wilford's testimony to Saints and defense of Manifesto. WWJ 9:168–170
Nov 6, 1891	Wilford decides temple recommends will be signed by Bishops and Stake leaders only, not by Church president.
Oct 13, 1892	President Harrison asks for the prayers of the First Presidency on behalf of his very ill wife. WWJ 9:222
Jan 5, 1893	Limited amnesty granted to former polygamists by President Harrison. WWJ 9:235

March 4, 1893	Grover Cleveland inaugurated as the twenty-fourth President of 44 United States.
April 6, 1893	Wilford dedicates the Salt Lake Temple at age 86. WWJ 9:246
Aug 29, 1893	Wilford attends World's Fair in Chicago. WWJ 9:259–264
Oct 17, 1893	Wilford meets with temple presidents to harmonize the endowment ceremony in all the temples. WWJ 9:267
Jan 12, 1894	Money taken by government under Edmunds–Tucker Act returned to the Church. WWJ 9:284
March 19, 1894	Wilford has dream about Benjamin Franklin. WWJ 9:293
April 6, 1894	Wilford receives revelation regarding sealing practices and the Law of Adoption. WWJ 9:296
April 8, 1894	Wilford announces end to practice of adoption. WWJ 9:296–7
April 18, 1894	Wilford present at first endowment ceremony in Salt Lake Temple. WWJ 9:298
July 17, 1894	President Cleveland signed the Utah Enabling Act which gave Utah admission into the Union. WWJ 9:311
Oct 25, 1894	Wilford inaugurates week day religious education classes (led to seminary and institute programs). WWJ 9:323
Nov 13, 1894	Wilford establishes the Genealogical Society of Utah. WWJ 9:326
Mar–May 1895	Eighth Constitutional Convention held; new constitution banning polygamy ratified Nov 5th. WWJ 9:342–351
Jun–Jul 1895	Wilford travels to Oregon, Washington, and Alaska for recuperating vacation. WWJ 9:357–363
Jan 4, 1896	Utah admitted to the Union as the forty-fifth state by President Grover Cleveland. WWJ 9:385–386
April 6, 1896	Wilford and Quorum of the Twelve issue Political Manifesto. WWJ 9:397
Aug 13–Sept 9, 1896	Wilford travels to Oregon and California for recuperating vacation with L. John Nuttall. WWJ 9:417–424
Nov 5, 1896	Wilford changes fast day from the first Thursday to the first Sunday of each month. WWJ 9:433
March 1, 1897	Wilford attends the celebration of his 90th birthday in the Tabernacle. WWJ 9:449
March 4, 1897	William McKinley inaugurated as twenty-fifth President of 45 United States.
Mar 12–19, 1897	Wilford records his testimony (only known recording of his voice).
April 1897	Publication of *Conference Report* begins; continues through 1965 (replaced by *Ensign* Conference issue).
July 20–24, 1897	Wilford joins 50th anniversary celebration of first pioneer company arriving in Salt Lake. WWJ 9:492–94
Sept 9–25, 1897	Wilford travels to Oregon and California for recuperating vacation. WWJ 9:507–11
April 10, 1898	Wilford's Conference address on his 1877 vision of the Signers of the Declaration of Independence. WWJ 9:544
July 24, 1898	Wilford dedicates Pioneer Park (site of fort he helped build in 1847); last public appearance WWJ 9:556
Aug 13, 1898	Wilford leaves Utah for recuperating vacation in California. WWJ 9:558
Sept 2, 1898	Wilford dies from complications of a medical procedure in San Francisco at age 91. WWJ 9:561
1900	Church membership 283,000; population of State of Utah 276,749; population of 45 United States 76,212,000.

Appendix 5: Wilford's Serious Accidents and Incidents

1810 fell into a cauldron of boiling water; nine months of recovery before his life was considered out of danger

1812 fell from the great beam of his family's barn, landed face first on the floor

1812 broke his arm when he fell down the stairs while playing at home

1812 broke his other arm when he fell off uncle's porch

1813 escaped being gored by a bull running after the pumpkin he took from it to give to his cow

1814 broke his leg in a sawmill accident; leg got caught between headlock and fender post

1814 saved from suffocation after wagonload of hay he stacked incorrectly overturned on top of him

1815 uninjured when a horse bolted down a hill and flipped the wagon he was riding in

1816 fell 15 feet from a tree, landed flat on his back, knocked unconscious; cousin told parents he was dead

1819 rescued after drowning in 30 feet of water and "suffered much in being restored to life"

1820 almost froze to death in a blizzard; saved by passerby who found him in a hollow tree

1821 split open his foot with an ax "nearly clear through," crippling him for nine months

1822 bitten by a rabid dog but the bite did not break through his skin

1823 thrown 16 feet over runaway horse's head; broke left leg in two places; dislocated both ankles

1827 almost crushed when helping to de-ice the wheel of sawmill

1831 almost crushed when helping to de-ice the wheel of sawmill

1831 suffered a severe bout of pneumonia

1833 dragged headfirst between a team of horses for more than 300 feet with his sleigh on top of him

1834 a rifle accidentally discharged and the ball passed within a few inches of his body

1834 a heavily-loaded musket pointed at his chest was accidentally discharged, but misfired.

1835 preserved from a mob of about fifty people, a black bear and a large pack of wolves

1835 rescued after wandering for five hours in a tremendous storm

1837 left unhurt when a tornado removed the building he was standing in

1839	thrown from the axle tree of a wagon, head and shoulder were dragged on the ground for ½ mile
1839	contracted malaria but left for England to serve his mission with members of Quorum of the Twelve
1841	survived shipwreck on Lake Michigan
1842	bedridden for 40 days with bilious fever and struggled between life and death
1843	survived train crash; passenger cars smashed, baggage cars caught fire, engineer killed
1844	helped ship captain extinguish fire on board the ship he was traveling on
1845	inspired to disembark one steamer and take passage on another (the first later sank)
1846	hit in the head by mob throwing rocks at him while baptizing converts; later baptized some of mob
1846	crushed by falling tree; broke breast bone and three ribs, suffered severe internal injuries
1848	survived shipwreck on Lake Michigan
1848	inspired to move carriage and family from spot near tree; 30 minutes later whirlwind uprooted tree
1856	poisoned by infected animal; temporarily lost senses and memory
1859	severe lung fever "nearly blew out the lamp of life" "spirit fluttering between life and death"
1860	thrown from mule, head and shoulders hit ground and he was dragged behind the mule
1864	stung by a scorpion and felt the "shock through [his] whole system"
1872	dragged by runaway horse, but narrowly avoided being run over by the wagon
1873	mild stroke "it seemed to be paralysis and death"
1874	trying to prevent his son's fall, fell ten feet from a ladder and landed on his shoulder and hip
1879	severe bout of bilious colic; attacks took his breath away and he didn't think he'd live through one more
1881	thrown with three others from wagon; landed on hands and knees and extricated another passenger from wheels
1886	mild heart attack or stroke; couldn't see or speak for about 30 minutes
1893	severest bout of bilious colic "lay at the point of death"

SELECTED BIBLIOGRAPHY

Alexander, Thomas G. *Mormons in Transition: A History of the Latter-Day Saints, 1890–1930*. Urbana and Chicago: University of Illinois Press, 1996.

———. *Things in Heaven and Earth: The Life and Times of Wilford Woodruff, a Mormon Prophet*. Salt Lake City: Signature Books, 1993.

———. "Wilford Woodruff and Zion's Camp: Baptism by Fire and the Spiritual Confirmation of a Future Prophet," *BYU Studies* 39, no. 1 (2000):130–146.

Allen, James B. "Line Upon Line," *The Ensign of The Church of Jesus Christ of Latter-day Saints* (July 1979): 32–39.

Allen, James B., Jessie L. Embry, and Kahlile B. Mehr. *Hearts Turned to the Fathers: A History of the Genealogical Society of Utah*, Provo, Utah: Brigham Young University Studies, 1995.

Allen, James B. and Glen M. Leonard. *The Story of the Latter-day Saints*. Salt Lake City: Deseret Book Company, 1976.

Anderson, Devery S., ed. *The Development of LDS Temple Worship, 1846–2000*. Salt Lake City: Signature Books, 2011.

Anderson, Devery S. and Gary James Bergera, eds. *Joseph Smith's Quorum of the Anointed, 1842–1845*. Salt Lake City: Signature Books, 2005.

———. *The Nauvoo Endowment Companies, 1845–1846*. Salt Lake City: Signature Books, 2005.

Anderson, J. Max. *The Polygamy Story: Fiction and Fact*. Salt Lake City: Publishers Press, 1979.

Andrew, Laurel B. *The Early Temples of the Mormons*. Albany: State University Press of New York, 1978.

Arrington, Leonard J. *Great Basin Kingdom: An Economic History of the Latter-day Saints, 1830–1900*. Urbana: University of Illinois Press, 2004.

Arrington, Leonard J., Susan Arrington Madsen, and Emily Madsen Jones. *Mothers of the Prophets*. Salt Lake City: Bookcraft, 2001.

Asay, Carlos E. "The Temple Garment: 'An Outward Expression of an Inward Commitment'," *The Ensign of The Church of Jesus Christ of Latter-day Saints* (August 1997): 11–19.

Bagley, Will, ed., *The Pioneer Camp of the Saints: The 1846 and 1847 Mormon Trail Journals of Thomas Bullock*. Logan: Utah State University Press, 2001.

Baugh, Alexander L. "'For This Ordinance Belongeth to My House': The Practice of Baptism for the Dead Outside of the Nauvoo Temple." *Mormon Historical Studies* Spring (2002): 47–58. http://mormonhistoricsites.org/wp-content/uploads/2013/05/MHS3.1Spring2002Baugh.pdf.

Baugh, Alexander L. and Susan Easton Black, eds. *Banner of the Gospel: Wilford Woodruff*. Salt Lake City: Deseret Book, 2010.

Bennett, Richard E. "'Line Upon Line, Precept Upon Precept' Reflections on the 1877 Commencement of the Performance of Endowments and Sealings for the Dead," *BYU Studies* 44 (2005): 47–53. https://ojs.lib.byu.edu/spc/index.php/BYUStudies/article/viewFile/7019/6668.

————. *Mormons at the Missouri: Winter Quarters, 1846–1852.* Norman: University of Oklahoma Press, 2004.

Bennion, Lowell L. *An Introduction to The Gospel.* Salt Lake City: Deseret Sunday School Union Board, 1959.

Benson, Ezra Taft. *The Teachings of Ezra Taft Benson.* Salt Lake City: Bookcraft, 1988.

————. *This Nation Shall Endure.* Salt Lake City: Deseret Book Company, 1977.

Berrett, William E. *The Restored Church.* Salt Lake City: Deseret Book Company, 1973.

Berrett, William E. and Alma P. Burton. *Readings in L.D.S. Church History from Original Manuscripts.* 3 vols. Salt Lake City: Deseret Book Company, 1958.

Best of the Frontier Guardian. Salt Lake City: University of Utah Press, 2009.

Bishop, M. Guy. "'What Has Become of Our Fathers?': Baptism for the Dead at Nauvoo," *Dialogue* 23 (Summer 1990): 85–97.

Black, Susan Easton, "'A Voice of Gladness for the Living and the Dead' (D&C 128:19)," *Religious Educator* 3, no. 2 (2002): 137–149. http://rsc.byu.edu/archived/volume-3-number-2-2002/voice-gladness-living-and-dead-dc-12819.

Black, Susan Easton, Larry C . Porter, *Lion of the Lord: Essays on the Life and Service of Brigham Young.* Salt Lake City: Deseret Book, 1996.

Bleak, James Godson, *Annals of the Southern Utah Mission 1847–1877,* MS 318. Church History Library, Salt Lake City. http://eadview.lds.org/finding aid/MS%20318/.

Bloxham, V. Ben, James R. Moss, and Larry C. Porter, eds. *Truth Will Prevail: The Rise of The Church of Jesus Christ of Latter-day Saints in the British Isles, 1837–1987.* Cambridge: The Church of Jesus Christ of Latter-day Saints, 1987.

Bradshaw, Gilbert. "The Council House as a House for Sacred Ordinances in the Early Church." *Office of Research and Creative Activities,* 2002. http://orca.byu.edu/Content/jug/2002reports/2002religion.html.

Bradshaw, Hazel, ed. *Under Dixie Sun.* St. George: Washington County Chapter D.U.P., 1950.

Briney, Drew. *Understanding Adam-God Teachings: A Comprehensive Resource of Adam-God Teachings.* Drew Briney, 2005.

————. *Silencing Mormon Polygamy: Failed Persecutions, Divided Saints & the Rise of Mormon Fundamentalism, Volume 1.* Hindsight Publications, LLC, 2008.

Brooks, Juanita. *John Doyle Lee: Zealot, Pioneer Builder, Scapegoat.* Logan: Utah State University Press, 1992.

————. *On the Mormon Frontier: The Diary of Hosea Stout, 1844–1861,* 2 vols. Salt Lake City: University of Utah Press, 1964.

Brown, Lisle G. "Chronology of the Construction, Destruction and Reconstruction of the Nauvoo Temple." February 2000. http://users.marshall.edu/~brown/nauvoo/chrono.html.

————. "'Temple Pro Tempore': The Salt Lake City Endowment House." *Journal of Mormon History* 34 (Fall 2008): 1–68.

————. "The Holy Order in Nauvoo." November 1995. http://www.robato.org/doc_other/nauvoo_holy_order.pdf.

Brown, Matthew B. *Exploring the Connection Between Mormons and Masons.* American Fork: Covenant Communcations, 2009.

Brown, Samuel M. "Early Mormon Adoption Theology and the Mechanics of Salvation." *Journal of Mormon History,* 37 (Summer 2011): 3–52.

Buerger, David John. *The Mysteries of Godliness: A History of Mormon Temple Worship.* San Francisco: Smith Research Associates, 1994.

Burton, Alma P. *Mormon Trail: From Vermont to Utah.* Salt Lake City: The Deseret Book Co., 1953.

Bushman, Richard L. *Joseph Smith and the Beginnings of Mormonism.* Urbana: University of Illinois Press, 1984.

Bushman, Richard Lyman. *Joseph Smith: Rough Stone Rolling, A Cultural Biography of Mormonism's Founder.* New York: Alfred A. Knopf, 2005.

Cannon, Abraham H. *Candid Insights of a Mormon Apostle: The Diaries of Abraham H. Cannon 1889–1895.* Salt Lake City: Signature Books, 2010.

Cannon, Donald Q., Larry E. Dahl, and John W. Welch. "The Restoration of Major Doctrines through Joseph Smith: Priesthood, the Word of God, and the Temple." *The Ensign of The Church of Jesus Christ of Latter-day Saints* 2 (February 1989): 7–13.

Cannon, Donald Q., and Lyndon W. Cook, eds. *Far West Record: Minutes of The Church of Jesus Christ of Latter-day Saints, 1830–1844.* Salt Lake City: Deseret Book Company, 1983.

Cannon, George Q. *A Review of the Decision of the Supreme Court of the United States, in the Case of Geo[rge]. Reynolds vs. the United States,* Salt Lake City: Deseret News Printing and Publishing Establishment, 1879). http://books.google .com/books/about/A_Review_of_the_Decision_of_the_Supreme.html?i d=xoYuAAAAYAAJ.

Card, Charles O., Donald G. Godfrey, and Brigham Y. Card, eds. *The Diaries of Charles Ora Card: The Canadian Years 1886–1903.* Salt Lake City: University of Utah Press, 1993.

Carter, Jared. *Journal of Jared Carter 1831–1833.* MS 1441. Church History Library, Salt Lake City.

Church of Jesus Christ of Latter-day Saints, The. *The Book of Mormon: Another Testament of Jesus Christ.* Salt Lake City, 1989.

———. *The Doctrine and Covenants.* Salt Lake City, 1989.

———. *The Pearl of Great Price.* Salt Lake City, 1989.

———. *The Holy Bible.* King James Version. Salt Lake City, 1986.

Clark, James R. *Messages of the First Presidency of The Church of Jesus Christ of Latter-day Saints 1833–1964.* 6 vols. Salt Lake City: Bookcraft, Inc., 1966.

———. *The Pearl of Great Price Through Sixty Centuries: A Series of Five Know Your Religion Lectures.* Provo: Brigham Young University, n.d.

Clayton, William, and George D. Smith. *An Intimate Chronicle: The Journals of William Clayton.* Salt Lake City: Signature Books in Association with Smith Research Associates, 1995).

Clayton, William. *Manchester Mormons: the Journal of William Clayton, 1840 to 1842,* James B. Allen and Thomas G. Alexander, eds. Salt Lake City and Santa Barbara: Peregrine Smith, 1974.

Collins, George Knapp. *Spafford, Onondaga County, New York,* Onondaga Historical Association, 1917. http://archive.org/details/spaffordonondaga01coll.

Compton, Todd. *In Sacred Loneliness: The Plural Wives of Joseph Smith.* Salt Lake City: Signature Books, 1997.

Corbett, Pearson H. *Hyrum Smith: Patriarch.* Salt Lake City: Deseret Book Company, 1971.

Cornwall, J. Spencer. *Stories of Our Mormon Hymns.* Salt Lake City: Deseret Book Company, 1963.

Cowan, Richard O. *Temple Building: Ancient and Modern.* Provo: Brigham Young University, 1971.

Cowley, Matthias F. *Wilford Woodruff: History of His Life and Labors As Recorded in His Daily Journals.* Salt Lake City: Bookcraft, 1964.

Daynes, Kathryn M. *More Wives Than One: Transformation of the Mormon Marriage System, 1840–1910.* Urbana: University of Illinois Press, 2001.

Death of President Brigham Young. Brief Sketch of His Life and Labors. Funeral Ceremonies with Full Report of the Addresses. Salt Lake City: Deseret News Steam Printing Establishment, 1877. https://archive.org/details/deathofpresident00 deserich.

Deseret News (Weekly Edition) 1850–1898. http://lib.byu.edu/digital/ deseret_news/.

Durham, G. Homer. ed. *The Discourses of Wilford Woodruff.* Salt Lake City: The Bookcraft Company, 1946.

———. *The Gospel Kingdom: Selections from the Writings and Discourses of John Taylor.* Salt Lake City: The Bookcraft Company, 1943.

Duyckinck, Evert A. *Portrait Gallery of Eminent Men and Women of Europe and America.* 2 vols. New York: Johnson, Wilson and Company, 1873.

Edmunds, John K. *Through Temple Doors.* Salt Lake City: Bookcraft, Inc., 1979.

Ehat, Andrew F. "Joseph Smith's Introduction of Temple Ordinances and the 1844 Mormon Succession Question." Master's thesis, Brigham Young University, 1982). http://www.scribd.com/doc/35205295/.

———. "'They Might Have Known That He Was Not a Fallen Prophet'—The Nauvoo Journal of Joseph Fielding," *BYU Studies* 19, no. 2 (Winter 1979), 133–166.

Ehat, Andrew F., and Lyndon W. Cook. *The Words of Joseph Smith,* 6 Vols. Salt Lake City: Bookcraft, Inc., 1981.

Ellis, Edward S. *Ellis's History of the United States.* St. Paul: Western Book Syndicate, 1899.

Encyclopedia of Mormonism. http://lib.byu.edu/digital/Macmillan//.

Endowment House Baptisms for the Dead. Microfilm Nos. 183384, 183388. Family History Library, Salt Lake City.

Esplin, Ronald. "Joseph, Brigham and the Twelve: a Succession of Continuity," *BYU Studies* 21, no. 3 (Summer 1981): 301–341.

Esplin, Ronald K., and Daniel Bachman, "Plural Marriage," *Encyclopedia of Mormonism,* ed. Daniel H. Ludlow, 4 vols. (New York: Macmillan, 1992), 3:1095.

Evans, John Henry. *One Hundred Years of Mormonism.* Salt Lake City: The Deseret News, 1905.

Faulring, Scott. *An American Prophet's Record: The Diaries and Journals of Joseph Smith.* Salt Lake City: Signature Books, 1987.

Ferris, Robert G., and Richard E. Morris. *The Signers of the Declaration of Independence.* Flagstaff: Interpretive Publications, Inc., 1982.

Firmage, Edwin Brown, and Richard Collin Mangrum. *Zion in the Courts: A Legal History of the Church of Jesus Christ of Latter-day Saints 1830–1900.* Urbana and Chicago: University of Illinois Press, 2001.

Flanders, Robert B. *Nauvoo: Kingdom on the Mississippi.* Urbana: University of Illinois Press, 1965.

Gaskill, Alonzo L. *Sacred Symbols: Finding Meaning in Rites, Rituals, & Ordinances.* Springville: CFI, 2011.

Gates, Susa Young. "The Temple Workers' Excursion." Edited by Susa Young Gates. *The Young Woman's Journal* 5 (August 1894): 505–516.

Gibbons, Francis M. *Wilford Woodruff: Wondrous Worker, Prophet of God.* Salt Lake City: Deseret Book Company, 1988.

Grant, Heber J., *Gospel Standards: Selections from the Sermons and Writings of Heber J. Grant.* Edited by Dr. G. Homer Durham. Salt Lake City: The Improvement Era, 1943.

Green, Forace, comp. *Cowley and Whitney on Doctrine.* Salt Lake City: Bookcraft, Inc., 1963.

Green, Harry Clinton, and Mary Wolcott Green. *The Pioneer Mothers of America.* 3 vols. New York: G. P. Putnam's Sons, 1912.

Hafen, LeRoy R., and Ann W. Hafen. *Handcarts to Zion: the Story of a Unique Western Migration.* Glendale: The Arthur Clark Company, 1988.

Handbook 2: Administering the Church, The Church of Jesus Christ of Latter-day Saints, 2010, Salt Lake City. https://www.lds.org/handbook/handbook-2-administering-the-church?lang=eng.

Harrington, Virginia S., and J. C. Harrington. *Rediscovery of the Nauvoo Temple.* Salt Lake City: Nauvoo Restoration, Inc., 1971.

Hartley, William G., "The Priesthood Reorganization of 1877: Brigham Young's Final Achievement", *BYU Studies* 20, no.1 (Fall 1979): 3–36.

Heinerman, Joseph. *Temple Manifestations.* Salt Lake City: Magazine Printing and Publishing, 1977.

Hill, Donna. *Joseph Smith: The First Mormon.* Midvale: Signature Books, 1977.

Hill, Marvin S. *Quest for Refuge: The Mormon Flight from American Pluralism.* Salt Lake City: Signature Books, 1989.

Hilton, Lynn M., Ph.D. *Levi Savage Jr., Journal.* Hilton Books, 2011.

Holloway, Laura C. *The Ladies of the White House or In the Home of the Presidents.* Philadelphia: Bradley & Company, 1882.

Horowitz, Jerome. *The Elders of Israel and the Constitution.* Salt Lake City: Parliament Publishers, 1970.

Howard, Nora Oakes. *Catch'd on Fire: The Journals of Reverend Rufus Hawley, Avon, Connecticut.* Avon: The History Press, 2011.

Howells, Rulon S. *The Mormon Story: A Pictorial Account of Mormonism.* Salt Lake City: Bookcraft, 1963.

Hullinger, Annette C. *The Illustrated Story of President Wilford Woodruff: Great Leaders of The Church of Jesus Christ of Latter-day Saints.* Provo: Steven R. Shallenberger, 1982.

Hunter, Milton R. *The Gospel Through the Ages.* Salt Lake City: Stevens and Wallis, Inc., 1945.

———. *Utah: The Story of Her People, 1540–1947.* Salt Lake City: The Deseret News Press, 1946.

Irving, Gordon. "The Law of Adoption: One Phase of the Development of the Mormon Concept of Salvation, 1830–1900," *BYU Studies* 14, no. 3 (1974), 291–314.

Ivins, Anthony W. *The Relationship of "Mormonism" and Freemasonry*. Salt Lake City: Deseret News Press, 1934.

Ivins, Stanley. "Notes on Mormon Polygamy," in *The New Mormon History: Revisionist Essays on the Past*. D. Michael Quinn, ed. Salt Lake City: Signature Books, 1992. http://signaturebookslibrary.org/?p=745.

Jenson, Andrew. *Encyclopedic History of the Church of Jesus Christ of Latter-day Saints*. Salt Lake City: Deseret News Publishing Company, 1941.

Jessee, Dean C., ed. *Letters of Brigham Young to His Sons, Volume One*. Salt Lake City: Deseret Book Company, 1974.

———. *The Personal Writings of Joseph Smith*. Salt Lake City: Deseret Book, 1984.

Jessee, Dean C., Ronald K. Esplin, and Richard Lyman Bushman, eds. *The Joseph Smith Papers*. 9 vols. Salt Lake City: Church Historian's Press, 2008–.

Johnson, Benjamin F. *My Life's Review*. Mesa: Press of Zion's Printing & Publishing Co., 1979.

Johnson, Clark V., ed. *Mormon Redress Petitions: Documents of the 1833–1838 Missouri Conflict*. Provo: Religious Studies Center, Brigham Young University, 1992.

Journal History of The Church of Jesus Christ of Latter-day Saints: 1830–1972. Church History Library, Salt Lake City.

Journal of Discourses. 26 vols. Liverpool and London, November 1, 1853–May 17, 1886. http://lib.byu.edu/digital/mpntc/az/J.php#journal-discourses.

Kelly, Charles. *Journals of John D. Lee, 1846–1847 and 1859*. Salt Lake City: Western Printing Co., 1938.

Kimball, Heber C. *On the Potter's Wheel: The Diaries of Heber C. Kimball*. Edited by Stanley B. Kimball. Salt Lake City: Signature Books in association with Smith Research Associates, 1978.

Klapthor, Margaret Brown. *The First Ladies*. Washington, D.C.: White House Historical Association, 1989.

Kraut, Ogden L. *John Nuttall: Diary Excerpts*. Salt Lake City: Pioneer Press, 1994.

Larson, Stan, ed., *A Ministry of Meetings: The Apostolic Diaries of Rudger Clawson*. Salt Lake City: Signature Books, 1993.

Late Corporation of the Church of Jesus Christ of Latter-day Saints v. United States. 136 US 1 (United States Supreme Court, 1890). http://supreme.justia.com/cases/federal/us/136/1/case.html

Latter-day Saints' Millennial Star. Manchester, England, May 1840–March 1842; Liverpool, April 1842–March 3, 1932; London. http://lib.byu.edu/digital/mpntc/az/M.php#latter-star.

Lesson Committee, comp. *An Enduring Legacy*. 8 vols. Salt Lake City: Daughters of Utah Pioneers, 1982.

———. *Chronicles of Courage*. 8 vols. Salt Lake City: Daughters of Utah Pioneers.

Linforth, James, ed. *Route from Liverpool to Great Salt Lake Valley: Illustrated with Steel Engravings and Wood Cuts from Sketches Made by Frederick Piercy*. Liverpool: Franklin D. Richards, 1855. https://archive.org/details/routefromliverp00linfgoog

Longacre, James B., and James Herring, ed. *The National Portrait Gallery of Distinguished Americans*. 2 vols. Philadelphia: Henry Perkins, 1835.

Ludlow, Daniel H. *A Companion to Your Study of the Doctrine and Covenants*. 2 vols. Salt Lake City: Deseret Book Company, 1978.

Ludlow, Daniel H., ed. *Encyclopedia of Mormonism*. 4 vols. New York: Macmillan Publishing Company, 1992.

———. *The Church and Society.* Salt Lake City: Deseret Book Company, 1992.

Lundwall, N. B., ed. *Exodus of Modern Israel by Orson Pratt and Others.* Salt Lake City: N. B. Lundwall, n.d.

———. *Masterful Discourses and Writings of Orson Pratt.* Salt Lake City: Bookcraft, Inc., 1962.

———. *Masterpieces of Latter-Day Saint Leaders.* Salt Lake City: Deseret Book Company, 1953.

———. *Temples of the Most High.* Salt Lake City: Press of Zion's Printing & Publishing Co., 1960.

Madsen, Carol Cornwall. *Journey to Zion: Voices from the Mormon Trail.* Salt Lake City: Deseret Book Company, 1997.

Madsen, Susan Arrington. *I Walked To Zion: True Stories of Young Pioneers on the Mormon Trail.* Salt Lake City: Deseret Book Company, 1994.

Marshall, Evelyn T., "Garments," in *Encyclopedia of Mormonism,* ed. Daniel H. Ludlow, 4 vols. (New York: Macmillan, 1992), 2:534.

Martineau, James Henry. *An Uncommon Common Pioneer: The Journals of James Henry Martineau, 1828–1918.* Edited by Donald G. Godfrey and Rebecca S. Martineau-McCarty. Provo: Religious Studies Center, Brigham Young University, 2008.

McBride, Bruce L., and Darvil B. McBride. *Against Great Odds: The Story of the McBride Family.* Anaheim: KNI Incorporated, 1988.

McConkie, Bruce R. *Mormon Doctrine.* Second edition. Salt Lake City: Bookcraft, 1966.

McConkie, Oscar W. Jr. *The Kingdom of God: A study course for priests under 21 and bearers of the Aaronic Priesthood over 21 years old in The Church of Jesus Chirst of Latter-day Saints for 1963.* Salt Lake City: The Presiding Bishopric, 1962.

McGavin, E. Cecil. *Mormonism and Masonry.* Salt Lake City: Bookcraft, 1956.

———. *Nauvoo the Beautiful.* Salt Lake City: Stevens & Wallis, Inc. Publishers, 1946.

———. *The Nauvoo Temple.* Salt Lake City: Deseret Book Co., 1962.

Miller, David E., and Della S. Miller. *Nauvoo: The City of Joseph.* Santa Barbara and Salt Lake City: Peregrine Smith, Inc., 1974.

Morris, Larry E. *A Treasury of Latter-Day Saint Letters.* Salt Lake City: Deseret Book Company, 2001.

Nauvoo Baptismal Record Index. Microfilm No. 820155. Family History Library, Salt Lake City.

Nauvoo Baptisms for the Dead, Salt Lake Temple Record. Microfilm No. 183379. Family History Library, Salt Lake City.

Nauvoo Sealings and Adoptions, 1846–1857. Microfilm No. 183374. Family History Library Special Collections, Salt Lake City.

Nauvoo Relief Society Minute Book, March 17, 1842–March 16, 1844. http://josephsmith papers.org/

Nauvoo Sealings, Adoptions, and Anointings: A Comprehensive Register of Persons Receiving LDS Temple Ordinances, 1841–1846. Salt Lake City: The Smith-Pettit Foundation, 2005.

Nibley, Hugh. "The Early Christian Prayer Circle," *BYU Studies* 19, no. 1(Fall 1978): 41–78.

Nibley, Preston. *Brigham Young: The Man and His Work.* Salt Lake City: Deseret Book Company, 1960.

———. *The Presidents of the Church.* Salt Lake City: Deseret Book Company, 1959.

Nielson, Carol Holindrake. *The Salt lake City 14th Ward Album Quilt, 1957: Stories of the Relief Society Women and Their Quilt.* Salt Lake City: The University of Utah Press, 2004.

Nuttall, L. John. *In the President's Office: The Diaries of L. John Nuttall, 1879–1892.* Edited by Jedediah S. Rogers. Salt Lake City: Signature Books, 2007.

Oliver, George. *The Antiquities of Free-masonry: Comprising Illustration of the Five Grand Periods of Masonry, from the Creation of the World to the Dedication of King Solomon's Temple.* London: 1823 and 1843. https://archive.org/details/antiquitiesoffre00oliv

Oxford Companion to American Military History. Edited by John Whiteclay Chambers II. Oxford: Oxford University Press, 1999).

Packer, Boyd K. *The Holy Temple.* Salt Lake City: Bookcraft, 1986.

Pease, Harold W., ed. *The Mind and Will of the Lord.* Springville: Bonneville Books, 1999.

Peterson, H. Donl. *The Story of the Book of Abraham: Mummies, Manuscripts, and Mormonism.* Salt Lake City: Deseret Book Company, 1995.

Pratt, Orson. *Orson Pratt's Works on the Doctrines of the Gospel.* Salt Lake City: The Deseret News Press, 1945.

Pratt, Parley P. *"A Voice of Warning and Instruction to All People: Or an Introduction to the Faith and Doctrine of the Church of Jesus Christ of Latter-Day Saints, commonly called Mormons."* New York: [W. Sanford, 1837]. http://contentdm.lib.byu.edu/cdm/compoundobject/collection/NCMP1820-1846/id/2824/rec/1.

———. *Key to the Science of Theology.* Salt Lake City: Deseret Book Company, 1948.

Proctor, Scot Facer, and Maurine Jensen Proctor, eds. *The Revised and Enhanced History of Joseph Smith by His Mother.* Salt Lake City: Bookcraft, 1996.

Reynolds v. United States, 98 U.S. 145 (1879). http://supreme.justia.com/cases/federal/us/98/145/case.html

Quinn, D. Michael. "Latter-day Saint Prayer Circles," *BYU Studies* 19, no. 1 (Fall 1978): 79–105.

———. "LDS Church Authority and New Plural Marriages, 1890–1904." *Dialogue: A Journal of Mormon Thought* 18 (Spring 1985): 1–68. http://www.dialoguejournal.com/wp-content/uploads/sbi/articles/Dialogue_V31N02_19.pdf

———. *The Mormon Hierarchy: Extensions of Power.* Salt Lake City: Signature Books, 1997.

———. *The Mormon Hierarchy: Origins of Power.* Salt Lake City: Signature Books, 1994.

———. "The Mormon Succession Crisis of 1844," *BYU Studies* 16, no. 2 (Winter 1976): 187–233.

Rasmussen, Victor J., and Myrtle Hancock Nielson. *The Manti Temple.* Manti: Manti Temple Centennial Committee, 1988.

Rich, Russell R. *Ensign to the Nations: A History of the LDS Church from 1846 to 1972.* Provo: Brigham Young University Publications, 1972.

Richards, Bradley W., M.D. *The Savage View: Charles Savage, Pioneer Mormon Photographer.* Nevada City: Carl Mautz Publishing, 1995.

Richards, LeGrand. *A Marvelous Work and Wonder.* Salt Lake City: Deseret Book Company, 1979.

Richards, Mary Haskin Parker. *Winter Quarters: The 1846–1848 Life Writings of Mary Haskin Parker Richards.* Edited by Maurine Carr Ward. 2 vols. Logan: Utah State University Press, 1996.

Ridley, Jasper. *The Freemasons: A History of the World's Most Powerful Secret Society.* New York: Arcade Publishing, Inc., 2001.

Roberts, B. H. *A Comprehensive History of the Church of Jesus Christ of Latter-day Saints.* 6 vols. Provo, Utah: Brigham Young University Press, 1965.

———. *Discourses of B. H. Roberts.* Salt Lake City: Deseret Book Company, 1948.

———. *Outlines of Ecclesiastical History.* Salt Lake City: The Church of Jesus Christ of Latter-day Saints, 1924.

———. *Rise and Fall of Nauvoo.* Salt Lake City: The Deseret News, 1900.

———. *The "Falling Away" or The World's Loss of the Christian Religion and Church.* Salt Lake City: The Deseret Book Company, 1950.

———. *The Life of John Taylor: Third President of The Church of Jesus Christ of Latter-day Saints.* Salt Lake City: Bookcraft, Inc., 1963.

Savage, Levi Mathers. *Journal of Levi Mathers Savage.* Provo: Brigham Young University Press, 1955.

Sill, Sterling W. *The Keys of the Kingdom.* Salt Lake City: Bookcraft, Inc., 1973.

Slover, Robert H. "A Newly Discovered Wilford Woodruff Letter," *BYU Studies* 15, no. 3 (Spring 1975): 355.

Smart, William B., ed. *Deseret 1776–1976: A Bicentennial Illustrated History of Utah by the Deseret News.* Salt Lake City: Deseret News Publishing Company, 1975.

Smith, George D. "Nauvoo Roots of Mormon Polygamy, 1841–46: A Preliminary Demographic Report." *Dialogue: A Journal of Mormon Thought,* 27 (Spring 1994):1–72.

Smith, John Henry. *Church, State, and Politics: The Diaries of John Henry Smith.* Edited by Jean Bickmore White. Salt Lake City: Signature Books, 1990.

Smith, Joseph Fielding. *Doctrines of Salvation.* Edited by Bruce R. McConkie. 3 vols. Salt Lake City: Bookcraft, 1960.

———. *Man: His Origin and Destiny.* Salt Lake City: Deseret Book Company, 1969.

Smith, Joseph Fielding, ed. *Teachings of the Prophet Joseph Smith.* Salt Lake City: Deseret Book Company, 1972.

Smith, Joseph. *History of the Church of Jesus Christ of Latter-day Saints,* 7 vols. Salt Lake City: Deseret Book Co., 1957.

Smith, Joseph Jr. *The Journal of Joseph: The Personal History of a Modern Prophet.* Edited by Leland R. Nelson. Provo: Council Press, 1979.

Smith, Lucy Mack. *History of Joseph Smith by His Mother.* Salt Lake City: Bookcraft, 1979.

Smith, Lucy Woodruff. "President Wilford Woodruff." *Young Women's Journal 9* (October 1898): 437.

St. George Temple Baptisms for the Dead. Microfilm No. 170843. Family History Library, Salt Lake City.

St. George Temple Endowments. Microfilm No. 170542. Family History Library, Salt Lake City.

St. George Temple Sealings. Microfilm No. 170595. Family History Library, Special Collections, Salt Lake City.

Staker, Susan, ed. *Waiting for World's End: The Diaries of Wilford Woodruff.* Salt Lake City: Signature Books, 1993.

Stapley, Jonathan A. "Adoptive Sealing Ritual in Mormonism." *Journal of Mormon History,* 37 (Summer 2011): 53–118.

Stapley, Jonathan A., and Kristine L. Wright. "'They Shall Be Made Whole': A History of Baptism for Health." *Journal of Mormon History* 34 (Fall 2008): 69–112.

Stewart, John J. *Joseph Smith: the Mormon Prophet.* Salt Lake City: Mercury Publishing Company, Inc., 1966.

Stuy, Brian H. Collected Discourses of President Wilford Woodruff, His Two Counselors, The Twelve Apostles and Others. 3 vols. Burbank: B.H.S. Publishing, 1986–1991.

———."Wilford Woodruff's Vision of the Signers of the Declaration of Independence," *Journal of Mormon History,* 26 (Spring 2000), 83–90. https://www.mormonhistoryassociation.org/cms-assets/documents/41529-138226.2000-2003-toc.pdf

Talmage, James E. *The House of the Lord: A Study of Holy Sanctuaries, Ancient and Modern.* Salt Lake City: Bookcraft Publishers, 1962.

Tate, George. "Prayer Circle," *Encyclopedia of Mormonism,* ed. Daniel H. Ludlow, 4 vols. (New York: Macmillan, 1992), 3:1120–1121.

Taylor, John. "The John Taylor Nauvoo Journal." *BYU Studies* 23 (Summer 1983): 1–105.

Taylor, Samuel W. *The Kingdom or Nothing: The Life of John Taylor, Militant Mormon.* New York: MacMillan Publishing Co., Inc., 1976.

The Joseph Smith Papers. http://josephsmithpapers.org/.

Times and Seasons. Nauvoo: The Church of Jesus Christ of Latter-day Saints. 1839–1846. http://lib.byu.edu/digital/mpntc/az/T.php#times-seasons

Tingen, James Dwight. "The Endowment House, 1855–1889." Senior History Research Paper, L. Tom Perry Special Collections, Harold B. Lee Library, Brigham Young University, Provo.

Tullidge, Edward W. *The Women of Mormondom.* Salt Lake City: Tullidge and Crandall, 1887. https://archive.org/details/womenofmormondom00tullrich.

Typescript of Autobiography of Zera Pulsipher (1789–1872). L. Tom Perry Special Collections, Harold B. Lee Library, Brigham Young University, Provo.

Van Orden, Bruce A. *Prisoner For Conscience' Sake: The Life of George Reynolds.* Salt Lake City: Deseret Book Company, 1992.

Van Wagoner, Richard S. *Mormon Polygamy: A History.* Salt Lake City: Signature Books, Inc., 2009.

Von Wellnitz, Marcus, "The Catholic Liturgy and the Mormon Temple," *BYU Studies* 21, no. 1 (Winter 1981]: 3–36.

Wade, Nicholas. *The Faith Instinct: How Religion Evolved & Why It Endures.* New York: Penguin Press, 2009.

Walker, Charles L., Andrew Karl Larson, and Katharine Miles Larson, *Diary of Charles Lowell Walker,* 2 vols. Logan: Utah State University Press, 1980.

Walker, Ronald W., Richard E. Turley Jr., and Glen M. Leonard. *Massacre at Mountain Meadows.* Oxford: Oxford University Press, 2008.

Ward, Maurine Carr, ed. *Winter Quarters: The 1846–1848 Life Writings of Mary Haskin Parker Richards.* Logan: Utah State University Press, 1996.

Watson, Elden J., ed., *Manuscript History of Brigham Young, 1801–1844.* Salt Lake City: Smith Secretarial Service, 1968.

———. *Manuscript History of Brigham Young, 1846–1847.* Edited by Elden Jay Watson. Salt Lake City: J. Watson, 1971.

West, Emerson R. *Profiles of the Presidents.* Salt Lake City: Deseret Book Company, 1977.

Whitney, Orson F. *Life of Heber C. Kimball.* Salt Lake City: Bookcraft, 1975.

Widtsoe, John A. *Evidences and Reconciliations.* Edited by G. Homer Durham. 3 vols. Salt Lake City: Bookcraft, 1965.

Widtsoe, John A., comp. *Discourses of Brigham Young.* Salt Lake City: Deseret Book Company, 1977.

———. *Priesthood and Church Government.* Salt Lake City: Desert Book Company, 1963.

Woodger, Mary Jane, ed., *Champion of Liberty: John Taylor.* Provo: Brigham Young University, 2009.

Woodruff, Wilford. *Leaves From My Journal.* Salt Lake City: Juvenile Instructor Office, 1881.

———. *Wilford Woodruff's Journals 1833–1898, Typescript.* Edited by Scott G. Kenney. 10 vols. Salt Lake City: Signature Books, 1983.

Yorgason, Blaine M., Richard A. Schmutz, and Douglas D. Alder. *All That Was Promised: The St. George Temple and the Unfolding of the Restoration.* Salt Lake City: Deseret Book, 2013.

Young, Brigham. *The Journal of Brigham: Brigham Young's Own Story in His Own Words.* Compiled by Leland R. Nelson. Provo: Council Press, 1980.

———. *Letters of Brigham Young to His Sons.* Edited by Dean C. Jessee. Salt Lake City: Deseret Book Company, 1974.

———. *Manuscript History of Brigham Young, 1801–1844.* Edited by Elden Jay Watson. Salt Lake City: Smith Secretarial Service, 1968.

———. *Manuscript History of Brigham Young, 1846–1847.* Edited by Elden Jay Watson. Salt Lake City: J. Watson, 1971.

Young Woman's Journal. Salt Lake City: Juvenile Instructor Office, Geo. Q. Cannon & Sons; and Deseret News. 40 vols. 1889–1929. http://lib.byu.edu/digital/mpntc/az/Y.php#young-journal.

IMAGE CREDITS

All images were cropped and/or edited for inclusion in this work.

Page	Description
Cover	Compilation of Wilford Woodruff circa 1880s and the St. George Utah and Salt Lake City Utah temples. Images courtesy of the Church History Library, The Church of Jesus Christ of Latter-day Saints.
vii	Giclée of "That We May Be Redeemed" by Harold I. Hopkinson. Courtesy of Alice Clarkson Turley.
3	Wilford Woodruff's childhood home in Connecticut PH 9391. Courtesy of the Church History Library, The Church of Jesus Christ of Latter-day Saints.
5	Wilford Woodruff in March 8, 1849 by Marsena Cannon PH 6821. Courtesy of the Church History Library, The Church of Jesus Christ of Latter-day Saints.
7	Wilford Woodruff in 1868 by Edward Martin PH 1600. Courtesy of the Church History Library.
11	Wilford Woodruff's Journal showing consecration of property December 31, 1834 MS 1352. Courtesy of the Church History Library, The Church of Jesus Christ of Latter-day Saints.
12	Wilford Woodruff in 1897 by C. W. Symons PH 2797. Courtesy of the Church History Library, The Church of Jesus Christ of Latter-day Saints.
17	Farmington mill of Cowles, Deming & Camp *Wilford Woodruff: History of His Life and Labors As Recorded in His Daily Journals,* (Salt Lake City: Bookcraft, 1964), 385.
19	Congregational Church in Avon, Connecticut built in 1819. Courtesy of Nora Oakes Howard.
23	View of Collinsville, Connecticut showing mill where Wilford Woodruff worked and housing for Collins Company employees. Sketch by John Warner Barber circa 1836. Courtesy of The Connecticut Historical Society.
25	Oswego County Map from David H. Burr, *An Atlas of the State of New York,* New York, 1829.
27	Zerah and Mary Pulsipher. Courtesy of Kathy S. Simkins.
29	Wilford Woodruff's Book of Commandments. Courtesy of Kenneth R. Mays.
31	Kirtland Temple by George Edward Anderson circa 1900 MSS P 1 20439. Courtesy of L. Tom Perry Special Collections, Harold B. Lee Library, Brigham Young University, Provo, Utah.
33	Wilford Woodruff's certificate of ordination to the office of Teacher in the Aaronic Priesthood by Zerah Pulsipher on January 2, 1834. MS 1352. Courtesy of the Church History Library, The Church of Jesus Christ of Latter-day Saints.

87	Nauvoo Temple circa 1847 by Louis R. Chaffin. Courtesy of the International Society Daughters of Utah Pioneers.

87   Nauvoo Temple circa 1847 by Louis R. Chaffin. Courtesy of the International Society Daughters of Utah Pioneers.

91   Wilford Woodruff February 18, 1850 by Marsena Cannon PH 100. Courtesy of the Church History Library, The Church of Jesus Christ of Latter-day Saints.

93   Wilford Woodruff's certificate of ordination to the office of Elder in the Melchizedek Priesthood signed by Warren Parrish on January 28, 1835 MS 1352. Courtesy of the Church History Library, The Church of Jesus Christ of Latter-day Saints.

95   Death masks of Joseph and Hyrum Smith. Courtesy of Val Brinkerhoff.

97   July 14, 1844 article on the death of Joseph and Hyrum Smith from the *Portland* [Maine] *Tribune*.

101   July 30, 1848 sketch of Nauvoo Temple baptismal font by Henry Lewis. Lewis made the only known drawings of the font in the Nauvoo Temple. This is one of his series of sketches of the interior and exterior of the Nauvoo Temple. Courtesy of the Missouri History Museum, St. Louis.

103   Nauvoo Attic floor plan. Courtesy of Lisle G. and Merry Brown.

107   Brigham Young circa 1851 by Marsena Cannon PH 598. Courtesy of the Church History Library, The Church of Jesus Christ of Latter-day Saints.

113   Nauvoo in 1846 by Lucien R. Foster PH 1456. Courtesy of the Church History Library, The Church of Jesus Christ of Latter-day Saints.

114   Wilford Woodruff's home in Nauvoo in 1907 by George E. Anderson PH 457. (Wilford only lived in this house for a total of six weeks.) Courtesy of the Church History Library, The Church of Jesus Christ of Latter-day Saints.

117   Thomas Bullock's map of Winter Quarters. Courtesy of L. Tom Perry Special Collections, Harold B. Lee Library, Brigham Young University, Provo, Utah.

121   Depiction of Mormon Trail from Illinois to Utah.

123   First Presidency as organized in 1847 PH 328. Courtesy of the Church History Library, The Church of Jesus Christ of Latter-day Saints.

124   Salt Lake City plat section from original made by J.B. Ireland p. 2 No. 27771. Used by permission, Utah State Historical Society, all rights reserved.

125   Map of proposed State of Deseret and Territory of Utah in 1850 p. 2 No. 9980. Used by permission, Utah State Historical Society, all rights reserved.

127   Utah Territorial Council House, Post Office, and Globe Bakery on Main Street in Salt Lake City in 1850s MS P174 002. Courtesy of L. Tom Perry Special Collections, Harold B. Lee Library, Brigham Young University, Provo, Utah.

129   Salt Lake Temple Block in 1855 with adobe Tabernacle and bowery by Marsena Cannon No. 6421. Used by permission, Utah State Historical Society, all rights reserved.

130   Endowment House and 1856 additions by Charles W. Carter PH 1300.
       Courtesy of the Church History Library, The Church of Jesus Christ of
       Latter-day Saints.

131   Layout of second floor of Endowment House (with some text
       removed). Courtesy of Lisle G. and Merry Brown.

133   Layout of main floor of Endowment House showing baptistery,
       completed in 1856, located between Endowment House and wall
       surrounding Temple Block. Courtesy of Lisle G. and Merry Brown.

138   List of questions asked during Reformation transcribed from Andrew
       Gibbons broadsheet of Reformation Questions MSS SC292 F1.
       Courtesy of L. Tom Perry Special Collections, Harold B. Lee Library,
       Brigham Young University, Provo, Utah.

139   Utah Territorial militia in front of their tents in 1850s p. 7 No. 14685.
       Used by permission, Utah State Historical Society, all rights reserved.

141   Wilford Woodruff in 1862 by Charles R. Savage 156 MSS P24 B2 F3.
       Courtesy of L. Tom Perry Special Collections, Harold B. Lee Library,
       Brigham Young University, Provo, Utah.

143   First Presidency and Quorum of the Twelve in 1868 by Charles R.
       Savage No. 27673. Used by permission, Utah State Historical Society, all
       rights reserved.

144   Salt Lake Temple construction with Endowment House and new
       tabernacle in background PH 1983. Courtesy of the Church History
       Library, The Church of Jesus Christ of Latter-day Saints.

145   Sign above Zion's Cooperative Mercantile Institution by Charles R.
       Savage PH 1772. Courtesy of the Church History Library, The Church
       of Jesus Christ of Latter-day Saints.

146   Salt Lake Temple foundation; adobe tabernacle and new tabernacle by
       Charles R. Savage PH 410. Courtesy of the Church History Library, The
       Church of Jesus Christ of Latter-day Saints.

148   St. George Temple construction in 1875 by J. Cecil Alter PH 388.
       Shown at the bottom of the image are George Brooks, Edward L. Parry,
       John O. Angus, Miles Romney, and Charles L. Walker. Courtesy of the
       Church History Library, The Church of Jesus Christ of Latter-day
       Saints.

151   St. George Temple construction in January 1876 PH 388. Courtesy of
       the Church History Library, The Church of Jesus Christ of Latter-day
       Saints.

153   Wilford Woodruff in 1874 by Charles W. Carter. Courtesy of W. Bruce
       Woodruff.

154   Wilford Woodruff's brother Azmon Woodruff circa 1862 by J. Ford
       Morris MS 19509. Courtesy of the Church History Library, The Church
       of Jesus Christ of Latter-day Saints.

155   St. George Temple construction February 28, 1876 showing red
       sandstone walls half covered with stucco by Jesse A. Tye PH 1145.
       Courtesy of the Church History Library, The Church of Jesus Christ of
       Latter-day Saints.

157   St. George, Utah and completed temple by George Edward Anderson
       circa 1903. MSS P 1 21110. Courtesy of L. Tom Perry Special

Collections, Harold B. Lee Library, Brigham Young University, Provo, Utah.

163   Page from David H. Cannon's 1894 journey with summary of St. George Temple baptisms MS 8540. Courtesy of the Church History Library, The Church of Jesus Christ of Latter-day Saints.

167   St. George Temple with new cupola on hill by J. Cecil Alter PH 388. Courtesy of the Church History Library, The Church of Jesus Christ of Latter-day Saints.

169   Brigham Young in 1874 by Charles R. Savage PH 1300. Courtesy of the Church History Library, The Church of Jesus Christ of Latter-day Saints.

173   L. John Nuttall in July 1888 by Davis in Washington, D.C. PH 1700. Courtesy of the Church History Library, The Church of Jesus Christ of Latter-day Saints.

173   John D. T. McAllister by Edward Martin PH 1600. Courtesy of the Church History Library, The Church of Jesus Christ of Latter-day Saints.

177   Wilford Woodruff in 1878 by Charles R. Savage PH 5087. Courtesy of the Church History Library, The Church of Jesus Christ of Latter-day Saints.

181   Female temple ordinance workers PH 1140. Courtesy of the Church History Library, The Church of Jesus Christ of Latter-day Saints.

183   Wilford and Sarah Brown Woodruff's sons David Patten and Brigham Young Woodruff PH 946. Courtesy of the Church History Library.

185   St. George Temple circa 1877 with original tower by James Booth PH 8601. Courtesy of the Church History Library, The Church of Jesus Christ of Latter-day Saints.

188-9   Pages from Wilford Woodruff's Journal on August 21, 1877 with list of eminent men MS 1352. Courtesy of the Church History Library, The Church of Jesus Christ of Latter-day Saints.

191   St. George Temple record of baptisms on August 21, 1877 pages 186–187 of Microfilm 170844. Courtesy of the Family History Library, The Church of Jesus Christ of Latter-day Saints.

193   St. George Temple record of baptisms on August 21, 1877 pages 188–189 of Microfilm 170844. Courtesy of the Family History Library, The Church of Jesus Christ of Latter-day Saints.

197   Salt Lake Temple construction in 1877 by Charles W. Carter p. 14 No. 6475. Used by permission, Utah State Historical Society, all rights reserved.

201   Prisoners in the Utah Territorial Penitentiary in 1885 by John P. Soule PH 349. Courtesy of the Church History Library, The Church of Jesus Christ of Latter-day Saints.

202   Wilford Woodruff's home on West Temple Street in Salt Lake City converted to Valley House Hotel shown in 1902 by Charles Anderson PH 1872. Courtesy of the Church History Library, The Church of Jesus Christ of Latter-day Saints.

249   September 25, 1890 article on polygamy in the *Salt Lake Herald.*
255   Wilford and Emma Woodruff by C. W. Symons March 1, 1897 on her 60th and his 90th birthday. Courtesy of Carolyn Woodruff Owen.
257   Salt Lake Temple capstone laying ceremony on April 6, 1892 by Charles W. Carter PH 2010. Courtesy of the Church History Library, The Church of Jesus Christ of Latter-day Saints.
261   United States flag from Utah's statehood celebration in 1896 hung on Salt Lake Temple in 1897 to mark the fiftieth anniversary of pioneers' arrival in Salt Lake Valley. P0184n1 05 60. Courtesy of Special Collections Dept., J. Willard Marriott Library, University of Utah.
264   Oxen for Salt Lake Temple baptismal font in Silver Brothers Iron Works foundry yard 1890 PH 2482. Courtesy of the Church History Library, The Church of Jesus Christ of Latter-day Saints.
265   Salt Lake Temple baptismal font from the January 1912 issue of *Popular Mechanics.*
267   Wilford Woodruff in his office on December 10, 1894 by John R. Hafen MS 19509. Courtesy of the Church History Library, The Church of Jesus Christ of Latter-day Saints.
269   Admission ticket to dedication of Salt Lake Temple PH 13160. Courtesy of the Church History Library, The Church of Jesus Christ of Latter-day Saints.
273   Wilford Woodruff with daughter Phebe Amelia, grandson Orion Snow and great grandson Orion Snow Jr. by Alma J. Compton PH 708. Courtesy of the Church History Library, The Church of Jesus Christ of Latter-day Saints.
277   St. George Temple with new cupola circa 1880s PH 2010. Courtesy of the Church History Library, The Church of Jesus Christ of Latter-day Saints.
283   Aphek Woodruff in 1861 by Edward Martin. Courtesy of the International Society Daughters of Utah Pioneers.
285   Wilford Woodruff with son Wilford Jr., grandson Wilford S. and great-grandson Charles Wilford Woodruff August 16, 1897 by Charles Ellis Johnson. Courtesy of Carolyn Woodruff Owen.
287   First Presidency of Wilford Woodruff on March 2, 1894 by Charles R. Savage PH 2497b. Courtesy of the Church History Library, The Church of Jesus Christ of Latter-day Saints.
291   Church Historian's Office in 1866 by Charles R. Savage PH 1103. Courtesy of the Church History Library, The Church of Jesus Christ of Latter-day Saints.
293   Wilford Woodruff in 1897 by Charles Ellis Johnson. Courtesy of Ron Fox.
295   Cache Valley and Logan Temple by Charles R. Savage 687 MS P24 B7 F13. Courtesy of L. Tom Perry Special Collections, Harold B. Lee Library, Brigham Young University, Provo, Utah.
297   Manti Temple in Sanpete Valley p. 2 No. 15503. Used by permission, Utah State Historical Society, all rights reserved.
299   Wilford Woodruff speaking at dedication of Pioneer Park on July 24, 1897 by Charles Ellis Johnson. Courtesy of Ron Fox.

INDEX

Page numbers set in italic type indicate entries for images.

Bradshaw, Gilbert (author), 334n460
Brontë, Charlotte: proxy ordinances
for, 190. *See also* eminent men and
women
Brown, Charles (father-in-law), 279,
376
Brown, Frances Cann, *181*, 345n633
Brown, Francis A., conviction of, for
polygamy, *201*, 351n691
Brown, Harry (father-in-law), 376
Brown, Lisle G. (author): 334n467;
Endowment House layout, *131,
133*; Nauvoo Temple attic layout,
103; Red Brick Store layout, *69*
Brown, Mary Arey (mother-in-law),
376
Brown, Matthew B. (author),
318n243
Brown, Moroni, conviction of, for
polygamy, *201*, 351n691
Brown, Rebecca: proxy sealing to
Wilford Woodruff, 279
Brown, Rhoda North (mother-in-
law), 376
Browning, Elizabeth Barrett: proxy
ordinances for, 190. *See also*
eminent men and women
Buchanan, James: Johnston's Army
and, 139–40; proxy ordinances
for, 187, 190. *See also* eminent men
and women
Buell, Prescindia Lathrop
Huntington: sealing to Joseph
Smith, 327n345
Bullock, Isaac: rebaptism of,
335n488
Bullock, Thomas: Winter Quarters
plat by, *117*
Bunker, Edward Sr.: priesthood
adoptions and, 281, 343n596
Burke, Edmund: proxy ordinances
for, 348n663. *See also* eminent men
and women
Burke, Jane Nugent: proxy
ordinances for, 348n663. *See also*
eminent men and women
Bushman, Richard Lyman (author),
311n123, 319n254

Cahoon, Reynolds: second anointing
of, 323n305
Cahoon, Thirza Stiles: second
anointing of, 323n305
Caine, John T.: and Manifesto,
360n843; rebaptism of, 335n488
Calhoun, Patrick: proxy ordinances
for, 191. *See also* eminent men and
women
calling and election: 323n298; and
second anointing, 84
Candland, David, children sealed to,
326n335
Candland, Mary Ann Barton,
children sealed to, 326n335
Cannon, Abraham H., diary of,
343n596, 352n711, 358n829,
364n916
Cannon, Angus, court case of,
350n689
Cannon, David H.: exile of, 210; and
endowment ceremony, 261; work
in St. George Temple, 344n611;
record of baptisms and, *163*
Cannon, George Q.: on Adam-God
teaching, 343n596; and written
endowment 341n590; on heirship
and proxy ordinances, 220; as
member of First Presidency, *217*,
242, 259, *287*; on Manifesto, 250;
on plural marriage, 224, 247–48;
on priesthood adoption, 287;
rebaptism by, 145; with Quorum
of the Twelve, *143*; and United
Order, 145; wanted poster for, *210*
Carrington, Albert: rebaptism of,
335n488, 336n489
Carroll, Charles, 347n657. *See also*
eminent men and women
Carter, Ezra (father-in-law): 376;
proxy second anointing of, 182
Carter, Jared, 309n87
Carter, Mary (sister-in-law): proxy
sealing to Wilford Woodruff, 132,
335n470
Carter, Sarah Fabyan (mother-in-
law), 376
Carthage Jail, 232, 327n347

Index

Custis, Daniel Parke: proxy ordinances of, 194, 349n671. *See also* eminent men and women

Cutler, Alpheus: second anointing of, 323n305

Cutler, Lois Lathrop: second anointing of, 323n305

Dame, William H.: rebaptism of, 335n488

David (King): and patriarchal marriage, 75

de Corday, Charlotte: proxy ordinances for, 190. *See also* eminent men and women

Deacon: church organization and, 45; responsibilities of, 338n526

Declaration of Independence, Signers of: 168, 347n657; proxy ordinances for, 190–94, 347n661, 348n665; Wilford Woodruff's vision of, *vii*, 185–87, *188–89*, 196, 205, 299

Democratic Party, 244

Derr, William: rebaptism of, 335n488

Deseret, State of, *125*, 334n458

divorce(s): regulation of, 200; of Wilford Woodruff, 81, 203, 351n695, 376

Doctrine and Covenants: and oath and covenant of the priesthood, 92; and patriarchal marriage, 75

dreams: of Brigham Young, 117–18; of spirit world, 198; of Wilford Woodruff, 116, 186–87, 256, 349n670

Dunford, Moreland, 376

Duyckinck, Evert A. (author), 187, 347n661

Dyer, Frank H.: and confiscation of Church property, 232, 240–41, 246, 357n811, 358n819

Edmunds Act: compliance with, 224; passed by Congress, 200, 223–24

Edmunds-Tucker Act: civil rights and, 245, 359n834; effects of, 201; confiscation of temples and, 241

Ehat, Andrew F. (author), 318n237, 319n245, 323n297, 323n304, 325n315, 333n456

Elder(s): Church organization and, 45; and endowment of power, 36; and keys of the kingdom, 68, 324n312; ordination to office of, 132, 160, 310n94; Wilford Woodruff ordained as, *93*

Elias (prophet): appearance of, 37, 312n128

Elijah (prophet): appearance of, 35, 310n103, 312n128; mission of, 33, 46, 61, 63, 89–90, 96, 100, 109, 266, 272–73, 283–84, 288, 290, 312n129, 338n526; sealing power and, 31-32, 37, 62, 312n128; spirit of, 89, 258

Elisha (prophet): instruction to Naaman, 58

Emancipation Proclamation, 142

eminent men and women: list in Wilford Woodruff's journal, *188–189*, 348n663; proxy ordinances for, 187–96, 207, 348n664, 349n671, 349n672; source for information on, 347n661; temple records of proxy ordinances for, *191, 193*. *See also* Declaration of Independence, Signers of

endowment: changes to, 172–74; and Book of Abraham, 66–67; ceremony of, 65; changes to, 172–74; in Council House, 127, 372; of eminent men and women, 191–93; in Endowment House, 150–52, 155–56, 372; on Ensign Peak, 126; and endowment of power in Kirtland, 70–71; introduction of, in Nauvoo, 68–69, 168–69; Masonry and, 69–71; in Nauvoo Temple, 94, 102–103, 108, 263, 298, 372; of Phebe Woodruff, 83, 370; prior to sealing, 105, 278; proxy, 53–54, 128, 151, 160,

Hartley, William G. (author),
340n580; 341n581
Haun's Mill, 45
Haven, Jesse, rebaptism of, 335n488
Hawkins, Leo: rebaptism of,
335n488
Hawley, Reverend Rufus: Woodruff
family and, 15–16
heirship: baptism and right of, 60;
and priesthood, 116, 118–19; in
proxy ordinances, 219-221,
345n632
High Priest: eminent men ordained
by proxy as, 194
Holmes, Elvira Annie Cowles:
sealing to Joseph Smith, 327n345,
330n391
Holy Ghost. *See* Holy Spirit
Holy Spirit: Adam-God and,
343n596; baptism in name of, 28,
47, 50; gift of, 17, 18, 36, 41, 42,
60; Brigham Young and, 122;
Joseph Smith on, 118, 332n422;
Manifesto and, 250; Wilford
Woodruff and, 23–28, 44, 252,
254. *See also* Holy Spirit of
promise; Spirit of God, the
Holy Spirit of promise, 72, 320n261
Hosanna shout: at Logan Temple
dedication, 226; at Nauvoo
Temple dedication, 114; at Salt
Lake Temple dedication, 257, 258
House of the Lord: 39, 132, 184. *See*
Endowment House; Kirtland
Temple; Logan Temple; Manti
Temple; Nauvoo Temple; Salt
Lake Temple
Howard, Nora Oakes (author),
308n48
Hyde, Marinda Johnson: children
sealed to, 326n335; officiates in
Endowment House, 132; sealing
to Joseph Smith, 327n345
Hyde, Orson: children sealed to,
326n335; and dedication of
Nauvoo Temple, 114, 331n411;
endowment of, 102; mission of,
25–26; sealing of, 319n253;

second anointing of, 323n306,
325n316; seniority of Apostles,
143, 354n754

Illinois: Saints move to, 45, 315n188;
Saints persecuted in, 102, 125,
327n347
Irving, Gordon (author), 330n390,
367n956
Isaac (prophet): blessings of, 278;
patriarchal marriage and, 224;
sacrifice of, 75–76, 235–36
Israel, House of: adoption into, 60,
105; blessings of, 92; gathering of,
29, 37–38; as kingdom of priests,
86; tribes of, 55
Ivins, Annie L., 344n611
Ivins, Anthony W. (author),
318n243, 362n894
Ivins, Stanley (author), 320n272

Jackson, Andrew: proxy ordinances
for, 187, 190, 347n660. *See also*
eminent men and women
Jackson, Elizabeth Lloyd (mother-in-
law), 376
Jackson, Rachel Donelson: proxy
ordinances for, 347n660. *See also*
eminent men and women
Jackson, William (father-in-law), 376
Jacob (prophet): blessings of, 278;
patriarchal marriage and, 224. *See
also* Israel
Jacobs, Zina Diantha Huntington:
181; sealing to Joseph Smith,
327n345
Jefferson, Martha Wayles: proxy
ordinances for, 347n660. *See also*
eminent men and women
Jefferson, Thomas: proxy ordinances
for, 51, 187, 190, 347n660. *See also*
eminent men and women
John the Baptist: conferral of
Aaronic Priesthood, 312n128,
338n526
Johnson, Aaron: rebaptism of,
335n488

174, 344n606; and written
endowment ceremony, 168, 170

oil, anointing: in Kirtland Temple,
36, 42–43, 312n141; in Nauvoo
Temple, 103

Old Testament: plural marriage in,
75–76, 86; practices and rituals in,
36, 42, 55, 70

Oliver, George: Masonry, book on
319n246

Olmstead, Harvey, first proxy
baptism by, 314n158

ordinances, higher, 86, 97, 192, 195

ordination. *See* priesthood ordination

Page, John E., 102, 319n253

Palmerston, Lord (Henry John
Temple): proxy ordinances for,
191. *See also* eminent men and
women

Parepa, Demetrius: proxy ordinances
for, 347n661. *See also* eminent men
and women

Parepa, Elizabeth Sequinn: proxy
ordinances for, 347n661. *See also*
eminent men and women

Parepa-Rosa, Euphroynse: proxy
ordinances for, 347n661. *See also*
eminent men and women

Parker, John D.: rebaptism of,
335n488

Parkinson, Esther, *181*, 345n633

Parrish, Warren, 93

Patriarch: 44, 68, 99, 123

patriarchal blessing: of Martha
Cragun Cox, 180; of Wilford
Woodruff, 44, 132

patriarchal marriage: Joseph Smith
on, 74–76; law against, 245;
Manifesto and, 251; Wilford
Woodruff and, 76–83, 212, 224.
See also plural marriage

Patten, David W., 312n128

Paul (Apostle): on adoption through
baptism, 60–61; on baptism for
the dead, 49; on marriage, 72; on
spiritual communication, 341n590

Peacock, George: rebaptism of,
335n488

Pentecost, in Kirtland Temple, 37

People's Party, 244

Perpetual Emigration Fund, seizure
by government, 201, 232, 236

Peter (Apostle): on calling and
election, 84, 323n298; on spirit
world, 301; conferral of
Melchizedek Priesthood, 105, 187,
338n526

Phelps, William W.: rebaptism of,
335n488; and "The Spirit of God"
hymn, 42

Phippen, Reverend George: baptizes
Wilford Woodruff, 22–23

Pierce, Franklin: proxy ordinances
for, 187, 190. *See also* eminent men
and women

Pingree, Job: conviction of, for
polygamy, *201*, 351n691

plan of salvation, 89, 297, 325n324

plural marriage: abandonment of,
199–200, 213–14, 230, 233,
353n723; amnesty for, 242, 256,
359n840; announcement of,
321n273; anti-polygamy legislation
and, 140, 224–25, 336n504;
compared to adultery, 79, 224;
implementation of, 72, 75–76;
John Taylor and, 74, 213, 232,
252, 350n688; Phebe Woodruff's
defense of, *77*; post-Manifesto,
254–55, 361n868; prevalence of,
320n272; punishment for, 199,
200, 224–25, 336n504, 351n697;
suspension of, 236, 248, 252–54;
test oath for, 231, 244, 357n811;
Ulysses S. Grant and, 353n741;
Utah Commission report on, 224;
Utah Constitution and, 230–31; of
Wilford Woodruff, 79–83, 376;
William Law and, 319n253,
327n347. *See also* Edmunda Act;
Edmunds-Tucker Act; Manifesto;
John Miles; Morrill Anti-Bigamy
Act; Poland Act; polyandry,

sealing of couples: 10, 86, 272,
335n487, 373; during exodus, 126;
of eminent men and women, 191,
194, 347n660, 349n672; in
Endowment House, 131; Joseph
Smith on, 71–74, 274; by proxy,
156, 178, 211, 373; in Nauvoo
Temple, 104, 274; in Salt Lake
Temple, 288–89; in St. George
Temple, 161, 178, 192, 207, 211;
of Wilford Woodruff, 74, 80, 126–
27
sealing of families: in Nauvoo
Temple, 90–92; Wilford
Woodruff's revelation on, 266,
272–75, 281–90.
second anointing: *85*, 373;
administered to couples, 86,
325n316; blessings of, 83–84; of
eminent men, 349n670; in
Endowment House, 132, 373; in
Nauvoo, 83–86, 97, 323n304–306,
324n313, 325n316; in Nauvoo
Temple, 330n396; by proxy, 182,
349n670, 373; recommend for,
265–66; reintroduction of, in Salt
Lake City, 142, 161–62, 337n508,
373; in St. George Temple, 162,
192, 207, 344n606; Wilford
Woodruff and, 85, 142, 349n670
Second Coming: preparation for, 24,
111, 158; timing of, 361n866;
Wilford Woodruff and, 150, 205,
212, 214, 230, 254, 302
Sessions, Patty Bartlett: sealing to
Joseph Smith, 327n345
Seventy, Quorum of, 40, 43
Shem, Ham, and Japheth, 205
Siloam, pool of, 58
Smith, Agnes Moulton Coolbrith:
endowment of, 102
Smith, Alvin, 34, 35
Smith, Bathsheba Bigler: children
sealed to, 326n335; officiates in
Endowment House, 131–32;
sealing of, 319n253; second
anointing of, 323n306

Smith, Don Carlos: endowment of,
102; proxy baptism by, 51,
349n671, *Times and Seasons,*
318n232
Smith, Edna Lambson, *181*, 345n633
Smith, Emma Hale: endowment of,
83; ordinances administered by,
83; sealing of, 72; second
anointing of, 85, 323n304; temple
ordinances after Joseph Smith's
death, 102, 106
Smith, George A.: *143*; on Brigham
Young, 342n594; children sealed
to, 326n335; endowment of, 102;
and proxy baptism of Wilford
Woodruff, 51, 328n368; sealing of,
319n253; second anointing of,
323n305; on Wilford Woodruff,
307n38
Smith, George D. (author), 320n272,
356n801, 363n895
Smith, Hyrum: 73; children sealed to,
326n335; criminal charges against,
327n347; death of, 95–6; death
mask of, *95*; endowment of, 68–9;
plural marriage and, 75; sealing of,
72, 319n253; performs sealing of
Wilford and Phebe Woodruff, 74,
334n462; second anointing of,
323n305; Wilford Woodruff's
vision of, 258
Smith, Jerusha Barden: children
sealed to, 326n335; proxy sealing
of, 319n253
Smith, John: endowment of, 102
Smith, John L., 344n611
Smith, Joseph: *71, 95*; and Abraham,
Book of, 66–67, 318n234; on
adoption, 60–63, 79, 92, 274,
332n422; adoption to, 106, 280–
81, 330n393; on baptism for
healing, 57–58, 60; on baptism for
the dead, 34–35, 47, 51–53, 56–57,
184; and Book of Mormon, 29; on
calling and election, 83–84,
323n298, 323n299; on celestial
kingdom, 71–72; on consecration,
337n511; death of, 95–96,

35177124R00252

Made in the USA
Middletown, DE
02 February 2019